AMERICAN POLICY TOWARD LAOS

AMERICAN POLICY TOWARD LAOS

Martin E. Goldstein

Rutherford • Madison • Teaneck
Fairleigh Dickinson University Press

Associated University Presses, Inc.
Cranbury, New Jersey 08512

Library of Congress Cataloging in Publication Data

Goldstein, Martin E
    American policy toward Laos.

    Bibliography: p.
      1. United States—Foreign relations—Laos.
2. Laos—Foreign relations—United States.
I. Title.
E183.8.L3G64   327.73'0594   72-416
ISBN 0-8386-1131-1

Printed in the United States of America

To my Mother and Father—they gave me all the values.

CONTENTS

TABLES

PREFACE

For over a decade and a half, the United States has been intimately involved in the affairs of the Kingdom of Laos. The purpose of this volume is to shed light on the symbiotic tie between these two nations.

Whoever sets out to investigate an area of current controversy is confronted by an unnerving difficulty: that of obtaining accurate information. Since so many of the major figures in this narrative remain alive and active in political life, and since a resolution of the struggle in Indochina has yet to occur at the time of this writing, many of the individuals and governments concerned seek to conceal information that may prove embarrassing to them. For instance, based on information currently available, it is impossible to ascertain the precise extent to which the Pathet Lao is controlled by North Vietnam or the degree of American responsibility for the fall of Souvanna Phouma's government in the summer of 1958. A complete explanation of Phoumi Nosavan's decision, in September 1960, to take up arms against Souvanna's government must await the disclosure of information still locked in official files. The same may be said of Soviet, Communist Chinese and North Vietnamese involvement in Laotian affairs. One suspects, furthermore, that presently undisclosed aspects of American participation in Laotian military matters, particularly after 1962, will come to light as time passes and documents become declassified.

An additional problem that the chronicler of current affairs must recognize is that of the veracity of available information. This matter assumes increasing significance to the extent that the writer relies on the recollections of the participants in the events he seeks to reconstruct. As even the best memories are fallible, and all individuals seek to present a decorous appearance when they stand before the tribunal of history, the

11

personal reminiscences of even the most upright individuals must be consumed with care. Since this volume relies heavily on such sources, the author has made every effort to confirm the information he has obtained thereby. Yet, it is possible that some distortions remain. Given these limitations, the author has tried to assemble as comprehensive an account of American-Laotian relations as his capabilities would allow.

The author has also made an attempt to further our knowledge about the phenomenon of conflict resolution. If mankind is to survive technology, including the technology of war, he must learn to settle his differences without the use of force. In 1961-1962, the statesmen assembled at Geneva fashioned a compromise, albeit a short-lived one. In attempting to extract and explain the essence of that compromise settlement, the author hopes that he has made a small contribution to advancing our knowledge about this method of settling disputes. And, when man does learn how to resolve his conflicts on the basis of compromise, it is the author's hope that the gentle, humane inhabitants of Laos be the first beneficiaries.

Finally, writing this book would not have been possible without the assistance of several inordinately kind and generous individuals. Dr. John F. Melby of the University of Guelph in Canada helped guide the original research that led to this study. Dr. Donald E. Smith, of the University of Pennsylvania, provided valuable advice and understanding while most of the work was in progress. Without his assistance, these efforts would never have come to fruition. Dr. J. Russell Andrus was kind enough to review the final chapter and make some helpful suggestions. I am also grateful to other individuals, too numerous to mention separately, who agreed to be interviewed or who corresponded with me. Finally, I owe an incalculable debt of gratitude to my wife Janet. Without her encouragement and understanding, her editing and typing, her culinary magic and gladdening smile, this project would have aborted many typewriter ribbons ago.

MARTIN E. GOLDSTEIN
Philadelphia, Pennsylvania

ACKNOWLEDGMENTS

The author would like to thank the following for permission to quote at length:

Dwight D. Eisenhower, *Waging Peace* (New York: Doubleday and Company, 1965).

John Foster Dulles, "A Policy for Security and Peace," *Foreign Affairs* 32 (April, 1954): 353-64.

AMERICAN POLICY
TOWARD LAOS

1

INTRODUCTION

"IF YOU WANT to get a sense of the universe unraveling, come to Laos. Complexities such as this have to be respected." The writer, Norman Cousins, former Editor of *Saturday Review,* was expressing the reaction of many who turn their attention to Laos. Perhaps the very complexities that Mr. Cousins so respected were instrumental in enticing the author of the present volume to plunge further into that unraveling universe. In any event, this book represents an effort to untie some of the knots, bind up the loosening threads, and weave the complexities of Laos into an intelligible pattern.

Previous attempts have been made to explain the dizzying events that whirled about Laos. Arthur J. Dommen's *Conflict in Laos* (New York: Frederick A. Praeger, 1964) and Bernard B. Fall's *Anatomy of a Crisis: The Laotian Crisis of 1960-61* (Garden City: Doubleday and Company, 1969) both offer highly useful day-to-day accounts of Laotian political history. *Storm Over Laos* (New York: Frederick A. Praeger, 1961), penned by Sisouk Na Champassak, a Laotian who participated in the events under consideration, sheds light on the period through 1960.

The present volume differs from those mentioned in several respects. In the first place, the author, as a political scientist, has not attempted to narrate the hour-by-hour sequence of events upon which the journalist and historian thrive. The emphasis in this book is on analysis; that is, we shall be concerned less with *what* happened than with *why* a particular event occurred and the consequences of that event. Accordingly, the reader will not find an exhaustive history of Laos within these pages. Various minor details and unimportant happenings have been omitted

17

(they can be found in the volumes previously cited) so that the reader can ponder the significance of the more important events. It has been necessary, of course, to include some smaller matters in order to render the larger events explicable. The author has attempted, however, to minimize superfluous detail in the interest of analysis and explanation as opposed to mere reporting.

A second way in which this account differs from others already published lies in its subject matter. Other writers have told the story of Laos from the vantage of Vientiane, the capital of that troubled land. In other words, they were concerned primarily with the problems facing the Laotian government and people, the ways in which they solved these problems, and the most likely course for Laos in the future. Such a story obviously needs to be told and, indeed, already has been. The present writer has taken a different point of departure. He has forsaken the noisy, dust-filled thoroughfares of Vientiane for the scarcely less turbulent city of Washington, D. C. This vantage point has afforded him the opportunity to focus on American perceptions, interests and policies with regard to Laos. While other works discuss American policy toward Laos only occasionally, American policy occupies stage center in the present volume.

Besides a detailed examination of American policy, the author is concerned with another matter that the previously mentioned writers elected not to discuss in a systematic manner. The Laotian conflict represented an unusual cold war struggle in that it was settled, at least temporarily, by a compromise agreement in 1962. That compromise might well have endured for several years, were it not for the escalation of the fighting in Vietnam in the middle 1960s. The United States and particularly North Vietnam found the territory of Laos to be of central strategic importance to the war in Vietnam. Hanoi sent men and supplies down the Ho Chi Minh Trail, which passes from North Vietnam through eastern Laos into South Vietnam. To interdict this flow, the United States dispatched its bombers against the trails in eastern Laos. Furthermore, each protagonist sought the assistance of its Laotian clients: Washington persuaded Souvanna Phouma's government to help stem the movement of men and material down the Trail. Hanoi and the Pathet Lao joined forces in mounting a resistance against the government in Vientiane. As Laos became a part of the battlefield on which the Vietnamese war was waged, the 1962 accords suffered unbearable strain and eventually snapped. But the fact remains that, at least for a time, a compromise settlement was achieved in Laos. It was far from inevitable that a compromise would be fashioned. The feuding Laotian factions could have chosen to continue their military contest until one side annihilated the other and demanded the fruits of total victory. The United States and the Soviet Union, principal external supporters of the Laotian fighting forces, could have urged their respective factions to keep fighting for unconditional surrender. Yet unconditional surrender, the rallying-cry in World Wars I and II, was dropped in favor of compromise settlement. The particular question the author seeks to answer is: why did these intense rivalries, heated to a glowing red by years of shootings, burnings, and vicious diatribe, end in compromise? Why did the parties, both in Laos and abroad, jettison unconditional surrender in favor of a compromise settlement? Such a question bears importance not only on the Laotian situation, but also on the entire spectrum of conflicts that colors today's world. If one could uncover the necessary and sufficient ingredients of compromise, then perhaps such factors could be force-fed into some of the quarrels that afflict mankind, from student–administration confrontations to labor–management disputes to international crises. The present volume represents an effort to add to the growing body of knowledge on the conditions leading to compromise. Much has been written on the causes of war. Surely it is not amiss to inquire into the causes of peace.

We begin our examination of American policy toward Laos in the following chapter, in which we consider America's stake in Laos. This chapter seeks to answer the question: Why should the United States be concerned with what happens in Laos? In answering this question, the author includes a thumbnail sketch of Laos, so that the reader may become better acquainted with the land that forms the subject of this study. Inasmuch as American policy toward Laos cannot be insulated from American policy toward the remainder of Indochina, we move on in the next chapter to an examination of Indochina in the context of America's overall strategic objectives.

The 1954 Geneva Conference may be considered the prologue to American involvement in Laos, since the delegates at Geneva mapped out a settlement that Washington tried to modify during the next decade. In Chapters 4 and 5, we examine the Geneva settlement as well as Washington's reaction thereto. Having glanced at America's larger interests in Indochina, in addition to the existing state of affairs in that area of the world as determined at Geneva, we focus in on Laos once again. In the following chapters, we concern ourselves with what occurred in Laos and what the United States was doing there; these topics comprise the major portion of this volume.

It is convenient, for the sake of analysis, to consider the years 1954–1962 as a distinct unit of time to be broken off and treated apart from the rest. Certainly, two international conferences—one in 1954 and the other in 1961–62—bracket this time span rather neatly. The Geneva Conference in 1954 seemed to clear the slate in Laos, to provide the opportunity for a fresh start. The second international conference, also at Geneva, had the appearance of a settlement, an end to the problems that had been generated since 1954. But as seasoned observers of human affairs realize, all time periods—whether they be as subjective as the Age of Reason or as objective as the fourteenth century—are artificial. In the topography of history, there are no canyons, only slopes. Events issue from one another and give rise to yet newer occurrences. With this fact in mind, the writer has attempted, albeit briefly, to show how the events of 1954–1962 stand in relation to what came before and what has followed. The communist organization in Laos, the Pathet Lao, as well as the Pathet Lao's possession of a base area in northern Laos, were both products of the fighting between the French and the Vietnamese in the decade leading up to 1954. These matters are discussed in the chapter on the Geneva Conference.

To evaluate the significance of the 1962 settlement, as well as succeeding events, is a bit more difficult. The chronicler of recent history is invariably afflicted with limited vision. What man, writing in 1502, could have perceived the vast significance of Columbus's voyage to the New World only ten years earlier? What man, today, can fathom the consequences of Astronaut Neil Armstrong's first footprint on the moon? Although the contemporary historian labors under certain handicaps, he must nevertheless attempt to fill the need for an interpretation of the world around him. Accordingly, the author has endeavored, in the closing chapter, to bring his narrative up to the present.

Let us begin with an examination of America's interest in Laos.

2
AMERICA'S INTEREST IN LAOS

ANYONE WITH AN interest in American policy toward Laos must at one time or another confront the simple question: Why should the United States display any concern with what happens in Laos? In this chapter, we shall attempt to answer this question, in the process presenting a thumbnail description of the kingdom.

TRADITIONAL BASES FOR INTERVENTION

In general terms, why does one country intervene in the affairs of another country? A complete answer to this question would require volumes. In the context of the present discussion, however, it is possible to suggest some answers that will shed light both on Laos itself and on America's interest in that country.

One reason why country A might feel called upon to interfere in the affairs of country B falls under the rubric of geopolitics. Any nation-state, by virtue of its location on the earth's surface, possesses certain qualities. Because these qualities are prime determinants of the nation's ability to influence other states, they are often referred to as the "elements of national power." Natural resources, climate, population, topography, and the state's location in relation to other states are generally included in a typical catalogue of the elements of national power. A few examples should make this explanation clearer. For no other reason than its location on the globe, West Germany has inherited the Saar Valley, which contains one of the richest iron and coal deposits in the world. Consequently, there is a strong likelihood that West Germany would become a mighty industrial power, enabling her to wield much influence in the international arena. China's enormous population has made her a major power on the Asian continent. The climate in Antarctica renders it improbable that that area will become a dominant power.

Returning to the matter of intervention, one traditional occasion for intervention is state A's concern with who controls the elements of power in state B. When the elements of power in B are of sufficient magnitude that they could be used to inflict serious damage on A, then A generally seeks to prevent B from falling into hands hostile to A. On the other hand, if B's elements of power are so miniscule that, even should they fall into the clutches of forces hostile to A, they could not cause serious damage to A, then A would have little interest in B's fate. For example, the United States has a vital interest in preventing the elements of power in West Germany or France or Great Britain from falling into hands hostile to the United States, because an enemy power could utilize the resources in these states to wreak serious destruction on the United States. However, the United States displays little concern with who controls Lesotho or Uganda because the elements of power in such states could not be used to threaten America. Obviously, there are gradations in between vital concern for who controls another state and no interest at all. As would be expected, America regards most states as falling somewhere toward the middle of this spectrum instead of at the extremities.

Where does Laos fall along this geopolitical continuum? Should its attributes of power place it high on the list of American priorities, on the ground that a power hostile to the United States could seize Laos and use its elements of power to seriously damage American interests? Could the United States utilize the elements of power in Laos to further American interests?

POPULATION

Let us first consider population. Generally, a state cannot become a major or even a middle power without a minimum level of population.[1] This condition applies even to a state extremely rich in resources. North America, one of the most resource-rich land masses in the world, was a negligible power until the Europeans colonized it. The European explorers brought two things to the New World: technology and people. It was only in the latter part of the nineteenth century, when a sufficient number of people applied an advanced technology[2] to the land, that the United

States began to emerge as a world power. An overcrowded state, even though well endowed with resources, cannot produce at maximum efficiency. Would not India and China carry more influence if they contained fewer people? An underpopulated area, such as Greenland, could enhance its influence by the addition of more people. A state which is both underpopulated and lacking in natural resources is likely to be discounted at the world's chanceries as little more than a wavelet on the seas of international politics.

Such a state is Laos. With an area of just over 91,000 square miles, Laos occupies about the same space as Idaho. No better indication of the level of development in Laos can be had than the simple fact that there has never been an official census in Laos. It is estimated, however, that from two to three million people inhabit Laos, about the same number of people as live in the metropolitan area of Philadelphia. Using a population figure of 2.5 million, we see that the population density in Laos is only 27 persons per square mile, a very low figure compared to that of most countries. Laos's small population is one of the factors that place it among the ranks of the world's mini-powers.

NATURAL RESOURCES

Another reason why Laos must be classified among those states least able to wield influence in international affairs may be traced to its share of natural resources.

Natural resources have traditionally served as a rationale for the intervention by one state into the affairs of another. This line of reasoning may take two forms. In the first place, it is desirable to prevent an enemy power from gaining control of resources that it could use to bolster its political power by increasing its military or industrial capacities or in some other manner. Such thinking may lead to "preventive intervention." One hears, for example, that the United States must establish a foothold in Southeast Asia in order to prevent the Chinese from seizing the rice yield there. The second argument states simply that a nation wishes to have for its own use the resources of the target state. Both of these ideas find their application in American relations with West Germany. The United States wishes to prevent the Soviet Union from gaining control of the natural resources of the Ruhr, for these would enable Russia to increase her military and industrial capabilities. In addition, the United States wants access to these resources to bolster her own capabilities as well as those of her allies in Western Europe.

What of Laos? Does she possess natural resources that a power hostile to the United States might use against the United States? Does she have natural resources that the United States deems important for its own use? Such questions are difficult to answer, because Laos has never been completely surveyed for natural resources. However, some mineral deposits have been located. Large deposits of iron ore have been discovered in Kieng Khoung. Magnesium and coal have been identified. French-operated tin mines are currently functioning at Phong Tiou. Laos has considerable timber resources and is beginning to export forestry products. Deposits of zinc, limestone, copper, lead, gold, salt, tungsten and phosphates have been found, although the extent of such deposits is not known. Except for the tin mines, the only sizable industry in Laos, these mineral resources have not been developed due to constant warfare. There is reason to believe, however, that development will begin when hostilities cease and the country can devote full attention to internal economic development.

As one can see, Laos is by no means a barren land. However, it is quite another matter to aver that Laos is so abundant in crucial resources that the United States has good reason, on this ground alone, to intervene in Laos on a massive scale. As Table 1 shows, the products that Laos exports hardly warrant large-scale American intervention.

TABLE I
LAOTIAN EXPORTS[a]

(In thousands of kips)[b]	1964	1965
Tin	165,745	147,246
Wood	12,716	19,122
Green coffee	15,123	11,104
Cardamon	2,977	1,200
Benzoin	496	26,845
Sticklac	180	225
Leather and hides	1,417	1,032
Others	14,691	33,395
Total	213,345	240,169

a Excluding gold
b 290 kips equals $1.00
Source: Laotian Ministry of Finance

Table 1 does not show receipts from the substantial but illicit export of opium.

Inasmuch as Laos has just begun to extract its resources from the ground, the table above provides a better indication of present grounds for intervention rather than potential future reasons to intervene. However, Laos possesses no resources that cannot be obtained elsewhere. The magnitude of already identified deposits remains unknown. In all likelihood, the United States has already spent more money on Laos than she could ever hope to regain in natural resources. There is good reason to conclude that Laos lacks natural resources in such quantity that they could be used with great effect either against American interests or to forward American objectives. Surely, there must be more convincing reasons to account for American intervention.

ECONOMY

Closely related to the natural resources rationale for intervention is the argument that the economy of the target country merits interference. Like the natural resources argument, the economy argument takes two forms. First, state A may intervene in state B in order to prevent a third state, hostile to A, from adding B's output to its own. Secondly, A may wish to intervene in B not for preventive reasons but to gain control of B's productivity.

As we cast our eyes at the Laotian economy, we find little that a state hostile to America could use and little that the United States could utilize. Economically, Laos is one of the least developed countries in the world. Its average annual per capita income is fifty dollars. When the French came, they found no industry. The French elected to extract wealth from Vietnam and use Laos as a buffer between Vietnam and Thailand, where the French rivals in Britain were trying to establish a foothold. Thus, when Laos received her independence in 1954, there was practically no industry to speak of, except for the tin mines and a few sawmills.

Farming provides the principal livelihood for the Laotian peasants, who make up about 90 percent of the population. Most of the farmers live at the subsistence level and still use methods dating to the stone age.[3] A picture of a typical Laotian farmer shows him gripping a wooden plow drawn by a beast of burden. Some of the tribes use an ancient agricultural method known as *ray* cultivation. The farmers burn down a certain area of forest and plant on the fertile ashes. The following year, the farmers move to another forested section, burn it down, and plant on the new ashes. This practice has injured the land and may eventually interfere with the forestry industries.

Stimulated by foreign assistance, the Laotian economy is beginning to make advances, but at a glacial pace. In the towns along the Mekong, one sees small market places, where food can be exchanged for goods made by craftsmen. This represents a change from the usual pattern of self-sufficient communities with no outside commercial contacts. Even today, many areas in Laos remain economically self-sufficient. During the rainy season—May to September—many sections of the country are isolated because of muddy and impassable roads. Thus, no trade occurs. A great many of Laotian villages remain cut off even in the driest weather; these villages occupy a jungle clearing and lack access except by helicopter.

Internal fighting in Laos since 1965 has hampered economic advance. Bridges, roads and other transportation facilities have been destroyed. Development projects have been largely confined to the towns,[4] since rural areas enjoy little security. The constant warfare has discouraged foreign private investors from undertaking enterprises in Laos.

In the larger cities, such as Vientiane, Luang Prabang and Pakse, retail trade and the processing of raw materials are beginning to develop. Chinese living in Laos dominate this aspect of the economy.

Cash crops are also making an appearance. Sweet corn, beans, sugar cane, pimento, tomatoes, potatoes, sweet potatoes, coffee, cotton, maize, and tobacco have been grown. None of these products has been cultivated in great quantity. The Laotians also produce livestock, but this has been poor in quality. The first bank in Laos, a branch of the *Banque de l'Indochine,* opened in 1953. Since then other banks have started, so a skeletal banking system exists. Many Laotians, however, distrust the banks and prefer to borrow money from local Chinese and Indian money-lenders.

If Laos could put an end to the warfare that has continued since 1954, she could make major strides in economic development.[5] If an enterprising and acquisitive ethic were to replace the traditional outlook of the peasantry,[6] agricultural advances could take place. Larger farms and more modern methods could increase output and free agricultural workers for work in capital goods industries. Laos could increase the quantity, quality and diversity of her farm output. She could grow more productive strains of rice, temperate fruits and vegetables, and better livestock. Food-producing plants could be kept busy by an increase in agricultural output. The Mekong offers opportunities to develop hydroelectric power. The vast wooded areas could be worked at a greater pace, so as to increase the forestry industries. Known mineral deposits could be worked, while the remainder of the country was being surveyed.

Given the primitive technology and traditional outlook of most Laotians, prospects for substantial economic development over the next two or three decades appear dim. Even if Laos were to exploit the resources at her disposal, she could not become a major industrial economy. Consequently, we are compelled to reject the contention that the United States intervened in Laos either to prevent strategic goods from falling into enemy hands or to gain control of the Laotian economy to add to America's capabilities. We must continue to search for a more convincing rationale for America's involvement.

SOCIAL STRUCTURE

Social structure is an important determinant of a country's capacity to act effectively in international affairs. Where the people stand united, a country is able to act more forcefully than where the population is riven by disagreements. In the late 1940s and 1950s, when nearly every American believed in the existence of a communist plot to take over the world, Presidents Truman and Eisenhower had little difficulty in persuading the American people to commit themselves to the defense of nations halfway around the globe. In the 1970s, many Americans question both the intentions and capabilities of the leaders in Moscow and Peking. Such doubts appeared most dramatically in wide-scale demonstrations against the war in Vietnam. Consequently, President Nixon must act more cautiously in committing the United States to the defense of faraway places with strange sounding names.

A nation with a unified cohesive social structure is better able to resist foreign penetration than a state where various elements welcome assistance in overthrowing the existing regime. The former condition is illustrated by South Korea, which has withstood North Korean efforts to mount a campaign of subversion and guerrilla warfare. In contrast, South Vietnam was highly vulnerable to foreign interference, because so many South Vietnamese felt alienated by the government of Ngo Dinh Diem and its successors.

As between these two extremes, the social structure in Laos lies closer to that typified by South Vietnam than to the South Korean model.[7] If one were to raise a pane of glass over one's head and smash it on the floor, the scattered distribution of glass splinters would bear a striking resemblance to the social structure in Laos.

The Laotian social structure is remarkable for its variety. It has been estimated that in this land of less than three million inhabitants, there are over 50 distinct ethnic groups, each as separate from and out of contact with each other as shards of glass spread about the floor.

The people of Laos may be divided into three basic groups. The largest segment is the Lao people, a branch of the Tai race, which originated in Yunnan. The second largest element is the tribal minorities who inhabit the hill country. National minorities, especially the Chinese and the Vietnamese, constitute the third major group in the Laotian social structure.

The people we know today as ethnic Laotians originally came from China. Beginning in the third century A.D. and extending up to the fourteenth century, the Chinese forced the Tai peoples living in China down through southern China into the Indochinese peninsula. These uprooted Tais settled across Yunnan (in southern China), northern Vietnam, Cambodia, Laos, Thailand, and the Shan states of Burma.[8]

The Tai people who settled in Laos are known today as the Lao people. The Lao make up from one-half to two-thirds of the total population of Laos. When the Lao people were driven from China, many of them built settlements along the Mekong River Valley. Today, practically all urban life in Laos is clustered in the Mekong towns where 10 percent of the population lives. The remainder of the Lao people inhabit many of the 10,000 villages scattered over the land in an irregular polkadot pattern.

The second major element in the Laotian social structure is the tribal minorities. Most of these tribes have retained their unique dialects, cultures, traditions, habits, and life-styles. Consequently, the traveler senses that he has entered a new land each time he passes from one tribal settlement to another. Many of the tribes, which cannot communicate with one another because of language differences,[9] feel hostile toward one another. Just as in pre-Columbian America, an Apache or an Iroquois was devoted to his tribe rather than a nation, so many Laotian tribesmen attach their supreme loyalty not to Laos but to their respective tribes. This parochialism is reinforced by the topography of Laos. Except for the Mekong Valley, most of Laos looks like an egg carton, with high mountains and steep ravines. The automobile and railroad have not penetrated to the hill country. Hence, each tribe lives in an isolated pocket, cut off from its neighbors except by a jungle trek that is likely to require several days, if it can be made at all.

The compartmentalization of the tribes has aggravated the problem of governing the country. Tribal antipathies, as well as the physical isolation of many settlements, have deprived the Vientiane government of control. These factors also provided opportunities upon which the communists skillfully capitalized to gather followers.

Even more important than the ill will among the tribes is the relationship between the tribal peoples and the dominant group in Laos, the ethnic Laotians. The latter have traditionally regarded the tribes as lazy, untutored primitives deserving only of contempt. The tribes have returned this disdain with a studied dislike for the Lao people, often coupled with a refusal to cooperate with them. Given the grave difficulties in governing the country caused by the antipathy between the tribes and the ethnic Laotians, and given the communist successes in finding recruits among the tribesmen, the Laotian government has followed a remarkably obtuse policy regarding the tribal peoples. Staffed almost completely by ethnic Laotians, the government seems bent on aggravating the differences between the tribes and the Laotians. The government has done little to integrate the tribes into the social structure dominated by the Laotians, so as to forge a national Laotian society. Few steps have been taken to raise the subsistence level of the tribal economies or to provide the tribesmen with educational opportunities. The Lao, in the process of maintaining their separate and privileged position, are gradually dissolving what few bonds of national unity exist.

The third principal segment of the Laotian social structure, the national minorities, dwells with the Lao in the towns along the Mekong. For the most part, the national minorities have been integrated into the mainstream of the Laotian economy. The most important national minorities are the Chinese and the Vietnamese.

Relations between the Laotians and the approximately 25,000 Vietnamese living in Laos may be characterized by an old Laotian proverb, "Dog and cat, Annamite [Vietnamese] and Laotian." Laotian–Vietnamese rivalry dates from a troubled history of conflicting border claims and warfare between the two states, aggravated by certain practices of the French colonial administration. Since the Middle Ages the Vietnamese have tried to establish a sphere of influence over the territory that is now Laos. In fact, North Vietnamese incursions into Laos in the late 1960s[10] could be viewed in part as a continuation of this historic struggle for influence. The occasional appearance of a powerful Laotian warrior-prince would force the Vietnamese back to their own land until a weakened Laos invited renewed Vietnamese aggression. This flux and reflux has left a residue of ill will between Laotians and Vietnamese, a situation not unlike the nationalistic hostilities between Poland and Russia or between Germany and Czechoslovakia. When the French moved into Indochina in the middle of the nineteenth century, they employed Vietnamese as minor administrators and teachers in Laos. Naturally, the Laotians were unhappy with the exalted position accorded to foreigners in their midst. This resentment has persisted, although the Vietnamese have been eliminated from their positions in the administration and the educational system.

The Chinese constitute the largest national minority in Laos. There are approximately 35,000 sons of the Middle Kingdom in Laos, making up nearly 2 percent of the total population. The Chinese have retained their own separate dialects and traditions. In fact, the Chinese, coming from six different regions in China, have difficulty communicating with each other, because the dialect from each area is unintelligible to the people from the other areas. As in other states in Southeast Asia, the Chinese operate their own schools,[11] their own community organizations, and in some towns even their own Chinese chambers of commerce. Another similarity between the Chinese in Laos and those in other Southeast Asian states is the position occupied by the Chinese in the economy. Throughout Southeast Asia, the clever and industrious Chinese have achieved an importance in the economy far in excess of their numbers.[12] In 1959 there were 2,951 business establishments in the seven major towns in Laos. Of these establishments, 1,392 or 47 percent were operated by Chinese who, as we have observed, constitute less than 2 percent of the population of Laos.[13]

One would expect some tension to exist when an outside minority enjoys such a favored position in a nation's economy. In Laos, there is hostility between the Laotians and the Chinese, but the two ethnic groups have worked out a coexistence that is quite admirable when compared to other nations faced with a similar problem. To a certain extent the Laotians envy the Chinese for their business ability and record of commercial achievements. The situation is hardly helped by the traditional Chinese attitude of superiority towards all non-Chinese. In order to limit Chinese domination of the economy, the Laotian government has enacted restrictions on Chinese commercial activity. Frequently, however, a Laotian and a Chinese will form a partnership in order to skirt these regulations. Typically, the Laotian "partner" is only a front man who shares the profits while the Chinese actually operates the business.

Bribery presents another source of ill feeling between the Chinese and Laotians. Some Lao government officials seem prone to offer lucrative commercial opportunities to Chinese in return for a bribe. Many Laotians accuse the Chinese of promoting government dishonesty by attempting to bribe officials. In all likelihood, the initiative comes from Lao officials in some cases and from Chinese in others. In any case, the problem has led to some nasty accusations on both sides.

The political affiliation of Chinese living in Laos represents a potential source of friction. Little is known about the political views of the Chinese living in Laos. In case of Red Chinese pressure upon Laos, would the Chinese residents provide a fifth column? Fears of such an eventuality have been voiced in Laos.

Despite these points of conflict, the Chinese and the Laotians have managed to get along quite well. Chinese and Laotians intermarry at all levels of society. In some respects, the Chinese have adopted the Laotian culture which surrounds them. Nevertheless, it remains unlikely (and is perhaps undesirable) that the Chinese will be assimilated and disappear as a distinct cultural entity in Laos.

In reviewing the social structure of Laos, the resemblance to a shattered pane of glass become apparent. This description applies particularly to the tribes which, as observed earlier, comprise approximately fifty distinct ethnic groups, speaking different languages, inheriting different cultures, and regarding each other with suspicion and hostility. Add to this the ethnic Lao people—practically a minority in their own land—and the condescending attitude of the Lao toward the tribes, and more lines of division in the Laotian social structure become visible. Finally, when one considers the presence of national minorities—particularly the Vietnamese and Chinese, but also the Thais, Indians, French, Cambodians, and still others—the kaleidoscope of peoples and cultures that is Laos is complete.

Let us return to the theme of American interests in Laos. Could a power hostile to the United States so mobilize the Laotian population as to threaten American interests? Could, on the other hand, the United States make use of the Laotian people to further its own designs? Either eventuality seems unlikely. Because of Laos's fragmented social structure, no government in Vientiane has been able to control all the people, and some regimes have not been able to control even a majority of the people. It remains doubtful that, should any other group seize power, it would enjoy greater success in uniting the people—the Lao, the tribes and the national minorities—on a single course. Furthermore, the Laotian population, less than three million, is just too small to make much of a difference, even in Southeast Asia. In light of these factors, the Laotian population, in terms of both cohesiveness and numbers, would not seem to call for large-scale American intervention. There must be other reasons why the United States decided to become involved in the affairs of Laos.

PROTECTION OF COMMERCIAL INTERESTS

A frequently expressed reason for intervention is the need to protect or advance the private commercial interests of the nationals of the intervening state. Such reasoning became one of the principal underlying tenets of nineteenth-century European expansion into the non-European world. In the early part of the twentieth century, this rationale was occasionally offered in defense of American intervention in Latin America. We can, however, dismiss this argument in the case of American involvement in Laos, inasmuch as there has been no substantial American private investment in that country. The bulk of foreign investment in Laos was French, an expected result of the French presence in the country since the middle of the nineteenth century.

Thus far, we have found no convincing explanation for American involvement in Laos. None of the factors considered as yet—population, natural resources, economy, social structure, or protection of commercial interests—which have traditionally served as reasons for intervention, seems to account for American interest in this small kingdom halfway around the globe.

STRATEGIC LOCATION

One geopolitical factor remains to be considered: strategic location. Strategic location has often been cited as a basis for intervention. In 1956 the British and French felt compelled to invade Egypt in order to keep open the Suez Canal, an area that has long enjoyed high strategic importance. Gibraltar, which commands the passage leading from the Atlantic Ocean to the Mediterranean Sea, has long been considered one of the world's most strategic locations. Another area that has dominated history because of its strategic importance is the Dardanelles. For centuries Russia has sought to control the Dardanelles, because this passageway governs the movement of ships from the Black Sea, on which Russia fronts, to the Mediterranean. Control of the Dardanelles would give Russia a warm water port and unrestricted access to the Mediterranean Sea, traditional objectives of Russian policy from the times of the Tsars.

What of Laos? Does this country which lies just below the Tropic of Cancer qualify as an area of important strategic location? The answer to this question depends upon the answer to another question, namely: is it vital to American security to keep Southeast Asia free from communist domination? If one answers the second question in the affirmative, then Laos does possess significant value in terms of strategic location. We shall explore the importance attached to keeping Southeast Asia out of the communist orbit in a later section. For the present, let us assume that American policy-makers thought it essential to prevent the communists from penetrating Southeast Asia.

If the communists were to exert external[14] influence in Southeast Asia, they would have to move in a north to south direction; that is, they would have to move from China and North Vietnam down into the southern portion of the Indochinese peninsula. The topographical configurations in Southeast Asia contain four routes capable of being transformed into north–south roads.[15] Two routes run through Burma—the

Ledo Road, running from the Brahmaputra Valley of Assam in India across Burma to Kunming in China, and the Burma Road, leading from Rangoon through Mogok to China. Burmese neutrality has prevented China from using these two routes along the western side of the Indo-chinese peninsula. A third potential north–south thoroughfare proceeds from China to Hanoi and then down the coast of Vietnam to the southern tip of the peninsula. The division of Vietnam after 1954 and the American presence in Vietnam have blocked this route. The fourth and final passageway goes down the Laotian side of the Annamite Mountains through northern Laos to the royal capital of Luang Prabang,[16] thence along an existing road to the political capital of Vientiane, and then either southward along the Mekong River or westward toward Bangkok by way of Korat in Thailand. Laos itself is too weak to prevent a determined effort by either the Chinese or North Vietnamese from utilizing this fourth route to the south. If the United States wished to close this road to the communists, Americans themselves would have to help the Laotians do the job. Having made the decision that the communists must be kept out of Southeast Asia, the United States had reason, on geopolitical grounds, to intervene in Laos to control this access route from China and North Vietnam to the remainder of Southeast Asia.[17]

We have finally uncovered a credible reason for American intervention in Laos. It remains to explore another rationale often used to justify interference in another country's affairs.

IDEOLOGY

Ideology as a basis for intervention can count its followers from the origin of the nation-state system in the Middle Ages. In the early feudal period, the Christian lands of the West joined together to do ideological battle against the Infidel in the Near East. More recently, the monarchs of early-nineteenth-century Europe crossed scepters in the Holy Alliance, formed for the purpose of protecting monarchical governments threatened by republican uprisings. In August 1968, the Soviet Union intervened in Czechoslovakia to protect that state from ideological "impurities" contained in the liberalized regime of Alexander Dubcek. Both the Holy Alliance and the Soviet Union intervened for the purpose of maintaining forms of government that shared the same ideology as the intervening party. Could American intervention in Laos be based on the need to maintain a form of government similar to that in the United States?

Ever since the emergence of Laos as a separate political entity between the ninth and fourteenth centuries, that country has been governed by

the very form of government against which our Founding Fathers re-
belled: monarchy. The emergence of national cohesion in Laos paralleled
the pattern of nation-state development in medieval Europe. Mighty
princes who controlled separate regions in the kingdom contested the
monarch for actual sovereignty.[18] In the late seventeenth and early
eighteenth centuries, Prince Soulingavongsa brought unruly Laotian princes
under his sway. During Soulingavongsa's reign, which lasted until his
death in 1711, Laos attained its "Golden Age" of national unity and
cultural achievements. After the Prince died, dynastic quarrels weakened
the state, easing the way for Annam, Burma, China and Siam to exact
tribute from Laos. The tendency for neighbors to take advantage of
internal strife in Laos, a pattern that commenced with the founding of
the Laotian state, is one reason why Laos remains so suspicious of her
neighbors today. The current involvement of North Vietnam and China
in Laos, on behalf of the Pathet Lao, is only the latest manifestation of
this pattern of Laotian history.

In the early nineteenth century, Prince Chou Anou nearly succeeded
in subduing independent-minded princes and reuniting Laos. After Chou
was defeated in an attack upon Bangkok, Laos fell again to internal
fighting and foreign domination. The Thais occupied much of the country,
while Annam controlled the eastern portion. In 1885 the French came
to Laos and, eight years later, established a protectorate. Welcomed as
liberators, the French easily gained Laotian cooperation in driving out the
Thais. When the French set up their protectorate over Laos in 1893, they
designated the Mekong River as the western boundary of Laos. This
boundary has never been accepted as final by the Laotians, inasmuch as
areas west of the Mekong had been recognized as Laotian territory before
Laos was defeated by Thailand in 1828. Irredentist claims to these
regions could lead to trouble between the Thais and Laotians, should a
strong man emerge in Laos to unite its people once again.

Since France's principal interest in Indochina lay in Vietnam, the
French did not upset the traditional princely administration of the Laotian
state. (On the other hand, the French did not prepare the Laotians for
independence by training them to run a modern state.) The Laotian
monarchical form of government has changed little to this day. At present,
Laos is a constitutional monarchy. The king appoints the upper house
of Parliament and the prime minister, who then nominates a cabinet,
which the king and National Assembly must approve. The National
Assembly, or lower house, is composed of 59 members elected at large by
the population every five years. In accord with the European parliamentary
system, a vote of no confidence by the National Assembly results in the
collective resignation of the cabinet. Then the king selects a new prime

minister, who in turn proposes a new cabinet to the king. By tradition the king is more of a symbol than an active participant in the government. The king, who rarely sojourns about the countryside, commands respect as an august personage who is occasionally heard of but seldom seen. Laotian politics are based primarily on personality. Political platforms give way to personal loyalties as the *raison d'être* of political parties. Since there are as many political parties as there are prominent individuals, parliamentary life resembles that of the French Fourth Republic more than Great Britain, where there is one party in power and another party in opposition. Government by coalition is the norm in Laos.

Can it be said, then, that the United States has taken an interest in Laos in order to preserve a form of government similar to its own? This would hardly seem to be the case, since the two countries have vastly different forms of government, and the United States began life in rebellion against the very principles which Laos has upheld since birth.

There is another sense, however, in which the United States could be said to share an ideological affinity with Laos. Both countries belong to that nonexistent entity known as the "free world." As everyone knows, of course, many governments in this "free world" allow no freedom whatsoever. Can states such as Paraguay, Greece, Brazil, and Spain really be said to be free in the same sense that we know freedom in the United States or Great Britain? There is no basis in reality for designating such states as members of the same "world." "Free world" has meaning, it seems, only if "free" is equated with "noncommunist." Such an interpretation ignores the fact that there are forms of tyranny other than, and sometimes worse than, communism.

Nevertheless, American intervention in Laos does find a plausible explanation in the "free world" argument. American policy toward Laos was forged in the Eisenhower era, when Washington undertook the task of sealing off the "free world" from communist penetration. In the process, Washington made formal security commitments to over forty nations, nearly half the noncommunist world. Although Laos was not favored with a formal American guarantee, Washington's involvement in Laos proceeded from the same rationale as America's involvement in Greece and Turkey, Berlin, Lebanon, Cuba, Vietnam and the Dominican Republic. All these interventions were grounded in the identical ideological prescription: preventing communists from gaining control of any country not already in the communist fold.

Although one may question the wisdom of this ideological crusade against communism, one cannot deny that it formed a strong basis for American intervention in Laos.

Bernard B. Fall, to whom every student of Southeast Asia remains indebted for his extensive research and writing on Indochina, suggests a further reason for American involvement in Laos.[19] By the early 1950s, Fall says, the United States was sorely in need of a foreign policy success in Asia. The Americans since World War II had suffered a number of policy defeats in Asia. The communists had expelled America's client Chiang Kai-shek to Taiwan. In the Korean War, the United States was compelled to accept a settlement that reestablished the boundary between the two Koreas almost exactly where it lay before the North Korean attack in June 1950. Thus the Korean War could hardly be termed a victory from the American point of view. Then, in 1954, America's ally France was defeated by the communist-led Vietminh. After this string of humiliations, the United States hungered for a foreign policy success in Asia. Laos was selected as the morsel to satisfy Washington's appetite.

Fall's argument might help account for a general attitude on the part of American officials that a foreign-policy victory in Asia was desirable. However, he fails to explain why the United States should take a stand in Laos in particular. Why not draw the line in Thailand or South Vietnam? Moreover, what was there about Laos that led American policy-makers to believe that they could achieve success there? Fall does not answer these questions, nor does he cite evidence to show that American policy-makers actually experienced as strong a desire for a foreign policy victory in Asia as Fall seems to feel they did. Even if the quest for a foreign policy success in Asia was high on America's list of priorities, Fall does not explain why Washington chose to make Laos the object of such efforts.

In reviewing possible reasons for American intervention in Laos, we have discovered two that seem highly plausible. One explanation lies in the geography of Southeast Asia. The only north–south route open to the communists for expansion into Southeast Asia passed through Laos. This outlet had to be plugged in order to prevent the communists from moving southward. The second plausible reason lies in the ideological struggle the United States was waging against communism and vice versa. This conflict, as it took shape in Southeast Asia, will be considered in the following chapter.

NOTES

1. One possible exception to this rule might be the case of a micro-state that obtains a nuclear weapon. For an amusing but instructive fictional account of such an occurrence, the reader is referred to the movie *The Mouse that Roared*.

2. Technology is a crucial factor. Besides having population and resources, a

state must possess the knowhow to convert raw material into a finished product. Primitive technology accounts for the low level of productivity in the Congo and other resource-rich territories in Africa.

3. Foreign assistance is beginning to introduce more modern agricultural methods, but the great majority of the farmers still use the most primitive techniques.

4. A fact that hardly endears the non-Lao hill tribesmen to the ethnic Laotians living in the towns.

5. Approximately 60 percent of the national budget is devoted to national security, principally to pay the salaries of about 80,000 soldiers.

6. The following tale illustrates the attitude of the typical Laotian farmer toward economic development. An American AID agent showed a farmer, living at the subsistence level, a new strain of rice with a yield four times as great as the rice the farmer had been planting. The farmer accepted the new strain and gleefully told his friends, "Now I only have to plant one-fourth my field."

7. A detailed description of the social structure in Laos may be found in Joel M. Halpern, *Government, Politics and Social Structure in Laos* (New Haven: Yale University, Southeast Asia Studies, Monograph Series Number 4, 1964).

8. This ten-century history of repression and expulsion accounts for the existence of a broad band of people in southern China and the northern reaches of Southeast Asia, all of whom share the same historical and cultural heritage. As students of nationalism in Europe know, any attempt to place people from a single ethnic strain on opposite sides of a national border will in all likelihood lead to trouble. Many of the difficulties in Southeast Asia, such as disputes between Thailand and Vietnam and between Vietnam and Cambodia, stem from this condition. On the basis of Wilsonian self-determination, it would make sense to redraw the boundaries in Southeast Asia so as to create a single state for the Tai people who inhabit Yunnan and the northern portions of Southeast Asia.

9. At least half the inhabitants of Laos are unable to communicate in the official Laotian language.

10. Prime Minister Souvanna Phouma estimated that at least 60,000 North Vietnamese troops were operating in Laos in January 1971 (*The New York Times,* January 31, 1971). Other estimates ranged down to 45,000. While the principal purpose of this expeditionary force may be to keep men and supplies flowing along the Ho Chi Minh Trail, running from North Vietnam through Laos into South Vietnam, it may be that Hanoi has intentions of establishing a base of influence in Laos which could be exploited after the conclusion of hostilities in Vietnam.

11. Special schools for the Chinese have had the effect of depriving the Chinese of higher education in Laos. The Chinese language is used and taught in the Chinese schools. The Chinese do not offer education beyond the junior high school level. In the more advanced Laotian schools the French language is used. Since the Chinese do not teach French in their own schools, Chinese children are unable to matriculate beyond the junior high school level. Many government jobs require education above that which is offered by the Chinese schools. Obviously, the Chinese lack the qualifications for such jobs.

12. The overseas Chinese have been called the Jews of Asia.

13. J. M. Halpern, *The Role of the Chinese in Laos Society,* Rand Corporation Research Report P-2161, March 1, 1961.

14. Another direction the communists could take, and did take, was to rely on communist sympathizers *within* each country, rather than imposing outside influence.

15. For a more detailed presentation of these geographical considerations, see Roger Hilsman, *To Move a Nation* (Garden City: Doubleday and Company, Inc., 1967), pp. 93–94.

16. Laos has two capitals. The king resides at Luang Prabang. The actual seat of government lies in Vientiane, further to the west.

17. No attempt is being made here to either praise or condemn this decision, but only to explain it. We shall evaluate the decision in a later chapter.

18. In Laos today, certain princely families, such as the Champassaks in southern Laos, exert strong influence in parts of the country they traditionally controlled. The internal fighting in Laos has overtones of family rivalries.

19. Bernard B. Fall, *Anatomy of a Crisis* (Garden City: Doubleday and Company, Inc., 1969), pp. 157–58.

3
AMERICA'S STANCE IN SOUTHEAST ASIA

AMERICA'S involvement in Laos in the later 1950s and 1960s was an outgrowth of American policy toward Southeast Asia as a whole. That policy, in turn, was part and parcel of the general policy taken by the United States toward the vast stretch of countries on the rim of the communist world, extending from the Baltic shores of Eastern Europe down along the Middle Eastern lands, then across southern China and North Vietnam up to Korea. This global policy has been given the name "containment."

In this chapter we shall discuss Washington's application of the containment policy to Indochina up to the Geneva Conference of 1954. First, we shall consider American involvement in the area up to, during, and immediately after World War II. Then we shall look at the crucial period in the winter of 1949–1950. Following this brief survey, we shall turn our attention to the views of President Eisenhower and his Secretary of State, John Foster Dulles, toward the threat posed by communism. Then, after consideration of Indochina's importance to American security, we shall review American actions with regard to Indochina and France in the years leading up to the 1954 Geneva Conference.

AMERICAN INVOLVEMENT IN INDOCHINA THROUGH WORLD WAR II

Before World War II, America's minimal involvement in Southeast

Asia, and Indochina in particular, reflected a general American attitude that this region was of little strategic value to the United States. As the historian Lawrence S. Finkelstein noted, "If strategic interest be calculated solely in terms of military defense of the United States against armed attack, it is difficult to project a situation in which Southeast Asia would be strategically vital to the United States."[1] Even apart from the immediate need for defending the United States against military assault, Americans attached little importance to Southeast Asia. Washington's principal involvement in the area centered on the Philippines, which the United States had fitfully acquired in 1899 as spoils from the Spanish-American War. Foreseeing a diminishing role for itself in that portion of the globe, Washington in 1935 accorded commonwealth status to the Philippines and granted that country independence on July 4, 1946.

As regards Indochina, the United States had every reason to assume that France was in control of the area. Consequently, there was no occasion for American concern. Besides, the French discouraged outside interference in their colonial affairs. In the years preceding World War II, then, the United States displayed minimal interest in Southeast Asia and Indochina.

This situation changed when Japan, bent on conquering all of Asia, began to occupy portions of Southeast Asia in 1940. Washington reacted to the extension of Japanese power first with verbal denouncements and later by freezing Japanese assets and denying Japan the scrap metal she needed to complete her domination of Southeast Asia. It is important to note, however, the quality of the change in America's position with regard to Southeast Asia. The United States did not resist Japan's encroachments because of the inherent importance of Southeast Asia to American security. Indeed, America survived the temporary "loss" of Southeast Asia in World War II rather well. What attracted American attention to the area was its importance as a *symbol*. If, it was argued, Japan were allowed to capture Southeast Asia, she would then turn her talons against the United States. Somewhere the line must be drawn. Since there was no place to draw the line between Southeast Asia and the west coast of the United States, America elected to resist Japanese aggression in Southeast Asia.

Southeast Asia, then, functioned as a symbol of American determination to resist Japanese aggression. It was in this respect that the area assumed importance to the United States in World War II. It is worth noting that Southeast Asia, and particularly Indochina, has continued to serve this role up to the present. In the latter half of the twentieth century it is communism, not Japanese militarism, that America has chosen to confront in Southeast Asia. And it has been Southeast Asia's misfortune to serve as the symbol of American resistance to communist expansion. At the same time, many Asian communists have also perceived Southeast Asia as a symbol—a symbol of peasant communism's capacity to defeat the industrialized, mechanized might of the West.

American policy toward Indochina from World War II to the hardening of the cold war in 1950 followed a zig-zag path. President Roosevelt had every intention of persuading France to grant independence to Indochina after the war. But with the passing of Roosevelt, French reluctance to abandon her colonies, and the onset of the cold war, United States policy shifted in favor of French retention of Indochina. We shall trace this reversal of American policy here.

To begin with, we may note that when Japan in 1940 began to train her sights on Indochina, Washington displayed a reluctance to become involved. This hesitation was consistent with America's minimal participation in Southeast Asian affairs before the war, and it provides further evidence that Washington did not regard the area as possessing great strategic importance.[2]

During the latter half of 1940, Japan took advantage of France's weakness to further her objectives in Indochina. One of Japan's aims was to close down the railroad that transported supplies from Haiphong to Chinese forces in Yunnan. On June 18, 1940, the day after France sued Germany for an armistice, Japan demanded that France shut down the Haiphong–Yunnan rail line. Faced with the threat of force, France had no choice but to comply.

Capitalizing on the Vichy government's impotence, Japan advanced her efforts to blockade China. On August 30 Japan compelled Vichy to grant her access rights to Indochina and permit her to establish bases there. On September 22, Vichy gave Japan the right to occupy Hanoi and Haiphong, use airfields in Tonkin (northern Indochina), and station troops there. Japan won Vichy's consent to station troops throughout all Indochina in July 1941.

America's bland reaction to these Japanese moves gives evidence that the United States attached little importance to Indochina at the time. On several occasions, Britain and France asked Washington for help in resisting these Japanese encroachments. In June 1940, the British Ambassador to the United States, Lord Lothian, asked America to pressure Japan by either placing an embargo on trade with Japan or dispatching warships to Singapore; Washington refused.[3] Later in June, once again during the summer of 1940, and once more in December 1940, Vichy appealed to America for help in resisting Japan's demands. All Washington would do was to express her sympathy and issue verbal condemnations of Japanese aggression.[4]

Washington's response to Japan's intrusions in Southeast Asia continued to take the form of verbal pronouncements until the summer of 1941. As 1941 progressed, the symbolic importance of resisting Japanese militarism in Southeast Asia was becoming more and more apparent in Washington. When Japanese forces began to occupy all of Indochina in the spring and summer of 1941, the Navy Department sent a major report on Indochina to President Roosevelt. The Navy report, dated July 21, said that American security depended on Britain's victory over Germany. Japan's occupation of Indochina, the report continued, might jeopardize Britain's position in Singapore and the Dutch position in the Netherlands East Indies (now Indonesia). This would weaken Britain and render her more vulnerable to defeat at the hands of Germany. Therefore, the report concluded, the United States has a close military interest in sustaining the status quo in Southeast Asia.[5] Three days later, Roosevelt registered a vigorous protest with the Japanese ambassador against Japan's occupation of southern Indochina. When Tokyo persisted, Washington on July 26 froze Japanese assets in the United States and placed an embargo on all trade with Japan.

The next major event in U. S.–Japanese relations occurred at Pearl Harbor. During the course of World War II, President Roosevelt reached the conclusion that Indochina should receive its independence after the war. At the Casablanca Conference in January 1943, where Roosevelt met with Churchill, the President told his son Elliott that colonialism in itself leads to war and therefore should be abolished. The President said,

> . . . the colonial system means war. Exploit the resources of an India, a Burma, a Java; take all the wealth out of those countries, but never put anything back into them, things like education, decent standards of living, minimum health requirements—all you're doing is stirring up the kind of trouble that leads to war.[6]

After the war, the President continued, France should be restored as a world power and entrusted with her colonies not as an absolute master but as a trustee, with the duty to report annually to the United Nations on her stewardship.[7]

One year later, Roosevelt wrote in a memo to Secretary of State Cordell Hull,

> France has had the country [Indochina]—thirty million inhabitants for nearly one hundred years, and the people are worse off than they were at the beginning.
> France has milked it [Indochina] for one hundred years. The people of Indo-China are entitled to something better than that.[8]

Roosevelt held fast to his trusteeship idea until late 1944. He abandoned

the plan partly because of British and French opposition to trusteeships—
they wanted their colonies back after the war—and partly because General
De Gaulle, whom Washington had by then recognized as the spokesman
for France, came to Washington in July 1944 and promised to grant
Indochina more representation within a postwar federal system.

When Roosevelt went to his grave in April 1945, his trusteeship idea
went with him. However, Washington continued for a time to hope for
and encourage eventual independence for Europe's colonies, including
Indochina.[9]

1945–1949

In the middle of 1945, as President Truman took over the reins of
power, American policy shifted in favor of supporting a French presence
in Indochina. The transition in American policy was a gradual one. A
policy paper prepared June 22, 1945, in the Department of State declared,
"The United States recognizes French sovereignty over Indochina." But
the paper reiterated, in very general terms, the hope that colonial people
everywhere would be prepared for eventual self-government.[10] On August 22, 23, and 25, three months after Germany's surrender, De Gaulle
met with Truman in Washington. Both leaders agreed that the communist
menace bore watching. According to De Gaulle's account of the meeting,
Truman voiced the opinion that the communist threat was so grave that
the United States must avoid dissension among its allies at all cost. With
regard to Franco-American relations, Truman told De Gaulle, "my government offers no opposition to the return of the French Army and
authority in Indochina."[11] The Truman–De Gaulle meeting settled once
and for all the question of American acquiescence in France's return to
Indochina. On October 20, John Carter Vincent, Director of the State
Department's Office of Far Eastern Affairs, supplied the definitive statement of American policy. In an important address, Vincent said, "With
regard to the situation in French Indochina, this Government does not
question French sovereignty in that area."[12] American policy had come
full circle from Roosevelt's plan for a trusteeship and his opposition to
France's return to Indochina.

While American policy was undergoing this shift, events in Indochina
were moving swiftly. Between August 1941 and March 1945, Japan had
controlled Indochina through the French Governor General, Jean Decoux.
On March 9, 1945, Japan decided to replace the French regime with a
native puppet regime which Japan hoped would be more subservient to
Tokyo's interests. To head this new regime, Japan chose Bao Dai. On

August 18–20, the Bao Dai regime was overthrown by the Viet Minh, a communist-dominated united front headed by Ho Chi Minh, which had been waging—with some American assistance—jungle warfare against the Japanese in Indochina. The Viet Minh proclaimed as its first objective total independence for Indochina. Upon seizing power in August, Ho declared Vietnamese independence and set up in Hanoi a Provisional Government of the Democratic Republic of Vietnam. Elections were scheduled for December 23, 1945.

Ho Chi Minh's proclamation of Vietnamese independence confronted the United States with a difficult choice: to recognize the new regime or to acquiesce in France's reassertion of domination over Indochina. Ho Chi Minh, who had once visited America, looked to the United States for encouragement and assistance. He knew of America's revolutionary heritage and its often proclaimed dedication to the principle of self-determination. In fact, the Vietnamese proclamation of independence opens with words from America's Declaration of Independence:

> All men are created equal. They are endowed by their Creator with certain inalienable rights, among these Life, Liberty, and the Pursuit of Happiness.

Furthermore, Ho expected something in return for his military actions against the Japanese and his provision of intelligence to Allied forces. In 1945 and 1946 Ho wrote eight letters to President Truman and the State Department, asking for American help in gaining independence from France.[13] The Defense Department analyst who wrote the section of the *Pentagon Papers* that refers to this matter could find no evidence that the U. S. Government answered any of Ho's letters.

Washington's failure to reply to Ho's letters was in part the product of a re-appraisal of international politics that was being made in the U. S. capital. Immediately after the end of World War II, Americans perceived a new threat to their security: communism. As we saw earlier, containment of communism was elevated to the highest priority in American foreign policy. The area of the world that Washington considered most in need of protection from communism was Western Europe. And in 1945 Western Europe seemed quite vulnerable. Massive destruction and dislocation were everywhere. The Red Army was camped on Western Europe's doorstep. Stalin was mouthing aggressive threats. The Communist Party in France and Italy was getting stronger. In Greece, communists were fighting a civil war to gain control of the country. In light of these threatening developments, American policymakers decided that France must be strengthened so that she could help resist communist encroachments in Western

Europe. Since most Frenchmen saw their empire as a symbol of French vitality, the United States concluded that it must support France's return to Indochina. This is not to say that American officials were insensitive to Ho Chi Minh's pleas. It was a matter of priorities, and the dominant sentiment in Washington was that the economic strength and political integrity of France was more important to American interests than self-determination for Indochina. Besides, Ho Chi Minh's stature in Washington was not helped by the fact that he himself was a communist. Another factor was Washington's traditional low estimation of Indochina's importance; it was thought that the United States could afford to displease the peoples there, by not supporting their drive for independence, without suffering substantial harm. The result of all these considerations was that the United States lent its support for France's return to Indochina, with the underlying but not too vigorously expressed hope of eventual independence for the colonies.

Until the 1950s, the United States refrained from providing France material assistance for her return to Indochina. Preoccupied with events elsewhere, Washington elected not to involve itself in France's contest with Ho Chi Minh concerning Vietnamese independence. However, the United States did not insist upon the return of lend-lease equipment that she knew France would use in the developing military confrontation in Indochina.

When French troops began to filter back into Indochina in September 1945, they found Ho Chi Minh in control and determined to obtain independence for Vietnam. The French attempted to work out a settlement that would bring Indochina back under French suzereignty, but with more freedom of action than previously. On March 6, 1946, an agreement was signed providing for French recognition of Vietnam as a "free state with its own government, parliament, army, and finances," and Vietnamese recognition that their country was to form "part of the Indochinese Federation and the French Union." This agreement proved difficult in the application, for the two parties could not agree on the extent of independence Vietnam was to enjoy. Further efforts to reach an understanding failed, and in December 1946, war between the French and the Vietnamese erupted.

Accounts of the Franco-Vietnamese war are so numerous that there is no need to repeat this story here. Instead, we shall examine this struggle only as it affected American policy.

During the very first years of the war, the United States maintained a stance of noninvolvement. The American people, weary from the World War, were not prepared to send their sons abroad to fight again, particularly in a colonial war. Besides, the United States was preoccupied with events in Europe, where Soviet communism threatened to extend its control.

It was not until 1949–1950 that the United States took an active role in the Indochina situation. Washington's heightened interest was occasioned by two occurrences, the installation in 1949 of Bao Dai as Vietnamese head of state and the Chinese communist victory in December of that year. Let us consider these in turn.

The quick military victory that France expected to win over the Viet Minh was proving increasingly elusive. In 1947 the French devised a new plan which they hoped would bring the war to a successful conclusion. The French scheme was to bring into being a Vietnamese government, comprised of all anti-communist nationalist forces, that would settle for the limited measure of independence France was prepared to grant. If Ho and his Viet Minh did not like the arrangement, they could fight it out with the new Vietnamese regime which, of course, would receive French support.[14] This strategy, if successful, would reduce the Viet Minh to just another faction in Vietnam, as opposed to its position as the standard-bearer of Vietnamese nationalism. The French hoped that their plan would so weaken the Viet Minh that they would have to come to terms with Paris.

As Buttinger points out, France's strategem was destined to fail, for the simple reason that most Vietnamese would not rally behind a regime that was willing to settle for anything less than total independence.[15] The French, lacking the benefit of such hindsight observation, went ahead with their plan. The individual they chose to lead the new native regime was Bao Dai, who had briefly headed the puppet government installed by the Japanese in 1945. After extended negotiations, Bao Dai concluded, on March 8, 1949, a number of accords with French President Vincent Auriol. These have become known as the Elysee agreements. These agreements extended a small measure of sovereignty to Vietnam, but defense and foreign relations remained in French hands. Total independence, the dream of Ho Chi Minh and most other Vietnamese, remained a distant hope. Nevertheless, in June 1949, Bao Dai was installed as head of state of Vietnam. As expected, the Viet Minh denounced Bao Dai's government as a puppet regime and rejected its authority. In January 1950, Peking and Moscow officially recognized Ho's regime as the official government of Vietnam.

THE WINTER OF 1949–1950

At this point American interest in Indochina began to quicken. With encouragement from Paris, Washington's perception of the Franco-Vietnamese conflict underwent a significant shift. American officials to an ever increasing degree began to view the struggle less as a colonial war than as an ideological one: an active theater in the global struggle between communism and the so-called free world. Recent developments in this confrontation were causing great alarm in Washington. In January 1949, the Chinese communists took Peking. Stalin was consolidating his control in Eastern Europe. Communist revolts had broken out in 1948 in Malaya, Burma, and Indonesia. These occurrences inclined Washington to look with growing sympathy upon the French anti-communist effort in Indochina. Accordingly, upon Bao Dai's installation as head of state, the United States sent him a message of welcome.[16] On December 30, 1949, France formally transferred authority over Vietnam to Bao Dai. By then, the Chinese communists had sent the Nationalists scurrying to Formosa, and the Soviet Union had exploded its first atomic bomb. In January 1950, the French National Assembly voted to treat Vietnam, Laos, and Cambodia as "independent" states within the French Union. Washington accorded diplomatic recognition to the three states one month later.[17] The Soviet Union and China continued to recognize Ho's regime as the official government of Vietnam. The lines between the communists, represented by Ho Chi Minh, and the noncommunists, represented by Bao Dai, were clearly drawn in Indochina.

The victory of the Chinese communists in December 1949, following in the wake of other communist advances already mentioned, had a major impact on American policy in Southeast Asia. Until the winter of 1949–1950, the United States remained only peripherally involved in this area. American interest accelerated in June 1949, when she welcomed Bao Dai as Vietnamese head of state, and gained still further momentum in February 1950, when Washington extended diplomatic recognition to the three Indochinese states in the French Union. The communist victory in China prompted a National Security Council study, designated NSC 48/2. On December 30, 1949, President Truman gave his approval to the document, which said,

> The United States on its own initiative should now scrutinize closely the development of threats from Communist aggression, direct or indirect, and be prepared to help within our means to meet such threats by providing political, economic and military assistance and advice where clearly needed to supplement the resistance of other governments in and out of the areas which are more directly concerned. . . . Particular attention should be given to the problem of French Indochina.[18]

An even more concise statement of Washington's appraisal of the communist threat on a global scale is contained in a secret paper prepared by the National Security Council in April 1950. This document, known as NSC-68,[19] summarized Washington's outlook toward communism and prescribed a broad basic strategy for the United States, especially with regard to the Soviet Union. Sixty days before North Korea invaded South Korea in June 1950, President Truman signed NSC-68, thereby making it official American policy. The United States response to the North Korean attack corresponded to the guidelines specified in NSC-68.

The document stated that there was a basic incompatibility between communist and democratic philosophies and that this incompatibility in all probability could not be bridged. This antagonism would place the communist and noncommunist worlds in conflict indefinitely. The United States and like-minded nations must be prepared to defend their principles by force if necessary. The paper recommended that the United States undertake a massive rebuilding of its defensive capabilities and the defensive capabilities of the rest of the noncommunist world. It went on to say that the United States should adopt the posture of an unflinching will to fight.

NSC-68 posed the likelihood that the Soviet Union was prepared to launch a military offensive on several fronts in an effort to extend her hegemony. The paper cited the Middle East, Europe, and Asia as the most probable danger spots. When the North Koreans stormed across the Thirty-eighth Parallel, the United States was not certain whether the drive was an isolated thrust or a diversionary tactic to conceal a major communist attack elsewhere. West Germany was considered the most likely target if another attack were planned. In any event, NSC-68 called for United States resistance to such attacks as the one in Korea, in cooperation with other noncommunist nations if possible and by use of armed force if necessary.

NSC-68 expressed the United States Government's official assessment of communist intentions during the latter portion of the Truman Administration. In brief, the document stated that the communists, particularly Soviet communists, were prepared to use armed force to extend their control; no limit was assigned to communist ambitions. The United States, the document recommended, must resist, with force if necessary, communist efforts to increase the dominions under their sway.

American policy toward Indochina in the 1950s followed the general principles laid down in NSC 48/2 and NSC-68. In February 1950, France requested American military aid for the war in Indochina. On May 8 Washington announced it would provide economic and military aid to France, beginning with a grant of $10 million.

Washington's decision to assist France, one might observe, came in opposition to the recommendations of an official U. S. mission sent out to survey the situation in Southeast Asia. This study mission, known as the Melby-Erskine mission, was dispatched in mid-1950 to estimate what American aid was needed in Indochina and elsewhere in Southeast Asia. Although the mission's report remains classified, one of its principal members, John F. Melby, who presently is a professor of political science at the University of Guelph, Canada, has written the following:

> I had not been in Saigon very long before I became convinced that not only had Ho Chi Minh captured the nationalist movement but also that all Vietnamese so hated the French that regardless of political persuasion, they would follow anyone who gave some promise of getting rid of the French. I was also convinced that no amount of aid could save the French and that any aid to Vietnam should be conditioned on an unqualified guarantee by the French to get out by a certain date. I was overruled. . . .[20]

It is sad that Dr. Melby's wise advice went unheeded.

The North Korean attack on South Korea in June 1950 acted as a stimulus to Washington's application of containment in Indochina and the rest of Asia. Responding to the invasion, President Truman gave a speech on June 27 in which he said the United States would increase its aid to the Philippines and strengthen its forces there, send a military mission to Indochina, and speed up aid to France and the Associated States of Vietnam, Laos and Cambodia. Truman also sent the Seventh Fleet into the Formosa Straits. The cold war was entering the period of deep-freeze.

ESTIMATION OF THE COMMUNIST THREAT — EISENHOWER ADMINISTRATION

In 1953 Dwight D. Eisenhower brought a Republican administration to Washington. Did this change of hands spell the death of such documents as NSC 48/2 and NSC-68? Let us examine the views of the principal foreign policy-makers in the Eisenhower Administration toward the communist threat.

The two chief American foreign policy-makers at the time of the 1954 Geneva Conference and immediately after were President Eisenhower and Secretary of State John Foster Dulles.

EISENHOWER

President Eisenhower was of the opinion that the aim of communism was to dominate the globe, and that the communists would attempt to do so by force. In a letter to Winston Churchill, in which the President urged England to join with the United States and other countries in a coalition to boost France's fading position in Indochina, Eisenhower said,

> If I may refer again to history; we failed to halt Hirohito, Mussolini and Hitler by not acting in unity and time. That marked the beginning of many years of stark tragedy and desperate peril. May it not be that our nations have learned something from that lesson? . . .[21]

Eisenhower specifically indicted the Soviet Union. He said,

> Hope ran high when, in 1945, many nations' representatives met in San Francisco to establish the United Nations Organization and a world in which law would supplant force as the arbiter in international disputes. That was hope's high point; from then onward every attempt to advance even a single step toward world peace encountered one unsurmountable obstacle—*the implacable purpose of men in the Kremlin to achieve Communist domination of the world.*[22] [Italics mine.]

Addressing the nation, the President said, "We all know something of the long record of deliberately planned Communist aggression. There has been, to this moment, no reason to believe that Soviet policy has changed its frequently announced hope and purpose—the destruction of freedom everywhere."[23]

Communist determination, Eisenhower said, respects no limitations. In his 1953 Inaugural Address, he described the democratic way of life in America and said,

> The enemies of this faith know no god but force, no devotion but its use. They tutor men in treason. They feed upon the hunger of others. Whatever defies them, they torture, especially the truth.[24]

Then he drew attention to the incompatibility between communism and democracy, reflecting the thinking in NSC-68,

> Here, then, is joined no argument between slightly differing philosophies. This conflict strikes directly at the faith of our fathers and the lives of our sons. No principle or treasure that we hold, from the spiritual knowledge of our free schools and churches to the creative magic of free labor and capital, nothing lies safely beyond the reach of this struggle.
> Freedom is pitted against slavery; lightness against the dark.[25]

In summary, Eisenhower believed that a monolithic communism was dedicated to extending its hegemony around the world. There was no hope for lasting compromise between communism and democracy. Unless communism underwent a radical change, or unless communism were miraculously to disappear, there was no hope for a world without conflict.

Let us see how Eisenhower's Secretary of State viewed the communist threat.

DULLES

An examination of Secretary Dulles's speeches and writing reveals that he and Eisenhower agreed in their assumptions about the communist threat.

Dulles outlined his position in an article he wrote for the April 1954 issue of *Foreign Affairs*.[26] "There is no evidence," he wrote, "that basic Soviet policies have been changed with the passing of Stalin. . . . The Soviet Communists have always professed that they are planning for what they call 'an entire historical era.' "[27] Dulles then described the nature of the Communist threat,

> The threat is not merely military. The Soviet rulers dispose throughout the world of the apparatus of international Communism. It operates with trained agitators and a powerful propaganda organization. It exploits every area of discontent. . . . It seeks to harass the existing order and pave the way for political coups which will install Communist-controlled regimes.
>
> By the use of many types of manoeuvres and threats, military and political, the Soviet rulers seek gradually to divide and weaken the free nations and to make their policies appear as bankrupt by over-extending them in efforts which, as Lenin put it, are "beyond their strength." Then, said Lenin, "our victory is assured." Then, said Stalin, will be the "moment for the decisive blow."[28]

Dulles reiterated this theme several times. He told the Senate Foreign Relations Committee, "The Soviet and Chinese Communist rulers are continuing to seek world domination. Nothing has happened to indicate any change in this purpose."[29]

"A tide of despotism" threatens to engulf the world, he said to an audience at Williamsburg. Soviet rulers are seeking to extend their rule, especially in Southeast Asia. "Their avowed aim is to bring all of mankind under the rule of their system."[30]

"The Soviet and Chinese Communist rulers are continuing to seek world domination," he stated.[31] "The destruction of free world unity is the principal goal of Soviet strategy."[32]

To summarize, in the period leading up to, including, and following the 1954 Geneva Conference, the two leading shapers of American foreign policy viewed the world in terms of a confrontation between the communist and noncommunist nations. The two sides faced each other much like two fighting cocks in an arena, their throats swollen with anger and their razor-sharp claws extended to strike.

INDOCHINA IN THE UNITED STATES SECURITY SCHEME

We have seen how the leading policy-makers in Washington viewed the confrontation between the United States and communism. Let us now turn to Indochina for a consideration of that area's position in the American security scheme. In particular, we should like to know what strategic importance Indochina possessed in the minds of American officials.

American policy-makers did not regard the population, resources, industrial capacity, or buying power of Indochina as vital to American security.[33] Rather, Indochina was regarded as a symbol, an area that would provide a crucial test of communist strength versus Western strength. It also served as a corridor for communist expansion into the rest of continental Southeast Asia, the island states of Indonesia, the Philippines, Australia and New Zealand, and even beyond to the Middle East and Europe.

A key to the government's thinking about Southeast Asia may be found in a policy statement drafted by the National Security Council toward the very end of the Truman Administration.

The document,[34] finalized in early 1952 and notable for its early formulation of the "domino" theory, said,

> Communist domination, by whatever means, of all Southeast Asia would seriously endanger in the short run, and critically endanger in the longer run, United States security interests.
> In the absence of effective and timely counter-action, the loss of any single country would probably lead to relatively swift submission to or an alignment with communism by the remaining countries of this group. Furthermore, an alignment with communism of the rest of Southeast Asia and India, and in the longer term, of the Middle East (with the probable exceptions of at least Pakistan and Turkey) would in all probability endanger the stability and security of Europe.
> Communist control of all of Southeast Asia would render the U. S. position in the Pacific offshore island chain precarious and would seriously jeopardize fundamental U. S. security interests in the Far East.

The document went on to say that the United States should continue to assure France that "the U. S. regards the French effort in Indochina as one of great strategic importance in the general international interest rather than in the purely French interest, and as essential to the security of the free world."

The United States, it continued, should provide increased aid on a high priority basis for France. Furthermore, if "the United States determines jointly with the UK and France that expanded military action against Communist China is rendered necessary by the situation in Indochina, the United States should take air and naval action in conjunction with at least France and the UK against all suitable military targets in China. . . . In the event the concurrence of the United Kingdom and France to expanded military action against Communist China is not obtained, the United States should consider taking unilateral action."

The United States had come a long way from Roosevelt's idea of an international trusteeship for Indochina.

President Eisenhower contended that if the United States did not stand firm in Indochina, the communists might conclude that America was giving them a free hand in Asia. As Eisenhower wrote,

> The loss of all Vietnam, together with Laos on the west and Cambodia in the southwest, would have meant the surrender to Communist enslavement of millions. . . . It would have meant that Thailand, enjoying buffer territory between itself and Red China, would be exposed on its entire eastern border to infiltration or air attack.
> And if Indochina fell, not only Thailand but Burma and Malaya would be threatened, with added risks to East Pakistan and South Asia as well as to Indochina.[35]

Communist seizure of Southeast Asia, Dulles explained, would place forces hostile to the United States astride the most direct and best-developed air and sea routes between South Asia and the Pacific. The communists would gain control of major air and naval bases. Communist control of Southeast Asia would pose a threat to the Philippines, Australia, and New Zealand, with whom the United States had treaties of mutual assistance.[36]

Vice-President Nixon extended the argument one point further. "If this whole part of Southeast Asia goes under Communist domination or Communist influence," he said, "Japan who trades and must trade with this area in order to exist, must inevitably be oriented towards the Communist regime."[37]

Communist aggressiveness in Indochina, Eisenhower said, "unless checked decisively and promptly . . . could really become alarming. We as a nation could not stand aloof—unless we were ready to allow free nations to crumble, one by one, under Communist pressure."[38]

Eisenhower viewed the struggle in Indochina as a manifestation of communist aggressiveness that became more intense after the victory of the Chinese communists in 1949. He wrote, "With the Communist victory on the Chinese mainland in 1949, the situation [in Asia] changed rapidly. Red China began providing support for the rebelling elements[39] in Vietnam. . . . The struggle became more intense and began gradually, with Chinese intervention, to assume its true complexion of a struggle between Communism and non-Communist forces. . . ."[40]

Eisenhower considered Indochina, then, as a testing ground in the struggle between the communist and noncommunist worlds. The real danger was not the Vietminh—no one expected Vietnamese junks to sail off the coast of California and demand American surrender—but China. "The developing scene," Eisenhower stated, "had ominous aspects. The Chinese Communists were constantly threatening aggressive action against Formosa and the government of Chiang Kai-Shek. . . . In the Philippines the Huk (Communist) activities had long created serious problems for that government."[41] He went on to say, "At this time, the spring of 1953, our main task was to convince the world that the Southeast Asian war was an aggressive move by the Communists to subjugate the entire area."[42]

Eisenhower viewed the Vietminh's efforts in Indochina as one aspect of communist determination to dominate Asia and then the world beyond. Like a life-giving force, China pushed the juices of aggression outward, first in Korea and then in Indochina. China and her communist allies in Indochina[43] must be stopped, not because Indochina in itself was so important, but because a communist victory there would only encourage the communists to wage further wars of expansion. The eventual result of communist victory in Indochina would only be wider war, when communist expansion had reached a point beyond which the requirements of American security could not allow it to pass.

With the added vision that hindsight provides, we can see that Eisenhower underestimated nationalistic and anti-colonial motivations on the part of the Vietminh. He considered Ho and those fighting under him to be merely agents of Peking. Eisenhower also subscribed to the predominant view at the time that all communists were, for practical purposes, identical. He saw no cause to make distinctions between communists in Hanoi and those in Peking or Moscow, not to mention other capitals in the communist world.

Dulles agreed that the real danger in Asia was China. He concurred in Eisenhower's judgment that Chinese communist expansion was at stake in the Indochina war. Addressing the American Legion in September, 1953, he said,

Communist China has been and now is training, equipping and supplying the Communist forces in Indo-China. There is the risk that, as in Korea, Red China might send its own army into Indo-China. The Chinese Communist regime should realize that such a second aggression could not occur without grave consequences which might not be confined to Indo-China.[44]

Some American officials believed that the validity of an American commitment was also at issue in the Indochina war. Dulles enunciated this rationale as follows:

A great danger in Asia is the fear of many non-Communist peoples that the United States has no real intention of standing firmly behind them. Already that fear has mounted to the danger point. . . .
If the non-Communist Asians ever come to feel that their Western allies are disposed to retreat whenever communism threatens the peace then the entire area could quickly become indefensible.[45]

At a meeting of the National Security Council on March 6, 1954,[46] while the decisive battle at Dienbienphu was raging, American policymakers reviewed the various reasons why Indochina and Southeast Asia were vital to American security. It was decided that Southeast Asia must be held at all costs. This conclusion merely confirmed an earlier American decision on the defense of Indochina expressed in a joint communique issued July 14, 1953, by the foreign ministers of the United Kingdom, France, and the United States. The communique noted that "they agreed that the struggle in defense of the independence of these three nations [Vietnam, Cambodia and Laos] against aggressive communism is *essential to the free world*. . . ."[47] (Italics mine.) Less than a year later, Dulles declared that "the imposition on Southeast Asia of the political system of Communist Russia and its Chinese Communist ally, by whatever means, would be a *grave threat* to the whole free community."[48] (Italics mine.)

AMERICAN AID TO FRANCE

We have seen what importance the Truman and Eisenhower Administrations attached to Southeast Asia. This in itself might have justified the provision of American aid to France to help that ally prosecute a war against communism in Indochina. But there was yet another reason why the United States elected to assist the French. To grasp this additional rationale, we find it necessary to take a detour to the prime area of America's security interest, Western Europe.

FRENCH COMMITMENT TO EUROPEAN DEFENSE

Events in Western Europe took an ominous turn shortly after the German surrender in 1945. While the American army precipitously demobilized, the Red Army used its bayonets to establish satellite states in Eastern Europe. A communist revolution erupted in Greece. The Soviet Union applied pressure on Turkey, which controlled the strategic Dardanelles. When Great Britain signified her inability to assist these Near Eastern nations, regarded as within Britain's sphere of influence, President Truman announced the Truman Doctrine in March 1947. The Doctrine signified a new American policy "to support free peoples who are resisting attempted subjugations by armed minorities or by outside pressure." One year later a communist coup succeeded in Czechoslovakia (February 1948). This was followed by the Russian blockade of Berlin, inaugurated in June 1948. Indeed, from the Western viewpoint, the situation in Europe looked grim. Communist actions seemed to support the contentions of those who warned that the Russians would invade Western Europe unless the West took immediate and drastic action. Such action was not long in coming. Under the Marshall Plan, the United States arranged to transfer billions of dollars to Europe to help the shattered continent rebuild. In April 1949, thirteen nations including the United States signed the North Atlantic Treaty (NATO).[49]

Communist successes in the late 1940s, combined with the prostrate condition of Western Europe, seemed to augur communist aggression westward across the Iron Curtain. The United States attached overriding importance to the need for building up Western defenses. Such concern increased with the detonation of the first Soviet atomic bomb in late 1949.

The single country in Western Europe that was most able to contribute to Western defenses was West Germany. Because it possesses a wealth of important resources, a large and highly skilled population with acquisitive values, and an effective political structure, West Germany had the wherewithal to become the most powerful country in Europe. Fully cognizant of this, American policy-makers wanted to capitalize on West Germany's ability to bolster Western defenses. However, armistice agreements then in effect precluded West Germany from possessing a national military force. In order to make the most of West Germany's potential, the United States sought a scheme to provide for West German participation in European defense without violating the armistice agreement which prohibited West Germany from fielding a national military force. The French came forth with such a plan, called the European Defense Community (EDC). EDC was to be composed of France, Italy, Belgium, the Netherlands, Luxembourg, and West Germany. These countries would pool their military forces to form a European army. No nation would thus have its own military force, and any fears of a revival of German militarism would be quieted.

The United States placed much importance on the formation of EDC. Dulles said,

> President Eisenhower is deeply convinced that there can be no long-term assurance of security and vitality for Europe, and therefore for the Western World including the United States, unless there is a unity which will include France and Germany.
>
> . . . .
>
> Until the goals of EDC are achieved, NATO, and indeed future peace, are in jeopardy.[50]

President Eisenhower viewed EDC as the keystone of a new organic unity in Western Europe.[51] The United States, joined with this new European organization, would confront a potential aggressor with an unbeatable military force, Western experts proclaimed.

EDC would also permit West Germany to recover her national independence under conditions favorable to the maintenance and growth of democratic institutions, tie West Germany to the West, and lay the groundwork for Franco-German cooperation. Thus, EDC would represent an advance toward European unity, another objective of American policy.

When, in April 1954, the Luxembourg Parliament approved membership in EDC, Italy and France were the only prospective members of the new organization that had not ratified the treaty. But the French were having second thoughts about EDC. Ever distrustful of the Germans, the French feared that West Germany might one day pull her troops out of EDC and confront the world with a separate West German army, an army that might seek to reverse the results of Hitler's defeat. In order to be prepared for such an eventuality, France would have to increase its military spending immediately. Indeed, the entire concept of EDC required additional military outlays. Paris was reluctant to devote more funds to defense because she needed money to rebuild her economy and, more importantly, to fight a full-scale war in Indochina. To encourage France to allocate more resources to European defense—including ratification of EDC—the United States decided to help France defray the cost of the Indochina war.[52]

American aid to France, therefore, had a dual purpose. On one hand, it was designed to help France prevent the communists from seizing Indochina. On the other hand, it was given in hope that it would encourage France to ratify EDC, which was to become the foundation of Western security in Europe.[53]

DULLES'S PLAN FOR ALLIED INTERVENTION IN INDOCHINA

In a speech to the Council on Foreign Relations delivered in January 1954, Dulles said, "The way to deter aggression is for the free community to be willing and able to respond vigorously at places and with means of its own choosing."[54] Indochina was one of the places where Dulles meant to respond vigorously.

The first official public mention of Western intervention in Indochina occurred on March 29, 1954, when Dulles addressed the Overseas Press Club in New York. After warning potential aggressors that "aggression might lead to action at places and by means of free-world choosing," the Secretary said,

Under the conditions of today, the imposition on Southeast Asia of the political system of Communist Russia and its Chinese Communist ally, by whatever means, would be a grave threat to the whole free community. The United States feels that that possibility should not be passively accepted but should be met by *united action*.[55] [Italics mine.]

Western diplomats had been discussing the possibility of Western intervention in Indochina for several days before Dulles's speech. On March 20, General Paul Ely, the French Chief of Staff, arrived in Washington for talks with American officials.[56] Ely explained that France was on the verge of negotiating with the Viet Minh, albeit from a position of weakness, unless outside help were forthcoming.

On March 25 Admiral Arthur H. Radford, Chairman, U. S. Joint Chiefs of Staff, made an unofficial suggestion to Ely that the United States provide tactical air support to the defenders at Dien Bien Phu.[57]

Ely took this proposal back to Paris. There, the French government asked General Navarre in Indochina whether such tactical assistance would prove beneficial. Navarre replied that such aid would ease the predicament of the French forces at Dien Bien Phu, which was completely surrounded by Viet Minh forces. On April 4 Premier Leniel and Foreign Minister Bidault asked Ambassador Dillon for American air support.

Meanwhile, on April 3, Dulles had called a secret conference in Washington.[58] In attendance were Senate Majority Leader Knowland and his Republican colleague Eugene Milliken, Senate Minority Leader Lyndon B. Johnson and his colleagues Richard B. Russell and Earle C. Clements, House Republican Speaker Joseph Martin and two Democratic House leaders, John W. McCormack and J. Percy Priest. Other participants were Admiral Radford, Undersecretary of Defense Roger Kyes, Secretary of the Navy Robert B. Anderson, and Dulles's Assistant Secretary for Congressional Relations, Thruston B. Morton.

Dulles ran the meeting, the purpose of which was to determine whether Congress would pass a joint resolution authorizing the President to use air and naval power in Indochina. The legislators advised Dulles that Congress would not pass such a resolution unless the Administration could produce allies who would join the United States in the operation. Dulles, therefore, set out to find allies for the intervention.

On April 5, Dulles replied to Dillon, who had forwarded the French government's request for military support. Dulles said that he had explained to Ely, in Radford's presence, that the United States could not involve itself in Indochina without a political agreement among the United States, France, and other powers and without Congressional approval. Dulles concluded by saying that the United States would seek agreements from other countries for unified action in Indochina.[59]

Immediately after meeting with the Congressmen on April 3, Dulles called on French Ambassador Henri Bonnet and asked him to sound the opinion of the French government on a coalition including the United States, France, the United Kingdom, Australia, New Zealand, Thailand, and the Philippines.[60]

On April 8 the French government replied that it did not believe the formation of such a coalition advisable because it might incite China to send troops into Indochina or at the least harden the communist position.[61]

Despite French rejection, Dulles attempted to gain support for his plan. On April 11 he flew to London. After he presented his proposal to Britain, Churchill and Eden said that Britain would not participate in such a coalition if the French did not ask them to join. They added that the West should try to extract as satisfactory a settlement as possible at Geneva before forming an alliance. They agreed, however, to explore the possibilities of forming an alliance after the Geneva Conference.[62] At the end of Dulles's visit, a joint communique was issued. It said in part, "We are ready to take part, with the other countries principally concerned, in an examination of the possibility of establishing a collective defense, within the framework of the Charter of the United Nations, to assure the peace, security and freedom of Southeast Asia and the Western Pacific."[63]

Dulles then flew to Paris, where on April 14 he tried to convince the French that a coalition would increase chances of Western success at Geneva. The French merely repeated the objections stated in their communication of April 8. A joint communique issued April 14 stated, "In close association with other interested nations, we will examine the possibility of establishing, within the framework of the United Nations Charter, a collective defense to assure the peace, security and freedom of this area [Southeast Asia and the Western Pacific]."[64]

When Dulles returned to Washington, he invited France, the United

Kingdom and other interested parties to join the United States in preparatory conversations on the formation of a coalition. Dulles was under the impression that France and the United Kingdom had already agreed to such exploratory talks. However, on April 18 British Ambassador Sir Roger Makris told Dulles he had received instructions not to participate. Britain, he stated, wanted no such talks until every chance for peace had been explored at Geneva.[65]

Dulles made one last effort to win allied support for united action in Indochina. Later in April he flew to Paris to attend a meeting of the NATO Council. On April 23 Bidault showed Dulles a message from Navarre; the General said that only a powerful airstrike by the United States in the next seventy-two hours could save the situation at Dien Bien Phu.[66] Bidault asked Dulles for air assistance.[67] Dulles then told Eden that if Britain would "stand with him," Dulles was prepared to ask the President for war powers, which would give him wide latitude in deploying military forces.[68] Eden and Churchill, however, stood firm in their conviction that the West should not intervene in Indochina until all attempts at a settlement had been made at Geneva. Later, Eden told Dulles that if a settlement were reached at Geneva, Britain would join in guaranteeing it.[69]

After Britain had rejected Washington's request for allied intervention in Indochina, President Eisenhower decided to deny Bidault's request for air assistance.

However, Dulles's hopes for American intervention were not yet dead. On May 7, with the news that Dienbienphu had just fallen, Eisenhower met with Dulles at the White House to consider intervention once again.[70] The two men discussed the possibility, as a last act to save Indochina, of going to Congress for permission to intervene, if certain conditions were met. These conditions included 1). a French promise to grant genuine freedom to the three Associated States in Indochina, 2). that the U.S. take major responsibility for training indigenous forces, 3). that the U.S. share responsibility for military planning, and 4). that French forces stay in the fight. It is noteworthy that British participation was no longer cited as a precondition. Dulles said he would pass along these ideas to French Ambassador Bonnet that afternoon.

The French responded to Dulles's conversation with Bonnet by requesting American intervention. On the evening of May 10, Eisenhower met with Dulles, Radford, and Secretary of Defense Wilson to discuss a course of action. During the meeting Eisenhower, apparently considering a retreat from his earlier decision against intervening, directed Dulles to prepare a resolution he could take before Congress, requesting authority to commit

American troops to Indochina. Such a resolution was prepared and circulated in the Departments of State, Justice and Defense.[71]

State and Defense then began contingency planning for intervention. The State Department drew up a timetable of diplomatic moves, while Defense prepared a memorandum on the U.S. forces that would be required.[72]

As the debate over intervention continued in the course of the following days, the Joint Chiefs contributed a memorandum to Secretary Wilson on May 26, stating their belief that, "from the point of view of the United States, with reference to the Far East as a whole, Indochina is devoid of decisive military objectives and the allocation of more than token U.S. armed forces in Indo-China would be a serious diversion of limited U.S. capabilities."[73]

The argument over intervention was not finally settled until the French Cabinet decided that the war-weary National Assembly would object to any further military action. In addition, the military situation in the Red River delta near Hanoi had deteriorated so badly in late May and June that Washington concluded intervention was useless. On June 15 Dulles informed Bonnet that intervention was no longer a possibility.

Having abandoned efforts at united action in Indochina, the United States was obliged to adopt a negotiating position at Geneva. On June 29, the United States and the United Kingdom agreed on the text of a joint communication to the French government, which was on the verge of entering into final negotiations at Geneva. The joint communication stated the willingness of the United States and the United Kingdom to respect an armistice agreement on Indochina which:

1. Preserves the integrity and independence of Laos and Cambodia and assures the withdrawal of Vietminh forces therefrom.

2. Preserves at least the southern half of Vietnam, and if possible an enclave in the delta; in this connection we would be unwilling to see the line of division of responsibility drawn further south than a line running west from Dong Hoi.

3. Does not impose on Laos, Cambodia or retained Vietnam any restrictions materially impairing their capacity to maintain stable non-Communist regimes; and especially restrictions impairing their right to maintain adequate forces for internal security, to import arms and to employ foreign advisers.

4. Does not contain political provisions which would risk loss of the retained area to Communist control.

5. Does not exclude the possibility of the ultimate reunification of Vietnam by peaceful means.

6. Provides for the peaceful and humane transfer, under international

supervision, of those people desiring to be moved from one zone to another of Vietnam; and

7. Provides effective machinery for international supervision of the agreement.[74]

The Geneva settlement did not drastically depart from these guidelines.

AMERICAN MILITARY AND FINANCIAL AID

The Eisenhower Administration's plan to intervene in Indochina was one measure of the importance that Dulles and Eisenhower attached to the area. Another measure was the aid that the United States gave to France to help her conduct the Indochina war.[75]

Various sources give different figures on American aid to France for the conduct of the war in Indochina. Therefore, one must allow for some latitude when considering the following data.

The Foreign Operations Administration, which carried out the foreign aid program, estimated that up to the time that the Geneva agreements were signed, the United States had in four years given about $1.2 billion to France for conducting the war in Indochina.[76] This figure represents the amount actually spent, not the amount programmed. An additional $1 billion was appropriated but not spent by the time that the fighting stopped and American aid payments ceased. For the fiscal year 1954, the United States programmed $745 million to aid France in fighting in Indochina.[77] Christian Pineau, a Socialist deputy in the French National Assembly, said on March 16, 1954 that the United States was carrying 78 percent of the cost of the Indochina war.[78] During the period 1950–54, France spent about $30 million in American aid money in Laos.[79]

NOTES

1. Lawrence S. Finkelstein, *American Policy in Southeast Asia* (New York: American Institute of Pacific Relations, 1951), p. 3.

2. An excellent account of American policy toward Indochina during World War II may be found in Edward R. Drachman, *United States Policy toward Vietnam, 1940–1945* (Rutherford, N. J.: Fairleigh Dickinson University Press, 1970). Also, much valuable material is located in various issues of the *Foreign Relations of the United States,* published by the State Department. Hereafter, citations of this series will take the form *Foreign Relations of the United States.*

3. Drachman, pp. 5–6.

4. *Ibid.*

5. For a text of this note, which was transmitted to President Roosevelt and Secretary of State Hull on July 21, 1941, see *Foreign Relations of the United States, Japan, 1931–1941,* 2:516–520.

6. Elliott Roosevelt, *As He Saw It* (New York: Duell, Sloan and Pearce, 1946), p. 74.

7. *Ibid.,* p. 76.

8. Memo from Roosevelt to Hull, January 24, 1944, in Allan W. Cameron (ed.), *Viet-Nam Crisis: A Documentary History* (Ithaca: Cornell University Press, 1971), 1:13.

9. These aspirations found expression in Washington's efforts in late 1944 and 1945 to prevent French forces from helping to liberate Indochina, on the ground that once French soldiers reestablished a footing, French colonial administrators would follow. See Cordell Hull, *The Memoirs of Cordell Hull* (New York: The Macmillan Company, 1948), 2:1597-98, and *Foreign Relations of the United States,* 1944, 5:1205-06.

10. Policy Paper Prepared in the Department of State, June 22, 1945, in Cameron, 1:39-43.

11. Charles De Gaulle, *The War Memoirs of Charles De Gaulle* (New York: Simon and Schuster, 1960), 3:242.

12. Cameron, 1:64-65.

13. The *Pentagon Papers,* as published by *The New York Times* (New York: Bantam Books, 1971), p. 4. Hereafter cited as *Pentagon Papers.*

14. For a fuller account of these developments, see Joseph Buttinger, *Vietnam: A Political History* (New York: Frederick A. Praeger, 1968), pp. 277-314.

15. *Ibid.,* p. 286.

16. Cameron, 1:129.

17. *Department of State Bulletin,* February 20, 1950, pp. 291-292.

18. *Pentagon Papers,* p. 9.

19. The gist of this secret paper was reported in *The New York Times,* April 13, 1954.

20. Letter from John F. Melby to the author, November 17, 1971.

21. Dwight D. Eisenhower, *Mandate for Change* (New York: Doubleday and Company, 1963), p. 347.

22. *Ibid.,* p. 137.

23. Address over radio and television, May 19, 1953, in U.S., President, *Public Papers of the Presidents of the United States,* 1953, pp. 306-07.

24. *Public Papers of the Presidents,* 1953, pp. 3-4.

25. *Ibid.*

26. John Foster Dulles, "A Policy for Security and Peace," *Foreign Affairs* 32 (April 1954):353-364.

27. *Ibid.,* p. 354.

28. *Ibid.,* p. 355.

29. U.S., Department of State, *Department of State Bulletin,* June 19, 1954, p. 921.

30. *Ibid.,* May 24, 1954, p. 779.

31. U.S., Congress, Senate, Committee on Foreign Relations, *Hearings, Mutual Security Act of 1954,* 83rd Cong., 2d Sess., 1954, p. 2.

32. *Ibid.,* p. 9..

33. Eisenhower did state that the loss of Indochina would mean the "loss of valuable deposits of tin and prodigious supplies of rubber and rice." See Eisenhower, p. 333. However, he did not place special emphasis on this reason for defending Indochina. Furthermore, he did not take into account the availability of synthetics (especially as a substitute for rubber) and alternative sources of supply.

34. For the complete text of the document see the *Pentagon Papers,* pp. 27–32. No exact date for the document was supplied.

35. Eisenhower, p. 333. Eisenhower did not say how this sequence of events would affect American security.

36. *Department of State Bulletin,* April 12, 1954, pp. 549–50.

37. Alan B. Cole (ed.), *Conflict in Indo-China and International Repercussions, A Documentary History, 1945–1955* (Ithaca: Cornell University Press, 1956), p. 174.

38. Eisenhower, p. 168.

39. It is interesting to note that Eisenhower referred to the Vietnamese fighters as rebels. Many observers considered them to be fighting for national independence, not rebels against legitimate foreign domination.

40. Eisenhower, pp. 166–67.

41. *Ibid.,* p. 168.

42. *Ibid.*

43. Eisenhower said, "Ho Chi Minh was, of course, a hard-core Communist, while the Vietminh, the forces under his command, were supported by the Chinese Communists in the North." Eisenhower, p. 333.

44. *The New York Times,* September 2, 1953, p. 4.

45. *Department of State Bulletin,* February 28, 1955, p. 330.

46. Reported in Jean Lacouture and Philippe Devillers, *La Fin D'Une Guerre* (Paris: Editions du Seuil, 1960), p. 72. Since then this valuable book has been translated into English.

47. *The New York Times,* July 15, 1953.

48. *Department of State Bulletin,* April 12, 1954, p. 540.

49. Greece and Turkey joined later.

50. *Department of State Bulletin,* January 25, 1954, p. 109.

51. See, for example, his statement on EDC in *Public Papers of the Presidents,* 1954, pp. 400–01.

52. Sherman Adams, *Firsthand Report* (New York: Harper and Brothers, 1961), pp. 120–21. See also Miriam S. Farley, *United States Relations with Southeast Asia* (New York: American Institute of Pacific Relations, 1955), pp. 1–5, and Eisenhower, p. 336.

53. France eventually voted against EDC, and the plan was dropped.

54. *Department of State Bulletin,* January 25, 1954, p. 108.

55. *Ibid.,* April 12, 1954, p. 540.

56. For an account of General Ely's visits see Lacouture and Devillers, pp. 71 ff.

57. *Ibid.,* p. 73.

58. An account of this conference may be found in Chalmers M. Roberts, "The Day We Didn't Go to War," *The Reporter,* 11 (September 14, 1954): pp. 31–35.

59. Lacouture and Devillers, p. 76.

60. *Ibid.,* p. 79.

61. *Ibid.,* p. 81.

62. *Ibid.,* p. 82.

63. *Department of State Bulletin,* April 26, 1954, p. 622. The communique was issued April 13, 1954.

64. *Ibid.,* p. 623.

65. Lacouture and Devillers, p. 84.

66. Anthony Eden, *Full Circle: The Memoirs of Anthony Eden* (Cambridge: Houghton Mifflin Company, 1960), p. 111.

67. Lacouture and Devillers, p. 88.

68. Eden, p. 113.

69. *Ibid.*, p. 121.

70. See Memorandum by Robert Cutler, special assistant to Eisenhower, May 7, 1954, in the *Pentagon Papers,* pp. 40–42.

71. *Ibid.,* pp. 12–13.

72. *Ibid.,* p. 13.

73. *Ibid.,* pp. 44–46.

74. Eden, p. 149.

75. During the Indochina war, American aid to Indochinese forces fighting on the side of France was channelled through France. See U.S., Congress, House, Committee on Government Operations, *U. S. Aid Operations in Laos,* 7th Report by Subcommittee on Foreign Operations and Monetary Affairs, 86th Cong., 1st Sess., 1959, p. 7. In addition to aid given for the purpose of conducting the war, the United States gave aid directly to Indochina for nonmilitary purposes. This aid, distributed under the Special Technical and Economic Mission (STEM) program, was used to finance such projects as village rehabilitation, sanitation, small business ventures, irrigation and public works. During fiscal years 1951–1954, $96 million was authorized for the STEM program. See U.S., Congress, Senate, Committee on Foreign Relations, *Report of Senator Mike Mansfield on a Study Mission to the Associated States of Indochina, Vietnam, Cambodia, Laos,* 85th Cong., 2d Sess., 1953, pp. 1–4.

76. *The New York Times,* August 2, 1954, p. 2.

77. U.S., President, *Report to Congress on the Mutual Security Program,* June 30, 1954, p. 37.

78. *The New York Times,* March 17, 1954, p. 3. Harold E. Stassen, Director, Foreign Operations Administration, said the United States was paying 65% of the dollar cost of the Indochina war. See U.S., Congress, House, Committee on Foreign Affairs, *Hearings, The Mutual Security Act of 1954,* 83rd Cong., 2d Sess., 1954, p. 35.

79. House Committee on Government Operations, *U.S. Aid Operations in Laos,* 1959, p. 7.

4
THE
1954 GENEVA CONFERENCE

THUS FAR, WE HAVE surveyed America's broader interests in Southeast Asia, as well as the application of the containment policy to Indochina during the war between the French and the Vietnamese. In order to examine in depth America's policy toward Laos in the aftermath of the 1954 Geneva Conference, we must now alter our perspective, taking in a smaller field but magnifying the details of that reduced region. In order to gain a full understanding of what the United States was attempting to accomplish in Laos, as well as the Laotian context in which Americans were obliged to operate, we must turn our attention to Laos in the years just before 1954. In particular, we must study the origin of the Pathet Lao, the organization which the United States identified as the instrument of communist expansion in Laos. Then, we shall have a look at the course of the Indochinese War as it was fought in Laos. Finally, as a prelude to examining the Geneva Conference of 1954, we shall consider the political and military situation in Laos at the time of the Geneva Conference.

EVOLUTION OF THE PATHET LAO[1]

Perhaps the most momentous consequence of World War II was the demise of colonialism and the emergence of the former colonies in Africa, Asia and the Middle East as fully independent nation-states. Since 1945, over sixty newly independent states have come into being. In some of these former colonies, the transition into independence was easy and abrupt, as in much of Africa and the Middle East. Other dependencies, however, were compelled to resort to force in order to sever colonial ties already frayed by World War II. Indonesia and Algeria fell into the latter category, as did the three Indochinese states of Cambodia, Laos, and Vietnam. In these countries that had to fight in order to achieve independence, various patriotic organizations sprang up to direct military action and organize affairs after independence had been won. The Vietminh was one such organization. Most of these groups, referred to as "united fronts," were composed of individuals who held political opinions ranging from fascism to communism. Opposition to the colonial country was the cement that held together these men of disparate political views. Just as a brick wall will collapse if the cement should be removed, so many of these united fronts fell in disunity when the colonial power was finally defeated and independence achieved. Such a fate befell an organization in Laos known as the Lao Issara, which led the struggle for national independence against the French.

THE LAO ISSARA

The six-month Japanese occupation of Laos ended in August 1945. In September, Prince Phetsarath, appointed Premier by King Sisavang Vong, formed an organization called the Lao Issara. Its goals were removal of French rule and unification of Laos.

Before French troops returned to assert French hegemony over Laos, Phetsarath, acting without the King's approval, declared the end of the French protectorate and the independence and unity of all Laos. The King, however, issued counterproclamations and dismissed Phetsarath from office. The Prince, supported by the Lao Issara, promulgated a provisional constitution, set up an assembly, nominated a government, and deposed the King.

In March 1946, returning French troops entered Vientiane, causing Phetsarath and the Lao Issara to flee to Bangkok, where they established new headquarters. In early May the King welcomed the French in the royal capital of Luang Prabang. The king annulled all acts of the Lao Issara and reaffirmed Laotian loyalty to France.

Soon after establishing themselves in Bangkok, the Lao Issara leaders fell into disagreement over matters of strategy. Phetsarath's half-brother, Prince Souphanouvong, advocated enlistment of Viet Minh support in a military campaign to eject the French. Phetsarath did not want to dilute the nationalist content of the Lao Issara by an alliance with the Viet Minh. Prince Souvanna Phouma, half-brother to Phetsarath and Souphanouvong, agreed with the former. Souvanna opposed military action against the French and favored a more gradual, peaceful evolution toward national independence.

In March 1947, Souphanouvong, commander-in-chief of the Lao Issara military, launched a general offensive against French forces in northern Laos. The campaign ended in total failure, as a result of which Souphanouvong insisted even more strongly on an alliance with the Viet Minh. The other Lao Issara leaders continued to oppose this move, and Souphanouvong found himself in conflict with the policies of the movement. In May 1949, the Lao Issara ousted him.

Satisfied by the Franco-Laotian Convention,[2] signed July 19, 1949, the Lao Issara leaders decided to return to Laos and render fealty to the Vientiane government. In October the Lao Issara dissolved itself, declaring that its principal aims had been accomplished with the signing of the Franco-Laotian Convention.[3]

THE PATHET LAO

After Souphanouvong's expulsion from the Lao Issara, he and his followers were not heard from until they appeared at Ho Chi Minh's mountain hideout in Tuyên-Quang, North Vietnam, where they proclaimed the establishment of a new organization called the Pathet Lao on August 13, 1950.[4] Opposed to the Royal Laotian Government, which followed a policy of compromise with the French (in the Franco-Laotian Convention), the Pathet Lao sought to eradicate the last vestige of French influence in Laos. Little is known about the activities—all covert—of the Pathet Lao in the few years following its formation. In November 1950, the Pathet Lao was supplemented by a front organization, the Neo Lao Issara (Free Lao Front), designed to attract noncommunist progressive elements. A full-fledged Laotian communist party was created in 1952; it called itself the Phak Khon Hgan Lao (Laotian Workers Party) and claimed about 75 members. These organizations were the predecessors of the Neo Lao Hak Xat, the political party of the Laotian communists today.

From the time of its founding, the Pathet Lao sought foreign support. In early 1951 the Vietminh sponsored a meeting in North Vietnam of communist front movements in Vietnam, Cambodia, and Laos. Souphanouvong represented the Pathet Lao at the gathering. The agreements made at this meeting provided for an alliance among communists in Vietnam, Cambodia, and Laos. The agreements also afforded a basis for Vietminh cooperation with the Pathet Lao. The Pathet Lao began to receive guns and uniforms from their Vietnamese comrades. Soon, Vietnamese advisers began to work with Pathet Lao military units.[5] In early 1953, as we shall see, the Pathet Lao and the Vietminh joined forces to launch the first of three invasions of Laos in an effort to expel the French. The pattern of cooperation between the Pathet Lao and the Viet Minh that started with the 1951 agreements has extended from the French-Indochinese War until the present.[6]

The Pathet Lao has succeeded so well in cloaking itself in obscurity that various questions about the nature of the organization in its early period still remain unanswered. For example, the Pathet Lao, as we have seen, was formed with the cooperation or perhaps the encouragement of Ho Chi Minh. It would be interesting to know the extent to which the members of the Pathet Lao accepted communist doctrine literally. Or were the Pathet Lao primarily nationalists who cared little about communism or any other doctrine, but who sought aid from anyone who would provide it, be they communists (like the Vietminh) or not?

Furthermore, to the extent that the Pathet Lao was a communist organization, what was the orientation of that communism? Was it heavily slanted in an anti-Western direction? Or was it concerned primarily with Laotian internal developments to the exclusion of the global cold-war conflict? Or was the nature of Pathet Lao communism never really defined by the Pathet Lao's members? Although lack of primary source material has precluded the author from definitively answering these questions, it is possible to present the United States Government's assessment of the Pathet Lao in its developing years. Two official documents express this American viewpoint. One of these sources says,

A few dissidents among the "Free Lao," most prominent among them Prince Souphanouvong, turned to the Vietnamese Communists (Viet Minh) for support in 1949. By September, 1950, Prince Souphanouvong had openly joined the Viet Minh movement. . . . The association with Hanoi . . . and Peiping has continued through the years.[7]

A State Department document states:

In March, 1951, the "Laotian National United Front" became associated with a similar organization for dissident Cambodians created by the Vietnamese Communists, and a tri-national "Vietnamese-Cambodian-Laos Alliance Bloc" was then created. The dependent roles of the Lao and Cambodian groups, however, were revealed in a Vietnamese Communist document issued in November, 1951, which noted that "the Vietnamese Party reserves the right to supervise the activities of its brother Parties in Cambodia and Laos." The document stated further that "the Central Executive Committee of the Vietnamese Workers Party has designated a Cambodian and a Laotian bureau charged with assisting the revolutionary movements in these countries. It organizes periodic assemblies of the three parties in order to discuss questions of common interest; it works toward the creation of a Vietnamese-Khmer-Laotian United Front. Militarily Vietnam, Cambodia, and Laos constitute a combat zone; Vietnam has substantially assisted Cambodia and Laos militarily as well as from all other points of view."[8]

A Pathet Lao statement lends credence to the State Department's allegation that the Vietnamese communists assisted Souphanouvong's organization. Thao Nou Hak, a Pathet Lao official, summarized the results of the April 1954 Viet Minh–Pathet Lao offensive into Laos by noting that the Pathet Lao had "liberated" nearly 40,000 square kilometers of territory. Then he said,

> This victory gives us a vast, wide, operational base full of obstacles, a base where paddy, forest products, and soil resources are abundant, a base which borders the free zone of *the friendly country of Vietnam.* In this place we will build up our Armed Forces, establish our authority, and reinforce our front.[9] [Italics mine.]

In summary, Washington interpreted the Pathet Lao to be not so much a nationalist party as a communist organization operating in coordination with other communists in Indochina to extend communist rule in Southeast Asia.

LAOS AS A BATTLEGROUND IN THE INDO-CHINA WAR

It has often been observed that a nation cannot win at the conference table what it has been unable to win on the battlefield. Accordingly, the compromises worked out at the 1954 Geneva Conference were organically related to what had been taking place on the battlefields of Indochina. A quick glance at what was happening on one of those battlefields, the indented face of Laos, will help us to appreciate the events in Geneva.

The Viet Minh, commanded by General Vo Nguyen Giap, staged three invasions of Laos: one in the spring of 1953, a second the following December, and the third in January 1954. The principal purpose of the invasions was to force the French to scatter their forces over as wide an area as possible.

"At the beginning of 1953, units of Vietnamese volunteers, co-operating with the Pathet Lao liberation army, began the campaign in Higher Laos which brought about the liberation of Sam Neua."[10] During the first three months of 1953, Viet Minh agents in Laos bought rice and stored it in dumps along projected invasion routes. In addition, guides were recruited and propaganda was intensified in villages along the frontier separating Laos from Vietnam.[11]

In the early spring of 1953—different sources give conflicting dates—Giap sent four divisions into Laos.[12] In the face of the Viet Minh advance, the French abandoned the garrison of Sam Neua. The Viet Minh seized the fortress, which controlled the province of Sam Neua, and presented it to Souphanouvong. The Pathet Lao leader set up his headquarters there and established a Resistance Government, which he declared to be the rightful government of all Laos.[13]

By the end of April, the Viet Minh had wrested control of northern Laos from the French, whose forces were isolated at Luang Prabang and on the Plaine des Jarres, twenty miles west of Vientiane. However, Giap's rapidly moving troops had outrun their supply lines. Lacking adequate supplies and facing heavily fortified French positions, the Viet Minh in May withdrew to Vietnam. But the brief invasion had served the strategic purpose of forcing the French to employ scarce reserves and to use air-supply power, which was also costly.

In December 1953, the Viet Minh launched a second offensive against Laos, this time in middle Laos.[14] In the course of this campaign, the Viet Minh gained military predominance in middle Laos, including Thakhek and Seno. One Viet Minh unit then headed south and, aided by local armed bands, captured the town of Attopeu. Exploiting their victory, the soldiers gained control of the entire Bolovens Highland in the south. Once again, the French were compelled to siphon off reserves.

In January 1954, Giap ordered a third drive into Laos. Driving down the Hou River valley, Giap's troops scored victories at Muong Khoa and came within striking distance of Luang Prabang. Meanwhile, another Viet Minh column captured the town of Phong Saly. "Thus," says Giap, "Navarre [General Henri Navarre, commander-in-chief of the French forces in Indochina] was obliged to scatter his forces still further."[15] In February, Giap called off the invasion of Laos in order to marshal his forces for the assault on Dien Bien Phu.

Thus, by the time that the 1954 Geneva Conference opened, the Viet Minh had shown themselves to be military masters of all of Laos except the Mekong River valley. The following map illustrates the extent of Viet Minh control in Laos at the time of the 1954 Geneva settlement.

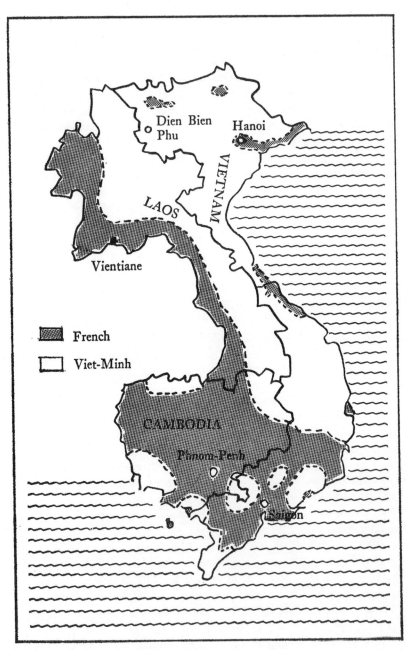

INDOCHINA, JULY 1954

From Bernard B. Fall, The Two Vietnams *(2d ed.; New York: Frederick A. Praeger, 1963), p. 128.*

THE MILITARY AND POLITICAL SITUATION IN LAOS AT THE TIME OF THE GENEVA CONFERENCE

As we have seen, the Viet Minh and its ally the Pathet Lao controlled about four-fifths of the territory of Laos when the diplomats sat down to convene the Geneva Conference. The Royal Laotian Government, which claimed about 20,000 weakly organized soldiers fighting under its banner, held only the Mekong River Valley. The Pathet Lao was comprised of a few incomplete companies—about 1500 men in all. A comparison of the numerical strength of the Royal Laotian Army and the Pathet Lao indicates that whatever dominance the Pathet Lao enjoyed in the countryside was due primarily to Viet Minh efforts, not to Pathet Lao might.

Turning to the political situation in Laos, the foremost issue in people's minds revolved around the legal status of the Pathet Lao. Was it a legitimate political organization, which represented the wishes of a significant segment of the Laotian people, and which therefore deserved an opportunity to voice its policies and viewpoints at Geneva? Or was the Pathet Lao an illegal rebel band that had no right to express its views at the Conference? This matter was discussed at the first plenary session of the Geneva Conference on May 8. Pham Van Dong, head of the delegation from the Democratic Republic of Vietnam, urged the Conference to adopt a resolution that representatives of the governments of Resistance Khmer (in Cambodia) and Pathet Lao be invited to participate in the Conference.[16] The Soviet Union and Communist China supported Pham Van Dong's proposal. Walter Bedell Smith, head of the American delegation, replied that the delegates at the Berlin Conference had decided that only France, the United Kingdom, the Soviet Union and the United States would have authority to propose inviting representatives to Geneva. Therefore, he said, Pham Van Dong's proposal was "a procedural evasion of previously-reached agreements." Smith then added a substantive reason for rejecting the North Vietnamese overture. "The United States cannot agree to the suggestion which has just been made that nonexistent, so-called governments or states such as the so-called Pathet Lao or Free Cambodians [Resistance Khmer] can in any way be considered as qualified for invitations to the Conference under the Berlin Agreement."[17]

Smith's remark introduced a key element in the dispute concerning the status to be accorded the Pathet Lao and the Free Cambodians. The communist delegates regarded these two movements as legitimate nationalist forces which represented the views of sizable proportions of their respective populations. This fact, combined with the political power allegedly wielded by the Pathet Lao and Resistance Khmer, merited the participation of these two organizations in the Geneva deliberations, the communists said. The noncommunist delegates, particularly the Americans, viewed the Pathet Lao and Resistance Khmer as troublesome insurgents who lacked popular support and who were wholly dependent upon the Viet Minh for their very existence. Smith's remark that the Pathet Lao and the Free Cambodians were not qualified for invitations to the Conference implied that they neither represented the views of a substantial portion of the populations in their respective countries nor were powerful enough to warrant consideration as important quantities in the power equations evolving at Geneva. Phoui Sananikone, head of the Laotian government delegation, joined Smith in opposing Pham Van Dong's proposal.

Despite the arguments vigorously put forth by the communists at Geneva, the noncommunist view prevailed. Neither the Free Cambodians nor the Pathet Lao were seated at the Conference.

THE GENEVA SETTLEMENT

The statesmen at Geneva arranged a comprehensive settlement for the entire area of Indochina. The remainder of this chapter will be concerned with those aspects of the settlement relating to Laos. The four principal documents pertaining to Laos are the Final Declaration, the Agreement on the Cessation of Hostilities in Laos, and two Declarations issued by the Government of Laos.[18]

INTERNAL AFFAIRS

Cease-Fire

Chapter I of the Agreement on the Cessation of Hostilities in Laos (hereafter: Agreement) declared that a cessation of all hostilities throughout Laos would occur on August 6. Withdrawals and transfers of military forces, supplies, and equipment were to be completed within 120 days after the Agreement entered into force (July 22). France stated its willingness to withdraw her troops from Laos, as well as Cambodia and Vietnam, at the request of the Governments concerned.[19] The Agreement provided that French and Vietnamese troops would assemble in five provisional assembly areas each (Article 12) and then depart from Laos (Article 13). In order to facilitate the implementation of the clauses in the Agreement relating to the cessation of hostilities and the withdrawal of foreign forces, the parties were to establish a Joint Commission (Article 28). The Joint Commission was to be staffed by representatives of the

Franco-Laotian side and the Vietnamese forces (Article 20).

The procedures for the cessation of hostilities and the withdrawal of French and Vietnamese forces from Laos were implemented satisfactorily.

Integration of the Pathet Lao into the National Community

The same cannot be said, however, for the arrangements to effect a reconciliation among all Laotians and to integrate the members of the Pathet Lao into the national community.

Article 15 of the Agreement stated, "Each party undertakes to refrain from any reprisals or discrimination against persons or organizations for their activities during the hostilities and also undertakes to guarantee their democratic freedoms." The Laotian Government, in its Declaration, affirmed its resolve "to take the necessary measures to integrate all citizens, without discrimination, into the national community and to guarantee them the enjoyment of the rights and freedoms for which the Constitution of the Kingdom provides." Finally, paragraph 9 of the Final Declaration said, "The competent representative authorities of . . . Laos . . . must not permit any individual or collective reprisals against persons who have collaborated in any way with one of the parties during the war, or against members of such persons' families."

In providing for a cease-fire and a reconciliation of all Laotians, the Geneva agreements laid the foundation for a permanent settlement of the difficulties in Laos. As we shall discover, however, during the next decade Laos was to experience civil conflict, overlaid with international rivalries, all of which culminated in another international conference.

The faithful implementation of the provisions calling for a cease-fire between the French and the Vietnamese and the withdrawal of their forces from Laos seemed to augur well for the final settlement of the Laotian portion of the Geneva agreements. The incorporation of the Pathet Lao fighting forces into the rest of the Laotian community did not proceed so happily, however. Since this matter proved to be the crux of future difficulties, it would be well to cast our attention upon the provisions of the Geneva agreements that described how the merger of these fighting forces was to take place.

The two most relevant provisions are Articles 12 and 14 of the Agreement. For the sake of convenience, these Articles are quoted herewith in full:

Article 12
   The Joint Commission in Laos shall fix the site and areas:
   Of the 5 provisional assembly areas for the reception of the Vietnamese people's volunteer forces—of the 5 provisional assembly areas for the reception of the French forces in Laos—of the 12 provisional

assembly areas, one to each province, for the reception of the fighting
units of "Pathet Lao."

The forces of the Laotian National Army shall remain *in situ* during
the entire duration of the operations of separation and transfer of foreign
forces and fighting units of "Pathet Lao."

Article 14

Pending a political settlement, the fighting units of "Pathet Lao,"
concentrated in the provisional assembly areas, will move into the
provinces of Phong Saly and Sam Neua except for any military personnel who wish to be demobilized where they are. They will be free to
move between these two provinces in a corridor along the frontier
between Laos and Vietnam bound on the south by the line Sop-Kin,
Na-Mi, Sop-Sang, Muong-Son.

Concentration shall be completed within 120 days from the date of
entry into force of the present agreement.

As shall be seen in the next chapter, the Pathet Lao and the Royal
Government attached different meanings to these provisions. In the first
place, the definition of "political settlement" (Article 14) remained open
to interpretation. Thus, to foreshadow, in the spring of 1959 the Laotian
government maintained that a political settlement had been reached, and
that therefore the Pathet Lao forces were no longer entitled to occupy the
two provinces of Phong Saly and Sam Neua. The Pathet Lao, on the
other hand, insisted that no such political settlement had taken place;
consequently, they said, they had a right to remain in the two provinces.
Nowhere does the Agreement define the term "political settlement." Another major disagreement arose over the nature of the control that the
Pathet Lao was entitled to exert in the two provinces. The Government
asserted that it had ultimate authority throughout the entire country,
including Phong Saly and Sam Neua. The Government, to support this
contention, cited the provision in Article 12 which said that, after the
Pathet Lao had assembled in the twelve provisional assembly areas, they
were to consolidate in the two provinces of Phong Saly and Sam Neua.
Thus the Government regarded these provinces as assembly areas under
Government control. The Pathet Lao insisted, however, that they had
exclusive control over the two provinces until a "political settlement" was
reached. Once again, the Agreement did not specify how the Pathet Lao
and the Government were to share authority in the two provinces.

The Agreement was clearly intended to effect a reconciliation between
the Government and the Pathet Lao. However, the wording of key provisions was sufficiently vague to permit differing interpretations, in the
event that either or both parties might seek to obstruct a final settlement.
What actually happened, as shall be seen below, is that the Pathet Lao
sought to retain an identity separate from the rest of the Laotian com-

munity, and they were frequently able to cite provisions in the Geneva agreements to justify their tactics.

The final step envisioned in the proposed integration was the conferral of political rights and privileges upon the Pathet Lao. In its Declaration, the Government said that it "affirms that all Laotian citizens may freely participate as electors or candidates in general elections by secret ballot." The Government also promised to "promulgate measures to provide for special representation in the Royal Administration of the provinces of Phong Saly and Sam Neua during the interval between the cessation of hostilities and the general elections[20] of the interests of Laotian nationals who did not support the Royal forces during hostilities."

At this point, it may be well to recapitulate the internal settlement planned for Laos. The Geneva accords provided for a cease-fire and the withdrawal of French and Vietnamese forces from Laos. In addition, the settlement called for the integration of the Pathet Lao into the national community. The Pathet Lao was to enjoy both civil liberties and political rights, including the right to vote and hold office. The fighting forces of the Pathet Lao were to regroup in the provinces of Phong Saly and Sam Neua, thereafter to join the national community when a "political settlement" was achieved.

Before passing to the international aspects of the Laotian settlement, we pause to consider the political map of Laos before and after the Geneva settlement. The following two maps illustrate the increase in territory controlled by the Royal Government as a result of the Geneva accords. Before the cease-fire, the Government's authority was restricted to the Mekong River Valley. The Geneva accords gave the Government physical control over all the country except the two provinces of Phong Saly and Sam Neua.

It would appear that the communists conceded considerable territory in Laos at the Geneva Conference. But one must, for these purposes, distinguish between Laotian and Vietnamese communists. If one accepts Champassak's estimate that the Pathet Lao had only 1,500 loosely organized troops,[21] then it appears incredible that they were capable of exerting mastery over all the shaded area in the left-hand map. In actuality, the shaded portion indicates the areas in which the Viet Minh enjoyed freedom of movement, which must be differentiated from control in the sense of conducting affairs. The truth of the matter was that no political organization had day to day control of these areas, the greater portion of which are mountainous and inaccessible except by helicopter or laborious jungle trek. Thus, when the communists agreed to allow the Laotian government to wield authority in these regions, they in effect agreed not to exercise their freedom of movement, something which would have been nearly

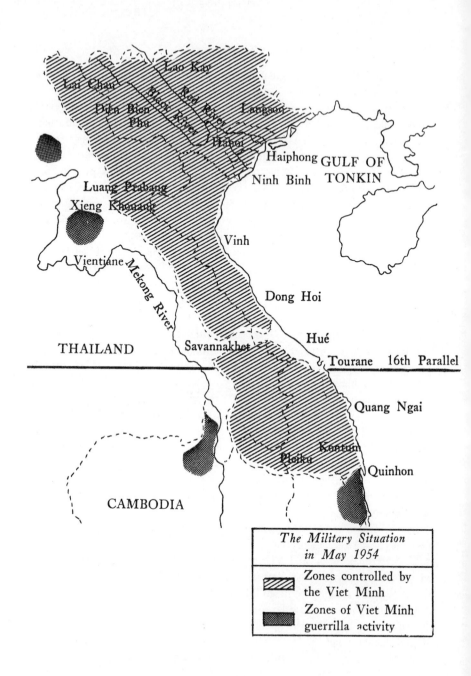

Lao Kay

Lai Chau

Red River

Dien Bien Phu

Black River

Langson

Hanoi

Haiphong GULF OF

Ninh Binh TONKIN

Luang Prabang

Xieng Khouang

Vinh

Vientiane

Mekong River

Dong Hoi

THAILAND

Savannakhet

Hué

Tourane 16th Parallel

Quang Ngai

Kontum

Pleiku

Quinhon

CAMBODIA

The Military Situation in May 1954

Zones controlled by the Viet Minh

Zones of Viet Minh guerrilla activity

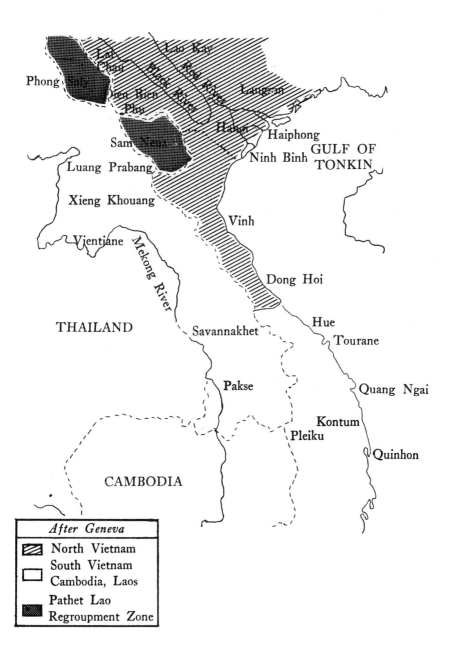

Phong Saly

Lao Kay

Lai
Chau

Black River

Red River

Dien Bien
Phu

Langson

Hanoi

Haiphong

Sam Neua

Ninh Binh

GULF OF
TONKIN

Luang Prabang

Xieng Khouang

Vinh

Vientiane

Dong Hoi

Mekong River

THAILAND

Savannakhet

Hue

Tourane

Pakse

Quang Ngai

Kontum

Pleiku

Quinhon

CAMBODIA

After Geneva

North Vietnam

South Vietnam
Cambodia, Laos

Pathet Lao
Regroupment Zone

impossible to exercise in any event. Furthermore, it seems clear that it was the Viet Minh, not the Pathet Lao, which was in a position to make this compromise. The Pathet Lao at that time possessed nuisance value. However, it was incapable of mounting a sustained offensive against the Royal Government, whose French-assisted army had 20,000 troops at the time of the Geneva Conference and 25,000 men six months later. In appraising the Pathet Lao's claim that it was entitled to control the provinces of Phong Saly and Sam Neua, one should consider that whatever territory the Pathet Lao obtained as a result of the Geneva agreements was due almost entirely to Viet Minh efforts. These Vietnamese, not the Pathet Lao, were in a position to demand a *quid pro quo* in return for agreeing to a cease-fire and making a political settlement.

EXTERNAL AFFAIRS

In addition to setting forth a plan for a cease-fire and the reconciliation of the factions within Laos, the Geneva settlement defined the obligations of foreign powers toward Laos. We shall take up these external matters under the headings of neutrality, foreign military assistance, and the International Commission for Supervision and Control in Laos.

Neutrality

Paragraph 12 of the Final Declaration contained the following: "In their relations with Cambodia, Laos and Viet Nam, each member of the Geneva Conference undertakes to respect the sovereignty, the independence, the unity and the territorial integrity of the above-mentioned States, and to refrain from any interference in their internal affairs." Various articles in the Agreement specified in more detail the rights and restrictions of foreign powers with regard to these obligations. Article 6 prohibited the introduction into Laos of "any reinforcements of troops or military personnel from outside Laotian territory." Article 7 precluded the establishment of "new military bases." Article 9 outlawed "the introduction into Laos of armaments, munitions and military equipment of all kinds," except for "a specified quantity of armaments in categories specified as necessary for the defense of Laos."[22]

In a separate document, the Laotian government pledged to pursue a neutral foreign policy. These promises were expressed in a second Declaration issued by that government at the Geneva Conference. This Declaration is printed in full as follows:

The Royal Government of Laos is resolved never to pursue a policy of aggression and will never permit the territory of Laos to be used in furtherance of such a policy.

The Royal Government of Laos will never join in any agreement with other States if this agreement includes the obligation for the Royal Government of Laos to participate in a military alliance not in conformity with the principles of the Charter of the United Nations or with the principles of the agreement on the cessation of hostilities or, unless its security is threatened, the obligation to establish bases on Laotian territory for military forces of foreign Powers.

The Royal Government of Laos is resolved to settle its international disputes by peaceful means so that international peace and security and justice are not endangered.

During the period between the cessation of hostilities in Viet Nam and the final settlement of that country's political problems, the Royal Government of Laos will not request foreign aid, whether in war material, in personnel or in instructors, except for the purpose of its effective territorial defense and to the extent defined by the agreement on the cessation of hostilities.[23]

Certain portions of this Declaration call for special comment, in light of events that occurred after 1954.

The word "aggression," which appears in the first paragraph, was never defined for the purposes of the Declaration. It has been argued that, in violation of paragraph 1, Laos was used for aggressive purposes by the Soviet Union (military aid and advisors), by the United States (also military aid and advisors), and by North Vietnam (military aid and advisors, invasions, and use of the Ho Chi Minh Trail for passage of North Vietnamese troops into South Vietnam). North Vietnam has accused Laos of violating its Declaration by sending troops into North Vietnam. In regard to the second paragraph of the Declaration, the Soviet Union, North Vietnam, and the United States have been charged with establishing bases on Laotian territory.

When accused of violating this Declaration, the Laotian Government has persistently responded by claiming that its "security is threatened." Since the Declaration does not state what shall constitute a threat to its security or who is to determine whether Laotian security is threatened, the Royal Government is left with an open-ended escape clause. As will be shown, the Royal Government did not always adhere to the spirit of paragraph 2.

The final paragraph of the Declaration prohibited Laos from requesting foreign military aid until "the final settlement" of Viet Nam's problems. This prohibition was qualified in that Laos was authorized to request such aid for the "purpose of its effective territorial defense." Although the final settlement of Viet Nam's problems has not been realized, regimes claiming to represent the Royal Government of Laos requested foreign military aid from both communists and noncommunists. In every case, the regime claimed it needed the aid for territorial defense. Once again, the Declaration specified no authority to determine whether such claims were justified. Thus the Declaration contained another open-ended escape clause.

One is tempted to blame much of the post-1954 strife on such inadequacies as escape clauses in this Declaration and on ambiguities regarding the definition of "political settlement" and the nature of control in Sam Neua and Phong Saly as expressed in the Agreement on the Cessation of Hostilities in Laos. To be sure, these documents do not rank among the masterpieces of diplomacy. Nonetheless, while the phrasing of diplomatic instruments is undoubtedly important, one can attribute more significance to it than it actually merits. The United States Constitution, the oldest written constitution still in use, contains its share of ambiguities; the meanings of the phrases "due process of law" and "clear and present danger" remain in flux to this day. Few people, however, criticize the Constitution for these and other ambiguities. In fact, many have credited these very uncertainties with enabling the Constitution to survive, for they have permitted the American people to adjust the Constitution to ever-changing conditions. Returning to Laos, if deficiencies are to be found anywhere, they lie not in the written word but in the minds of men. The American people were able to convert the seeming liability of ambiguities in their Constitution into assets because there was sufficient agreement on their meanings and because the Americans were willing to accept the rulings of the judiciary rather than upset orderly government. Such was not the case in Laos. No amount of verbal calisthenics could have prevented the Laotian government and the Pathet Lao from disputing their conflicting claims to control over Sam Neua and Phong Saly. Similarly, no written strictures—unless backed by force—could have obviated the Royal Government from seeking outside military assistance, once it perceived a threat to its very existence. Though few realized it at the time, the objectives of the Royal Government and the Pathet Lao were so opposed that any written document was doomed to suffer repeated violations.

Foreign Military Assistance

It will be recalled that Article 6 of the Agreement prohibited the introduction into Laos of any reinforcements of troops or military personnel from outside Laotian territory. The second paragraph of that article contained an exception to this rule. The paragraph said, "Nevertheless, the French High Command may leave a specified number of French military personnel required for the training of the Laotian National Army in the territory of Laos; the strength of such personnel shall not exceed one thousand five hundred (1,500) officers and non-commissioned officers." In addition to a military training mission, the French were granted two bases. Article 8 provided:

> The High Command of the French forces shall maintain in the territory of Laos the personnel required for the maintenance of two French military establishments, the first at Seno and the second in the Mekong valley, either in the provinces of Vientiane or downstream from Vientiane.
>
> The effectives maintained in these military establishments shall not exceed a total of three thousand five hundred (3,500) men.

Thus France was authorized to keep 5,000 soldiers in Laos to staff two bases and a military training mission. The Geneva agreements permitted no other power to have bases in Laos or train the Laotian army. In effect, as Anthony Eden notes,[24] the invading Viet Minh were required to withdraw from Laos while the Laotians, with French help, could build up their forces to deal with a recurrence of trouble. As we shall see, the French devoted only half-hearted efforts to establishing a military presence in Laos. They never maintained their mission at the full complement of 5,000 men, a fact which was to displease the Americans at a later time.

International Commission for Supervision and Control in Laos

As a means of making sure that the provisions relating to the cease-fire were honored, the powers at Geneva created an international inspection commission. This body was known as the International Commission for Supervision and Control in Laos (hereafter: ICC).

Article 27 of the Agreement defined the tasks of the ICC:

> The International Commission shall be responsible for supervising the execution by the parties of the provisions of the present Agreement. For this purpose it shall fulfill the functions of control, observation, inspection and investigation connected with the implementation of the provisions of the Agreement on the cessation of hostilities, and shall in particular:—
>
> (a) Control the withdrawal of foreign forces in accordance with the provisions of the Agreement on the cessation of hostilities and see that frontiers are respected;
> (b) control the release of prisoners of war and civilian internees;
> (c) supervise, at ports and airfields and along all the frontiers of Laos, the implementation of the provisions regulating the introduction into Laos of military personnel and war materials;
> (d) supervise the implementation of the clauses of the Agreement on the cessation of hostilities relating to rotation of personnel and to supplies for French Union security forces maintained in Laos.

It should be pointed out that the ICC was a supervisory body, not an international policeman with enforcement powers. Article 24 of the Agreement stated specifically that "Responsibility for the execution of the Agreement on the cessation of hostilities shall rest with the parties." Thus prime responsibility for performance of the Agreement was placed upon the parties; that is, on the French and the Vietnamese, not on the ICC. Article 25 stipulated that the ICC would be responsible for "control and supervision of the application of the provisions of the Agreement on the cessation of hostilities in Laos." Therefore, the ICC was not to act like a policeman with a nightstick, but rather as a mediator to help the parties reach agreement when possible and report on disputes as well as violations of the Agreement.

Article 25 said that the ICC would be composed of representatives from Canada, India, and Poland.[25] The Indian delegate was to be chairman.

Article 26 provided that the ICC set up fixed as well as mobile inspection teams, composed of an equal number of officers from each of the three member states. These teams were created in order to enable the ICC to keep track of developments throughout Laos. The mobile inspection teams were to follow events in the regions bordering the land frontiers of Laos. "Within the limits of their zones of action, they shall have the right to move freely and shall receive from the local civil and military authorities all facilities they may require for the fulfillment of their tasks. . . . They shall have at their disposal such modern means of transport, observation and communication as they may require" (Article 26). In later years, however, the ICC was often prevented from performing its duties because it was denied the necessary facilities to perform its tasks.

Since the ICC was composed of representatives from rival international camps—referring specifically to the Polish and Canadian delegates—voting procedures assumed critical importance. Obviously, if unanimous decisions were required, any member could paralyze the ICC if the ICC threatened to act in a manner prejudicial to the interests of the Laotian party that member favored. On the other hand, a majority vote would give much power to the chairman, the representative from India, who presumably was less tied than the Canadian or the Pole to the Laotian communists or noncommunists. A compromise was therefore adopted at Geneva. According to Article 34 of the Agreement, the ICC was permitted to adopt recommendations by majority vote with the exception of those matters specified by Article 35. That article stated:

> On questions concerning violations, or threats of violations, which might lead to a resumption of hostilities and, in particular,
> (a) refusal by foreign armed forces to effect the movements provided for in the withdrawal plan,

(b) violation or threat of violation of the country's integrity, by
   foreign armed forces,
the decisions of the International Commission must be unanimous.

As we shall discover, the most important disputes that the ICC was called
upon to resolve fell directly under the provisions of Article 35, thus
requiring unanimous decisions. Disagreement within the ICC often dis-
abled the Commission, rendering it virtually useless in its most vital
function.

The diplomats at Geneva attempted to facilitate the ICC's task by
obligating the parties to cooperate with the Commission. Article 20 instructed the commanders of both the Franco-Laotian and the Vietnamese
parties to "afford full protection and all possible assistance and cooperation
to the . . . International Commission and its inspection teams. . . ."

Finally, the Geneva settlement included a plan for keeping the international community informed of developments in Laos. Article 36 contained this scheme.

If one of the parties refuses to put a recommendation of the International Commission into effect, the parties concerned or the Commission
itself shall inform the members of the Geneva Conference.

If the International Commission does not reach unanimity in the
case provided for in Article 35, it shall transmit a majority report and
one or more minority reports to the members of the Conference.

The International Commission shall inform the members of the
Conference of all cases in which its work is being hindered.

Paragraph 13 of the Final Declaration stated that the members of the
Conference agree "to consult one another on any question which may be
referred to them by the International Supervisory Commission, in order
to study such measures as may prove necessary to ensure that the agreements on the cessation of hostilities in Cambodia, Laos and Viet Nam
are respected."

These arrangements for continuing international surveillance of Laos
did not constitute a means of enforcement, but only a plan for disseminating
information. Just how members of the Conference, by agreeing "to consult
one another on any question which may be referred to them by the International Supervisory Commission" could thereby see to it that "the agreements on the cessation of hostilities . . . are respected" was never explained. In the course of the next few years, to foreshadow once again,
this system of information and consultation proved highly unwieldy and
ineffective. The lack of standing machinery to enforce the Geneva agreements and resolve conflicts within the ICC was a serious deficiency.
There seemed to be no way of enforcing ICC recommendations upon the

recalcitrant parties in Laos short of convening another conference of the
Geneva powers. As everyone is aware, there is a wide gap between the
obligation to "consult one another," which everyone was willing to do,
and the application of pressure upon an intractable party, which few were
willing to carry out. What actually happened was that the foreign ministers of Great Britain and the Soviet Union, the Co-Chairmen of the
Geneva Conference, became overseers of the agreements. The ICC developed the practice of forwarding its reports to the Co-Chairmen, who then
took whatever action they deemed appropriate. In most cases, such action
amounted to pleas to the parties to act "reasonably." The ICC, which was
supposed to lead the parties in Laos to a harmonious agreement, was
actually debilitated by internal disunity and the absence of authority to
force the parties in Laos to follow its recommendations. Consequently, the
ICC, like a friend at the bedside of an ailing patient, was reduced to the
role of a frustrated onlooker.

NOTES

1. More detailed information on the origins of the Pathet Lao may be found
in Donald Lancaster, *The Emancipation of French Indo-China* (London: Oxford
University Press, 1961), pp. 150-152; Roger M. Smith, "Laos," *Government and
Politics of Southeast Asia,* ed. George McTurnan Kahin (2d ed.; Ithaca: Cornell
University Press, 1964), pp. 527-94; Sisouk Na Champassak, *Storm over Laos*
(New York: Frederick A. Praeger, 1961), pp. 12-19.

2. Text in Katay Don Sasorith, *Le Laos* (Paris: Berger-Levrault, 1954), pp.
117-30. The Convention, similar to the Élysée Agreement signed by France and
the Vietnamese government of Bao Dai, included French grant of independence
to Laos, which affirmed its adherence to the French Union as an Associated State.
Laotian independence, however, was qualified. Foreign policy was to be framed
in accordance with French Union policy, thereby giving France a veto over
Laotian foreign policy. In a state of war, the Laotian army was to be pooled
with other armies of the French Union under French command. French citizens
in Laos were granted extraterritorial rights and were placed under jurisdiction
of courts of the French Union.

3. Text of the decree dissolving the Lao Issara may be found in Sasorith, pp.
131-35.

4. Bernard B. Fall, "The Laos Tangle," *International Journal* 16 (Spring 1961):
140. This was not Souphanouvong's first visit to Vietnam. A communist source
affords the following account of an earlier visit: "When the Japanese invaded
Indo-China, Souphanouvong was in Vietnam. He contacted the revolutionary
movement there and was impressed by their ardor and self-sacrificing spirit and
by their organization, the practical way in which they were planning an eventual
seizure of power. Once he met Ho Chi Minh and asked him for advice. 'Seize
power from the colonialists,' was the reply." Wilfred Burchett, *Mekong Upstream*
(Hanoi: Red River Publishing House, 1957), p. 258.

5. Bernard B. Fall, *Anatomy of a Crisis* (Garden City: Doubleday and Company, 1969), pp. 44–45.

6. For the most detailed available account of Pathet Lao-North Vietnamese relations see Paul F. Langer and Joseph J. Zasloff, *North Vietnam and the Pathet Lao: Partners in the Struggle for Laos* (Cambridge: Harvard University Press, 1970).

7. U. S., Department of Defense, Armed Forces Information and Education Office, "Laos: Hot Spot in Cold War," *For Commanders*, 1 (May 24, 1962): 1.

8. U.S., Department of State, *The Situation in Laos*, 1959, pp. 2–3.

9. Article in newspaper *Lao-Issala*, broadcast by Vietnam News Agency, April 24, 1953, quoted in A. M. Halpern and H. B. Fredman, *Communist Strategies in Laos* (Santa Monica: The Rand Corporation, RM-2561, 1960), p. 3.

10. Vo Nguyen Giap, *People's War, People's Army* (New York: Frederick A. Praeger, 1962), p. 23.

11. Edgar O'Ballance, *The Indo-China War* (London: Faber and Faber, 1964), p. 188.

12. A detailed account of this campaign may be found in O'Ballance, pp. 188–92, and Bernard B. Fall, *The Two Vietnams*, 2nd ed. (New York: Frederick A. Praeger, 1963), pp. 120–22.

13. Great Britain, Parliamentary Papers, Accounts and Papers, Cmd. 2834, December, 1965, "Documents Relating to British Involvement in the Indo-China Conflict 1945–1965."

14. Giap discusses the strategy underlying this campaign in *People's War*, pp. 156, 160–62, and 200–04.

15. *Ibid.*, p. 204.

16. Great Britain, Parliamentary Papers, vol. 31 (*Accounts and Papers*, vol. 12), Cmd. 9186, June, 1954, "Documents Relating to the Discussion of Korea and Indo-China at the Geneva Conference, April 27–June 15, 1954," pp. 112–13.

17. *Ibid.*, p. 114.

18. Texts of these documents may be found in Great Britain, Parliamentary Papers, vol. XXXI (*Accounts and Papers*, Vol. XII), Cmd. 9239, August, 1954, "Further Documents Relating to the Discussion of Indo-China at the Geneva Conference, June 16–July 21, 1954."

19. Declaration by the Government of the French Republic, Geneva, July 21, 1954, in Great Britain, Cmd. 9239, p. 42.

20. According to the Laotian constitution, nationwide elections were to be held in April 1955. The elections were held during that month, except in the provinces of Phong Saly and Sam Neua.

21. Champassak, p. 31.

22. This exception proved controversial when Laos began accepting American military aid in the summer of 1959.

23. Great Britain, Cmd. 9239, pp. 41–42.

24. Anthony Eden, *Full Circle: The Memoirs of Anthony Eden* (Cambridge: Houghton Mifflin Company, 1960), pp. 157–58.

25. International political considerations certainly played a role in the selection of the countries to be represented on the ICC. One observes the presence of a communist nation (Poland), a Western nation (Canada), and a nonaligned state (India).

5
THE UNITED STATES AND
THE GENEVA CONFERENCE

AT THE CONCLUSION of the Geneva Conference, most Laotians were hopeful that a basis had been laid for an end to civil strife and a reconciliation between the Pathet Lao and the rest of the country. In Washington, however, officials were not so sanguine. In the eyes of many American policy-makers, the Geneva accords offered the communists opportunities to further their political ambitions in Southeast Asia. American officials were still smarting because of the spectacular communist advances since World War II. In the immediate postwar years, it will be recalled, communists had seized Eastern Europe, the Chinese mainland, North Korea and North Vietnam. The Korean War was at best a dubious victory for the United Nations forces, as the truce line was drawn practically in the same place as the boundary between the two Koreas before hostilities had erupted. The Korean War, in the eyes of many Westerners, failed to demonstrate to the communists that aggressive warfare was too costly.[1] It could even be argued that the communists had scored a triumph, in proving themselves capable of matching America's prowess on the battlefield. The Geneva agreements appeared to many American officials as another failure to halt communist aggression. Having gained international recognition of a communist regime in northern Vietnam, the communists would in all likelihood press for additional gains in Southeast Asia.

In this chapter we shall explore the American reaction to the Geneva Conference. We shall first examine the actions of the American delegation

88

at Geneva as the Conference completed its work. Then we shall study Washington's attempts to reinforce collective defense in Southeast Asia as the United States braced itself in expectation of further communist thrusts.

THE UNITED STATES REFUSES TO SIGN THE GENEVA AGREEMENTS

At the final session of the Geneva Conference, Under Secretary of State Walter B. Smith, head of the American delegation to the Conference, read an official Declaration of American policy. The United States, the Declaration said, "takes note of the agreements concluded at Geneva on July 20 and 21, 1954" and states that it will "refrain from the threat or the use of force to disturb them . . . ; and (ii) it would view any renewal of the aggression in violation of the aforesaid agreements with grave concern and as seriously threatening international peace and security." The Declaration concluded, "We share the hope that the agreements will permit Cambodia, Laos and Viet-Nam to play their part, in full independence and sovereignty, in the peaceful community of nations, and will enable the peoples of that area to determine their own future."[2]

At a press conference on July 21, President Eisenhower echoed Smith's words. The President noted that the United States "has not been a belligerent in the war.[3] The primary responsibility for the settlement in Indochina rested with those nations which participated in the fighting. . . . Accordingly, the United States has not itself been party to or bound by the decisions taken by the Conference. . . . The agreements contain features which we do not like, but a great deal depends on how they work in practice." The President, it seems, was doing his utmost to disassociate America from the documents drafted at Geneva. The United States, Eisenhower continued, "is not prepared to join in the Conference declarations, but, . . . the United States will not use force to disturb the settlement. We also say that any renewal of Communist aggression would be viewed by us as a matter of grave concern." The President added that "as evidence of our resolve to assist Cambodia and Laos to play their part, in full independence and sovereignty, in the peaceful community of free nations," the United States is requesting the agreement of those countries to the appointment of an American Ambassador or Minister to reside in their respective capitals. Finally, Eisenhower said that Washington was holding talks with other nations on the organization of collective defense in Southeast Asia.[4]

The above statements indicate that, while Washington was not entirely pleased with the agreements signed at Geneva, she would not attempt to upset them by the use of force or the threat of force. At the same time, the United States warned the communists that Washington would view any renewal of communist aggression "as a matter of grave concern." No one seemed to raise the question of how Washington could reconcile a forceful reaction to a renewal of communist aggression with the pledge to refrain from upsetting the Geneva agreements by the use or threat of the use of force.

In meetings on August 8 and 12, the NSC concluded that the Geneva settlement was a "disaster" that "completed a major forward stride of Communism which may lead to the loss of Southeast Asia."[5]

Perhaps the most meaningful measure of Washington's evaluation of the Geneva Conference and the post-Geneva situation in Southeast Asia was Washington's attempt to create an alliance system in that area. To this topic we now turn.

THE FORMATION OF SEATO

PRELIMINARY NEGOTIATIONS

According to Anthony Eden, SEATO was first discussed at a meeting in London in June 1953 of representatives of France, the United Kingdom, and the United States. During the formal discussions, Maurice Schuman of France proposed the creation of a permanent military organization to study the situation in Southeast Asia and plan measures that could be taken for the defense of the region.[6] This topic was again considered in April 1954, when Dulles flew to London and Paris for talks. At the conclusion of their conversations, Dulles and Eden issued a communique which said, in part, "We are ready to take part, with the other countries principally concerned, in an examination of the possibility of establishing a collective defense, within the framework of the Charter of the United Nations, to assure the peace, security and freedom of South-East Asia and the Western Pacific."[7] The following day, Dulles and Bidault, meeting in Paris, issued a communique which said, "In close association with other interested nations, we will examine the possibility of establishing, within the framework of the United Nations Charter, a collective defense to assure the peace, security and freedom of this area."[8] [Southeast Asia and the Western Pacific.]

On June 3, after the fall of Dien Bien Phu, military staff talks among representatives of the United States, the United Kingdom, France, Australia, and New Zealand began in Washington.[9] The State Department announced that the talks would supplement conversations being held among the United States and other countries. In Manila, Secretary of Defense Wilson was conferring with the Philippine government; in Geneva, American officials were talking with representatives of Laos, Cambodia, and Vietnam; and in Washington, the American government was consulting with the Thai Embassy. The United States was sounding the opinions of prospective members of a collective defense pact in Southeast Asia.

Toward the end of June, Eden and Churchill visited Washington. Eisenhower and Churchill issued a joint statement on June 28 in which they said, "We will press forward with plans for collective defense" *whether or not* a settlement on Southeast Asia is concluded at Geneva.[10] As a result of this visit, an Anglo-American study group on Southeast Asia was set up at the official level and began to meet in Washington at the beginning of July. The ANZUS powers,[11] meeting in Washington on June 30, also discussed collective security. They issued a communique which said, "All three representatives at the ANZUS meeting agreed on the need for immediate action to bring about the early establishment of collective defense in Southeast Asia."[12] In yet another forum, the practical implications of collective military action were being examined at a conference of Australian, British, French, and American military officers at Singapore starting July 6.[13]

THE MANILA CONFERENCE

These various negotiations culminated in the signing of a collective defense treaty in Manila on September 6, 1954, by representatives of the following states: France, the United Kingdom, Thailand, Pakistan, the United States, Australia, New Zealand, and the Philippines.

Secretary Dulles's opening remarks at the Manila gathering provide a clear indication of how the United States envisioned such a collective defense system. The Secretary of State stressed the defensive nature of the proposed scheme.

What we do is directed against no nation and no people. We are exercising what the [UN] Charter refers to as the inherent right of collective self-defense.

The United States itself has no direct territorial interests in Southeast Asia. Nevertheless, we feel a sense of common destiny with those who in this area have their life and being.

We are united by a common danger, the danger that stems from International Communism and its insatiable ambition. We know that wherever it makes gains, as in Indochina, those gains are looked upon not as final solutions, but as bridgeheads for future gains. That is the fact which requires each of us to be concerned with what goes on elsewhere.[14]

Dulles believed that miscalculation was one of the major causes of war.[15] Therefore, he felt, war in Southeast Asia might be averted by unequivocally notifying potential aggressors that they would face overwhelming force in the event of aggression. Dulles incorporated this idea into his Manila speech, saying,

We can greatly diminish that risk [of war through miscalculation] by making clear that an attack upon the Treaty area would occasion a reaction so united, so strong and so well placed that the aggressor would lose more than it could hope to gain.

So, our association should bind the members to develop both individual and collective capacity to resist armed aggression.[16]

Explaining that the states represented at Manila could not match the "vast land armies, of which International Communism disposes in Asia," Dulles said that "we can best serve by developing the deterrent of mobile striking power, plus strategically placed reserves."[17]

Dulles recognized that armed aggression was not the only danger posed by communism. He warned of the threat of subversion and other forms of indirect aggression. He expressed the opinion that opportunities for international communism would decrease if trade relations helped the noncommunist nations strengthen their respective economies.

Then he made a statement that foreshadowed the Protocol to the SEATO treaty. He said,

Some countries, which have a close relationship to the prospective Treaty area, are not here. Among them are Cambodia, Laos and Vietnam. Their Government and their people can know that we shall have them much in our mind, and I hope that we shall be able to throw over them some mantle of protection.[18]

The SEATO Treaty

The SEATO Treaty and Protocol were signed September 8, 1954, by all eight countries in attendance at Manila.[19]

The Treaty duplicates commitments undertaken by the United States in its mutual defense treaty with the Philippines and under the ANZUS Pact. Article IV (1) names "aggression by means of armed attack in the treaty area" as the condition that would precipitate a response by the SEATO powers. In the event of such armed attack, each party "agrees that it will . . . act to meet the common danger in accordance with its constitutional processes." Article IV (1) also says that each party recognizes that such an attack "would endanger its own peace and safety." A comparison with the NATO Treaty is revealing. Article 5 of the NATO Treaty states that each signatory would regard an armed attack against one member as "an attack against them all." The Article goes on to say that each party "will assist the Party or Parties so attacked by taking forthwith, individually and in concert with the other Parties, such action as it deems necessary, including the use of armed force." The SEATO Treaty, in specifying that each member will decide upon what action to take "in accordance with its constitutional processes," affords a less definite commitment to action than the NATO Treaty.

The SEATO Treaty under Article IV (1) does not oblige a signatory to consult with the other parties before reacting to external aggression. Article IV (1) permits each party to decide if an act of aggression has occurred and what measures it will take in response to it. However, Dulles in his report to the Senate said "in its understanding with reference to Article IV, Paragraph 1, the United States affirms that in the event of any aggression it will observe the consultation provisions of Article IV, Paragraph 2."[20] Paragraph 2 states that if any party is "threatened in any way other than by armed attack . . . the Parties shall *consult* immediately in order to agree on the measures which should be taken for the common defense." (Italics mine.) Once again, the commitment to action is vague. The SEATO Treaty does not seem to fulfill Dulles's intention of notifying a potential aggressor that he will be met unequivocally by "a reaction so united, so strong and so well placed that the aggressor would lose more than it could hope to gain." However, the Treaty does provide the United States with a basis for intervening in the treaty area. In this regard, Article IV (3) takes on added meaning. That paragraph states that "no action on the territory of any State designated by unanimous agreement under paragraph 1 of this Article or on any territory so designated shall be taken except at the invitation or with the consent of the government concerned." The United States was entitled to intervene, in other words, only if requested to do so.

In an Understanding attached to the Treaty, the United States declared that, for the purposes of an American response, aggression and armed attack under Article IV (1) applied only to communist aggression. In the event of other aggression or armed attack, the United States would consult under the provisions of Article IV (2).

Although Laos was not a signatory to the Manila Treaty, that country was brought under SEATO "protection" through a special Protocol to the Treaty. The Protocol said in part, "The Parties to the Southeast Asia Collective Defense Treaty unanimously designate for the purposes of Article IV of the Treaty the States of Cambodia and Laos and the free territory under the jurisdiction of the State of Vietnam." Thus the American alliance network embraced Laos, as well as Cambodia and the non-communist portion of Vietnam. The signing of the Protocol occasioned the following riposte from the Soviet Union,

> The governments of the USSR and the Democratic Republic of Viet Nam resolutely condemn the attempts to involve South Viet Nam, Laos and Cambodia in the sphere of action of the aggressive military bloc in Southeast Asia (SEATO), attempts which are contrary to the Geneva agreements. They have also drawn attention to the incompatibility with the Geneva agreements of the attempts of certain foreign powers to interfere in the domestic affairs of South Viet Nam, Cambodia, and Laos, and of attempts to impose agreements of a military nature on these countries.[21]

The Pacific Charter

The representatives of the eight powers at Geneva also signed another document, the Pacific Charter.[22] In this document, the parties agreed to "uphold the principles of equal rights and self-determination of peoples, . . . to promote self-government and to secure the independence of all countries whose peoples desire it and are able to undertake its responsibilities, . . . to cooperate in the economic, social and cultural fields," and "to prevent or counter by appropriate means any attempt in the treaty area to subvert their freedom or to destroy their sovereignty or territorial integrity."

One week after the Manila Conference adjourned, Secretary of State Dulles delivered a radio and television address to the American people. In the following terms he justified American participation in the security pact for Southeast Asia.

> Any significant expansion of the Communist world would, indeed, be a danger to the United States, because international communism thinks in terms of ultimately using its power position against the United States. Therefore, we could honestly say . . . that Communist armed aggression in Southeast Asia would, in fact, endanger our peace and security and call for counteraction on our part.
>
> . . . .
>
> I believe that the Manila Pact will, in fact, make a substantial contribution to preserve free governments in Southeast Asia and to prevent communism from rushing on into the Pacific area, where it would seriously threaten the defense of the United States.[23]

THE UNITED STATES FORTIFIES ITS COMMITMENT TO SOUTHEAST ASIA

At the same time that Washington was promoting collective defense through the Manila Treaty, the United States took measures to strengthen bilateral ties with the countries of Southeast Asia. On his way to Manila, Dulles participated in a meeting of the Philippines-United States Council set up under the 1951 mutual defense treaty between the two countries. According to a communique issued September 4, 1954, the American Secretary stated "in the most emphatic terms" that in the event of an attack on the Philippines, the United States would honor its commitments under that treaty and "would act immediately."[24]

At the end of September 1954, representatives of France and the United States held talks in Washington on the subject of Indochina. A communique issued September 29 said,

> The representatives of France and the United States reaffirm the intention of their governments to support the complete independence of Cambodia, Laos and Viet-Nam. Both France and the United States will continue to assist Cambodia, Laos and Viet-Nam in their efforts to safeguard their freedom and independence and to advance the welfare of their peoples.[25]

President Eisenhower sent a letter to Ngo Dinh Diem, President of the Council of Ministers in Vietnam, on October 23, 1954, offering him United States aid in resettling refugees from North Vietnam and for other projects. "The purpose of this offer," the President said in his letter, "is to assist the Government of Vietnam in developing and maintaining a strong, viable state, capable of resisting attempted subversion or aggression through military means."[26]

In February and March of 1955, Secretary Dulles underscored America's commitment to Southeast Asia by making a trip to the area. During this journey he attended the first meeting of the SEATO Council and visited six Southeast Asian capitals. His first stop was Manila, where he met with President Ramón Magsaysay on February 21. The next day, he arrived in Bangkok for the initial SEATO Council meeting.

SEATO COUNCIL MEETS

Article V of the Manila Treaty stipulated that the signatories should establish a Council "to consider matters concerning the implementation" of the Treaty. The Council, on which all eight members were to sit, was to "provide for consultation with regard to military and any other planning as the situation obtaining in the Treaty area may from time to time require." With the exception of France, where the Mendès-France government had just fallen, all eight countries were represented at Bangkok by their foreign ministers.[27] The meeting lasted from February 23 to February 25.

In his opening speech, Dulles reaffirmed the United States' "solid intention" to aid any state covered by the Manila Treaty that became the victim of aggression. He cited communist control of the Laotian provinces of Phong Saly and Sam Neua. The Secretary expressed his preference for using mobile power to strike where needed, instead of stationing large forces throughout the area.[28]

On the next day, the delegates set up a military staff group and a committee to deal with problems of the alliance. They also established a secretariat. The military staff group was to function under the secretariat. A body of experts on subversion and an economic group were also created and placed under the aegis of the secretariat.

On February 25 the Council delegates signed a communique[29] in which they reaffirmed the aim of their governments "to prevent or counter by appropriate means any attempt in the Treaty area to subvert their freedom or to destroy their sovereignty or territorial integrity." They also said, "Realizing the importance to the security of Southeast Asia and the Southwest Pacific of the States of Cambodia, Laos, and of the free territory under the jurisdiction of the State of Viet Nam, the Council reaffirmed the determination of the member governments to support these three States in maintaining their freedom and independence as set forth in the Protocol to the Treaty." Each signatory agreed to designate a Military Adviser to its representative on the SEATO Council. These advisers, who were to meet as the situation required, were given the responsibility of making recommendations on military cooperation to the Council.

From the time of this very first meeting of the Council, SEATO proved to be a weak organization. All the bodies set up by the Council were purely advisory. The Council's communique obligated the members to do little beyond promising to cooperate and exchange information. No force in being or unified command was created.[30] Since SEATO did not play a determining role in American policy toward Laos,[31] the alliance will hereafter be referred to only obliquely. We pause only to note that Katay Don Sasorith, a prominent Laotian political leader, attended the inaugural meeting of SEATO as an observer.[32]

DULLES TOURS SOUTHEAST ASIA

After attending the SEATO Council meeting in Bangkok, Secretary

Dulles traveled to four other Southeast Asian countries as well as Formosa.

From Bangkok, the Secretary went to Burma, where he conferred with Premier U Nu. During these talks Dulles told U Nu about the SEATO Council meeting and invited his country to join the alliance.

The following day, Dulles visited Laos, where he told Crown Prince Savang Vatthana that the United States would defend Laos under the Manila Treaty. In return, Dulles asked that Laos fight subversion within the country and preserve the principle of liberty. Savang agreed. Dulles also proposed that Laotian officers and men be sent to Thailand[33] to be trained by U. S. Army officers.

On February 28, Dulles arrived in Cambodia. He assured King Norodom Sihanouk—who abdicated three days later—that SEATO would afford Cambodia protection against communism.

The following day found the American statesman in Saigon, where he gave Premier Ngo Dinh Diem similar assurances.

At Taipei on March 3, Dulles and Foreign Minister George K. C. Yeh exchanged instruments of ratification of their mutual defense treaty signed December 2, 1954. The treaty made the United States and Formosa formal allies.

On the next day it was revealed that President Eisenhower had written on February 19 a letter to Bao Dai, Chief of State of South Vietnam, promising to "continue and expand support for free Vietnam."

On March 8, back in Washington, Dulles reported to the American people on his Asian tour.[34] Underlining the United States commitment to Southeast Asia, Dulles said, "We must, if occasion offers, make it clear that we are prepared to stand firm and, if necessary, meet hostile force with the greater force that we possess." In the speech he referred specifically to Laos, saying,

> To illustrate this connection between direct and indirect aggression I may mention the situation in Laos. In two of its provinces there are disloyal elements, supported by the Chinese and Viet Minh Communists. The Laos Government is seeking to reestablish control over its own territory. But it is worried lest, if it suppresses the Communists within, it will be struck by the Communists from without. I hope that that worry is now allayed by their better understanding of the protective nature of the Manila Pact.

Shortly after Dulles returned from Asia, the United States took measures to reinforce its mutual security design in Southeast Asia. On April 27, 1955, the United States and the Philippines signed an executive agreement providing for the equipping and training of a new Philippine army division. The project was to be financed by a $9.5 million grant-in-aid from the United States under the mutual defense agreement between the two countries. From May 2 to 6, 1955, Thai Prime Minister Field Marshal Pibul Songgram paid an official visit to Washington, where President Eisenhower presented him with the Legion of Merit, the highest award Washington can give to a noncitizen.[35] In mid-December, 1955, the Foreign Operations Administration increased defense support to Thailand to $36.7 million, an increase of $28.2 million for that fiscal year. The additional money was to be spent primarily on electric power, a road network and telecommunications. Throughout Southeast Asia, the United States appeared to be settling in for a long stay.

The purpose of this review of American policy in Southeast Asia through 1954 and 1955 has been to provide a necessary backdrop for an in-depth examination of American policy in Laos. A full understanding of that policy is possible only in the context of Washington's broad objectives in Southeast Asia as a whole. Before we focus on events in Laos in the following chapter, a brief summary of chapters 4 and 5 may be in order.

The problems facing American policy-makers concerned with Laos after the 1954 Geneva Conference arose out of the Laotian nationalist movement, born at the close of World War II. Until 1954, the United States did not interfere with French administration in Laos. During this period of American abstention from Laotian affairs, the Lao Issara emerged. Counting among its members both Souvanna Phouma and Souphanouvong, the Lao Issara sought Laotian freedom from French control. In 1949 Souphanouvong broke with the Lao Issara for two reasons. He wanted the Lao Issara to ally itself with the Viet Minh, and he was not satisfied with anything less than complete independence from France. Souphanouvong formed the Pathet Lao, connected with the Viet Minh, and demanded total independence from France.

During the years 1949–54, the Pathet Lao drew apart from other political elements in Laos. After the signing of the Franco-Laotian Convention in July, 1949, the members of the Lao Issara returned to Vientiane to take up the task of governing the country. The Pathet Lao, on the other hand, remained in the hills, opposed to the accommodation other Laotian leaders had reached with the French. Thus, in the years 1949–1954, the Pathet Lao consolidated itself as a separate force in Laotian politics.

The question arises as to whether Washington could have taken any action that would have prevented the formation of a communist-oriented political movement in Laos. The sole action that the United States might have taken was to apply more pressure on Paris to grant complete independence to Indochina. Such a move by France would have deprived the Pathet Lao of many of its non-communist, nationalist followers and might have robbed the organization of its *raison d'être*. The United States, however, considered France's role in European security to be more important than developments in Indochina. In order to gain French acquiescence to German rearmament and the formation of a European defense community, Washington did not wish to offend France by meddling in her relations with the Indochinese states. Given Washington's assignment of priority of Europe over Southeast Asia, as well as France's central role in European security, the United States was not in a position to prevent the formation of the Pathet Lao.

At the end of the Indochinese war, Viet Minh–Pathet Lao forces were supreme in Laos. The Viet Minh had mounted three successful invasions of Laos, the Pathet Lao following in their wake. Although the United States succeeded in keeping the Pathet Lao from being recognized as a party at the Geneva Conference, Washington was unable to prevent the Viet Minh–Pathet Lao from receiving a separate regroupment area which, following Viet Minh withdrawal, fell entirely to the Pathet Lao.

Washington's refusal to sign the Geneva accords signified American uneasiness over the existence of a communist regime in northern Vietnam, as well as a communist-oriented movement in Laos.

In order to put the communists on notice that further efforts at expanding the territory under their control would trigger an American response, the United States took the lead in forming SEATO. SEATO was the most salient feature of Washington's containment policy as applied to Southeast Asia. Other pacts, such as ANZUS and the mutual defense treaty with the Philippines, were formed at an earlier date in accordance with the containment policy. Laos was brought under the umbrella of containment by the Protocol to the Manila Treaty and by Secretary Dulles's assurances, in his 1955 visit, that the United States would meet its SEATO obligations should the communists menace Laos.

NOTES

1. President Eisenhower's domino theory seems to suffer in light of North Vietnam's efforts to take over the South, despite North Korea's setback.

2. *Department of State Bulletin*, August 2, 1954, pp. 162–63.

3. Eisenhower said nothing about American aid to France to enable her to prosecute the war.

4. *Documents on American Foreign Relations*, 1954, pp. 317–18.

5. *Pentagon Papers*, p. 14.

6. Anthony Eden, *Full Circle: The Memoirs of Anthony Eden* (Cambridge: Houghton Mifflin Company 1960), p. 94.

7. Great Britain, Parliamentary Papers, Accounts and Papers, Cmd. 2834, December, 1965, "Documents Relating to British Involvement in the Indo-China Conflict 1945–1965," pp. 66–67.

8. *Documents on International Affairs,* 1954 (London: Royal Institute of International Affairs, Oxford University Press, 1957), pp. 122–23.

9. *Collective Defense in Southeast Asia* (London: Royal Institute of International Affairs, 1956), pp. 2–3. These military representatives formed the Five-Power Staff Agency which had been in existence since January, 1953.

10. *Documents on American Foreign Relations,* 1954, p. 63.

11. New Zealand, Australia and the United States.

12. *Documents on American Foreign Relations,* 1954, p. 281.

13. *Collective Defense in Southeast Asia,* p. 5.

14. Republic of the Philippines, *The Signing of the Southeast Asia Collective Defense Treaty, the Protocol to the Southeast Asia Collective Defense Treaty, and the Pacific Charter* (Manila: Manila Conference of 1954, Secretariat, Committee on Publicity, 1954), p. 41.

15. He told correspondent James Shepley, "The important thing is that the aggressor know in advance that he is going to lose more than he can win. He doesn't have to lose *much* more. It just has to be *something* more. If the equation is such that the outcome is clearly going to be against him, he won't go in." James Shepley, "How Dulles Averted War," *Life* 40 (January 16, 1956): 78.

16. Philippines, *The Signing of the Southeast Asia Collective Defense Treaty,* p. 41.

17. *Ibid.,* p. 42.

18. *Ibid.,* pp. 42–43.

19. Texts may be found in *Department of State Bulletin,* September 20, 1954, pp. 393–95.

20. *Collective Defense in Southeast Asia,* p. 13.

21. Cole, p. 243.

22. Text in *Documents on American Foreign Relations,* 1954, pp. 318–19.

23. *Department of State Bulletin,* September 27, 1954, pp. 431–32.

24. *Collective Defense in Southeast Asia,* p. 6.

25. *Documents on American Foreign Relations,* 1954, p. 365.

26. *Ibid.*

27. France was represented by Henri Bonnet, former Ambassador to Washington.

28. *The New York Times,* February 24, 1955.

29. Text in *Documents on American Foreign Relations,* 1955, pp. 323–27.

30. The day before the Council meeting opened Marshal Pibul Songgram, Thai Foreign Minister, called for the formation of a permanent military force under the Manila Treaty. According to unofficial reports, the United States opposed the Thai suggestion. Dulles viewed Southeast Asia, the Far East and the Western Pacific as a single strategic entity. He did not want to commit American forces specifically to only one of these three potential theaters. See *Collective Defense in Southeast Asia,* pp. 121–22.

31. At a news conference on March 20, 1961, held by Secretary of State Dean Rusk, the following exchange took place:

"Q. Mr. Secretary, is our military aid program to Laos in any way linked or conditioned by our membership in the Southeast Asia Treaty Organization?"

"A. No. I think there is no direct organic relation there. We have been interested in the stability and the peace of all these countries in Southeast Asia.

"Military and economic assistance in Laos were undertaken within the framework of the Geneva accords and in full cooperation with the suggestion of the

Laotian Government. That has not been linked to the activities of the Southeast Asia Treaty Organization."
See *Department of State Bulletin,* April 10, 1961, p. 522.

32. Wilfred G. Burchett, *The Furtive War: The United States in Vietnam and Laos* (New York: International Publishers, 1963), p. 163.

33. Under the Geneva agreements, United States troops were prohibited from entering Laos.

34. Text of speech in U. S., Department of State, *The Bangkok Conference of the Manila Pact Powers, February 23-25, 1955,* 1955.

35. On July 13, 1954, the Department of Defense announced it had approved "a new and additional military assistance program" for Thailand. This intensified program included "accelerated development of junior officers, non-commissioned officers and technical personnel," provision of "weapons, equipment and technical training assistance" and construction of a $3 million highway through central Thailand. The U. S. Military Assistance Advisory Group (MAAG) of more than 200 men was to be enlarged. Finally, the number of Thai officers being trained in the United States—503—was to be increased. See *The New York Times,* July 14, 1954.

6
LAOS SWINGS TO THE LEFT

THUS FAR IN our study we have focused the bulk of our attention on the viewpoints and policies of Washington. In examining America's containment policy as applied to Southeast Asia, we have noted the evaluation of the communist threat made by important policy makers in the United States. We have also reviewed the actions taken by the United States in pursuit of containment—aid to France, the formation of SEATO, and the strengthening of America's security arrangements in the South Pacific.

In the years that followed the Geneva Conference in 1954, Washington began to take a greater interest in Laos itself. In order to understand why the United States should have become so involved in a small, remote country as unlike the United States as any state could be, we must delve into the sequence of events that was unfolding in Laos.

A simple analogy may prove useful in describing the course of events in Laos in the years after 1954. Consider a pendulum swinging back and forth between the extremes of the Pathet Lao on the left and the conservative elements on the right. This pendulum will represent political power in Laos. As the pendulum moves toward the left, the Pathet Lao gains a prominent role in determining the affairs of state. Various ministries are headed by Pathet Lao leaders. The Pathet Lao's political party is permitted to compete openly for the popular vote. Pathet Lao officials run for election to the National Assembly. When the pendulum swings to the right, conservative elements reduce the amount of influence that the Pathet Lao is able to bring to bear in Laos. Ministries are removed from Pathet Lao hands. Their political party is declared illegal and prevented from operating, except underground. Pathet Lao leaders are put in jail.

The entire political history of Laos after 1954 can be described in terms of this analogy. In the period from 1954 through the middle of 1958, the pendulum swung to the left, representing the movement of the Laotian government toward accommodation with the communist-led Pathet Lao. From the summer of 1958 until the spring of 1961, the pendulum swayed to the right, as the Pathet Lao lost power to the conservatives. From the spring of 1961 to the summer of 1962, when an international conference on Laos concluded its business, the pendulum moved toward the left once again, as the Pathet Lao won many political rights. After 1962, the pendulum began to move toward the right once again. Whether it will eventually settle in the center, on the right, on the left, or perhaps keep swinging indefinitely remains to be seen.

In this chapter we shall follow the pendulum as it swings to the left, in the direction of rapprochement with the Pathet Lao.

ROYAL GOVERNMENT DISPUTE WITH THE PATHET LAO

The Geneva agreements, it will be recalled, stipulated the means by which the Pathet Lao was to be integrated into the rest of the Laotian community. Article 11 of the Agreement on the Cessation of Hostilities in Laos called for the concentration of Pathet Lao forces in provisional assembly areas within fifteen days after the cease-fire. Article 12 specified that a Joint Commission—composed of an equal number of representatives from the commands of both sides—should be established to fix the sites and boundaries of twelve provisional assembly areas, "one to each province," for the reception of Pathet Lao military personnel. Article 14 provided that, "Pending a political settlement, the fighting units of 'Pathet Lao,' concentrated in the provisional assembly areas, shall move into the Provinces of Phongsaly and Sam-Neua, except for any military personnel who wish to be demobilized where they are." This concentration was to be completed within 120 days after the Agreement entered into force, that is, by November 19.

In October, representatives of the Laotian government and the Pathet Lao met at Khang Khay and set up the Joint Commission, designed to "facilitate the implementation of the clauses of the Agreement on the Cessation of Hostilities relating to the simultaneous and general cease-fire" (Article 28). Although the establishment of the Joint Commission was a gesture in the spirit of conciliation, the wording of the Khang Khay communique led to an aggravation of the dispute between the Royal

Government and the Pathet Lao. The communique stated that the Pathet Lao should regroup in six provisional assembly areas, but made no mention of such areas in the provinces of Phong Saly or Sam Neua.

The Pathet Lao claimed, on the basis of Article 14 of the Agreement and the Khang Khay communique, that "the whole of the two provinces of Phong Saly and Sam Neua constitutes the final regroupment area for all the fighting units of 'Pathet Lao.' "[1] More specifically, the Pathet Lao argued that the wording of Article 14 meant that they should station themselves throughout the two provinces because "the term 'province' implies the totality of the territory within its limits and, if it had been otherwise, the wording would have been that the fighting units of 'Pathet Lao' would move *into a zone within the two provinces.*" The Pathet Lao also noted that the Khang Khay communique named six provisional assembly areas but made no reference to the provinces of Phong Saly and Sam Neua. "This provision clearly indicates," the letter concluded, "that the two provinces of Phong Saly and Sam Neua constitute in their totality the final regroupment area for the forces of 'Pathet Lao'. . . ."[2]

The Laotian government offered a conflicting interpretation of these documents, saying:

> The Agreements and Final Declaration of the Geneva Conference recognize that the sovereignty of the Royal Laotian Government extends over the whole of the territory of Laos. That Government, therefore, must be able to re-position its administration in the provinces of Phong Saly and Sam Neua, as an expression of its sovereignty.[3]

Article 12 of the Agreement, the letter went on to say, states that the Pathet Lao shall be stationed in twelve provisional assembly areas, that is, one area per province, including Sam Neua and Phong Saly. The letter also stated that the two provinces were not mentioned in the Khang Khay agreement because the government tried to facilitate the signing of the agreement by avoiding controversial matters.

On November 4, 1954, the Commander of the Pathet Lao fighting forces, Colonel Singkapo, made a declaration that signaled a mellowing of the dispute between the Royal Government and the Pathet Lao. The Colonel said, "As representative of the 'Pathet Lao' at the Joint Armistice Commission for Laos, I declare that the 'Pathet Lao' forces recognize the Royal Government and that *in principle* the administration of 'Pathet Lao' in the two provinces of Sam Neua and Phong Saly is classified under the Supreme Authority of the Royal Government."[4]

Despite Singkapo's statement, the Pathet Lao and the Laotian government drifted further apart during the ensuing fall and winter. The two parties found themselves in disagreement regarding the continuation of the Joint Commission—set up in October at Khang Khay—and the Joint Groups formed under it. Arguing that the withdrawal of foreign troops had been completed, the Laotian government alleged that further activity of the Joint Groups constituted "a foreign interference in the affairs of the Kingdom."[5] The Pathet Lao insisted that the Joint Commission and Joint Groups should function until the Geneva agreements had been fully implemented.[6] The dispute was ended in February 1955, when the Laotian government unilaterally recalled its representatives from the Joint Commission and the Joint Groups.

Meanwhile, additional talks between representatives of the Laotian government and the Pathet Lao had begun in January. These dilatory conversations lasted until March 9, when the two parties issued a communique. In the communique each side promised that it would not permit any hostile acts against the other party.[7] However, outstanding disputes were not resolved.

On April 22, the Pathet Lao communicated to the ICC a proposal which seems to have expressed the minimum conditions that the Pathet Lao was prepared to accept in regard to its political future. The proposal called for free general elections and the formation of a coalition government including representatives from the Pathet Lao. The Vientiane government, led by Premier Souvanna Phouma, rejected this request.[8]

Vientiane's denial of the Pathet Lao's proposal indicated to the communists that their attempts to gain a voice in the government through political means were not likely to succeed. Accordingly, the Pathet Lao was soon to adopt an alternative method: military force.

A review of the genesis of the dispute between the Pathet Lao and the Royal Government reveals that the Pathet Lao was willing to integrate itself into the remainder of the Laotian community. The communists, however, insisted upon certain conditions. The Pathet Lao's proposal of April 22 listed one of these conditions, namely, Pathet Lao participation in a coalition government. Perhaps such an arrangement was what the communists envisioned as the "political settlement" called for in Article 14 of the Agreement. Until the communists had achieved what in their opinion was an acceptable political settlement, they were unwilling to forfeit their military power. Such power depended on an independent base of operations (the provinces of Phong Saly and Sam Neua) and an independent army. In the absence of what was, to them, a satisfactory political settlement, the Pathet Lao steadfastly refused to yield control of either of these necessities of life.

The Laotian government, on the other hand, urged that the dissolution of the Pathet Lao fighting units must be the first, not the last, step in the arrival at a final political settlement. Refusing to accord the Pathet Lao a voice in the government, the Vientiane regime claimed that the Pathet Lao's refusal to disband—and thereby place its trust in the Royal Government, which it had just fought—was the sole impediment to a political settlement.

In sum, the dispute between the Pathet Lao and the Laotian government concerned the political influence the communists would wield once a final political settlement were realized. The communists insisted upon a position in the Royal Government; the political leaders in Vientiane sought to deprive the communists of political influence. This conflict of interests soon reached a crisis; military clashes were the result.

THE CIVIL WAR BEGINS

From the spring of 1955 until the fall of 1956, the Royal Government and the Pathet Lao each accused the other of violating the cease-fire agreement negotiated at Geneva. In its report covering the period, the ICC characterized the military situation in the provinces of Sam Neua and Phong Saly as "unsatisfactory." The report said that "numerous clashes occurred between the troops of the Royal Government and the Fighting Units of Pathet Lao." These hostilities, the report continued, ceased in August 1956, but occasional incidents continued to occur after that date. "The need for vigilance therefore continues," the report warned.[9] The ICC tabulated complaints and petitions received from the Laotian government and the Pathet Lao during the period July 1955–September 1956. These figures appear below:

TABLE 2

COMPLAINTS AND PETITIONS RECEIVED BY THE ICC DURING JULY, 1955–SEPTEMBER, 1956[a]

Type of Complaint	Filed by	
	Government	Pathet Lao
1. Military nature	113	117
2. Mine laying	30	2
3. Democratic freedom	37	27
4. Forced recruitment	2	—
5. Miscellaneous	20	8
6. Petitions	2	42
Total	204	196

[a]Great Britain, Cmd. 314, p. 82.

On several occasions the Government charged that North Vietnam had aided the Pathet Lao.[10] The Pathet Lao countered with the accusation that 3,000 Chinese Nationalists had infiltrated the provinces of Phong Saly and Sam Neua upon American instructions.[11] None of these allegations was substantiated with convincing evidence.

Ideally, the ICC should have investigated these charges to determine their validity. However, as the ICC admitted, it was hindered in carrying out its work by lack of transportation facilities and interpreters and failure of the parties to cooperate at all times.[12] The ICC, for instance, received nine complaints alleging the presence of North Vietnamese troops in the provinces of Phong Saly and Sam Neua during the period July 1, 1955–May 16, 1957. The ICC was able to undertake only four investigations. It found no Vietnamese troops in these areas. However, the ICC acknowledged that long delays occurred in carrying out these inquiries. Since the delays were sufficient to permit Vietnamese troops that may have been in the area to leave before the ICC investigators arrived, the ICC investigations did not prove or disprove the presence of Vietnamese troops in the provinces at the times that the Government filed its complaints.[13]

The ICC's inability to make timely investigations of the Laotian government's accusations did not preclude Washington from making its own assessments of the Royal Government's claims. The official American interpretation of the relationship between the Pathet Lao and the North Vietnamese was contained in a white paper on Laos released in 1959.[14] According to this document, the North Vietnamese actually controlled the administration in the provinces of Phong Saly and Sam Neua. A central mission of ranking North Vietnamese responsible for guiding the Pathet Lao leadership was located near Pathet Lao headquarters in the town of Sam Neua. This mission was directed by a special North Vietnamese staff situated in North Vietnam. Vietnamese advisors were attached to Pathet Lao ministries and also assisted the Pathet Lao at lower levels of administration. On occasion, the State Department document goes on to say, Viet Minh troops entered Sam Neua province and engaged in joint maneuvers with Pathet Lao military units, which had permanent Viet Minh advisers on their staffs. In North Vietnam, the Viet Minh operated training facilities for Pathet Lao military personnel and undercover agents.

Unhappily, the State Department did not choose to document its charges. It can be seen, however, that Washington pictured the Pathet Lao as a mailed fist on the arm of the North Vietnamese. And if the arm belonged to North Vietnam, then the central nervous system which controlled its movements was located in Peking or Moscow, or perhaps in both. In Washington's eyes, the Laotian civil conflict was not an isolated instance of internal violence; rather, it was but one manifestation of an attempt by Asian communists to exert hegemony over all of Southeast Asia. Significantly, the United States began giving aid to Laos at the same time the Viet Minh, according to Washington, was helping the Pathet Lao. For fiscal 1955 the United States appropriated $40.9 million for Laos, principally to pay the salaries of the army and the civil administration.[15]

THE BANDUNG CONFERENCE

On the diplomatic front, both Laos and North Vietnam sent delegates to the Bandung Conference which met in April 1955. In the presence of Nehru and Chou En-lai, North Vietnamese Foreign Minister Pham Van Dong concluded the following written agreement with Katay Don Sasorith, Prime Minister of Laos:

> First, the Government of the Democratic Republic of Vietnam considers that the settlement which is due to take place between the Royal Government of Laos and the "Pathet Lao," by virtue of the Geneva agreements, is a question of internal order which the Royal Government and the "Pathet Lao" are entirely free to solve in the best way possible in the higher interests of the country and people of Laos.
> Second, the Government of the Democratic Republic of Vietnam and the Royal Government of Laos will develop and harmonize the good neighborly relations which tie and should tie these countries to each other, within the framework of the Five Principles defined in the Sino-Indian Agreement of April 29, 1954.[16]

At the conference, Chou En-lai said that China would respect Laotian independence and promised not to trespass on Laotian territory.[17]

It was not long, however, before Laos charged North Vietnam with violating the April agreement. In November 1955, Foreign Minister Phoui Sananikone accused North Vietnam of attaching political commissars and military cadres to the Pathet Lao, in addition to sending military and food supplies to them.[18] The tenor of these accusations corresponded with the theme of the American white paper released later.

By charging the Pathet Lao with accepting outside support, the Royal Government was building a case for soliciting foreign intervention on its own behalf.

THE 1955 ELECTIONS

According to the Laotian constitution, elections for the National Assembly were to be held throughout the country in 1955. These elections were originally scheduled for August 28. In the hope that the Government and the Pathet Lao would reach a reconciliation, however, the National Assembly postponed the date for elections until December 25.

The Pathet Lao, which exercised actual control over the provinces of Phong Saly and Sam Neua, suggested that the Government entrust it with the continued administration of these provinces until the elections. The Pathet Lao maintained that full freedom and fairness in the elections would best be assured if joint committees of Pathet Lao and Government representatives supervised the electoral proceedings in the two provinces. The Government rejected this proposal on the basis that such an arrangement would enable the Pathet Lao to determine the outcome. The two parties held talks on these matters until September 5, when the meetings adjourned after the two sides had failed to resolve their differences.

Subsequent talks were held in Rangoon between October 9 and 15. The chief negotiators were Prime Minister Sasorith and Prince Souphanouvong, leader of the Pathet Lao. On October 11 the parties signed a written agreement.[19] Like so many compacts between the government and the Pathet Lao, this document was in essence a declaration of intention, rather than a blueprint for action. The parties reaffirmed their declaration of March 9, 1955, and promised to take measures to prevent the occurrence of violence between their forces. Perhaps the only reason that the parties were able to sign an agreement at all was that the document failed even to mention the cardinal differences that separated the parties. The negotiators reached no accord on establishing Government administration in the provinces of Sam Neua and Phong Saly, nor did they devise a scheme for holding elections there. On the most important matter of all, the future status of the Pathet Lao fighting forces, the negotiators agreed to postpone discussion. The two sides met again at the end of October, but were unable to harmonize their views.

The elections were held as scheduled. The Pathet Lao boycotted the elections and unsuccessfully urged the rest of the country to do likewise. All 39 seats in the Assembly were at stake. Since the Government was unable to administer the elections in the provinces of Sam Neua and Phong Saly, no voting was held in these provinces. Katay Sasorith's National Progressive Party[20] won 21 seats; Phoui Sananikone's Independent Party captured 8; and various smaller parties divided the remaining 10 seats.[21] The election results presaged a continuance of the policies of the Sasorith government.

THE AGREEMENTS OF 1956

Although elections were held, the Pathet Lao and the rest of the Laotian community remained as far apart as ever. The Pathet Lao still retained exclusive control of their base area in Phong Saly and Sam Neua. Military clashes continued.

In an effort to move things off center, the ICC, with Poland dissenting, adopted a resolution on January 7, 1956, which said that "without further delay the Royal Administration should be re-established in the provinces of Sam Neua and Phong Saly and the Royal Government should concurrently take necessary measures to bring about the integration of Pathet Lao fully and without discrimination into the national community."[22] The Government accepted the resolution. The Pathet Lao, however, took note of it but neither accepted nor rejected it.[23]

In the latter half of 1956, the two parties renewed their efforts to reach agreement. In July, Souphanouvong flew to Vientiane for talks with the Royal Government, whose Prime Minister was now his half brother Souvanna Phouma.[24] These talks culminated in the issuance of two joint declarations, one on August 5 and the second on August 10.[25] In the first declaration, the parties agreed to set up political and military joint commissions to work out details of a cease-fire, the administration of the provinces of Phong Saly and Sam Neua, and the integration of the Pathet Lao fighting forces into the Royal Army. Of more importance was the agreement, embodied in the August 10 communique, to establish a National Union Government that would include representatives of the Pathet Lao. This communique marked the Government's first agreement to accept Pathet Lao representatives in a coalition government. The communique of August 5 stated that the Pathet Lao's political party, the Neo Lao Hak Xat (henceforth: NLHX), "can undertake their activities in the legal forms as the other political parties."

On October 31, 1956, the Joint Military Committee set up pursuant to the August communiques issued a program[26] for maintaining a cease-fire. The Committee members decided to create two Joint Military Teams, one for each of the two troubled provinces. These teams, composed of representatives from both sides, were to spread word of the August joint declarations, prevent the resumption of hostile acts, settle any incidents that might occur, and receive and execute orders from the Joint Military Committee. This self-enforcing agreement worked satisfactorily, for the ICC said in its report covering the period to May 16, 1957, that "the Military situation in the two northern provinces improved considerably from August [1956] onwards. . . ."[27]

The Joint Political Committee established in August released its report on November 2, 1956. In this document the parties agreed that Laos would follow a foreign policy of peace and neutrality, establish diplomatic relations with all countries, and seek aid from any country that would provide it "without any political or economic strings and without any control or supervision on the use of that aid." The agreement also said, "Our country shall resolutely resist any interference whatever in the internal affairs of our country, so as to safeguard the national sovereignty and independence." By confining itself to noncontroversial external matters, the Joint Political Committee managed to achieve consensus. However, the report did not treat the most urgent political problems, which involved internal affairs, not foreign policy.

In order to settle these internal matters, Souvanna and Souphanouvong held further talks. On December 24, the two princes announced that they had reached an agreement. They affirmed the NLHX's right to conduct political activities like any other Laotian political party, and they guaranteed that Pathet Lao members would enjoy the same rights and democratic freedoms that other Laotian citizens enjoyed. The parties also stated that "the Pathet Lao cadres . . . shall be integrated in the administration and the various technical services of the Kingdom at all levels, without discrimination and on an equal footing. . . ."

On December 28, Souvanna and Souphanouvong published a second communique in which they noted "that the atmosphere of great cordiality and perfect mutual understanding went on increasing between the Parties. . . ." The two princes agreed to expand the government to include Pathet Lao representatives. They also decided that, after the formation of the coalition government, the administration as well as the fighting forces in the provinces of Phong Saly and Sam Neua would be placed under the authority of the new government.

While these 1956 agreements signified a growing accord between the Government and the Pathet Lao, certain contrary features of the documents merit attention. Each agreement was a declaration of intention, which committed the parties to little else than a continuing effort to resolve their basic differences. Even the announcement of plans to admit Pathet Lao members into the Royal Government was more a statement of principle than a schedule for action. Nothing was said about which ministries would be awarded to the Pathet Lao. Either party could suddenly reject any of these agreements without penalty. The most divisive issue, existence of independent Pathet Lao fighting forces, was not settled in any of these agreements. So long as a military force independent of the Royal Army existed in the country, political stability remained distant. The parties failed to reach consensus on which was to come first, integration of the Pathet Lao fighting forces into the Royal

Army or establishment of a coalition government. The 1956 agreements could not lead to political action until these more fundamental differences were settled. Hence, the effusively cordial joint statements of 1956, while signaling a growing spirit of cooperation, should not be overrated in terms of their political significance.

SOUVANNA PHOUMA VISITS HANOI AND PEKING

Taken at face value, the 1956 agreements signified a shift of the Laotian pendulum toward the left. In other words, the Laotian government seemed to be moving in the direction of compromise with the Pathet Lao, instead of refusing to bargain and pressing for capitulation. The one factor that gave the most momentum to the leftward swing of the pendulum was the agreement to form a coalition government. An additional push was provided, or so it seemed, when Prime Minister Souvanna Phouma paid a visit to Hanoi and Peking in August 1956.

The Prince himself wrote about this trip five years later.[28] Despite American and Thai opposition, Souvanna said, he visited the two Asian capitals, where he proposed a policy of strict neutrality and good neighborliness. He obtained a pledge from each country that it would not interfere in Laotian internal affairs. In exchange, they requested him not to accept an American base and to oppose American meddling in Laotian military affairs. The joint statement issued by Chou En-lai and Souvanna Phouma on August 25 reflects these mutual promises. It stated,

> The Government of the Kingdom of Laos declares that it is firmly resolved to carry out a policy of peace and neutrality, that it will not form any military alliance as long as its security is not menaced and that it will not allow the installation on its territory of any foreign military base, other than as provided in the Geneva agreements. The Government of the People's Republic of China affairs [sic] that it will respect and wholly support the aforementioned position of the Government of the Kingdom of Laos.[29]

Proceeding to Hanoi, Souvanna signed a declaration of peaceful coexistence with North Vietnam.

Western observers, particularly those in Washington, tend to regard with displeasure any visit by an important political figure in a nonaligned state to a communist capital. Such visits, it is generally felt, indicate a bond of friendship between the nonaligned leader and his communist host and provide the latter with an opportunity to exert influence upon the former. Such views were voiced by Westerners, notably Americans and Thais, upon the announcement of Souvanna's trip to Peking and Hanoi. The Americans in particular condemned Souvanna's journey, believing that, along with the August agreements between the Laotian government and the Pathet Lao, it signified a growing rapprochement between the Laotian Prime Minister and the communists. It was true, as Souvanna later wrote, that one purpose of the visit was to form the basis for friendly relations between Vientiane on one hand and Peking and Hanoi on the other.[30] At the same time, however, as Americans totally failed to recognize, Souvanna was trying to improve his chances of containing communism within Laos. While Souvanna was in Peking, the Chinese asked him to allow the Communist Chinese and the North Vietnamese to set up consulates in Vientiane. Such consulates would have made it possible for the communists to increase their contacts (and consequently their influence) with the Laotian people, both private citizens and government officials. The communists would also acquire better access to information about Laos and would possess a center for gathering intelligence and perhaps organizing activities against Souvanna's government. Realizing this, Souvanna explained that he could not permit the Red Chinese or the North Vietnamese to operate consulates in Laos. Vientiane, the Prince said, had not recognized Formosa. To recognize Hanoi and Peking without extending diplomatic recognition to Formosa, or vice versa, would have unbalanced Laotian neutrality, Souvanna stated.[31] Just as important, we learn from a member of Souvanna's traveling delegation, was Souvanna's desire to deprive the Pathet Lao of assistance from abroad. Sisouk Na Champassak, who was later to become information minister in a subsequent pro-Western government in Laos, wrote that one reason for Souvanna's trip to Peking and Hanoi was to obtain pledges of noninterference from Peking and Hanoi. Such promises would boost Souvanna's position in his dealings with the Pathet Lao, particularly in regard to negotiating specifics in the aftermath of the agreements of August 5 and 10.[32]

Considering all the evidence, it is highly questionable whether Souvanna's visit to Red China and North Vietnam signified movement toward a rapprochement with communism. Regarding external affairs, one can argue that the Prince did desire to establish friendly relations with the communist capitals. Nevertheless, Souvanna refused to permit Peking and Hanoi to set up the consulates they requested. If Washington considered his trip as a sign of warmth toward communism, Peking and Hanoi must have felt a chill when Souvanna rejected their requests for the consulates. Concerning internal affairs, it is much less clear that Souvanna was preparing to give in to the communists. This is not to say that Souvanna was not inclined to make a compromise with the Pathet

Lao. This he was certainly ready to do, as proved by the agreements of August 1956. Some compromise was necessary, in Souvanna's eyes, to end the fighting in Laos and restore orderly government. Without compromise, the Pathet Lao would have no reason to lay down its arms. Compromise, however, is not the same as capitulation. Champassak's observation on Souvanna's effort to cut off the Pathet Lao from outside support shows that the Prime Minister, while willing to meet some of the Pathet Lao's demands, was not prepared to give in to all of them. In trying to minimize the Pathet Lao's bargaining power, Souvanna was hardly acting like a fellow traveler or a communist dupe, as some people in the West alleged.

SPRING 1957 CABINET CRISIS

Inasmuch as the 1956 agreements between the Laotian government and the Pathet Lao were phrased in general terms, it was necessary to work out the details of each accord. For this purpose, the Laotian government and the Pathet Lao began holding talks in January 1957. These conversations proceeded into the spring with negligible results. On May 16 the ICC, beginning to lose patience with the glacial pace of the Government–Pathet Lao negotiations, adopted a resolution that expressed "concern and regret . . . that the Parties have encountered difficulties of various kinds, so that they have not been able to achieve a final political settlement. . . ."[33]

The ICC was not the only party displeased by the paucity of results which Souvanna's policy of reconciliation had thus far produced. Souvanna's policy of incorporating the Pathet Lao into the national community and giving the communists ministerial portfolios did not meet favor with all Laotian political elements in Laos. Disenchanted with the inconclusive Government–Pathet Lao conversations, the majority in the National Assembly lost faith in Souvanna's policy of reconciliation and voted against continuing negotiations with the communists. In view of the Assembly's repudiation of his policy, Souvanna submitted his resignation on May 30.

During June and July, three unsuccessful attempts were made to form a new government. Finally, on August 9, the National Assembly approved a new government, headed once again by the seemingly indispensable Souvanna Phouma. In his investiture speech, the Prince signaled that he would resume the policies he had followed previously.[34] He identified the reestablishment of Laotian unity as the cardinal national imperative. Reviving the spirit of the 1956 agreements, Souvanna said that when the Pathet Lao was integrated into the national community, the government would be enlarged to include Pathet Lao representatives. National elections would follow. Finally, the Prince stated that Laos would "entertain neighborly relations with all its neighbors" (a reference to Hanoi and Peking) and would accept foreign aid from any source provided no strings were attached (also a reference to Hanoi and Peking).

Souphanouvong announced his support for Souvanna's new government, and the Pathet Lao asked Souvanna to resume negotiations. Talks were begun on September 25. On October 18 the National Assembly enacted a law guaranteeing civil rights to members of the Pathet Lao.

The Government's new efforts to reach a compromise with the Pathet Lao represented a setback for American policy. The United States had hoped that after Souvanna's resignation the King would appoint a hardliner who would refuse to negotiate with the communists. The United States had favored two Western-minded former premiers, Katay Sasorith and Phoui Sanikone, both of whom failed to win Assembly approval in June and July.[35]

One reason the United States disapproved of Souvanna can be traced to contrary interpretations of the Pathet Lao. Souvanna denied that the Pathet Lao was or ever had been a communist organization, although he admitted that it contained some communist members. He described the Pathet Lao as an organization of ultranationalists who leaned toward the left. He claimed that the Pathet Lao had been forced to seek help from North Vietnam, but that it had not allowed itself to become absorbed by the Viet Minh. These views were summarized in remarks made by Souvanna in February 1958:

> I have always considered the Pathet Lao to be a united front, comprising within itself people of diverse tendencies. I have reached the conviction that components of this movement consist essentially of a majority of ultranationalists, intellectuals tending toward the Left and finally, quite likely, a weak minority of Communists.[36]

Washington officials, on the other hand, regarded the Pathet Lao as a fully developed communist organization subservient to higher headquarters, be they in Hanoi, Peking, or Moscow. Souvanna considered reconciliation with the Pathet Lao as a step toward normality, that is, toward national unification. Washington, in contrast, regarded such a move as abnormal, to be equated with according foreigners (the leaders of international communism and their servants, the Pathet Lao) a voice in Laotian affairs. In accordance with the containment psychology then prevalent in Washington, any concessions to the Pathet Lao would advance what Washington believed to be the objective of international communism, which was to remake the world in its own image. Much of Washington's disenchantment with Souvanna can be traced to this divergence of views regarding the Pathet Lao.

THE NOVEMBER 1957 AGREEMENTS

In November 1957, Souvanna Phouma brought his policy of reconciliation to a climax, expressed in another set of agreements with the Pathet Lao.

On November 2 the parties agreed to enlarge the Government to include representatives of the Pathet Lao; this had already been stated in the 1956 negotiations. Before presenting the expanded government to the National Assembly, the provinces of Phong Saly and Sam Neua, as well as the Pathet Lao fighting units, would be placed under the jurisdiction of the Royal Government. The enlarged government would follow the policies set forth by Souvanna in his investiture speech of August 8. The parties further agreed to recognize the NLHX as a political party. Souphanouvong consented to surrender to the Royal Government all arms and ammunition held by the Pathet Lao. Finally, the Premier promised to appoint Pathet Lao civil cadres to suitable posts in the Kingdom's administrative and technical services.

Two additional agreements were signed ten days later. The first concerned reestablishment of royal authority in the provinces of Phong Saly and Sam Neua. Both sides agreed that the provinces would be placed under the jurisdiction of the Government. Half of the officials in each province would belong to each party. The head of Sam Neua province would be a Government official; the head of Phong Saly, a Pathet Lao representative. Elections would be held in the two provinces three months after the Government assumed control of them.

The second agreement signed on November 12 concerned the integration of the Pathet Lao fighting forces into the Royal Army. The parties agreed that, owing to budgetary ceilings, the Royal Army would accept no more than 1,500 Pathet Lao soldiers. The rest of the Pathet Lao's forces would return to civilian status. Two provisions that later proved of key importance were included in this document. First, the agreement said that until all the final details of integration were settled, the 1,500 Pathet Lao troops would remain grouped in units. This meant that, in case these details should never be settled, the Pathet Lao would retain its military capability. Secondly, when these units were fused—as separate units, not by dispersing the men throughout various divisions of the Royal Army—into the Royal Army, they would possess the same proportion of officers, NCO's, and privates as Royal Army units. Military integration was to take place within sixty days after the formation of the coalition government.

Shortly thereafter the two parties began to implement the November accords. On November 18 the National Assembly unanimously approved a National Union Government led by Souvanna Phouma. The new regime included two Pathet Lao representatives. Souphanouvong became Minister of Plans, Reconstruction, and Urbanism, a post which placed him in charge of administering foreign—including American—aid, and Phoumi Vongvichit was Minister of Cults and Fine Arts. On the same day the NLHX initiated its activities as a legitimate political party.

The Government set May 4, 1958, as the date for supplementary elections in the provinces of Phong Saly and Sam Neua. Souphanouvong transferred the province of Sam Neua to the Royal Government on December 8, 1957; he transferred Phong Saly four days later.

After a visit to Sam Neua on March 1, 1958, the Political Committee of the ICC "learnt that integration was proceeding smoothly."[37] The Royal Government had sent sixty officials to the province; these officials were working "in complete harmony" with the Pathet Lao officials who had been there since the Geneva Conference. The Committee reported that the Acting Commander of the Laotian National Army stationed in the province had said that "an atmosphere of calm existed throughout the province."[38]

At a special ceremony at the Plain of Jars on February 18, 1958, about 1,500 Pathet Lao army personnel were integrated into the Royal Army in a symbolic ceremony. Actual reassignment and conferment of rank were to take place at a later date. Over 4,000 additional military personnel were processed for discharge. The ICC reported, "Complete integration of former Pathet Lao Military Personnel into the Laotian National Army has been achieved."[39]

Short of a communist takeover, the pendulum had swung about as far left as it could go.

THE MAY 1958 ELECTIONS

It will be recalled that when elections for the National Assembly were held in December 1955, voting did not take place in the provinces of Sam Neua and Phong Saly, where the Government was unable to supervise the voting. Supplementary elections in these two provinces were scheduled for May 4, 1958. Twenty seats were assigned to the provinces, increasing the number of seats in the National Assembly from 39 to 59. One additional vacancy had to be filled, owing to the death of a legislator, making a total of 21 seats at stake in the election. The voting took place on May 4 as planned. When the returns were tallied, the results showed that the NLHX (political party of the Pathet Lao), which had nominated 14 candidates, had won 9 seats. Four additional seats were won by the Santiphab (Peace) Party, a leftist grouping including among its membership Quinim Pholsena and Bong Souvannavong. The neutralist and conservative factions had won only 8 of the 21 seats. The outcome of the elections represented a startling victory for the forces on the left. The election results, however, did not accurately reflect the popular vote. The neutralists and rightists had nominated 85 candidates for the 21 seats. By thus scattering their strength, they greatly reduced their chances of electing their candidates to office. "The wide range of competing government candidates and their total lack of method were the essential factors in the victory."[40] Actually, the Pathet Lao and their leftist allies won only 35 percent of the popular vote.[41] The candidate who garnered the most votes was Souphanouvong.

The result of the May 1958 elections stimulated a process of self-examination by the neutralists and conservatives. Although the Pathet Lao and their leftist allies controlled only 13 of the 59 seats in the National Assembly, the balloting showed that about one-third of the voters were displeased with the way the country was being managed. A number of prominent political figures, among them Foreign Minister Phoui Sananikone, feared the leftist success might be the wave of the future, and he voiced doubts about Souvanna's policy of working with the Pathet Lao. The election also provoked questioning about the use of American aid. A major NLHX campaign strategy had been to decry the corruption made possible by U.S. aid. This tactic appeared to have worked, and so the politicians in Vientiane began to concern themselves with the matter. One concrete result of the election was a coalescence of the noncommunist political parties. Everyone realized that had the noncommunists put up fewer candidates they would have won more seats. In order to reduce the fragmentation of the noncommunist forces, Phoui Sananikone's Independent Party and Katay Sasorith's Nationalist Party merged to form the Rally of the Laotian People, known as the RPL (*Rassemblement du Peuple Laotien*). The RPL, formed in early June, selected Souvanna to head the new combination. The RPL vowed to wage a united struggle against communism and subversion.

What can be said about Souvanna's policy of trying to incorporate the Pathet Lao into the Laotian national community? Was it a wise course of action? Or should Souvanna have tried to liquidate the leftist movement?

The answers to these questions depend largely on the view one takes of the Pathet Lao. Souvanna's policy of reconciliation reflected his evaluation of the Pathet Lao: the neutralist prince did not consider the Pathet Lao as a threat to Laotian independence or as an agent of a foreign power. Instead, he viewed the Pathet Lao as a legitimate nationalist element deserving to be part of the Laotian state. His objective was national unification, an essential condition for a return to normal political life in Laos. Souvanna also realized that Laos, as a weak state, would have to adjust its policies to those of its more powerful neighbors, as well as those of the United States. Accordingly, he tried to follow a course that would antagonize no one. Unfortunately for Laos, the views of those governments among whom Souvanna sought to steer a neutral course were too disparate to permit compromise. Hanoi, Peking, and Moscow wished to see the Pathet Lao incorporated into the Laotian government. Washington, on the contrary, considered such an expansion of the Laotian government as the first stage in the loss of Laotian independence to an external conspiracy, a view that naturally followed from Washington's assessment of the Pathet Lao as an agent of a foreign power. The 1956 agreements in principle to form a coalition government, combined with Souvanna's visit to Peking and Hanoi, the formation of a coalition regime after the November 1957 accords, and the leftist victory in the May 1958 elections, persuaded Washington that Souvanna was leading Laos into the communist camp. Souvanna's willingness to accept American aid, as well as his refusal to countenance a Chinese or North Vietnamese consulate in Vientiane, was not sufficient to convince Washington that Souvanna desired to maintain ties with the West as well as the East.

In choosing to bring the Pathet Lao into the Laotian government, Souvanna destroyed the last vestige of support he had from Washington. Indeed, Souvanna's policies called forth an even stronger American reaction than he had dreamed possible.

NOTES

1. Letter No. 129/VL, October 20, 1954, from the Pathet Lao to the ICC, in Great Britain, Parliamentary Papers, vol. XIX (Accounts and Papers, vol. XII), Cmd. 9445, May, 1955, "First Interim Report of the International Commission for Supervision and Control in Laos, August 11–December 31, 1954," pp. 70–73.

2. Ibid.

3. Letter No. 820/C.M.L., October 10, 1954, from the Franco-Laotian Delegation to the ICC, in Great Britain, Cmd. 9445, pp. 74–75.

4. Great Britain, Cmd. 9445, p. 43.

5. Great Britain, Parliamentary Papers, vol. XLIV (Accounts and Papers, Vol. XVI), Cmd. 9630, November, 1955, "Second Interim Report of the International Commission for Supervision and Control in Laos, July 1, 1955–May 16, 1957," p. 6.

6. Ibid., pp. 6–7.

7. *Ibid.*, p. 34.

8. *Ibid.*, p. 10.

9. Great Britain, Parliamentary Papers, vol. XXX (Accounts and Papers, vol. XII), Cmd. 314, December, 1957, "Third Interim Report of the International Commission for Supervision and Control in Laos, July 1, 1955–May 16, 1957," pp. 13–14.

10. *The New York Times,* January 15, 1955; April 15, 1955; July 10, 1955; August 19, 1955.

11. *Ibid.,* March 9, 1955.

12. See, for example, Great Britain, Cmd. 9445, p. 15.

13. According to Professor Russell Fifield, an authority on Southeast Asia, the Government allegations were substantially true. Fifield says that between 1954 and 1957, the Viet Minh provided a special staff near the Laotian border. In addition, they furnished advisers to the Pathet Lao's various "ministries." Furthermore, North Vietnam provided on its own soil training facilities for Pathet Lao forces, sent advisers to the Pathet Lao, and sometimes permitted Pathet Lao troops to come to North Vietnam for joint maneuvers. Finally, Fifield says, North Vietnam gave the Pathet Lao military equipment. Unfortunately, Fifield does not give the sources for this information. (Russell H. Fifield, *Southeast Asia in United States Policy* [New York: Frederick A. Praeger, 1963], p. 182.) Two investigators for the Rand Corporation, Paul F. Langer and Joseph J. Zasloff, conducted interviews with Pathet Lao defectors and North Vietnamese prisoners that appear to confirm the Royal Government's charges and Fifield's findings. Langer and Zasloff say the North Vietnamese were particularly active in providing military training and political instruction for Pathet Lao personnel. See Paul F. Langer and Joseph J. Zasloff, *North Vietnam and the Pathet Lao: Partners in the Struggle for Laos* (Cambridge: Harvard University Press, 1970), pp. 62–63.

14. U. S. Department of State, *The Situation in Laos,* 1959.

15. Arthur J. Dommen, *Conflict in Laos* (New York: Frederick A. Praeger, 1964), p. 104. Dommen uses A.I.D. figures.

16. George McTurnan Kahin, *The Asian-African Conference* (Ithaca: Cornell University Press, 1956), p. 27.

17. *The New York Times,* April 24, 1955.

18. *Ibid.,* November 13, 1955.

19. Text in *Ibid.*

20. In Laos, political parties form themselves around prominent politicians. It is not uncommon for parties to come into being after elections instead of before elections. Laotian parties possess little discipline.

21. *The New York Times,* January 9, 1956.

22. Great Britain, Cmd. 314, p. 48.

23. *Ibid.,* p. 51.

24. Souvanna Phouma became Prime Minister March 21, 1956.

25. Texts in Great Britain, Cmd. 314, pp. 54–57.

26. Text in *Ibid.,* pp. 57–59.

27. *Ibid.,* p. 11.

28. Souvanna Phouma, "Laos: le fond du problème," *France-Asie,* 17 (March–April, 1961): 1825.

29. *New China News Agency,* August 25, 1956.

30. Souvanna Phouma, *France-Asie,* 17: 1825.

31. *Ibid.*

32. Sisouk Na Champassak, *Storm over Laos* (New York: Frederick A. Praeger, 1961), pp. 49–50.

33. Great Britain, Cmd. 314, p. 13.

34. Text of speech in Great Britain, Parliamentary Papers, vol. XXXIV (Accounts and Papers, vol. XV), Cmd. 541, October 1958, "Fourth Interim Report of the International Commission for Supervision and Control in Laos, May 17, 1957–May 31, 1958," pp. 44–51. Such an improbable reversal of sentiment in the National Assembly, which approved as Prime Minister the man they had rejected three months earlier, is not abnormal in politics, Laotian style.

35. Another Laotian who made an unsuccessful attempt to form a government was Bong Souvannavong, an extreme leftist.

36. *The New York Times,* February 25, 1958.

37. Report of the Political Committee on a Visit to Sam Neua on March 1, 1958, in Great Britain, Cmd. 541, p. 72.

38. *Ibid.*

39. Telegram from ICC Chairman Dr. S. S. Ansari to Indian Foreign Office, March 5, 1958, in Great Britain, Cmd. 541, p. 74.

40. Champassak, p. 62.

41. Testimony of Walter S. Robertson, Assistant Secretary of State for Far Eastern Affairs, in U. S., Congress, House, Committee on Foreign Affairs, *Hearings, Mutual Security Act of 1959,* 86th Cong., 1st Sess., 1959, p. 1123.

7
DEVELOPMENT OF
UNITED STATES POLICY

IN DESCRIBING THE events related in the previous chapter—the beginning of the civil war, the 1955 elections, the agreements of 1956 and 1957, Souvanna's visit to Peking and Hanoi, the Spring 1957 cabinet crisis, and the elections in May 1958—American policy has been referred to only sporadically. It is now time to examine that policy in detail.

American policy toward Laos in the years after 1954 may be divided into two periods. The first period, which came to a close just after the Laotian elections in May 1958, may be characterized as one of limited involvement, of reacting to events rather than shaping them. Beginning with a Laotian cabinet crisis in the summer of 1958, American policy entered the second phase, during which Washington became involved in making and unmaking governments and in fighting the cold war on the battlefields of Laos.

In this chapter we shall discuss the development of American policy during the first period; that is, through the elections of May 1958, in which the leftists captured 13 of 21 Assembly seats.

It was not long after the 1954 Geneva Conference that the United States began to woo Laos into joining the Western fold. As we have seen, the Protocol to the SEATO Treaty placed a security umbrella over Laos by designating it as falling within Article IV of the Treaty. On his way home to Washington after the Manila Conference in September 1954, Secretary Dulles became the first American Secretary of State to set foot in Laos. Dulles assured the Laotians that the United States was prepared to defend them with air and sea power against communist invasion.

Less than a year later, in August 1955, the United States and Laos celebrated their growing cordiality by raising their diplomatic missions from legations to embassies. Charles .J. Yost became the first American ambassador to Vientiane.

So long as the Laotian government persisted in resisting the demands of the Pathet Lao, based in Sam Neua and Phong Saly, the United States continued to give encouragement and support to Vientiane. When, however, Souvanna Phouma attempted to strike a compromise with the Pathet Lao, the smiling view that Washington had taken toward the Laotian government's policies creased into a frown. This new outlook was in harmony with the opinion toward neutralism shared by many American policymakers.

AMERICAN ATTITUDE TOWARD NEUTRALISM

We have seen that when the King reappointed Souvanna Phouma Prime Minister in August 1957, following his resignation three months earlier, Souvanna announced a policy of neutrality. This policy had two aspects, internal and external. Internally, neutralism consisted of bringing Pathet Lao members into the government, allowing the Pathet Lao's political party, the NLHX, to function, merging the Pathet Lao's fighting forces with the Royal Army, and granting Pathet Lao personnel full civil and political rights. With the exception of the consolidation of the fighting forces, Souvanna accomplished these measures in the aftermath of the agreement of November 1957. Neutralism as concerned foreign affairs meant a willingness to have diplomatic relations with all countries, regardless of their political ideologies, and a readiness to accept foreign aid from any country that did not attach too many strings to its assistance.

While Souvanna considered neutralism to be the only means of bringing peace and political order to Laos, American policymakers had far less charitable views on the wisdom of such a course. In late 1954 President Eisenhower succinctly stated his attitude toward neutralism. He said,

> There are some who have believed it possible to hold themselves aloof from today's world-wide struggle between those who uphold government based upon human freedom and dignity, and those who consider man merely a pawn of the state. The times are so critical and the difference between these world systems so vital and vast that grave doubt is cast upon the validity of neutralistic argument.[1]

In June and July 1956, American foreign policymakers issued a number of statements on neutralism. On June 7, the White House issued a statement to clarify remarks made by the President the preceding day. The explanatory statement said, "The President does believe that there are special conditions which justify political neutrality but that no nation has the right to be indifferent to the fate of another, or, as he put it, to be 'neutral as between right and wrong or decency or indecency.' "[2] The President seemed to be saying that no nation has the right to pursue its self-interest if that policy renders the nation indifferent to the fate of another; yet how many foreign policies can take into account the well-being of all other nations? Such an interpretation denies the existence of sovereignty—a state's freedom to act as it chooses within the limits of its capabilities. It is, of course, open to question who has the authority to define "right and wrong" in international affairs.

In his denunciation of neutralism, Vice-President Nixon countenanced a nation's decision against joining in a security treaty with the United States. "But there is still another brand of neutralism," he said, "that makes no moral distinction between the Communist world and the free world. With this viewpoint, we have no sympathy. . . . Is freedom the same as tyranny?"[3] Nixon, like Eisenhower, denied neutral countries the right to remain neutral regarding the Cold War.

The most extreme and controversial statement on neutralism to come from an American official was uttered by Secretary Dulles. Mutual security treaties abolish, he felt, "the principle of neutrality, which pretends that a nation can best gain safety for itself by being indifferent to the fate of others. This has increasingly become an obsolete conception and, except under very exceptional circumstances, it is an immoral and short-sighted conception."[4] One month later, the Secretary was asked whether he still believed that neutralism was immoral. He replied,

I believe what I said, which is that the kind of neutralism which is indifferent to the fate of others and which believes security can best be sought in isolation and without concern for others—I said that kind of neutrality, I believe, is immoral. I did not say neutralism of all kinds is immoral.[5]

These statements made by leading American policymakers suggest common attitudes toward neutralism in the very highest echelons of the Eisenhower Administration. These attitudes may be summarized as follows. The Cold War is a conflict between two separate entities, the communist countries and the noncommunist ones. This is a conflict between good and evil. A state does not have the right to be neutral in the Cold War. In other spheres, however, a country may remain neutral.

Given Washington's outlook on neutralism, it was hardly surprising that the United States was not deeply pleased with Souvanna's policies. On April 16, 1957, while Souvanna was trying to work out specific details of the 1956 general agreements with the Pathet Lao, the United States delivered a note to the Laotian Ambassador in Washington. This note contains a neat summary of American policy toward Laos, a policy that remained unchanged until President Kennedy modified it in early 1961.

The note said that "the government of the United States confirms its interest in the peace, sovereignty, independence, unity, and territorial integrity of the Kingdom of Laos." The note continued,

> The Government of the United States therefore continues fully to support the principle of the complete authority of the Royal Government of Laos over all its territory. It maintains the hope that a political settlement and the reunification of Laos will be effected in accordance with the principles of the Geneva Agreements on Laos of July 1954 and the Resolution of the International Control Commission of January 7, 1956.
>
> The Government of the United States regrets that these objectives have so far been made impossible because the Pathet Lao forces, in spite of these agreements and of the Resolution of the International Control Commission, have sought to place extraneous conditions upon their acceptance of the authority of the Royal Government and upon their reintegration into the national community. The Government of the United States welcomes the firmness with which the Kingdom of Laos has resisted this maneuver and is confident that the Royal Government will continue in its determination that the political future of the Kingdom of Laos shall not be dictated by dissident groups enjoying no constitutional status.[6]

This note clearly shows that Washington wanted no part of Laotian neutralism if it meant the continued existence of the Pathet Lao as an independent political and military force. What Washington sought was a settlement that would erase the Pathet Lao as a political and military factor in Laos. Thus, in its note the United States supported the Royal Government's contention that it had undivided authority over all territory in Laos, including, of course, the two northern provinces that the Pathet Lao claimed until a complete political settlement had been reached.

The parties in Laos had not been able to attain such a final accord, the note went on, because of Pathet Lao intransigence. The Royal Government was absolved of blame for the failure of the two parties to settle outstanding disputes. The United States heralded the Royal Government's "firmness" in refusing to bow to Pathet Lao demands. Finally, Washington reaffirmed its contention that the Pathet Lao lacked constitutional status and any legitimacy whatsoever. As we have noted before, this estimation of the Pathet Lao contrasted with that of Souvanna Phouma, who considered the Pathet Lao to be an integral part of the national community, as a party that had legitimate demands and that was entitled to representation in the government.

Subsequent developments in Laos revealed that, in condemning the Pathet Lao on legal and moral grounds, the United States applied erroneous criteria. The United States, in other words, failed to ask the right questions about the Pathet Lao. It was legitimate to inquire whether the Pathet Lao was a legal organization. It was, in addition, fair to question whether the Pathet Lao followed moral standards. But the most important query, from the standpoint of formulating effective foreign policy, was whether the Pathet Lao had a significant power base. In fact, the Pathet Lao did have a substantial power base, as well as a sophisticated political organization and a fighting force which, despite its small numbers, often outperformed the Royal Army. In treating Pathet Lao power as though it had no right to exist, the United States managed to avoid the more difficult problem of how to overcome that power.

The situation in Laos required a choice: either to compromise with the Pathet Lao and include it in the government as Souvanna Phouma proposed, or to try to defeat it militarily. In either case, one had to recognize the existence of the Pathet Lao as a real political and military force; this the United States hesitated to do in its early years of involvement with Laos.

The Government–Pathet Lao agreements of November 1957 aroused concern in Washington, for they signified that the communists were making quiet headway in Laos. American policy strongly opposed the formation of a coalition government including communists.[7] Shortly after the November 1957 agreements were signed, a State Department Press Officer said Washington regarded a coalition government with communists as "a perilous course" about which the United States Government was "seriously concerned."[8]

It was later revealed that the United States attempted to prevent the inclusion of the Pathet Lao in the Laotian government. In 1959 James Graham Parsons, American Ambassador to Laos when the coalition government was formed, told a Congressional committee, "I struggled for 16 months to prevent a coalition."[9] At the same hearing Walter S. Robertson, Assistant Secretary of State for Far Eastern Affairs, said, ". . . we did everything we could to keep it [coalition government] from happening. And I don't know of anybody who worked more against it than he [Parsons] did. He wasn't trying to get a coalition there. He was trying to prevent it."[10] Eric Kocher, Director, Office of Southeast Asian Affairs, Department of State, also said the State Department had opposed the formation of a coalition government. "We bent every effort," he said, "to withstand and try to prevent the coalition government."[11] At a later date Souvanna Phouma corroborated these statements by saying that the United States "did everything possible to prevent the integration of the Pathet Lao into the Government in 1957, and when, despite their efforts, I succeeded, the United States continued to sabotage me."[12]

AMERICAN AID TO LAOS

A nation trying to influence affairs in another country may take advantage of various means that have long been used for this purpose. The most obvious instrumentality is military force. In many cases, however, it is either embarrassing or inconvenient for one country to send a military expedition to a second country. Not even the most powerful state the world has ever seen possesses sufficient military resources to dispatch an expeditionary force to every country where it wishes to exert influence. Consequently, means less extreme than military force have been developed for the purpose of influencing affairs abroad. Trade—both the promise to increase it and the threat to reduce it—has been bartered for influence in the councils of nations. Credits have also proved useful. Propaganda, more effective than ever in this age of transmitters and spy-satellites, has been used by states from as far back as the memory runs. Sometimes a state attempts to influence events in another country by aiding a particular faction in that country, as when the United States assisted the Greek government against the communists just after the Second World War. Such help may come in the form of advice, military supplies, military training, equipment, food and other nonmilitary aid, and money.

In attempting to influence the course of events in Laos during the first few years after 1954, the United States elected to rely primarily upon military and economic aid. The American aid program in Laos had its inception in a pentalateral agreement among the United States, Cambodia, France, Laos and Vietnam in December 1950.[13] The following December the United States established a Mutual Security Program in Laos under the Mutual Security Act of 1951[14] and in 1955 set up a USOM (U. S. Operations Mission) in Laos to administer the aid program. Under this agreement, Laos consented to "make, consistent with its political and economic stability, the full contribution permitted by its manpower, resources, facilities, and general economic conditions to the development and maintenance of its own defensive strength and the defensive strength of the *free world*."[15] (Italics mine.)

OBJECTIVES OF AMERICAN AID

Foreign aid has become one of the least understood elements of American foreign policy. The unnecessary confusion and bickering over foreign aid within the United States has issued in large part from a rather simple misunderstanding. When American policymakers communicate with the American public about foreign aid—through speeches, press releases, public forums, and so on—they generally emphasize American *generosity*. Why does the United States distribute so much aid? Because Americans are the richest people on earth and sense a moral obligation to share their bounty. So goes the argument one hears from the men who make foreign aid policy and must justify it before the people. As a result of this public relations campaign, carried out with much success, most Americans have come to believe that foreign aid is an altruistic gesture on their part, free of the taint of self-interest. The fact of the matter is, however, that many, if not most Americans resent this "giveaway," for, in truth, they do not feel nearly so concerned with their less fortunate brethren across the seas as their policymakers tell them they should. Accordingly, as the inflation-gripped American economy gradually imposes more and more difficult economic burdens on its citizens, Americans have grown more and more opposed to sharing their ever-dearer dollars just for the sake of helping others. It is only when our own desires are satisfied that we are willing to contribute to charity. As a consequence, the American people have become so resistant to foreign aid that such aid has been pared to virtually negligible proportions.[16]

Much of the debate over foreign aid could probably be eliminated if government spokesmen would explain to the American people the true rationale for this expenditure. While no one should deny that a degree of compassion enters into the American foreign aid program, the principal purpose of foreign aid is to advance the security and well-being of the American people. Secretary Dulles enunciated this fact in the following terms: "In giving economic and military assistance to friendly countries to improve their capacity to defend themselves against aggression or subversion, the United States is guided primarily by consideration of its own national interest to help in the economic and social advancement of all free nations."[17] In other words, foreign aid is hardly "aid" at all. Instead, it is simply one of various means a government has at its disposal to influence events in another country, with the ultimate purpose of advancing its own interests. In this sense, foreign aid falls along a continuum of influence stretching from military force at one extreme to diplomatic cocktail conversation at the other. Foreign aid, therefore, is just one of the weapons in a country's arsenal that is used to promote that nation's self-interest.[18] If those officials responsible for American foreign aid would only explain the program to the American public on this basis, many more Americans would acknowledge the need for foreign aid. It would be regarded as only incidentally for the purpose of helping others (and it does not always accomplish this). Its true purpose, people would realize, is to help Americans. Seen from this perspective, foreign aid would in all likelihood command the support of many Americans, who would realize that foreign aid is a relatively inexpensive means of gaining influence abroad.[19]

As regards American policy in Laos, military and economic assistance was the principal instrument of influence used by Washington in the early years of its involvement there. American officials were quite candid in discussing the purpose of the American aid program in Laos.

Testifying before the House Subcommittee on Foreign Operations and Monetary Affairs, Under Secretary of State for Economic Affairs C. Douglas Dillon said,

> The principal objective of our foreign policy in Laos since the ceasefire in the Indochina war in 1954 has been to assist the Royal Government to overcome Communist efforts to overthrow it from within. Our basic policy has been to encourage the establishment of the strongest practicable non-Communist government, and the development of the broad popular support which such a government would require in order to defend and strengthen its independence.
>
> Specifically it has been and is our policy to assist the Royal Lao Government in reducing the internal Communist threat by the extension of economic and military assistance. . . .[20]

This statement underscores the position that the rationale for American aid to Laos was not generosity but "to assist the Royal Lao Government in reducing the internal Communist threat," an objective perceived to be requisite for American security.

In general, a country can select from two basic approaches in helping another government deal with an internal threat. Both of these approaches were included in Secretary Dillon's statement. In the first place, one can assist the government in winning the support of its people, who will then presumably cooperate with the government against factions opposed to it. This approach was covered in Dillon's reference to "development of the broad popular support." Such support can be won by such devices as tax reduction, land reform, flood relief, bridge and road construction, educational programs, providing security to harassed villagers, and various other methods, depending on the circumstances. Such a program often goes under the name of civic action or, as in Vietnam, pacification. A second way of helping a government combat an insurgency is to help the government conduct military and police operations against the insurgents.

This can be done by training paramilitary forces, paying the salaries and expenses of the army and police, providing equipment, flying troops into combat zones, air-dropping equipment to isolated outposts, establishing communications networks, and so on. The United States has successfully carried out such operations in cooperation with the government of Thailand, which has been faced with low-level insurgency in the northeastern part of the country. For maximum effectiveness, both approaches can and should be used simultaneously.

The American aid effort in Laos placed much greater emphasis on the second of these two approaches. That is, much more aid was expended on enabling the Royal Army and police to inflict military defeat on the Pathet Lao than on strengthening popular support for the Vientiane regime. A State Department memorandum described the objectives of United States aid in these terms:

> The principal purpose of our aid program in Laos is not to finance the economy of Laos, it is largely for *military budget support*. The entire cost of maintaining the Lao army is met from MSP [Mutual Security Program] funds. Assistance to the Lao National Police Force is next in importance.[21] [My italics.]

The memo went on to say that "in an effort to bolster internal security and to increase popular support for the government," additional money was being provided to support a civic action program.

To state the matter in stark but not exaggerated terms, the primary purpose of American aid to Laos was to destroy the Pathet Lao by financing the complete cost of the Laotian army and police forces. Later on we shall have occasion to inquire into the wisdom of allocating so high a proportion of American aid to supporting the Laotian military and police force, instead of using the money to broaden the base of popular support for the central government. We shall also discuss, in the following chapter, the all-important matter of the impact of American aid on Laos. For the present, however, we merely note Washington's decision to devote the bulk of its aid to financing the Laotian military and police.

Washington's decision to underwrite the Royal Army was not reached easily. Indeed, this policy was arrived at in a highly unorthodox manner.

The standard procedure for determining "force objectives"—the number of troops in a particular country that the United States should support— was to consult the Joint Chiefs of Staff and the Department of Defense. The Joint Chiefs would then study the matter and make a recommendation to the Secretary of Defense. He, in turn, would review the JCS recommendation and forward his views on this essentially military question to the White House, where a final decision would be made. In the case of Laos, however, a rather unusual procedure for setting force objectives was followed.

In late 1954, not too long after the Geneva Conference, the Joint Chiefs of Staff were requested to recommend a "force objective" for Laos. The JCS, appraising the military situation in Laos, and taking into account the inclusion of Laos under SEATO's umbrella, believed that the only reason Laos needed an army was for the purpose of internal policing. The existing Laotian army, which numbered approximately 15,000 men, was already too large for this task. Besides, the State Department interpreted the Geneva agreements as prohibiting the establishment of a U. S. Military Assistance Advisory Group (MAAG) in Laos. Since no Americans would be present in Laos to conduct the training, the JCS could not be certain that effective training would occur and therefore hesitated to recommend military aid. In accordance with the above considerations, the JCS in November 1954 advised Secretary of Defense Charles E. Wilson that "No force levels are recommended for this country."[22]

By the end of 1954, it was becoming clear to various officials in the State Department that the Pathet Lao was unwilling to submerge itself in a greater Laotian community. Fears were voiced that the Pathet Lao might refuse indefinitely to disarm, and a number of policymakers expressed the view that a lengthy struggle might develop between the Vientiane regime and the Pathet Lao. Should this conflict materialize, it was said, the noncommunist government of Laos would need to mobilize its resources and enlist the patriotic support of the citizens throughout the country. But here a problem presented itself. In this newly independent, primitive country, there were practically no established institutions to bind the people together with the government in a united effort against the Pathet Lao. In the opinion of many observers, particularly at State, the only institution that could perform this vital unifying function was the army. There were several valid arguments to sustain this view. The officer corps was one of the few repositories of educated Laotians. The army was the only agency of the government with the capability of penetrating isolated areas and establishing a government presence there. As a highly visible entity, the army could act as a national symbol, a focus for the expression of patriotic sentiment. Also, various army-directed civic action projects—road building, school construction, health care—could win popular support for the Vientiane government, which many Laotians equated with the tax collector and nothing more. In short, a well-financed Laotian army could serve a valuable *political* purpose, by helping the Laotian government mobilize the nation against the Pathet Lao in Sam Neua and Phong Saly. It should be pointed out that, in this view, the

Laotian army's essential mission was not military but political, an area in which the Joint Chiefs of Staff were generally not called upon to make judgments.

Nevertheless, in January 1955, the Joint Chiefs were asked to review their decision on troop levels in Laos, taking into consideration the political factors discussed above. The Joint Chiefs replied to Secretary Wilson that their views "as previously conveyed to you . . . have not changed." As before, support of the Laotian army could not be recommended from the *military* point of view. However, the JCS memorandum continued, they would acquiesce in such support "should *political* considerations be overriding."[23] (Italics mine.) Wilson communicated these views to the Secretary of State, and added that he concurred in the JCS recommendation but that he too would agree to support the Laotian army "for political reasons."

Shortly after it received this communication, State asked the U. S. Mission in Vientiane to recommend a level of Laotian military forces that the U. S. should support. The Mission advised that the level should be 23,600 men. American financial aid for the Laotian army began to flow soon after.

In January 1956, the Joint Chiefs were again approached on the subject of military aid to Laos. This time, the JCS were asked to consider financing an increase in the size of the Laotian army to 25,000 men. The JCS, affirming their earlier views regarding the military usefulness of supporting the Laotian army, agreed to the increase, but only on the ground that it seemed necessary "from a psychological, political and morale aspect."[24] Accordingly, the Laotian army was enlarged to 25,000.

The disagreement between State and Defense concerning support of the Laotian army persisted until 1960. As late as fiscal year 1958, the Defense Department continued to list Laotian troops as being "not within force objectives." Finally, in fiscal year 1960, Defense concurred in the support of the Laotian army without protest.

One may very well raise questions about the decision-making process that led the United States to assume the burden of financing, in its entirety, the cost of the 25,000-man Laotian army. According to mutual security program procedures, the level of funding was supposed to rest on the recommendations of the Joint Chiefs of Staff, who utilized their military expertise to make a judgment. In the case of Laos, however, the advice of the JCS was ignored. Not only was the opinion of the JCS set aside, but they were repeatedly requested to consider support for the Laotian army on political rather than military grounds. However well versed the Joint Chiefs may be on political matters, they are not equipped by training or experience to judge the *political* necessity for supporting foreign armies. If the decision to finance the Laotian army was to be based on political grounds, one wonders why the Joint Chiefs were consulted in the first place. Presumably, the State Department is better suited to decide such matters. A congressional investigating committee expressed its concern over these irregularities in the following words,

> *U. S. support of a 25,000-man army, of the entire military budget, and of segments of the civilian economy is, in fact, based on a political determination, made by the Department of State contrary to the recommendations of the Joint Chiefs of Staff.* In Laos, the only country in the world where the United States supports the military budget 100 percent, military judgments have been disregarded.[25]

At a later point in this narrative we shall inquire whether that assistance did in fact bring about the stability and popular support for Vientiane that the State Department hoped for.

DISTRIBUTION OF AMERICAN AID

The best indication of what Washington hoped to accomplish with its aid may be obtained by considering the sums of money spent on various projects. Similar reasoning applies to a business firm. Suppose an investigator wished to ascertain what the directors of a company thought the firm should do in order to maximize its profits. Did the directors feel that more research was vital? Did they think that expanding the sales force was the key to higher profits? Or did they believe that more advertising was the answer? Perhaps they felt that expanding the plant was the best means of increasing income. How could our investigator find out what he wished to know? One means would be to read the company's glossy brochures. Another possibility would be to listen to speeches delivered at meetings of stockholders or boards of directors. But the best method would be to examine the budget. Where was the money going? Was the company spending more on hiring additional salesmen or on sponsoring television spectaculars? Was it building additional plants or establishing new research laboratories? The answers to such questions would reveal the priorities held by the directors of the firm.

We can ask the same kind of questions to discover how officials administering the American aid program in Laos viewed their priorities. For example, was more money spent on building schools or on procuring tanks for the Laotian army? It is to questions like these that we now turn.

American aid first flowed to Laos under the Mutual Security Program in 1955, after the Defense Department had yielded to State. During that fiscal year, the United States gave Laos $28.2 million in cash grants for defense support.[26] In fiscal years 1956 and 1957, the United States programmed economic aid to Laos as shown in Table 3.

TABLE 3

U.S. ECONOMIC AID OBLIGATIONS TO LAOS
(IN MILLIONS OF DOLLARS)[a]

	Fiscal Year 1956	Fiscal Year 1957
Economic Aid by Category:		
Total	48.7	44.5
Technical cooperation	1.0	1.5
Defense support	47.7	43.0
Economic Aid by Type:		
Project aid	6.6	6.0
Nonproject aid	42.1	38.5

[a]Source: House Committee on Foreign Affairs, *Mutual Security Act of 1958*, p. 1743.

In 1957, a typical year, the breakdown of project and nonproject assistance is illustrated in Tables 4 and 5.

TABLE 4

PROJECT PROGRAM BY FIELD OF ACTIVITY IN 1957
(IN THOUSANDS OF DOLLARS)[a]

Total, All Fields	5,978
Agriculture and natural resources	277
Industry and mining	391
Transportation	2,311
Health and sanitation	297
Education	185
Public administration	965
Community development and housing	403
General and miscellaneous	1,149

[a]Source: House Committee on Foreign Affairs, *Mutual Security Act of 1958*, p. 1744.

TABLE 5

NONPROJECT PROGRAM BY MAJOR COMMODITY GROUP IN 1957
(IN THOUSANDS OF DOLLARS)[a]

Total, nonproject program 38,480
    Fuel 800
    Raw materials and semifinished products 3,928
    Machinery and vehicles 2,300
    Miscellaneous and unclassified 700
    Cash transactions 30,752

[a]Source: House Committee on Foreign Affairs, *Mutual Security Act of 1958*, p. 1744.

Tables 3–5 reveal significant information about the thrust of the American aid program in Laos. Table 3 clearly shows that Washington placed the highest priority on defense support, not on helping the central government win the allegiance of the peasants. In 1956, for example, the United States spent $47.7 million on defense support and only $1 million on technical cooperation. Table 4 shows the specific projects undertaken with the small portion of aid classified as "project aid" ($6 million out of a total aid package of $44.5 million in 1957). Nearly half the project assistance funds were spent on transportation. This project, essentially a road-building program, was organically related to the military aspect of the aid program. The army needed roads to move men and equipment into remote areas where the Pathet Lao operated. Table 5 offers some revealing information about nonproject aid, which bulked much larger than project aid in 1956 and 1957. The preponderance of nonproject aid falls under the category of "cash transactions" (nearly $31 million out of over $38 million spent on nonproject assistance in 1957). The money designated as cash transactions was used to pay the salaries and all other costs of maintaining Laos's army, police, and civil administration. In transferring these funds, the United States was paying well over half the total expenses of the Royal Government. (For the sake of comparison, imagine that another country was financing the American military as well as the salaries of all state officials, from the President on down.)

A report accompanying Tables 3–5 presented some further data concerning the uses of American aid funds.

Substantial amounts of nonproject aid have been given in the form of cash transfers, to assure timely payment of military costs. Smaller amounts have financed the importation of industrial commodities needed to maintain consumption and production, and to provide an offset to the inflationary effect of large military expenditures. The local currency generated by the sale of these imports has financed the military budget and has provided funds to meet the local costs of economic projects.[27]

In addition to the aid covered in Tables 3–5, the United States provided some military equipment. "The United States military program has provided limited material assistance, largely from residue assets of the old Indochina program, which has been used to build a reliable army."[28] The exact amount of this aid has not been made public.

The figures presented above indicate beyond doubt that Washington intended its aid to help the Laotian government suppress the Pathet Lao militarily. The General Accounting Office has provided a different breakdown of United States aid to Laos for the period 1955–1957. These figures are presented in Table 6. Significantly, the data in Table 6 also show that most of the aid was earmarked to assist the Royal Government in putting down the Pathet Lao by force.

TABLE 6

DOLLAR FUNDS (IN MILLIONS OF DOLLARS)[a]

	1955	1956	1957	Total	Percent of Total
Generation of local currency					
Cash grants	28.2	33.7	32.7	94.6	70.0
Commodity import program	3.4	12.9	8.5	24.8	18.4
Administration	.3	.2	.9	1.4	1.0
Project assistance	1.4	6.6	6.3	14.3	10.6
Total[b]	33.3	53.4	48.4	135.1	100.0

[a]Source: U. S., Congress, House, Committee on Foreign Affairs, *Mutual Security Program in Laos,* Hearings before the Subcommittee on the Far East and Pacific, 85th Cong., 2d Sess., 1958, p. 3.
[b]These figures exclude the cost of military hardware, which the Defense Department supplied under the Military Assistance Program.

Table 6 reveals that from 1955 through 1957, the United States provided $135.1 million in aid to Laos, exclusive of military hardware. Of this amount $94.6 million, or 70 percent, was in the form of cash grants. Table 7 shows how these cash grant dollars were allocated.

TABLE 7

GENERATED LOCAL CURRENCY 1955–1957
(IN MILLIONS OF DOLLARS)[a]

	Amount	Percent of Total
Deposits to special account	98.5	100.0
Withdrawals by Laotian government:		
Military support	84.4	85.7
Public administration projects	4.0	4.1
Transportation projects	3.0	3.0
Other projects	4.4	4.5
Other items	.5	.5
Total	96.3	97.8
Balance on deposit	2.2	2.2

[a]Source: House Subcommittee on the Far East and Pacific, *Mutual Security Program in Laos*, 1958, p. 3.

The figures in Table 7 confirm our earlier finding that the preponderance of American aid was devoted to military support. Table 7 shows that most of the cash grant funds ("deposits to special account") were for military support. During the three years covered by Table 7, $84.4 million or over 85 percent of United States cash grants were so used.

In fiscal year 1958, American aid to Laos dropped from previous levels. This reduction reflected a devaluation of the Laotian currency, the kip, in October 1958, from 35 kip to a dollar to 80 kip to a dollar. Since $1 was now worth 80 kip instead of 35, fewer dollars were needed to generate a constant amount of kip. The devaluation was made retroactive to cover part of fiscal 1958. For that fiscal year, the United States programmed $1.7 million for development grants and technical cooperation, $29.8 million for budget support (principally to pay the salaries of the army and civil administration), and $5.4 million to purchase military equipment, making a total of $36.9 million.[29] In fiscal 1959, American aid declined still further. The United States programmed approximately $31 million in aid to Laos for fiscal 1959.[30]

American aid to Laos during the period fiscal 1955 to 1959 is summarized in Table 8.

TABLE 8

UNITED STATES AID TO LAOS
(IN MILLIONS OF DOLLARS)

Fiscal Year	Total Aid
1955	33.3
1956	53.4
1957	48.4
1958	39.6
1959	30.7
Total	205.4

In tracing the development of American policy toward Laos, we have taken a detailed look at the principal instrument of American policy, foreign assistance. As we have seen, the major purpose of American aid was to help the Laotian government overcome the Pathet Lao by strengthening the army and police. American policy in Laos was clearly in line with the strategy of containment. Washington was trying its best to equip the Royal Army to defeat the Pathet Lao once and for all. But persuading Prime Minister Souvanna Phouma to use his army to deal a death blow to the Pathet Lao instead of compromising with it was quite another matter. Thus American officials, in order to impress their views on the Laotian Prime Minister, arranged for him to visit Washington.

SOUVANNA PHOUMA VISITS WASHINGTON

Souvanna came to Washington on January 13, 1958, and departed two days later. The Laotian Prince met with President Eisenhower, Secretary Dulles, and other American officials. At the conclusion of the visit, Souvanna and Eisenhower issued a joint communique. This document revealed that the Prince's neutralism, so upsetting to Washington, could incline toward the West as well as the East. The communique stated,

Reaffirming Laos' membership in the Free World and its traditional friendly ties with the West, the Prime Minister declared that his Government would continue vigilant and strong in its determination to defend Laos' independence against any attempted alien domination. Prince Souvanna Phouma recognized that the Communist ideology is a danger to the Free World, and stressed that any system which throttled the dignity and freedom of the individual could have no appeal for the Lao people.

President Eisenhower confirmed the willingness of the United States to offer, within the limitations of Constitutional processes, its moral and material support to the Kingdom of Laos so long as such support could assist the Government of Laos in its effort to maintain its independence.[31]

Such a document brings into question Washington's practice of urging foreign officials to sign pledges of an ideological nature. Just how meaningful was Souvanna's affirmation of Laos's membership in the "Free World"? Washington may have been heartened by Souvanna's recognition that "the Communist ideology is a danger to the Free World"; contrary to Washington's expectations, however, Souvanna did not regard the Pathet Lao as merely an agent of an aggressive conspiracy with global ambitions. If the Prince had intended to assuage Washington, yet not commit his government to refrain from developing amicable relations with the Pathet Lao and neighboring communist countries, then he succeeded in his mission.

Whatever comfort Washington derived from the Prime Minister's visit, as well as his signature to a communique liable to charges of "right-leaning neutralism," was of short duration. Just two months after Souvanna's visit, Assistant Secretary of State for Far Eastern Affairs Walter S. Robertson summed up Washington's view of developments in Laos as follows:

A delicate situation exists in Laos. The 1954 Geneva Accords provided for unification of the country under the central government. The Communist-dominated Pathet Lao, however, refused to turn over to the Royal Government the two provinces under their armed control, using their defiance of this international agreement to negotiate successfully in November 1957 a coalition government which netted them two cabinet positions, other administrative participation, and legal status as a political party. This may extend Communist influence dangerously in Laos.[32]

A situation seemed to be developing in Laos that the United States could no longer tolerate.

NOTES

1. *Peace with Justice: Selected Addresses of Dwight D. Eisenhower* (New York: Columbia University Press, 1961), p. 97.

2. U. S. Department of State, *American Foreign Policy,* 1956, p. 32.

3. Address at Manila on Tenth Anniversary of Philippine Independence, July 4, 1956, in *Department of State Bulletin*, July 16, 1956, p. 94.

4. Commencement Address, Iowa State College, June 9, 1956, in *Department of State Bulletin* (June 18, 1956), pp. 999-1000.

5. *Department of State Bulletin*, July 23, 1956, p. 147.

6. *Department of State Bulletin*, May 13, 1957, pp. 771-72.

7. Communique signed by Great Britain, France, and the United States, April 24, 1957, in *The New York Times*, April 25, 1957.

8. *The New York Times*, November 21, 1957.

9. U. S. Congress, House, Committee on Government Operations, *United States Aid Operations in Laos*, Hearings before the Subcommittee on Foreign Operations and Monetary Affairs, 86th Cong., 1st Sess., 1959, p. 195.

10. *Ibid.*, p. 196.

11. *Ibid.*, p. 40.

12. *The New York Times*, January 20, 1961.

13. Agreement for Mutual Defense Assistance in Indochina between the United States of America and Cambodia, France, Laos, and Vietnam, December 23, 1950, in U.S., Department of State, *United States Treaties and Other International Agreements*, vol. 3, part 2, TAIS 2447, 1953.

14. *Mutual Security Agreement with Laos*, December 31, 1951, in U. S. Department of State, *United States Treaties*, vol. 3, part 4, TAIS 2613, 1953.

15. United States Note to Laos, December 18, 1951, in *Mutual Security Agreement with Laos*.

16. For fiscal year 1969, Congress voted $1.9 billion in foreign aid, less than one percent of the American GNP and the lowest amount since the program began in 1946.

17. Letter from Dulles to Foreign Minister Nong Kimny of Cambodia, April 19, 1956, in *Department of State Bulletin*, April 30, 1956, p. 727.

18. Whoever doubts this might note that the recipients of American aid are not necessarily the poorest nations but those nations, on the periphery of communist countries, who are willing to cooperate with the United States in containing communism. Such countries include India, Pakistan, Turkey, South Vietnam, Thailand, Laos, Formosa, Greece, Iran, and South Korea. Furthermore, as President Nixon stated in his foreign aid message to Congress on May 28, 1969, "over 90 per cent of all A.I.D. expenditures and virtually all purchases of goods will be made in the United States." (*The New York Times*, May 29, 1969.)

19. It is interesting to compare the statements made by AID officials to the public and to congressional committees holding hearings on foreign aid. In the first forum, they usually dwell on American generosity and lack of self-interest. In the second, they turn the emphasis around 180 degrees.

20. House Subcommittee on Foreign Operations and Monetary Affairs, *Hearings, United States Aid Operations in Laos*, 1959, p. 3.

21. U. S., Congress, House, Committee on Foreign Affairs, *Hearings, Mutual Security Act of 1958*, 85th Cong., 2d Sess., 1958, p. 568.

22. House Committee on Government Operations, *U. S. Aid Operations in Laos: 7th Report*, 1959, p. 8.

23. *Ibid.*

24. *Ibid.*

25. *Ibid.*

26. House Committee on Foreign Affairs, *Mutual Security Act of 1958*, p. 1807.

27. *Ibid.,* p. 1744.

28. *Ibid.*

29. Agency for International Development statistics as presented in Arthur J. Dommen, *Conflict in Laos* (New York: Frederick A. Praeger, 1964), p. 104.

30. *The New York Times,* August 26, 1959.

31. U. S., Department of State, *American Foreign Policy: Current Documents,* 1958, pp. 1242–43.

32. Testimony before Senate Committee on Foreign Relations, March 28, 1958, in *Department of State Bulletin,* April 28, 1958, p. 701.

8

LAOS SWINGS TO THE RIGHT

WE HAVE SEEN that the pendulum of political power in Laos, starting from an approximately central position at the conclusion of the 1954 Geneva Conference, swung steadily toward the left. Under the government of Souvanna Phouma, the Pathet Lao was gaining ever more political influence. The documents signed at Geneva stated that the Pathet Lao was to regroup in two provinces prior to their amalgamation with the rest of Laotian society. Afterward, the Pathet Lao consolidated their actual control over the provinces of Sam Neua and Phong Saly, established a legal political party (the NLHX), and managed to place two of its leading members as ministers in a coalition government. This course of events proved highly troublesome to Washington's stage-managers of containment. A coalition government containing communists, it was believed, would lead only to a communist takeover.

The Pathet Lao's political gains, however, had set in motion a wave that threatened to engulf and destroy the Pathet Lao's ultimate source of power: their armed forces. The agreements of 1956 and 1957 stipulated that in return for gaining participation in the Laotian government, the Pathet Lao would demobilize its fighting forces, except for 1,500 troops which would be integrated into the Royal Army. The Pathet Lao contingent would comprise only a small faction of the entire Royal Army of more than 20,000 soldiers, which was controlled by political leaders who were either opposed to the Pathet Lao or at best neutral toward it. Lacking a military arm, the Pathet Lao would find itself unable to protect its newly won political position in case of a future falling out between the Pathet Lao and other political forces. Furthermore, without a military component, it was doubtful that the Pathet Lao could extract further political concessions. Therefore, while in Washington's eyes the Pathet Lao leaders should have been rejoicing over the results of the 1957 agreements, the Pathet Lao chiefs were actually beset with a problem of large proportions. Should they trust those political forces that controlled the Royal Army enough to disband their fighting forces? Would Souvanna Phouma or one of his successors go back on the 1957 agreements, eject the Pathet Lao officials from their two ministries, and oust other Pathet Lao personnel from administrative positions?

CABINET CRISIS OF SUMMER 1958

By the summer of 1958—a full six months after the agreements of November 1957 and following the expansion of the Royal Government to include two Pathet Lao ministers—the Pathet Lao still refused to merge its fighting forces into the Royal Army. After having dealt with the Pathet Lao for so long, and after having met what he considered to be their reasonable demands, Souvanna Phouma himself began to lose faith that a final political settlement could be agreed upon. These doubts reached a climax on July 22, 1958, when the Prime Minister resigned, saying, "If I am appointed to form the new Government, I will try to keep the Neolao Hakxat [NLHX] Deputies out of Cabinet posts because I have doubts about their political views."[1]

Having lost patience with the Pathet Lao, Souvanna wanted to make certain that it could no longer take advantage of disunity in the ranks of the moderates and conservatives. In the back of Souvanna's mind was the memory of the May 1958 elections.

At the same time that Souvanna and other moderates were questioning the Pathet Lao's ambitions, the so-called "Young Ones" made their first appearance in Laotian politics. The Young Ones were students just returned from abroad, junior officials, and young army officers. They attributed internal discord in Laos to the ineptness, corruption and self-seeking of an older generation of politicians. According to one of their leaders,

. . . . these young people were shocked to find their country plunged once more into apathy and uncertainty. It angered them above all to see how nicely the ex-Pathet Lao Communists had used the corruption and glaring mistakes of the government, and the sudden fortunes dubiously acquired by particular ministers and high officials. The young men saw that as long as certain families continued to divide titles and prerogatives among themselves, as long as ministerial posts either cloaked the most disgraceful trafficking or were traded about like currency, as long as the wealthy in Vientiane flaunted their luxuries before the eyes of an astounded populace, any anti-Communist campaign would be pointless. These public scandals were better Communist propaganda than tons of newspapers and pamphlets.[2]

The Young Ones held their initial meeting on June 17, 1958. They sympathized with the RPL's political program but wanted to disassociate themselves from the senior politicians, whom they held responsible for past errors and the present situation. At their first meeting the Young Ones formed a political party called the Committee for the Defense of the National Interests (henceforth: CDIN).[3] The new party, strongly conservative in its political persuasion, declared war against corruption and communist subversion.[4]

One target of the CDIN was Souvanna Phouma. After his resignation in July, Souvanna tried to form a new government. This attempt failed because the CDIN, whose support in the National Assembly Souvanna needed, refused to accept a cabinet that contained some former ministers suspected of corruption. The King then asked Phoui Sananikone to form a government. Phoui succeeded, and on August 18, 1958, the National Assembly approved the new Cabinet. The eleven-man Cabinet contained four members of the CDIN and no members of the NLHX. This regime was to last eighteen months.

What role, if any, did the United States play in this change of government? To be sure, Washington had little sympathy for Souvanna's successful efforts to form a coalition regime with the communist Pathet Lao. Souvanna's resignation could occasion nothing but joy among American policymakers. But this is not to say that the Americans engineered his resignation. Those who wish to argue that Washington was more than a passive force in the change of government can point to Washington's encouragement of the Young Ones, who stood opposed to Souvanna. They can also cite Souvanna's allegation, three years later, that Ambassador Parsons was responsible for his resignation.[5] The Prince, however, did not say what Parsons had done to topple his regime. Perhaps he had in mind the suspension of American aid payments that took effect July 1, 1958. The then Under Secretary of State, C. Douglas Dillon, has said, however, that Washington interrupted the payments in an effort to persuade the Royal Government to devaluate the Laotian currency, not to topple Souvanna's government.[6] The Assistant Secretary of State for Far Eastern Affairs, Walter S. Robertson, denied that the United States was instrumental in the change of government. During a Congressional hearing, Representative Porter Hardy noted that during the summer of 1958 a Laotian government was formed that excluded communists. "What took place to bring that about?" he asked. To quote from the record:

> Mr. Robertson. I think they got a tremendous jolt when they ended up by losing those elections [of May, 1958].
> Mr. Hardy. It wasn't anything that we did.
> Mr. Robertson. Nothing that we did, no.[7]

Robertson's testimony seems to contradict Souvanna's accusation. America's responsibility for the Laotian government crisis remains a beclouded area in United States–Laotian relations. The public record contains no other information that sheds light on the issue. Until additional material becomes available, we must suspend final judgment of America's role in the events of the summer of 1958.

Before Souvanna resigned, his government took an action that was to have international repercussions. On March 13, 1958, the Souvanna government asked the ICC to terminate its activities in Laos as of May 4, the date of the scheduled supplementary elections in Phong Saly and Sam Neua. In his letter making this request, Souvanna wrote, "The Royal Government considers in fact that the supplementary elections of 4 May, 1958, constitute the last phase of the implementation of the Geneva Agreements of 20 July, 1954, on the cessation of hostilities in Laos."[8] On July 18, 1958, the ICC, Poland dissenting, adopted a resolution to adjourn *sine die*.

THE PHOUI SANANIKONE REGIME

With the accession of Phoui Sananikone, the pendulum of political power in Laos swung toward the right. The first indication of Phoui's new course was his decision to exclude Pathet Lao members from the government. In his investiture speech on August 18, Phoui gave further indications of the direction in which his regime would travel. "Our objective is to preserve our newly won independence and unification," the Prime Minister said. "We must guard against the most threatening danger, which will undermine our independence and unification. This danger is Communism." Commenting on the composition of his cabinet, he said, "I have selected members of political parties who desire to oppose communist expansion in Laos to participate in the government. The policy of the government that I have formed is as follows: To oppose the threat of this dangerous ideology . . ."[9]

On the subject of foreign policy, Phoui stated,

As far as peaceful coexistence is concerned, we shall clearly inform neighboring countries and the world that we shall coexist with the Free World only. We trust only those countries that really and sincerely support us.[10]

In stark contrast to the neutralist orientation of the previous Souvanna Phouma government, the Phoui regime—as the above quotations indicate —took a decided stand against the communists. It can be argued that the Pathet Lao should have merged its military units with those of the Royal Army when Souvanna Phouma's government seemed amenable to a compromise solution. Instead, the Pathet Lao elected to stall on military integration. This tactic, combined with leftist political victories in the May 1958 elections, caused many neutralists and moderates to suspect that the Pathet Lao sought not genuine compromise but victory. Many moderates felt that action should be taken before the nation-wide elections scheduled for 1959, when it was feared that the left would repeat its success of May 1958—this time on a national scale. The result of these political trends was the formation of the Phoui Sananikone regime, one of whose cardinal tenets was anticommunism. Many Laotian moderates, in rallying to the Phoui government, had given up hope of reaching a lasting compromise with the Pathet Lao. The Pathet Lao, in their eyes, desired not compromise but domination.

One of Phoui's first acts was to devalue the kip. In October 1958 he devalued the kip from the rate of 35 to one dollar to that of 80 to one dollar and abolished the import licensing system. These measures led to a decrease in corruption connected with American aid.

Shortly thereafter, Phoui took a major stride away from his predecessor's neutral foreign policy. In December 1958, Phoui recognized Nationalist China and approved the establishment of a Nationalist Chinese consulate in Vientiane. This step aroused the ire of Peking and Hanoi, who recalled Souvanna's refusal—during his 1957 visit to the two communist capitals—to countenance the establishment of North Vietnamese and Chinese Communist consulates in Vientiane. Souvanna's rationale for this refusal, it will be recalled, was that acceptance of a Chinese Communist consulate without also granting a consulate to the Chinese Nationalists would be inconsistent with Laos's neutral foreign policy. Souvanna had also assured his communist hosts that Vientiane had no intention of recognizing Taiwan.[11] Phoui's subsequent recognition of Nationalist China, as well as his decision to permit the Nationalists to establish a consulate, clearly signaled a departure from a neutralist foreign policy. It is therefore perhaps not surprising that, later in December, fighting erupted on the border between Laos and North Vietnam. Laos charged that Hanoi occupied a small frontier area, Huong Lap, near Tchepone in northern

Laos. North Vietnam countered that the territory belonged to her, not to Laos. The most likely explanation for this brief flareup is that North Vietnam launched the pin-prick attacks to show her displeasure at Laos's drift from neutralism toward anticommunism, particularly as manifested by Laos's acceptance of a consulate from Taiwan.[12]

Phoui further incensed the communists by inviting Ngo Dinh Nhu, brother of South Vietnam's chief of state, to visit Vientiane. No corresponding invitation was sent to a North Vietnamese official. A few weeks later the Laotian legation at Saigon was elevated to an Embassy.

The new year brought with it a further drift to the right. On January 14, 1959, Phoui asked the National Assembly for permission to reorganize his government and to govern for twelve months without the National Assembly; the Assembly consented, and also granted him power to enact programs of sweeping economic, social and political reform.

Despite Souphanouvong's insistence that these measures were illegal, Phoui proceeded to form a new fourteen-member cabinet. As in his previous government, no Pathet Lao representatives were included. Phoui's new cabinet was even more conservative than his former one. The CDIN received five portfolios. Two others went to army men closely associated with the CDIN. Colonel Phoumi Nosavan, a CDIN leader noted for his hostility toward communists, was appointed Secretary for Defense and Veterans Affairs. Phoui awarded six portfolios to members of his own RPL party.

Phoui's moves effectively deprived the Pathet Lao of any political power that could be exercised through government channels. Not only was the Pathet Lao eliminated from the cabinet, but the National Assembly, in which the NLHX occupied nine seats as a result of the 1958 elections, had adjourned for one year.

This acceleration of anticommunism inspired a second response from North Vietnam. Premier Pham Van Dong sent Phoui a series of protests against the alleged Laotian border violations of the previous December. The North Vietnamese Premier also asked the ICC to "resume its activities to conduct investigations and examinations of . . . violations" [of the Geneva agreements], and to "take appropriate and energetic measures to insure respect for, and correct implementation of, the Geneva agreements."[13]

In February 1959, Phoui further accelerated his assault against the Pathet Lao. At a press conference on February 11, he issued a lengthy statement on the situation in Laos.[14] He began by noting communist accusations that the Laotian government had violated the Geneva settlement of 1954. "The Royal Government considers that the agreement on the cessation of hostilities in Laos has been completely fulfilled," Phoui said. In subscribing to the Geneva agreement, he explained,

. . . the Royal Government voluntarily contracted two obligations: to achieve a cessation of hostilities and a reintegration within the national community of those Laotian citizens who were not on the side of the Royal forces during the said hostilities.

The cessation of hostilities has been a fact for several years. The elections of May 4, 1958, . . . permitted those Laotian citizens who had not been on the side of the Royal forces during the hostilities to be reintegrated within the national community without discrimination.

With respect to that interpretation of the agreements which consists of declaring that they are applicable to Laos so long as the reunification of Vietnam has not taken place,[15] the Royal Government cannot accept it. It is contrary to the spirit and the letter of agreements. No government worthy of the name may mortgage the political future of its territory on the basis of the situation existing in a neighboring country.

The same is true with regard to a certain Laotian political party and to certain foreign powers aiming at the revival of the ISCC [ICC] in Laos in order to have it arbitrate internal and international affairs of which Laos is a part.

The Kingdom of Laos, an independent and sovereign country, cannot tolerate intervention in its internal affairs. The Kingdom of Laos, . . . only recognizes arbitration originating from the [United Nations].

Phoui's remarks precipitated an international furor,[16] in response to which the Laotian government issued clarifying statements on February 16 and 17. These explanations said that the Phoui government repudiated only that portion of the Geneva settlement relating to the ICC. The Government argued that Laos, as a sovereign state that had—in the opinion of the Phoui government—fulfilled the obligations imposed by the Geneva agreements, was entitled to question the prerogative of an outside agency (the ICC). Underlying this attitude was the Government's suspicion of the Polish member of the ICC. The Government believed he was acting more as a communist espionage agent than as a functionary of an international organ. Furthermore, the Government did not want the ICC with its communist member to serve as an arbiter in Laotian politics when called upon to do so by the NLHX.

Did Phoui commit an infringement of the Geneva agreements by denying that the ICC had authority in Laos, on the ground that the Government had carried out the obligations imposed upon it at Geneva? On legal grounds a case could be made against the Government's declaration. Article 27 of the Agreement on the Cessation of Hostilities in Laos said the ICC "shall be responsible for supervising the execution by the parties of the provisions of the present Agreement." Clearly, so long as two units of the Pathet Lao's military forces remained an independent force within the country, the provisions of the Agreement had not been fully implemented, regardless of who was at fault. The "political settlement" called for in Article 14 of the Agreement could not be realized until the Pathet Lao's military forces were absorbed into the Royal Army. Therefore, it would seem that, until a political settlement materialized, the ICC could usefully perform its functions of "control, observation, inspection and investigation connected with the implementation of the provisions of the Agreement. . . ."

On the other hand, the essence of the Agreement was the cease-fire, which had existed for some time. The Royal Government had performed its obligations regarding the cease-fire as specified by the Geneva agreements. Furthermore, the Laotian government had not agreed to allow the ICC to function in Laos in perpetuity. The diplomats at Geneva expected that the merger of the Pathet Lao and the remainder of the national community would occur in the near future. How long was the ICC to have the prerogative of interfering in Laotian affairs? In the opinion of Phoui's government, the ICC was entitled to exercise authority in Laos for only a "reasonable" length of time, and this time had expired.

On balance, it would seem that Phoui's declaration did violate the spirit as well as the letter of the Geneva accords, which pointed to a final political settlement, not just a cease-fire. Whether or not the Government was responsible for the failure of a final political settlement to materialize, the Government was not justified in declaring itself exempt from part of the Geneva settlement before the entire settlement had been realized.

INTEGRATION OF PATHET LAO TROOPS

Phoui's campaign against the Pathet Lao gained further momentum during the spring of 1959.

It will be recalled that two units of the Pathet Lao fighting forces remained intact, awaiting integration into the Royal Army, as provided in the November 1957 agreements. These two units totalled 1,500 men.[17] The Royal Army now numbered 29,000.

The accords of November 1957 specified that the Pathet Lao units were entitled to the same proportion of officers to enlisted men as the Royal Army. On this issue the negotiations on merger broke down.[18]

Originally, the Pathet Lao had requested a ratio of officers to men far in excess of the standard proportion in the Royal Army. After prolonged bargaining, the Government and the Pathet Lao reached a compromise. The Government agreed to award Colonel Singkapo, commander of the Pathet Lao fighting forces, a colonel's commission in the Royal Army;

Singkapo was the only Pathet Lao to receive this rank. Without giving any notice, however, Singkapo did not appear at the ceremony—attended by many dignitaries—at which his rank in the Royal Army was to be conferred. Instead, he sent the Government an abusive letter refusing the commission. According to Champassak, "This was the end of serious negotiations with the Pathet Lao."[19]

Before the Singkapo affair, the Government had unilaterally designated May 11, 1959, as the date on which the Pathet Lao troops would receive ranks in the Royal Army, thus effecting the military integration envisaged in November 1957. Several days before May 11, Prince Souphanouvong sent a protest to the Government, disapproving the nominations and forbidding his men to accept the new ranks, on the ground that Singkapo was not among those to be commissioned. The Government had refused to reinstate the colonel.

On the morning of May 11, Laotian dignitaries and soldiers took their places on the reviewing stand for the integration ceremony. The Pathet Lao soldiers did not appear. Subsequently, the Government commanded the Pathet Lao troops to integrate. One Pathet Lao unit, consisting of about half of the 1,500 troops, was quartered at Xieng Ngeun in Luang Prabang province. The other was camped on the Plaine des Jarres. In these sectors, the Royal Army had only a few hundred troops, most of them without battle experience. The Government published a decree saying that those Pathet Lao troops who wished to serve in the Royal Army should present themselves to the proper authorities, who would confer ranks on them. Those who did not wish to serve in the Royal Army were ordered to lay down their arms and return to civilian life. The Government set a deadline of noon on May 13, 1959. After this hour, all Pathet Lao troops who refused to accept ranks in the Royal Army or lay down their arms would be considered rebels. Shortly before the deadline, Royal troops surrounded both Pathet Lao battalions. The unit stationed at Xieng Ngeun accepted the Government's conditions for integration into the Royal Army. The other battalion refused and, under cover of night, slipped through the cordon of troops surrounding it.

On May 15, the Government placed the residences of Souphanouvong and other leading Pathet Lao officials under police guard and detained the occupants under house arrest, in order to discourage subversive activity and preclude attempts to join the rebel battalion. On May 22 the Government declared the NLHX illegal.

For the Pathet Lao, the consequences of Phoui's policies were grave indeed. By the close of 1957, the Pathet Lao was represented by two ministers in the Royal Government; the following May, the Pathet Lao and their leftist allies captured 14 seats in the National Assembly. The political future of the Pathet Lao seemed bright. By the middle of 1959, after Phoui Sananikone had replaced Souvanna Phouma as prime minister, the Pathet Lao had lost these positions of power. Phoui had excluded the Pathet Lao from his cabinet, and as a result of the suspension of the National Assembly, the Pathet Lao was unable to exert influence through this channel. The NLHX was outlawed. Now the Pathet Lao's sole remaining source of leverage, their fighting forces, came under attack. Half of the 1,500 men under Pathet Lao arms joined the Royal Army; the remainder was scattered in flight across the hills of northeast Laos. In addition, Souphanouvong and other Pathet Lao leaders were under house arrest in Vientiane.

These developments drastically altered the range of choices open to the Pathet Lao. Before Phoui became prime minister, the Pathet Lao could have chosen from among three broad policy alternatives. One choice was to disband and merge with the rest of Laotian society. Another possibility was to adopt a fighting stance and, either alone or in combination with a foreign power, try to win a military victory over other political groups in Laos. A third policy was to seek political power by working within the normal channels of government; that is, by building a base of popular support, trying to win elections, gaining positions in the cabinet, and so on. Under Souphanouvong, the Pathet Lao had elected the last alternative. Now, Phoui had closed off that option. The Pathet Lao faced a grim choice: give up and disband, or resort to military means to achieve power. In a last-ditch effort to avoid having to make such a choice, the Pathet Lao attempted to keep alive the middle road, namely, gaining power within the normal political process. On June 1, 1959, the Pathet Lao issued what appears to have been a final call for the resumption of efforts toward a political settlement. This statement, purported to come from the vice-chairman of the NLHX Central Committee, decried Phoui's policies as a means of "eliminating all democratic freedoms" and turning Laos into "a colony and military base of the U. S. imperialists."[20] The statement called the Government's decision to outlaw the NLHX "an open provo-cation of civil war in Laos." Finally, the statement listed the following demands:

1. Withdrawal of army units attacking the remaining Pathet Lao battalion
2. Repeal of the order placing NLHX leaders under house arrest
3. Release of all Pathet Lao cadres jailed throughout the country
4. Assurance of democratic freedoms
5. Respect for parliament as provided in the constitution [that is, calling the National Assembly back into session]

6. Implementation of Government–Pathet Lao agreements
7. Implementation of the Geneva agreements, including resumption of ICC activities.

The Government, predictably, rejected these proposals.

REBEL OFFENSIVE BEGINS—JULY 1959

Finding political channels blocked, the Pathet Lao chose the only other route to political power—military force. On July 2 the NLHX issued what amounted to a declaration of war.[21] After declaring its dedication to "struggle to the end" to force the Royal Government to observe the Geneva agreements and the agreements of November 1957, the Pathet Lao listed conditions that the Government would have to meet in order to effect a reconciliation. These demands were essentially identical to those posited in the NLHX's statement of June 1, except that on July 2 the NLHX insisted upon the formation of a coalition government, establishment of diplomatic relations with all neighboring countries—a reference to Communist China and North Vietnam—and a renunciation of alleged servitude to the United States. The statement also indicated that the Pathet Lao would seek recruits among members of the many national minorities in Laos.[22]

Toward the middle of July 1959, the Pathet Lao launched its military offensive. Bernard Fall divides the Pathet Lao campaign into three phases.[23] During the first stage, which lasted from July 18 to July 31, the Pathet Lao concentrated their efforts on isolating Sam Neua province from the rest of Laos. This effort failed. The second stage lasted from August 1 to August 29. During this period the Pathet Lao tried to create a situation of general insecurity with a stress on pinprick attacks in almost every province.[24] From August 30 through September, the last phase of the offensive, the Pathet Lao resumed heavy localized attacks against Lao Army posts in Sam Neua, with some thrusts toward Luang Prabang and Vientiane.

The summer campaign was marked by indecisive skirmishes which left the military balance of power in Laos unchanged. The Royal Government charged that these military actions were carried out not by the Pathet Lao battalion that had refused integration, but by men who "represent new elements entirely armed, equipped and stiffened [encadrés] by the Democratic Republic of North Viet Nam."[25] Laotian Foreign Minister Khamphan Panya said the Pathet Lao had at least 2,000 men in the field.[26]

Meanwhile, the Government announced that it was removing Souphanouvong and other NLHX leaders placed under house arrest to a special camp outside Vientiane to await trial.

UNITED NATIONS MISSION
VISITS LAOS

On August 4, 1959, the Laotian Foreign Minister sent a letter to Secretary General Dag Hammarskjold, informing him that since July 16 "serious fighting" had flared in Sam Neua province. The Minister added that the trouble would not have occurred if:

1. Radio Hanoi, with support from Radio Peking, had not encouraged the Pathet Lao to take up arms.
2. North Vietnam had not given arms to the Pathet Lao fighters.
3. North Vietnam had not sent supplies to the Pathet Lao.
4. North Vietnam had not armed ethnic minority elements who were cooperating with the Pathet Lao.
5. Radio Hanoi had not allowed Royal Army deserters to use its broadcasting facilities.

The letter also accused North Vietnam of violating the Geneva agreements, which included noninterference in the domestic affairs of signatory countries.[27]

One month later, Laos sent a second communication to the Secretary General, alleging that since July 16, 1959, foreign troops had been crossing the frontier and engaging in military action against garrison units of the Royal Army stationed along Laos's northeastern frontier.[28] "It is obvious that these attacks would not have taken place if the attackers had not come from outside the country and would not have continued if the attackers had not been receiving reinforcements and supplies of food and munitions from outside," the letter charged. Referring to an August 30 attack against Royal Army posts at Muong Het and Xieng Kho, the letter stated, "Elements from the Democratic Republic of Viet-Nam took part in the attack, which was supported by artillery fire from the other side of the frontier." Finally, Laos requested United Nations assistance under Article 1, paragraph 1, and Article 11, paragraph 2, of the United Nations Charter. "In particular, Laos requests that an emergency force should be dispatched at a very early date in order to halt the aggression and prevent it from spreading."

On September 7, after rejecting the Soviet Union's contention that Laos should not be placed on the Security Council's agenda, the Council held a special meeting on the Laotian question. The Council voted 10–1

(USSR) in favor of the following procedural resolution, introduced by the United States, France and the United Kingdom:

> The Security Council
> Decided to appoint a sub-committee consisting of Argentina, Italy, Japan and Tunisia, and instructs this sub-committee to examine the statements made before the Security Council concerning Laos, to receive further statements and documents and to conduct inquiries as it determines necessary, and to report to the Council as soon as possible.

The United Nations subcommittee arrived in Laos on September 15, 1959, and left on October 13, 1959. The subcommittee considered its task as one of reviewing information supplied by the Laotian Government, not conducting its own investigation in the field. The subcommittee utilized three sources of information: statements made before it and the Security Council at the United Nations in New York, documents provided to it at United Nations headquarters, and information made available to it while in Laos.

In Laos, the subcommittee questioned eight civilian officers (district chiefs, village chiefs and their assistants) of the Royal Government, six members of the Laotian Army, fourteen peasants, one pagoda warden, one widow of a fallen soldier, and twelve Pathet Lao prisoners taken by the Royal Army. All the prisoners were of Laotian nationality. The subcommittee also visited nine wounded men in Luang Prabang and eighteen wounded men in Vientiane; it was shown fragments of shells and bullets allegedly extracted from wounded men. In addition, the subcommittee was presented with weapons, uniforms, and equipment allegedly captured in the northern and northeastern provinces during July–September, 1959.

In its final report, the subcommittee said,

> Practically all witnesses (forty out of forty-one) stated that the hostile elements received support from the territory of the D.R.V.N. consisting mainly of equipment, arms, ammunition, supplies, and the help of political cadres. The same emerges from the official Laotian documents submitted and from some of the material exhibits.[29]

The subcommittee, however, did not accept the Laotian Government's display of evidence as conclusive. The subcommittee's principal finding was, "The ensemble of information submitted to the Sub-Committee did not clearly establish whether there were crossings of the frontier by regular troops of the D.R.V.N."

The subcommittee's report therefore did not settle the question of whether there had in fact been aggression from North Vietnam. One immediate problem that presented itself was the definition of aggression. Does military aid, advice, or supplies constitute aggression? Or should aggression be more narrowly defined as the crossing of a national boundary by regular army troops of another country? Since aggression has never been defined to the satisfaction of the members of the world community, the United Nations subcommittee was operating under a semantic handicap. A second difficulty was pointed out by Champassak, Laotian Minister of Information at the time of the investigation. Champassak said that the subcommittee had not found material proof of North Vietnamese aggression because as soon as the subcommittee arrived, the alleged invaders ceased their activities and retired to North Vietnam.[30] Certainly, between September 7, the day the Security Council decided to dispatch the mission, and September 15, the day on which the subcommittee reached Laos, any invaders would have had time to vacate Laos. Thus, the fact that the subcommittee did not actually *see* any North Vietnamese troops in Laos does not preclude the possibility of their having been there. Failing to identify any North Vietnamese cadres in Laos, the subcommittee was compelled to rely on observations made by others. The subcommittee did precisely this, but refused to accept such second-hand evidence as conclusive. (One point arguing in favor of the subcommittee's published conclusion is the Laotian Government's failure to produce any North Vietnamese prisoners.)

If one accepts the evidence presented to the subcommittee as valid, then one must conclude that North Vietnam did violate the provision of the Geneva agreement that prohibited interference in the internal affairs of Laos. The fact that the Laotian government supplied the evidence to the subcommittee detracts from the credibility of that evidence to the extent that the Government had an interest in presenting information that would lead the subcommittee to a certain conclusion.

Regardless of its findings, the very presence of the subcommittee had an effect on the situation in Laos. From the time of the subcommittee's arrival, fighting in Laos declined to negligible proportions. The Pathet Lao's summer campaign came to an end.

PHOUMI HEADS SUCCESSFUL MILITARY COUP

The term of the Laotian legislature, which had not met since Phoui had received authority to govern without it in January 1959, was due to expire on December 25, 1959. As this date approached, political differences arose between Phoui's RPL party and the CDIN. There differences were reflected in a personal dispute between Phoui and his Minister of Foreign Affairs, Khamphan Panya, a leading member of the CDIN. On December 15 Phoui reshuffled his cabinet and discharged Khamphan, Minister of Information Champassak, Secretary of State for Defense Colonel Phoumi Nosavan, and Minister of Defense General Southone. A leftist, Bong Souvannavong, was named Minister of Postal Services and Telecommunications. Phoui himself assumed the following posts: Foreign Minister, National Defense Minister, Veterans Minister, Minister of Public Works and Rural Affairs, and Minister of Information, Sports, and Youth.

On December 18 the National Assembly set April 3, 1960, as the next election date and voted to extend its mandate until the elections were held.

One week later, on the day the original Assembly mandate was to have expired, Colonel Phoumi reacted to the expulsion of himself and other conservatives in Phoui Sananikone's government by calling for Phoui's resignation. When Phoui stalled for time, Phoumi's troops surrounded his residence. Meanwhile, on December 29, an important event occurred: the death of former premier Katay Sasorith, president of the RPL. Phoui was vice-president of this party, which controlled 36 seats in the 59-seat Assembly. However, Phoui commanded the personal loyalty of only one-fourth of the RPL; the remainder of the RPL looked for inspiration from Katay, who had supported Phoui's government. Katay's death gravely weakened Phoui's political support. On December 30 the King sent Phoui a letter declaring the end of his government. That night, Phoumi's troops occupied the ministries and government buildings. Phoui resigned. Without bloodshed, the army took over. On January 5, 1960, the King designated a new Premier, Kou Abhay, a respected elder statesman who was to rule symbolically until elections were held in April. The King and Kou then chose members of a provisional government, which included the recently ousted Khamphan Panya as Foreign Minister and Colonel Phoumi as Minister of Defense. Assembly elections were scheduled for April 24. The new Premier declared in his first radio address that under his government Laos would adhere to a "vigilant neutrality."

THE APRIL ELECTIONS RETURN A RIGHT WING REGIME

As the date of the April elections neared, Laotians began to wonder whether the Pathet Lao would repeat its victory of 1958. The Kou government acted to prevent the Pathet Lao from achieving another electoral triumph. Electoral districts were revised in order to break up Pathet Lao zones of influence. Eligibility requirements for candidates were stiffened.

In order to run for office, a businessman had to have paid for a trade license for five years. Election deposits were doubled; minimal educational standards were raised, requiring either an elementary school certificate or a *maha* of the third grade. This last requirement particularly penalized the Pathet Lao, since more than half of its leaders lacked schooling. Nine Pathet Lao leaders, including Souphanouvong, had been incarcerated for almost a year and were barred from running for office or campaigning on behalf of others. The few Pathet Lao leaders left at large were relatively unknown among the masses.

The army was entrusted with the task of supervising the elections. "The army decided that, wherever possible, it would suppress Communist propaganda in the provinces to insure the victory of the government candidates."[31] Phoumi Nosavan assumed control of this task.

The election results testified to the effectiveness of these anticommunist measures. Of the 59 seats in the Assembly, the RPL and its affiliates won 27 and the CDIN captured 32. Not one of the nine NLHX candidates was elected.

By most accounts the Laotian elections were the model of fraud and dishonesty, even for Laos. Not one communist candidate was elected, not even from the communist strongholds in the provinces of Sam Neua and Phong Saly. In the former province, the communist candidate, according to the official tally, received only four votes! In another area of Pathet Lao strength, the communist candidate received four votes, while the CDIN candidate garnered 18,189.[32] Such vote counts defy the limits of credulity—unless, of course, the elections were rigged. There is little doubt that this was the case. Souvanna Phouma in 1961 called them a sham (*truquées*).[33] Quinim Pholsena, a leader of the leftist Santahip Party, and Bong Souvannavong, another prominent leftist, complained that the elections were rigged.[34] In view of the electoral procedures followed by the Government, as well as the election returns that were reported, it does not seem that these charges were unfounded.

After the elections, the King named Tiao Somsanith, a former RPL member who switched to the more conservative CDIN, as Premier. Phoumi Nosavan became Minister of Defense and "exercised great influence within the new cabinet."[35] The rightist CDIN, with its 32 Assembly seats, was now, along with the army, in control of the Government.

One final development marked the spring of 1960. During the night of May 24, Prince Souphanouvong and the other Pathet Lao members arrested with him escaped into the jungle, with the help of the men assigned to guard them.

The events between Souvanna Phouma's resignation in July 1958 and the elections of April 1960 moved political power in Laos about as far to the right as it could go. Phoui Sananikone made clear that instead of compromising with the communists, he would try to put an end to their movement in Laos. Disregarding the agreements of November 1957, Phoui relieved the two Pathet Lao representatives from their ministerial posts. In winning approval for governing for a year without the National Assembly, Phoui neutralized the political power wielded by the Pathet Lao in that body. Phoui's ultimatum in May 1959 brought half of the Pathet Lao's fighting forces into the Royal Army. The remaining half, about 750 men, was scattered in flight from the Royal Army's nearly 30,000 troops. Colonel Phoumi Nosavan, who engineered a coup in December 1959, organized the elections of April 1960 so that not one Pathet Lao candidate won, even in those regions which were known to be Pathet Lao strongholds.

In the middle of 1960, Washington's containment policy appeared to be prospering in Laos. It is generally believed that the United States was the moving force behind the activities of the CDIN, which prevented Souvanna Phouma from forming a new government following his resignation in July 1958. The CDIN also pressured the Phoui Sananikone regime to drive the Pathet Lao up against the wall. Washington hailed the cabinet Phoui selected in January 1959—a staunchly anticommunist government that excluded the Pathet Lao. The United States also supported Phoui's statement of February 11, 1959, in which he denounced that part of the Geneva accords pertaining to the ICC. With American support, Phoui threatened the Pathet Lao's military forces with surrender or annihilation, placed Souphanouvong and other Pathet Lao leaders under arrest, and declared the NLHX illegal.

Finding normal political channels blocked, the Pathet Lao, in desperation, resorted to military force in the summer of 1959. The resulting fighting had two major consequences. In the first place, it provided both sides with an opportunity to make a preliminary assessment of their relative military strength. The hostilities demonstrated that each side was capable of withstanding the military blows of its opponent. Hence, there appeared to be no need for either side to capitulate. The second important consequence of the fighting proved to be the internationalization of the Laotian dispute. The United States supplied energetic assistance to Phoui in his effort to eliminate the communist movement from Laos. Phoui's anticommunist policies elicited Soviet protests as well as Soviet support for the Pathet Lao. One year later, external forces were to overtake events in Laos, in that outsiders seemed to acquire more influence in Laotian politics than the Laotians themselves.

In subsequent chapters we shall trace the growing involvement of foreign influences, starting with the United States.

NOTES

1. *The New York Times,* July 23, 1958. The reasons for the Prince's resignation are not clear. The article in the *Times* said that he yielded his post because he had lost faith in the Pathet Lao. In 1961, Souvanna said in an interview that the United States was responsible for his resignation. He did not elaborate. See *The New York Times,* January 20, 1961.

2. Sisouk Na Champassak, *Storm over Laos* (New York: Frederick A. Praeger, 1961), p. 63.

3. According to Roger Hilsman, the impetus for the creation of the CDIN came from the CIA, which feared that discord among the noncommunists in Laos would allow the communists to make greater political gains than their strength warranted. The author has been unable to obtain reliable information regarding the exact role of the CIA in the affairs of the CDIN. It is the author's opinion, based on sketchy reports, that the CIA was involved in the creation and activities of this political group. This opinion seems to be supported by two facts. In the first place, one of the leaders of the CDIN, General Phoumi Nosavan, was to receive CIA support when he embarked upon his campaign to unseat Souvanna Phouma in the last quarter of 1960. (See Chapter 10.) Secondly, Souvanna Phouma's personal aide told the author that, in the aftermath of the Kong Le coup of August, 1960, the CDIN requested the United States to provide extensive aid to the forces arrayed against Souvanna; these forces were backed by the CDIN. (Interview with Khamchan Pradith, New York, December 28, 1966.) A final account of the nature and extent of CIA involvement in the CDIN will have to await the release of information currently classified.

4. Champassak, pp. 63–64.

5. *The New York Times,* January 20, 1961. Five years later Souvanna said that he was forced to resign because of continued American opposition to his neutral policies. (*The Christian Science Monitor,* April 14, 1966.) In a personal interview with the author, Mr. Parsons denied responsibility for Souvanna's resignation.

6. U. S., Congress, House, Committee on Government Operations, *U. S. Aid Operations in Laos,* Hearings before the Subcommittee on Foreign Operations and Monetary Affairs, 86th Cong., 1st Sess., 1959, p. 8. When the devaluation took place in October 1958, under Phoui Sananikone's government, American aid was resumed.

7. *Ibid.,* pp. 191–92.

8. Letter from Prime Minister Souvanna Phouma to Chairman of the ICC, Vientiane, March 20, 1958, in Great Britain, Cmd. 2834, p. 131.

9. U. S., Department of State, *The Situation in Laos,* p. 14.

10. Quoted in Bernard B. Fall, "The Laos Tangle," *International Journal* (Toronto), 16 (Spring 1961):142.

11. Souvanna later said that Phoui's decision to allow Taiwan to set up a consulate general in Vientiane irked the Chinese and North Vietnamese and was one of the earliest steps in the internationalization of the Laotian crisis.

12. Jean Lacouture and Philippe Devillers, *La Fin D'Une Guerre* (Paris: Editions du Seuil, 1960), p. 359.

13. Letter from Pham Van Dong to Chairman, ICC, January 19, 1959, in A. M. Halpern and H. B. Fredman, *Communist Strategy in Laos* (Santa Monica: The Rand Corp., RM–2561, 1960), p. 28.

14. Text in Halpern and Fredman, pp. 30–31.

15. In its Declaration of July 21, 1954, the Laotian government said, "During the period between the cessation of hostilities in Viet Nam and the final settlement of that country's political problems, the Royal Government of Laos will not request foreign aid, . . . except for the purpose of its effective territorial defense." (Great Britain, Cmd. 9239, p. 42.)

16. The Chinese Communists, for example, called Phoui's statement "a grave act of unscrupulous violation of the Geneva agreements and forms a part of the U. S. imperialist plot of aggression against Indo-China." (Statement by Foreign Minister Chen Yi, February 18, 1959, in *Concerning the Situation in Laos* [Peking: Foreign Languages Press, 1959], p. 1.)

17. The numerical strength of the Pathet Lao has never been reliably determined and has received widely varying estimates. Fall states that the Pathet Lao's 1,500 regulars could count on the support of over 4,000 trained reserves who had fought with the Pathet Lao prior to their demobilization as a consequence of the November 1957 agreements. In addition, Fall says that the Pathet Lao could rely on further support from White and Black T'ai mountaineers from North Vietnam, who are very close in race and language to their brothers in Laos. (Bernard B. Fall, *Anatomy of a Crisis* [New York: Doubleday and Company, 1969], pp. 116-17.)

18. The following account is based on Champassak, pp. 77-80 and a Royal Government broadcast of May 17, 1959, printed in Halpern and Fredman, pp. 53-55. Champassak was the Minister of Information in Phoui's Government. The Pathet Lao's version of these events has not been published.

19. Champassak, p. 78.

20. Text of statement in Halpern and Fredman, pp. 71-72.

21. Text in Halpern and Fredman, pp. 75-78.

22. The generally favorable response of the tribes—with the significant exception of the Meos—to the Pathet Lao's appeal underscores the government's mistake in neglecting the welfare of the tribesmen and treating them with contempt.

23. Bernard B. Fall, *Street Without Joy* (Harrisburg: The Stackpole Company, 1961), pp. 302-303.

24. A senior French officer in close and frequent contact with the Laotian army said on August 11 that most Pathet Lao attacks were executed by units of ten to fifteen men armed with old weapons. See *The Times* (London), August 12, 1959.

25. Statement by the Laotian Government, July 29, 1959, in *Documents on International Affairs*, 1959, p. 261.

26. *The Times* (London), August 5, 1959.

27. Text of letter in U. S. Department of State, *The Situation in Laos*, pp. 19-20.

28. Letter from Laotian Foreign Minister Khamphan Panya to United Nations Secretary General Dag Hammarskjold, September 5, 1959, United Nations document S/4212, in U. S. Department of State, *American Foreign Policy: Current Documents*, 1959, p. 1228.

29. United Nations, Security Council, Official Records, Supplement for October, November, and December, 1959, *Report of the Security Council Sub-Committee under Resolution of 7 September, 1959*, S/4236, November 5, 1959.

30. *Le Monde,* October 17, 1959.

31. Champassak, p. 141.

32. *The New York Times,* April 26, 1960.

33. Souvanna Phouma, "Laos: le fond du problème," *France-Asie* 17 (March-April, 1961), p. 1825.

34. *The New York Times,* April 27, 1960.

35. Champassak, p. 148.

9
AMERICAN POLICY
THROUGH MID-1960

SO LONG AS Souvanna Phouma, as prime minister, had tried to effect a reconciliation with the Pathet Lao, outside countries did not become involved in Laotian affairs to an exceptional degree. When, however, Phoui Sananikone instituted his harsh policy against the communists, Laos began to attract the attention of other governments the way a burning building draws a crowd.

Foreign involvement in Laos had at least two major consequences. In the first place, it intensified the civil conflict. Utilizing nothing but its own resources, each side in the Laotian dispute simply was unable to wage war on a major scale. However, when outside governments began to pour in money, automatic weapons, ammunition, artillery, and so forth, the Laotian factions were able to conduct their fighting in a manner befitting the barbarism we have come to associate with the twentieth century. A second major result of foreign intervention was the prolongation of the internal struggle. In many contests—whether between father and son, labor and management, or one army and another—the weaker party eventually yields, either voluntarily or as a result of force. It may take a lengthy period of time for one party to establish itself as the master of the situation and for the other side to recognize this fact. This period was stretched in Laos because of foreign involvement. As often happened, the weaker party in Laos would not give in because it expected—and often received—outside assistance that rendered it once again the equal of its adversary. Succeeding chapters will reveal how external involvement in

161

Laos both aggravated the internal conflict and extended its duration.

In our consideration of foreign intrusion in Laos, we shall be primarily concerned with the policy of the United States. Our probe of American policy will be divided into two parts. In the present chapter, we shall direct our attention to Washington's diplomatic activities against the background of international politics as they swirled about Laos. In the following chapter, we shall make a studied examination of Washington's major instrument of policy in Laos: economic aid.

THE DIPLOMATIC SETTING

The first sign of foreign displeasure with Phoui Sananikone's anticommunist policies came from North Vietnam. As we have seen, Hanoi sent soldiers across the border near the Laotian town of Tchepone in December 1958, with the probable intention of demonstrating the North Vietnamese vexation with Phoui's tactics.

Wide-scale internationalization of the Laotian conflict began with Premier Phoui's statement of February 11, 1959, in which he declared that Laos was no longer bound by certain provisions of the Geneva agreements. On February 19, Chinese Foreign Minister Chen Yi wrote a letter to the British and Soviet foreign ministers, Co-Chairmen of the 1954 Geneva Conference, protesting Phoui's alleged "unilateral repudiation of the Geneva Agreements."[1] He also accused the State Department of supporting Phoui[2] and sending "large numbers of military personnel and arms to Laos."

The Chinese note, we may observe, followed a procedure that became standard for the diplomacy of the Laotian conflict. At the 1954 Geneva Conference, the foreign ministers of Great Britain and the Soviet Union were designated as Co-Chairmen and overseers of the accords. It followed that a government could most readily make known its views on Laos by transmitting a note to either or both of the Co-Chairmen.

On April 7 the United Kingdom commented on the Chinese note.[3] The British note referred to the clarifying statement issued by the Laotian Prime Minister on February 17, 1959, which stated that the Laotian Government had not repudiated the entirety of the Geneva agreements. The British also denied the Chinese accusation that the United States was introducing large numbers of military personnel and arms into Laos.

The Laotian Government's partially successful attempt, in May 1959, to coerce the two Pathet Lao battalions to disband or join the Royal Army occasioned another diplomatic exchange. On May 25, Chen Yi wrote a second letter to the Co-Chairmen, in which he stated that since his earlier note the situation in Laos had "continued to deteriorate." The Chinese Foreign Minister cited the Laotian Government's attempt to disarm the Pathet Lao and the house arrest of Pathet Lao leaders, calling these actions "the gravest violations of the Geneva agreements." He added that the Laotian Government took these measures "at the direct instigation and with the direct support of the United States. . . . These actions are re-kindling the flames of war which were extinguished for several years; they pose a serious threat to the peace of Indo-China and greatly aggravate tension in Southeast Asia." Chen then requested the Co-Chairmen to adopt measures to stop "these grave actions of the Royal Laotian Government violating the Geneva agreements," and specifically asked the Co-Chairmen to instruct the ICC to resume its activities.[4]

On June 22, Great Britain once again replied to the Chinese. Her Majesty's Government declared itself "unable to see any possible grounds for maintaining that the Laotian Government's actions in regard to the integration of the two ex-Pathet Lao battalions have in any way constituted a violation of the Geneva Agreement (or the agreements between the Laotian Government and the Pathet Lao of November, 1957)." "Nothing in the actions of the Laotian Government has created a threat to the peace and security of Indo-China," the note stated. In reference to the Chinese request that the Co-Chairmen instruct the ICC to resume its activities, the British note went on to say that "any attempt to re-establish the International Commission for Laos without the concurrence of the Royal Laotian Government would be inconsistent with the duty resting on all members of the Geneva Conference to respect the sovereignty and territorial integrity of Laos and to refrain from any interference in Laos's internal affairs."[5]

The diplomatic situation preceding the Pathet Lao's summer 1959 offensive was shaping into a confrontation between the British co-chairman of the 1954 Geneva Conference on one hand and Communist China (joined by other communist powers) on the other. The communist governments accused the Laotian government of violating the Geneva agreements and the November 1957 agreements with the Pathet Lao. The communist powers most vehemently objected to Prime Minister Phoui's statement of February 11, 1959, and the actions taken by the Laotian Government against the two Pathet Lao battalions in May. The communist states also called for the ICC to resume its activities. The United Kingdom, however, denied that the Laotian Government had violated either the Geneva agreement or the agreement of November 1957. Britain also counseled against forcing the ICC upon a sovereign Laotian government that had expressed its reluctance to allow the Commission's re-activation.

UNITED STATES SENDS MILITARY
MISSION TO VIENTIANE

The Pathet Lao opened its attacks on Government positions in July 1959. On July 29, the Laotian Government issued a statement which declared that recent attacks by rebel bands in Sam Neua had created "a new situation." The Government added that the attackers "represent new elements entirely armed, equipped and stiffened [*encadrés*] by the Democratic Republic of North Viet Nam."[6] In a statement on August 1, the United States voiced its concern over the outbreak of violence in Laos. "It is obvious that the former Pathet Lao rebels and their north Vietnamese Communist patrons wish to deny to the Kingdom of Laos the period of tranquillity this small young nation desires," Washington said. The United States accused the Pathet Lao, "backed by their Communist coconspirators across the jungle borders of Laos," of having never ceased "intriguing and agitating to prevent the consolidation of a non-Communist neutral Laos." The United States warned, "With this new outbreak of fighting it may be that the Communist imperialists in the Far East are seeking to provoke a serious crisis. The United States does not believe that the use of force should be rewarded by concessions contrary to the will of the Royal Lao Government." Washington closed with the admonition that it "views with concern what may be a deliberate effort of insurgent elements, apparently backed by Communists from outside, to provoke a crisis in Laos, a sovereign nation and a member of the United Nations."[7]

The Soviet Union added its voice to the diplomatic chorus inspired by the summer violence in Laos. On August 17, the Soviets issued a lengthy statement on the situation.[8] Echoing previous Chinese statements, the Soviet Government placed responsibility for the "threat of civil war" on the Phoui Sananikone regime which, the Soviets alleged, had violated the Geneva agreements of 1954 and the Vientiane agreements of 1956 and 1957. Moscow accused Phoui of launching a campaign of reprisals and persecutions against Pathet Lao followers. The Soviets said that Phoui further violated the Geneva agreements by importing military material and weapons into Laos; Phoui also "flooded the country with United States servicemen." Furthermore, Moscow charged, the Laotian Government, in violation of the Geneva agreements, concluded a treaty legalizing the presence of American servicemen in Laos and transferring the Laotian army to United States control.[9] By delegating military observers to sessions of the SEATO Council and to SEATO military exercises, the Laotian Government ignored its obligation to refrain from joining military alliances and to follow a policy of peace and neutrality. In defiance of the popular will as expressed in the May 1958 elections, the Laotian Government excluded NLHX representatives from the Laotian Government. The Soviet Union attributed the violence in Laos not to Chinese or North Vietnamese interference in Laotian internal affairs, but to popular dissatisfaction allegedly aroused by Phoui's policies. In the same statement, Moscow leveled the following charge at the United States:

> The facts show irrefutably that it is not the Democratic Republic of Viet Nam or the Chinese People's Republic, but the United States, that is introducing military equipment and material and also military personnel into Laos. The introduction of numerous military advisers into the royal army and the government machinery of Laos clearly shows who it is that is really interfering in the internal affairs of Laos.

In their statements on Laos, both the Soviets and the Chinese levelled charges of illegal interference by the United States. It now behooves us to learn what the Americans were actually doing in Laos.

The 1954 Geneva settlement had authorized France to maintain in Laos a military training mission not to exceed 1,500 men. France was also permitted to maintain two military bases in Laos, to be staffed by a total of no more than 3,500 officers and enlisted men.[10] Largely on account of the Algerian War, France never fully manned these military establishments. According to an estimate in February, 1959, the French garrison at Seno numbered 750 men and the training mission numbered 200 persons, including office workers and other administrative and maintenance personnel.[11] France never did set up a second military base.

The United States was piqued at France for not maintaining as large a training mission as possible and training the Royal Army to the fullest possible extent. After all, the Royal Army remained the ultimate weapon in the American containment effort against the Pathet Lao. The Pathet Lao's military attacks during July 1959 lent special urgency to bringing the Royal Army to maximum effectiveness. During that month, American, French, and Laotian negotiators sat down to work out an agreement whereby the Americans would share responsibility for training the Royal Army. These talks led to a Franco-Laotian communique in late July, which announced that Laos would ask the United States to attach some civilian technicians to the French military training mission for the purpose of helping to train Laotian troops.[12] *The New York Times* reported on August 10 that France and the United States would begin joint training of Laotian military forces later that month. The French would instruct the Laotians on tactics, while the Americans would teach the Laotians how to use and maintain weapons and other equipment. The report said that 107 Americans would participate in the training program; this figure included military personnel.

The initiation of direct American instruction to Laotian military forces represented a qualitative change in the relationship between the Laotian military and the United States. The United States had interpreted the Geneva agreements as prohibiting the establishment of a U. S. Military Assistance Advisory Group (MAAG) in Laos.[13] Consequently, in order to gain a hand in training the Royal Army, the United States resorted to the somewhat devious tactics described below by Admiral Harry D. Felt, Commander-in-Chief, Pacific.[14] The Admiral cited a pentalateral agreement signed in 1950,[15] under which the United States gave military assistance to France, which was fighting in Indochina. After the 1954 Geneva Conference, Admiral Felt continued, the United States supplied military hardware to Laos under this pentalateral agreement. In order to receive and oversee the equipment and make sure it was properly used, the United States established a Program Evaluation Office (PEO) attached to the U. S. Mission (USOM) in Laos. The PEO personnel were technically civilians, although many of them had had recent military experience.[16] The PEO did not train Laotian troops; France retained exclusive prerogative over troop training. The United States restricted itself to supplying military equipment to the Laotians.[17]

During the summer of 1959, a round of agreements among France, Laos, and the United States produced a system under which the United States established a training mission to instruct Laotians in the use of equipment supplied by the United States. Thus, by the end of October 1959, Washington had two military missions in Laos. The PEO, staffed with nearly 200 persons under the direction of General John A. Heintges, continued to oversee military equipment supplied by Washington. The newly created training mission, consisting of about 100 persons, was responsible for training Laotians in the use of this equipment. France, however, continued to retain exclusive responsibility for the Laotians' tactical training.[18]

At the same time that the United States established the training mission, Washington set up a contingency task force of soldiers and logistical support. This force, located on Okinawa under the command of General Donald M. Weller, was assigned to intervene in Laos if the need arose. The force was known as Task Force 116.[19]

Did the presence of American military aid violate the Geneva agreements, as the communists charged? The Agreement on the Cessation of Hostilities in Laos prohibited (a) "the introduction into Laos of any reinforcements of troops or military personnel from outside Laotian territory"—except for the French authorization—(Article 6), (b) "the establishment of new military bases" (Article 7), and (c) "the introduction into Laos of armaments, munitions and military equipment of all kinds

. . . with the exception of a specified quantity of armaments in categories specified as necessary for the defense of Laos" (Article 9). It is not clear whether the military equipment supplied by the United States fell under the limitation included in Article 9, since the Agreement did not designate the permissible level of armaments or who should determine the kinds and quantity of armaments covered by the qualification. By staffing the PEO with civilians, the United States did not violate the letter of the provision prohibiting "the introduction into Laos of any reinforcements of troops or military personnel." However, since many PEO personnel were either recently retired from the military or on detached service, it would seem that Washington did violate the intent of Article 6. When, in the fall of 1959, the United States established a military training mission to instruct Laotian troops in the use of American-supplied equipment, Washington clearly violated Article 6.[20]

Before castigating the United States, however, one should observe that the Geneva agreements had not remained inviolate before the American infringement. The Laotian Government alleged that North Vietnam violated the agreements well before the United States established its military training mission. The Royal Government claimed that Pathet Lao fighters received military training in North Vietnam, that North Vietnam sent military supplies to the Pathet Lao, and that North Vietnamese troops joined Pathet Lao troops in combat. It is true that Laos was never able to prove these accusations. One must, however, consider the findings of the United Nations Security Council subcommittee, which lent support to the accusation of North Vietnamese indirect aggression. Furthermore, the witnesses that the Laotian government supplied to the subcommittee recounted numerous instances of North Vietnamese aid to the Pathet Lao. The history of Pathet Lao–Viet Minh relations, especially their collaboration during the war against the French, suggests the logic of Viet Minh assistance to the Laotian communists. If, then, one accepts the likelihood that both North Vietnam and the United States violated the Geneva agreements, one is led to conclude that these agreements had become largely meaningless by the end of 1959. After the fall of 1959, when each side believed the other had violated the Geneva agreements, each side justified further violations by citing the illegal acts of its adversary.

It is tempting to blame the violations of the Geneva agreements on ambiguous language in the original documents. One cannot, however, attribute the violations to the wording of the agreements. The parties concerned regarded the Laotian conflict as touching upon their national security; they refused to qualify their responses by legal considerations, regardless of how the documents were phrased. The cardinal defect in the

Geneva arrangements lay not in the provisions themselves, but in the lack of devices to prevent states from allowing so-called political necessity to supersede international agreements.

Meanwhile, the fact of outside intervention was providing the basis for an intensified and prolonged struggle within Laos.

FURTHER DIPLOMATIC MOVES

In late August, the United States undertook a diplomatic campaign to justify further American intervention in Laos. On August 19, 1959, Washington replied to the Soviet accusations of August 17. The American note[21] said, in part,

> Contrary to implications in the Soviet statement, the Lao army is controlled exclusively by the sovereign Government of Laos. It is not under the direction of United States military personnel. The few American technicians in Laos are there at the request of the French and Lao Governments. Their function is to help the French military mission by training the Lao National Army in the use and maintenance of World War II type American equipment. We also have a few clerical and fiscal personnel assisting the Lao Army's administration. No American personnel are commanding, advising, or serving with Lao units. No American personnel are directing military operations. We have no troops in Laos. We do not have in Laos, nor have we provided that country, any heavy or modern equipment. We have no bases in Laos, nor airstrips. . . .

The American note further stated that the Laotian Government had not violated the Geneva agreements or the agreements of November 1957. The current violence in Laos was due to the Pathet Lao, one of whose battalions had "revolted" and escaped to North Vietnam, "thus providing further evidence of the link between the Pathet Lao and north Viet-Nam."[22] In mid-July, the note continued, the Pathet Lao and its political party, the NLHX, "perpetrated insurrection with outside help and direction. It is this Communist-directed action which has broken the peace in Laos."

One week later, on August 26, the State Department issued a statement justifying additional military aid in Laos. The statement said:

> The United States strongly supports the determination of the Royal Lao Government to resist Communist efforts to undermine the security and stability of Laos. Contrary to repetitious allegations from Hanoi, Peiping, and Moscow, the United States reiterates that it has no military bases, airstrips, or other military installations in Laos. The few Ameri-

can technicians in Laos are there at the request of the French and Lao Governments to help in the training of the Lao National Army in the use and maintenance of certain World War II type equipment.

The United States will continue to support reasonable approaches to achieve a peaceful solution to the current situation in Laos. Unlike the Sino-Soviet bloc, the United States does not believe that there should be recourse to the use of force in resolving this matter. However, the Communists have posed their threat to Laos in terms that require adequate military and police countermeasures if that nation's integrity is to be preserved. The United States has, therefore, responded to specific requests from the Lao Government for improving its defense position by authorizing sufficient additional aid to permit temporary emergency increases in the Lao National Army and in the village militia which provides local police protection. The additional aid will permit the specific increases desired by the Government of Laos. The United States has also in the course of the past week taken steps to help improve the mobility of the Royal Lao Army and to otherwise help give that small nation better means to withstand what appears even more clearly to be an extensive Communist design to disrupt and subvert Laos.[23]

The United States soon followed up this note with shipments of military equipment. The first shipment of small arms arrived in Vientiane on September 8. The next few days saw arrivals of American rifles, grenades, webbing equipment, mosquito nets, and water bottles—all for the Laotian army. About 100,000 hessian bags for rice were brought in from Thailand, to be used in airdropping rice to army outposts. Subsequent airlifts brought in unspecified amounts of Browning automatic rifles, machine guns, pistols, carbines, and wireless equipment to aid in communications.[24]

It was announced that with American aid, the Laotian army was to be increased from 25,000 to 29,000 and the village militia from 16,000 to 20,000.[25]

The United States argued that such aid did not violate the provisions of the 1954 Geneva Conference. The Geneva accords permitted replacement of arms and prohibited only modern arms, which the United States alleged it had not transferred to Laos. Even after the planned increase of the Laotian army, the total number of soldiers would still be fewer than the 30,000 men who had been under arms when the Geneva agreements were signed, Washington officials said.[26]

With as little publicity as possible, Major Clifton L. Speer, an officer in the U. S. Air Force Reserve and a civilian employee at Fort Hiachuca in Arizona, organized a group of fliers to quell Pathet Lao attacks. This allegedly private group, not sponsored by the U. S. Government, was called American Fliers for Laos. By the end of September, nine fliers had already gone to Laos.[27] The author has not been able to uncover such additional information about American Fliers for Laos, as whether they were actually in the employ of the U. S. Government at the time they went to Laos.

The United States added diplomatic support to its military assistance on behalf of Phoui's anticommunist government. It will be recalled that on September 4, 1959, Laotian Foreign Minister Khamphan Panya addressed a letter to UN Secretary General Dag Hammarskjold, accusing North Vietnamese elements of participating in attacks on Laotian border garrisons and requesting the dispatch of an emergency force to Laos. The following day the State Department promised to support United Nations consideration of the Royal Lao Government's appeal. The statement went on to level several accusations against the communists. Washington accused North Vietnam of giving "active support" to forces attacking Royal Army forces in the northeast on August 30. The statement continued,

> It is now clear that the Communist bloc does not intend to permit the sovereign Lao Government to remain at peace. The Communist bloc apparently intends to foment and direct a rebellion within Laos and to give extensive support to the attempt to seize important areas and otherwise to prevent the establishment of those peaceful conditions necessary to implement basic economic and social programs. In short the Communist intervention is apparently aimed at preventing the Lao people from realizing their just hopes for a better life.

The note then listed four factors allegedly demonstrating outside communist intervention in Laos:

1. Certain assistance, including supplies and military weapons, given to the Pathet Lao. Since such material was unavailable in Laos, the Pathet Lao could have obtained it only from external sources.
2. Propaganda emanating simultaneously from Hanoi, Peking, and Moscow to the effect that the United States was instigating the Laotian Government to start a civil war.
3. Propaganda from Hanoi, Peking, and Moscow aimed at confusing world opinion and saying that the United States was using Laos as a military base.
4. The fact that the military outbreak in Laos followed conferences in Moscow and Peking between Ho Chi Minh and Soviet and Chinese leaders and also conferences in Moscow between two members of the North Vietnamese Politburo and Soviet Deputy Prime Minister Anastas Mikoyan.[28]

Finally, Washington warned that "any further augmentation of the invading force or continued material support thereof by Communists in north Viet-Nam will require a major change in the nature and magnitude of the Royal Lao Government's need for support."[29]

The four points of evidence cited by the State Department seem hardly conclusive. The first point most clearly indicates outside communist intervention in the form of providing supplies and military equipment. However, simultaneous propaganda broadcasts do not establish intervention in the form of direct support to fighting forces. Nor did Ho Chi Minh's visit to Moscow and Peking prove that communist leaders had decided to intervene in the Laotian conflict; more would have to be known concerning what transpired during the visit before one could arrive at such a conclusion.

However ambiguous Washington's evidence may have been, we may note that the United States took the position that the Pathet Lao was receiving aid from outside. Thus, from September 1959, both the United States and the communists based their policies on the assumption that the *other* side in the Laotian civil war was receiving external assistance. In response, each outside agent increased aid to its faction in Laos. This upward spiral of foreign help had the dual effect of intensifying the dispute and protracting it.

THE AMERICAN WHITE PAPER

Toward the end of 1959, it had become apparent to American officials that Phoui would need additional United States aid if he were to drive the communist threat from Laos successfully. American policymakers, while prepared to render further assistance, did not wish to appear to violate the agreements signed in Geneva in 1954. Consequently, Washington issued a major statement on Laos in September 1959. The main purpose of the white paper, entitled *The Situation in Laos*,[30] was to explain and justify as legal American intervention in that embattled country.

A passage from the preface summarized the tone of the white paper. The selection stated, "The fighting which began in Laos in July 1959 . . . is part of the pattern of Communist bloc aggressiveness that is basic to much of the tension existing in the world today."

The history of alleged outside aid to the Pathet Lao was a major theme in the white paper. The document said,

> The Communist forces that now threaten the independence of Laos owe their strength to the direction and support they have received from Communist countries, especially Communist China and even more particularly Communist north Viet-Nam. The history of the past ten years is witness to the determination of the Communists and particularly of

north Viet-Nam . . . to prevent the people of Laos from progressing freely and peacefully toward the social and economic development of their country.[31]

After the Geneva Conference, the State Department paper noted, the Pathet Lao increased its military forces from 1,000 men in 1954 to 6,000 in February 1958. This increment, the State Department admitted, could have been accomplished without outside help. "The corresponding increases in Pathet Lao military equipment, however, could have resulted only from supply movements originating in or passing through north Viet-Nam in clear violation of the Agreement on the Cessation of Hostilities in Laos (Articles 9 and 10)."[32]

When the Pathet Lao regrouped in the provinces of Sam Neua and Phong Saly, the white paper alleged, a nucleus of well-indoctrinated propagandists remained throughout Laos. These propagandists constituted a subversive network whose mission, the document claimed, included preparation of arms caches and the reception of agents sent from Sam Neua. These agents were dispatched from Sam Neua throughout Laos starting in May 1955.[33]

By the middle of 1956, the white paper continued, the Pathet Lao and North Vietnam were concentrating on entrenching their position in Sam Neua and Phong Saly and extending their operations throughout Laos. By that time the Pathet Lao had recruited over 3,000 partisans in the two northern provinces. As a result of this increased manpower, the Pathet Lao could afford to release hard-core communists from Sam Neua for service on clandestine missions throughout Laos. The white paper alleged that several hundred such agents were dispersed throughout Laos during 1956. These cadres established administrative committees, contacted Pathet Lao sympathizers, established arms depots and recruited manpower for guerrilla and intelligence work. Most of these cadres operated in areas occupied by the Viet Minh in 1953 and 1954, especially the following provinces: Vientiane, Luang Prabang, Xieng Khouang, Savannakhet, and Thakhek. The cadres also infiltrated the region of the Bolovens Plateau, which encompassed parts of Saravane, Champassak, and Attopeu provinces.[34]

In detailing communist assistance to the Pathet Lao, the United States was clearly trying to justify its own intervention in Laotian affairs. According to Washington, American aid to the Royal Government came only in response to communist support for the Pathet Lao. The Americans were not the aggressors. Quite the contrary; the United States was only trying to maintain the status quo against an insurgent movement.

The American white paper foreshadowed additional American aid for the purpose of containing communism in Laos. This support was next to come in the realm of diplomacy.

UN MISSION VISITS LAOS—AMERICAN REACTION

The United States was well aware that the international community would not accept at face value the American accusations of outside communist interference in Laos. After all, Washington was hardly an impartial observer. What better way to gain confirmation of these charges, reasoned American policymakers, than by sending a United Nations mission to Laos? Accordingly, Washington supported Laos's request for the dispatch of a United Nations team to Laos. In fact, the United States, along with France and the United Kingdom, sponsored the Security Council resolution calling for the appointment of a subcommittee to investigate the situation there. In introducing the draft resolution to the Security Council, Ambassador Henry Cabot Lodge said,

> The United States believes that there is no doubt at all that aggression is being committed. The newspapers are full of it. It is common knowledge. But we realize of course that there may be those around this table who do not agree.[35]

The United Nations subcommittee visited Laos from September 15 to October 13, 1959. The key passage in the subcommittee's report, discussed in a previous chapter, said, "The ensemble of information submitted to the Sub-committee did not clearly establish whether there were crossings of the frontier by regular troops of the D.R.V.N."[36]

The subcommittee's findings disappointed American officials, who had hoped that the United Nations would hold up North Vietnamese violations of Laotian territory for the world to see and condemn. The subcommittee's report, however, did not discount the possibility that North Vietnamese who were not members of the regular army may have assisted the Pathet Lao. The report noted that certain of the guerrilla operations that had occurred between July 16 and October 11 "must have had a centralized co-ordination." The report also said, "Practically all witnesses (forty out of forty-one) stated that the hostile elements received support from the territory of the D.R.V.N. consisting mainly of equipment, arms, ammunition, supplies, and the help of political cadres." Elsewhere the report stated, "Witnesses reported that in certain cases there had been participation of armed elements with ethnic Viet-Namese characteristics, but they did not identify them as belonging to North Viet-Namese regular army units."[37] American charges of North Vietnamese intervention did not specify that such interference was limited to North Vietnamese regular army troops. Therefore, American endorsement[38] of the subcommittee's report in no way implied American admission that North Vietnam was not supplying aid of various sorts to the Pathet Lao.

Washington's attitude toward the subcommittee's findings was most clearly revealed in a State Department release issued January 7, 1961. The relevant passage cited the launching by the communists of a series of military actions in Laos starting in mid-July 1959. The document continued,

> These actions were made possible through external direction and assistance. Then, following a Lao appeal to the United Nations, this Communist military advance terminated almost simultaneously with the appearance on the scene of a subcommittee of the Security Council, and every attempt was made by the Communists to erase evidences of external support.[39]

The United States, in other words, adhered to its view that outside communist sources supported the Pathet Lao's campaign of violence in the summer of 1959. The United States continued to act on this assumption after the Security Council's subcommittee filed its report. The above-quoted passage indicates that, in Washington's thinking, the subcommittee may have been unable to establish proof of North Vietnamese aggression because when the subcommittee reached Vientiane, the communists tried "to erase evidences of external support." This statement implies that the subcommittee's report failed to prove that North Vietnam had not supported the Pathet Lao both before and after the investigation. In summary, the United States, while not overjoyed at the subcommittee's report, did not find in the report any reason for discontinuing its aid to the Royal Government of Laos.

As we have noted previously, the Pathet Lao halted their military campaign at about the time that the United Nations subcommittee visited Laos, except for occasional jabs. The rivalry between the Government and the Pathet Lao shifted from the military to the political sphere. On October 24 the Government postponed the trial of Souphanouvong and seven other Pathet Lao leaders held in custody; no new date was set.[40]

The first half of 1960 witnessed a further movement of the Laotian government toward an authoritarian if pro-Western position. As we have already seen, Phoumi Nosavan led a *coup d'état* against Phoui Sananikone, who seemed to be inclining toward a more compromising position with regard to the Pathet Lao. The April 1960 elections returned a decidedly right-wing regime.

American economic and military aid continued to flow to Laos. In fiscal 1960 the United States gave Laos $13,542,000 in military aid and $42,124,000 in economic aid, making a total of $55,666,000.[41] This sum represented an increase of $24,666,000 over the amount appropriated for fiscal 1959.

In this chapter we have traced the early stages in the internationalization of the Laotian dispute, particularly America's increased involvement. In July 1959, the United States established a second military mission, with the purpose of training Laotians in the use of military equipment supplied in growing quantities by Washington. The Soviet Union and Red China also became more involved in the Laotian conflict during 1959 and the first half of 1960. In a series of diplomatic notes, these two communist countries supported the Pathet Lao and accused Phoui's government of violating the Geneva accords. The communists also criticized the United States for supplying aid to the Royal Army, which was fighting the Pathet Lao.

As the Laotian internal conflict prepared to lunge toward its climax in the next two years, we may make two observations about the effect of the developments described in this chapter upon the future course of events in Laos.

In the first place, neither the United States nor the Soviet Union, each of which was to play a crucial role in the neutralization settlement of 1962, chose to define the Laotian conflict as a matter of vital interest. Neither power served notice that its position, whether in support of the Royal Government or the Pathet Lao, was nonnegotiable. Both nations left room for retreat and compromise, without ever saying so. In 1961 and 1962, when the United States and the Soviet Union decided to compromise on Laos, this restraint—in not branding Laos a matter of vital interest— proved invaluable. Assuredly, both the Soviets and the Americans would have had much more trouble in backing down from their original stances in Laos had they stated, back in 1959 and 1960, that compromise in Laos was equivalent to abandoning a vital interest or a sacred commitment.

It may further be noted that foreign intervention gave neither the Pathet Lao nor the pro-Western government in Vientiane much incentive for reducing its demands and agreeing to a compromise settlement. The Americans urged Phoui's regime to carry out repressive measures against the Pathet Lao, including the destruction of their fighting forces. In addition, the United States supplied equipment and training to the Royal Army, thereby heightening Phoui's expectation that further support would be forthcoming. The American commitment, instead of persuading Phoui and the regime that succeeded him to moderate their positions, encouraged them to assume an increasingly rigid stance.

Similarly, Soviet and North Vietnamese support for the Pathet Lao gave the communists reason to believe that they had no need to capitulate or reduce their demands. The Pathet Lao no doubt assumed that they would receive additional external support if needed. Therefore, neither the Pathet Lao nor the Vientiane government had substantial incentive to moderate its bargaining position in the direction of compromise.

By strengthening the belief that increased outside assistance was forthcoming, the foreign powers prolonged and aggravated the Laotian conflict in 1959 and the first half of 1960.

NOTES

1. *Documents on International Affairs,* 1959, pp. 252–53.

2. After Phoui's statement, Lincoln White, State Department press officer, said,

Obviously the Laos Government considers the provisions of the Geneva agreement applicable to Laos have been complied with.

We respect that determination. Further, we consider the Prime Minister's statement as a reaffirmation by the Laos Government of its ideal of peace and adherence to the principles of friendly relationships with its neighbors as expressed in the Charter of the United Nations.

Laos is a small nation that poses no threat to anyone and we hope it will be allowed to work out its own problems without outside interference. (*Ibid.,* p. 254.)

3. *Documents on International Affairs,* 1959, pp. 253–55.

4. *Ibid.*

5. *Ibid.,* pp. 256–59.

6. *Ibid.,* pp. 260–61.

7. U. S. Department of State, *American Foreign Policy,* 1959, p. 1223.

8. Text in *Documents on International Affairs,* 1959, pp. 261–65.

9. The American military training mission is discussed later on in this chapter.

10. *Agreement on the Cessation of Hostilities in Laos,* Articles 6 and 8, in Great Britain, Cmd. 9239, p. 20.

11. *The New York Times,* February 13, 1959.

12. *Le Monde,* July 28, 1959.

13. See testimony of Captain Berton A. Robbins, Jr., Director, Far East Regional Office, Office of the Assistant Secretary of Defense for International Security Affairs, in U. S. Congress, House, Committee on Foreign Affairs, *Hearings, Mutual Security Act of 1957,* 85th Cong., 1st Sess., 1957, p. 1114. The State Department concurred in this limitation. (House Committee on Government Operations, *United States Aid Operations in Laos: Seventh Report,* 1959, pp. 8–9.)

14. U. S. Congress, House, Committee on Foreign Affairs, *Hearings, Mutual Security Act of 1961,* 87th Cong., 1st Sess., 1961, p. 338.

15. Agreement for Mutual Defense Assistance in Indochina between the United States of America and Cambodia, France, Laos, and Vietnam, December 23, 1950, in U.S. Department of State, *United States Treaties and Other International Agreements,* vol. 3, part 2, TAIS 2447, 1953.

16. Massachusetts Representative Silvio O. Conte, who visited Laos in 1959, described the PEO as follows, "They were all ex-Marines and Army boys. . . ." (U.S. Congress, House, Committee on Appropriations, *Hearings, Foreign Opera-*

tions Appropriations for 1962, 87th Cong., 1st Sess., 1961, p. 589.) General John A. Heintges, Chief of the PEO from late 1958 to January 1961, called the PEO "a civilian organization very similar to a MAAG." (U.S. Congress, Senate, Committee on Armed Services, *Military Cold War Education and Speech Review Policies,* Hearings before the Special Preparedness Subcommittee, Part V, 87th Cong., 2d Sess., 1962, p. 2371.) The PEO's first Chief was a Reserve Officer named Unger; he was not retired when he went to Laos. His successor, Brigadier General Rothwell H. Brown, arrived in Laos in February 1957, just after his retirement. Brown was succeeded by General Heintges.

17. This equipment consisted mostly of standard World War II items, including rifles, 105 mm. howitzers, small machine guns, mortars, bazookas, anti-tank guns, light tanks, armored cars, trucks, small observer planes and C-47 transport planes. (*The New York Times,* October 25, 1959.)

18. As of October 25, 1959, Laotian forces consisted of 25,000 army troops. An auto-defense force (village militia) also existed. The third element in the Laotian force was the corps of 3,000 policemen. The army included 27 battalions of 750 men each. There were 24 infantry battalions, 2 airborne battalions and 1 artillery battalion. (*Ibid.*)

19. Arthur J. Dommen, *Conflict in Laos* (New York: Frederick A. Praeger, 1964), p. 137.

20. The first paragraph of Article 6 says, "With effect from the proclamation of the cease-fire the introduction into Laos of any reinforcements of troops or military personnel from outside Laotian territory is prohibited." The *only* ones exempted from this restriction were the French (Articles 6 and 8).

21. Text in U. S. Department of State, *American Foreign Policy,* 1959, pp. 1225-26.

22. It has never been confirmed whether the escaped battalion went to North Vietnam or remained in hiding in Laos.

23. U. S. Department of State, *American Foreign Policy,* 1959, p. 1227.

24. The reports of American aid were contained in *The Times* (London), September 9, 10, and 18, 1959.

25. *The New York Times,* August 27, 1959.

26. *The Times* (London), August 28, 1959.

27. *The New York Times,* September 27, 1959.

28. Ho Chi Minh spent about a month in the Soviet Union, departing from Moscow August 1. He subsequently spent the period August 13–25 in Peking.

29. The full text of the note is printed in U. S. Department of State, *American Foreign Policy,* 1959, pp. 1228–30.

30. U. S. Department of State, *The Situation in Laos,* 1959.

31. *Ibid.,* preface.

32. *Ibid.,* p. 8.

33. *Ibid.*

34. *Ibid.*

35. U. S. Department of State, *American Foreign Policy,* 1959, p. 1230.

36. *Ibid.,* p. 1244.

37. *Ibid.*

38. Replying to a question at a news conference on November 12, 1959, Secretary of State Herter said,

I think that, on the whole, considering the facilities that the sub-committee had, it made a very objective and good report. As you know, paragraph . . . referred particularly to the witnesses who had been interviewed, all of whom, or 40 out of 41 of them, had testified to the effect that the Pathet Lao or enemy groups that the witnesses had come in touch with had received their supplies, equipment, logistical assistance, and the help of political cadres, from across the border.

(*Ibid.*, p. 1245.) Note that Secretary Herter, while endorsing the subcommittee's conclusion, took the opportunity to list several forms of indirect aggression allegedly engaged in by North Vietnam.

39. *The New York Times,* January 8, 1961. The American position coincides with that taken by Champassak.

40. *Le Monde,* October 25–26, 1959. Souphanouvong and the other leaders escaped before the trial took place.

41. U. S. Congress, Senate, Committee on Appropriation, *Hearings, Foreign Assistance and Related Agencies Appropriations for 1962,* 87th Cong., 1st Sess., 1961, p. 297.

10
THE AMERICAN AID PROGRAM

AS THE PREVIOUS chapter makes clear, American aid to Laos was a major issue in the diplomacy of the Laotian conflict. Much of the diplomatic correspondence concerned itself with either condemning or justifying such assistance. American aid, as we shall see, also figured heavily in the dramatic events of the latter half of 1960 up to the final settlement in July 1962. In view of the central role occupied by American aid in the Laotian drama, it becomes advisable to devote some pages to the American aid program.

American aid to Laos has acquired a fair degree of notoriety. The American aid program in Laos has been held up as a model of the iniquity in which an aid program can wallow if administered with a sufficient quantity of ineptitude combined with a full measure of exuberance. It is tempting, in fact, to conclude from the Laotian experience that all foreign assistance is wasteful if not downright criminal, and that the American foreign aid program should be cancelled in its entirety. Such reasoning, however, reveals a lack of maturity and perspective. It should be expected that any program involving billions of dollars, as has American foreign aid since its inception after World War II, would exhibit some irregularity. Why should the men distributing or receiving such monies be more honest or able than people involved in other projects in which questionable practices come to light but do not occasion the publicity that attaches to foreign aid?

I have chosen to preface this chapter on American aid to Laos with these remarks in order to warn the reader not to draw unwarranted conclusions about the entire aid program from the single case of Laos. Practically every error that could be made in the American aid program to Laos was made. However, to conclude from this that American foreign aid should be discontinued would be equivalent to arguing that the space program should be cancelled because one missile exploded on its launching pad.[1]

Before delving into the operation of the American aid program we should pause, perhaps, to recall the purpose for which the aid was given. As we discovered in Chapter 9, the primary purpose of American aid was to help contain communism in Laos. A certain portion of assistance was devoted to economic development and raising the general living standard, but the great bulk of aid supported the Royal Army and police. Indeed, the level of American aid to Laos—approximately $40 million per year— was based primarily upon the cost of maintaining the armed forces, for which the United States had assumed the full cost (salaries, equipment, and so on). Much of the assistance allegedly for economic development, such as the highway-building program, was actually intended less for economic development that for facilitating the army's task of combatting the Pathet Lao. It has already been noted that the strategy for containing communism in Laos was to help the army defeat the Pathet Lao, not to assist the government in gaining the support of the people in exchange for desired social services.

MECHANICS OF THE AID PROGRAM

Most economic aid[2] to Laos was distributed either through the commercial import program or by cash grants. The commercial import program worked as follows. The U. S. Government would open a bank account in the United States and authorize the bank to pay dollars to American exporters who sold goods to importers in Laos. In other words, the United States paid for the goods and then saw that they were transferred to Laotian importers. The latter did not pay any money to American exporters. Instead, when the Laotian importer gained title to the goods, he paid the Bank of Laos an amount of kip equal to the dollar value of the merchandise. This account was called the counterpart fund. The Laotian government then used the counterpart fund to purchase local goods and services, just as it would use tax revenues. Thus, the United States was able to finance the Laotian government to the extent that importers in Laos brought in goods from the United States. This means of generating economic development, it can be seen, had a severe limitation. The amount of American aid that could be supplied by this system was restricted by the volume of goods that Laotian importers wished to bring into the country.[3] In Laos, where per capita income averaged about $50 per year, demand for imported goods was not high.

In order to funnel more aid to Laos than the commercial import program could provide, Washington utilized cash grants. According to the cash grant method, the United States deposited dollars in the Laotian central bank. The Laotian government then borrowed the dollars and set aside an equivalent amount of kip in a special counterpart fund, in which the dollars backed the kip. The Laotian Government then used the kip in the counterpart fund to purchase local goods and services. In order to repay the central bank, the Laotian Government sold the dollars it borrowed to Laotian importers, who paid for the dollars in kip. The Government then used the kip to repay the central bank. The importers used the dollars to buy imports. Under this program, the United States could supply unlimited funds to Laos. There was, however, a danger of inflation, if Laotian importers could not be induced to purchase dollars from the Laotian Government and to import merchandise of equal dollar value.

In order to control imports under both the cash grant and the commercial import program, the Laotian Government issued licenses to Laotian importers to bring in goods. Thus, in theory, the Laotian Government retained direction over what goods entered the country.

CRITICISM OF AMERICAN AID

The American aid program in Laos has been subjected to two Congressional investigations. In May 1958, the House Committee on Foreign Affairs held hearings on the mutual security program in Laos. In the spring of 1959, the House Committee on Government Operations sponsored hearings and then issued a report on American aid to Laos. Much of the following material is based on these sources.

During the spring of 1958, the Subcommittee on the Far East and Pacific, of the House Committee on Foreign Affairs, conducted hearings on American aid to Laos. These hearings brought to light an internal United States report on American aid to Laos filed by the General Accounting Office (GAO). A GAO official, Robert F. Keller, testified before the subcommittee on deficiencies in the American aid program to Laos, based upon the findings of the GAO report.[4] Keller listed the following areas of the aid program that called for improvement:

1. *Need for monetary reform.* Keller called the existing official exchange rate of 35 kip to a dollar "unrealistically low." The exchange rate in Thailand and Hong Kong was 100 kip to a dollar. The official rate, Keller said, "substantially increases the cost of United States aid." Use of this rate contributed to certain abuses, such as profiteering, diversion of commodities, and political influence in obtaining import licenses.[5]

2. *Malpractices in the importation of commodities.* Most of these irregularities, Keller said, were related to the use of cash grants.

   (a). Improprieties in issuing import licenses. The International Cooperation Administration (ICA), which ran foreign aid, was supposed to approve Laotian issuance of import licenses for permission to use foreign exchange. However, Keller said, there were no systematic import plans, no adequate statistical data to determine commodity requirements, no definite criteria for identifying legitimate importers, and insufficient trained personnel to administer the operation properly. Laotian government officials were financially interested in some importing firms. Sometimes the Laotian Government bypassed the ICA in issuing licenses.

   (b). Diversions and overpricing of commodities. Some merchandise consigned to Laos was diverted enroute (thereby defeating the anti-inflationary purposes of the commodity import program). Some goods that reached Laos were later illegally shipped out of the country. Laotians overpriced goods by falsifying invoices and delivering inferior goods.

3. *Ineffective control of commodity program.* Keller said that ICA control procedures had not corrected the various malpractices listed above. The U. S. Mission was not able to conduct adequate end-use inspections because of insufficient personnel, Laotian reluctance to permit such inspections, and inadequate information concerning commodities purchased with cash grants. Keller said, "Of the relatively few inspections made, several evidenced unsatisfactory use of ICA-financed goods or improprieties in one form or another but little positive action appears to have been taken."[6]

4. *Military budget support.* Keller warned that the United States may be paying more than is necessary.[7]

5. *Project assistance.*

   (a). Roads. Much of ICA-financed equipment was abused. Property controls were inadequate.

   (b). Civil police administration. Although the police force was expanded from 800 to 2,900 men, only 400 had received police training.

One fact that emerged from these hearings was the lack of American control over cash-grant funds once they were handed over to the Laotian Government. The following exchange took place between Representative Kelly and a GAO official, George Staples:

> Mrs. Kelly. When this money is put in the bank in the United States, to the credit of the foreign government—
> Mr. Staples. It is placed to the credit of the foreign government.
> Mrs. Kelly. Have we no control over that, at that point?
> Mr. Staples. Generally not; no.
> Mrs. Kelly. No one has control over it? The Government deposits it in the foreign government's name at that point and we cannot control it?
> Mr. Staples. That is right.[8]

After Staples completed his testimony, J. Graham Parsons, Deputy Assistant Secretary of State for Far Eastern Affairs and a former Ambassador to Laos,[9] took the stand. He was asked to comment on GAO's findings.

Parsons stressed the political benefits that, in his opinion, the aid program had netted for the United States. Referring to the elections of May 4, 1958—the results of which were not yet fully in—Parsons said that early information concerning the results for fifteen seats indicated that the Pathet Lao would win only two. (In fact, the communists captured nine seats and their leftist allies won four.)

> We therefore have some basis for hoping that when the present Government resigns, as it is committed to do after the elections, a government may be formed which does not include Communists. If that comes about, the situation in Laos will have arrived at a point where the fighting has been ended, the Communists have been rolled back in the two Provinces, the Communists will have been eliminated from the Government, and Laos will be united and independent. It is also a country which has no Soviet, Communist Chinese, or other Communist bloc diplomatic representation, and a country which has not as yet accepted any aid from Communists.
> If this is the situation . . . it will be due, in part, to our aid and will, I hope, indicate, in part, what you gentlemen and the rest of us will have received in value for our aid money. . . . The main point is that the integrity and independence of Laos in the free world will have been preserved.[10]

Parsons added that negotiations with the Lao Government to modify the exchange rate were pending.[11] He said that procedures recently imple-

mented prohibited issuance of import licenses unless countersigned by a
U. S. representative.

Another witness at the hearing was Carter DePaul, Deputy Assistant
to the Director for Liaison, ICA, and former Chief of the U. S. aid program in Laos.[12] DePaul was asked about the GAO report, which said,
"At the time of our field examination [March 1958], no end-use inspections
were being made, principally because the Embassy had restricted ICA
mission representatives from contacting Lao nationals."[13] DePaul said
that the Laotian Government had complained that it did not want Americans roaming around. The communists, he said, were charging that the
Royal Government had done nothing but exchange French masters for
American ones, and they cited as proof the fact that Americans were
going about looking into the affairs of the Laotian government. DePaul
also explained that imports brought in under the commercial-import program were bought by Laotian importers with cash-grant dollars paid for
by the Laotian Government. After the Laotian Government bought these
dollars (with kip), he said, the dollars became the property of the Laotian
Government and passed beyond American control. End-use investigations
would have to be carried out among the private importing community in
Laos, not with the Laotian Government. DePaul said,

> I, myself, had a clear interpretation of this problem from the Comp-
> troller of the ICA. It was my understanding that the full force of our
> legal provisions could not and did not apply to dollars of this kind.[14]

To remedy this lack of American control, DePaul explained, USOM
tried to work out an arrangement with the Laotian Government whereby
the Laotians and the Americans would consult together on the ultimate
disposition of the aid funds. Until December 1956, when the Laotian
Government issued four import licenses outside of regular channels, those
consultations had worked satisfactorily. Even after the consultations had
taken place, however, USOM was not authorized to check on Laotian
adherence to the agreements. "The Lao Government is most reluctant to
permit us to have full entree and full scope of operation in this field,"
DePaul said.[15]

Testifying at a later date, DePaul acknowledged many of the deficiencies
cited by the GAO report. He added, however, that he knew no way to
stop diversions of goods before they reached Laos or after they had been
brought into the country. He cited the 600-mile river boundary with
Thailand, which, he said, was nearly impossible to patrol. To curtail
diversions, he recommended strengthening the services of the Lao Government.

DePaul favored continuance of American aid despite the lack of control over it. He stated,

> Here you have a linkage between a commercial import problem and paying the troops. Obviously you cannot lightly suspend the money to pay the troops in an army which is sitting just south of the Communist border in a country which is under extreme harassment and perhaps on certain of these occasions a country whose chief officers—let us say almost the entire Cabinet—are visiting Peking, and being given red carpet treatment in that city.[16]

DePaul's statement brings to mind the remarks by former ambassador Parsons cited earlier. Both officials sounded the theme that American aid had been successful. As evidence, they highlighted the fact that the communists had made little headway in Laos. Neither statement, in point of fact, actually demonstrated that the communists had been stymied *because* of American aid; they merely assumed that American aid had done the trick. Of more relevance for our purposes, however, is the fact that both officials were willing to overlook inefficient use of American resources as well as corruption on the part of Laotian officials. What matter such trivialities, they argued, so long as the aid was contributing to the containment of communism? Americans were soon to discover, however, that measures useful for containing communism in the short run do not necessarily have the same effect in the long run. In fact, some of these short run methods may actually enhance communist chances later on. What is the effect, for instance, of a foreign aid program which supports a regime under which the distribution of wealth favors a few but condemns the many to a marginal existence? Does a central government, trying to gain the support of a wary populace, truly advance its cause (and consequently strike at a communist movement) by engaging in well-publicized corruption, which swells the pockets of the favored few but deprives the masses of what they had been promised? These factors, as well as others that American officials were willing to disregard, assume particular importance in a country where the people have grown skeptical of the central government and are inclined to listen patiently to a clandestine movement that promises them a better life. Later on in this narrative, we shall find occasion to explore these matters in more detail. For the present, however, we must content ourselves with noting that American officials were satisfied with an aid program that bolstered the various elements in Laos that were most actively waging the struggle against the Pathet Lao: the army, the police, and the civil administration.

A few months after the House subcommittee conducted its hearings, an

American aid official who had left ICA wrote about his experiences in Laos.[17] The official, Haynes Miller, had been an end-use auditor in that country. His function was to make sure that aid funds were being used efficiently for the purposes to which they were assigned. Miller described several irregularities that he had personally confronted while helping to administer the aid program in Laos. For example, while investigating all rice shipments purportedly imported into Laos in 1956, he found:

1. The value of the rice was not $133 per ton—the price approved by the ICA and the Laotian Import-Export Board—but approximately $45 per ton; hence the United States was paying three times the value of the rice. Needless to say, someone was reaping a handsome profit from the difference.

2. At least $2 million of the $3.3 million spent for rice in 1956 represented a fraudulent dollar profit.

3. Although Laos was producing more than enough rice for its own needs, $3.3 million was spent in 1956 to import 24,000 tons of glutinous rice. "I could find no proof, except in one case involving only one hundred tons, that any rice at all had actually been imported into Laos during 1956," Miller wrote.[18]

The president of the Varivarn Company, an exporting firm in Bangkok, told Miller he had given his letterhead to a Laotian, Bouachan Intavong, who filled out the necessary documents to simulate the importation of 1,400 tons of rice, which was never brought into Laos.

In another transaction, Intavong received a license from the Import-Export Board to import twenty German-made generators from Thailand. Actually, these generators were American and had originally been sold to the U. S. Army in 1943 or 1944 for a total of $14,900. They were imported into Laos under an import license on which the United States paid $162,000 in Bangkok.

Miller's duties had brought him into contact with the road-building program, the largest single item under the category of project assistance. According to Miller, the road-building program started in 1955, when ICA employed Transportation Consultants Inc. (TCI) of Washington, D. C., to design a basic road pattern for Laos. Road equipment worth $1,760,000 was imported from the United States. The following year, two Americans, Willis Bird and G. A. Peabody, organized the Universal Construction Company in Bangkok. Within a year Universal had obtained six contracts with ICA and additional contracts with the Laotian government, whose officials said they had met Peabody through USOM's public works director, Edward T. McNamara. Universal received all of the heavy road-building equipment paid for with American funds as well as almost all of the equipment financed under the Colombo Plan. Within six months, Miller said, Universal's untrained operators had damaged 40 percent of the equipment.

Peabody obtained two contracts to receive, service, and catalogue the equipment and do some work on a short stretch of road outside Vientiane. USOM's public works division, headed by McNamara, certified Universal's performance, and Peabody was paid a total of $75,000. Yet, Miller stated, his investigation showed that Universal had fulfilled neither contract.

In May 1957, Universal was awarded a contract, allegedly handed out by TCI, which was working for ICA, to construct a ferry ramp and customs compound at what Miller called an "exorbitant" price. Shortly after TCI signed the contract with Universal, the TCI representative who had negotiated the contract quit TCI and went to work for Universal. One year later, McNamara left ICA and went to work for TCI.

Miller wrote that after inspecting Universal's performance,

> I concluded that the company had not executed any single contract; that none of its contracts contained adequate specifications; that the contract quotations were exorbitant; that the contractor did not have personnel adequate either in number or training to complete any of its contracts; and that ICA personnel appeared to be interested in some of the contracts.
>
> I had of course begun to report my findings to ICA, but I was soon ordered to drop my investigations of the possibly fraudulent aspects of Universal's activities and to make no examinations of its books. This was precisely what Peabody had told me would happen when I first asked permission to examine his records—and was refused.[19]

During the spring of 1959, Congress conducted its second series of hearings on the subject of American aid to Laos. This time, the Subcommittee on Foreign Operations and Monetary Affairs of the House Committee on Government Operations managed the proceedings.[20] In a subsequent report, the subcommittee summarized its findings.[21] The report listed twenty-two criticisms of American aid, including the following:

1. Giving Laos more foreign aid than its economy could absorb hindered rather than helped the accomplishment of the objectives of the Mutual Security Program.

2. Excessive cash grants forced money into the Lao economy at a faster rate than it could be absorbed, causing:

   (a) An excessive Lao Government foreign exchange reserve, reaching at one point $40 million, equal to a year's aid.[22] (A comparison of Laotian domestic revenues with foreign aid is shown in Table 9.)

TABLE 9

CENTRAL LAO GOVT FINANCES, 1956–58[a]
(MILLIONS OF DOLLARS)

Item	1956[1]	1957[2]	1958[3]
A. Revenue:			
1. Total	55.59	65.99	60.71
2. From domestic sources[4]	8.28	17.71	17.59
a. Direct taxes:			
Issues			2.01
Receipts			.99
b. Customs duties			13.93
c. Other			.66
3. US grants	40.11	40.11	38.51
4. Other foreign grants[5]	7.19	8.17	4.59
B. Expenditure:			
1. Total	63.02	77.42	66.91
2. Natl def[6]	34.91	35.19	25.99
3. All other current (civil)[7]	15.99	29.11	25.22
4. Capital outlay (civil)[8]	12.39	13.11	17.11
a. Financed by US	5.19	4.94	12.51
b. Financed by other countries	7.19	8.17	4.59
C. Deficit:			
1. Before foreign grants	—54.99	—59.71	—49.31
2. After non-US grants	—47.79	—51.54	—44.71
3. After all foreign grants	—7.71	—11.42	—6.19
D. Financing the deficit:			
1. Advances to Treasury	3.39	2.79	9.59
2. Changes in financial assets	4.31	8.62	—3.39

1. Fiscal yr is Apr 1955 to Mar 1956
2. Fiscal period is Apr 1956 to June 1957 & comprises 15 months
3. Fiscal yr is Jul 1957 to June 1958 (Budget)
4. Essentially customs receipts
5. Mainly from France
6. Entirely US financed
7. Financed by US and other foreign grants
8. Includes certain amounts for current civil expenditure which cannot be separated and reclassified.

a Source: International Cooperation Administration, in House Subcommittee on Foreign Operations and Monetary Affairs, Hearings, U. S. Aid Operations in Laos, 1959, p. 820.

    (b) Inflation, doubling the cost of living from 1953 to 1958.

    (c) Profiteering through import licenses and false invoices, which made possible the purchase of U. S. cash grant dollars for 35 kip.

Those dollars could be resold in the free market for as much as 110 kip.

3. Much of the overspending was the direct result of a decision to maintain a 25,000-man Lao Army. In general, the determination of force objectives, a military decision, is made by the Joint Chiefs of Staff or the Department of Defense. In Laos, however, the State Department made the decision to maintain a 25,000-man army, despite contrary recommendations from the Joint Chiefs of Staff who in 1954 advised, "No force levels are recommended for this country." This was a political decision in a military field. There is no evidence that it was essential to support a 25,000-man army, the committee report stated. Significant military opinion has suggested a force of 12,000 to 15,000.[23]

4. The discrepancy between the official exchange rate of 35 kip to the dollar and the open market rate of up to 110 kip to the dollar was a basic difficulty in the entire aid program. The State Department and ICA did not rectify this difficulty for four years.

5. Concentration of aid benefits in Vientiane and other population centers, in addition to enrichment of and speculation by Lao merchants and public officials, lent credence to communist allegations that the Lao Government was corrupt and indifferent to the needs of the people.[24]

6. Neither the first Director (Carter DePaul) of the U. S. Operations Mission nor his successor (Carl Robbins) "showed any clear awareness of the problems that confronted the program or any expertness in meeting them."

7. The USOM public works and industry officer, Edward T. McNamara, accepted bribes totalling at least $13,000 from officers of the Universal Construction Company in return for helping them secure lucrative contracts and overlooking deficiencies in their performance.[25]

8. After USOM's area transportation adviser performed an instrumental role in securing the award of a contract for supply of ferry barges to the Hong Kong Transportation Company, he went to work for an affiliate of the company.

9. An engineering consultant employed by ICA for the purpose of assisting in the selection of construction projects was simultaneously under retainer to Vinnell Company, which was seeking to obtain such contracts with ICA in Laos.

10. Although ICA/Washington had received continuing information from at least five sources—including end-use auditor Haynes Miller and other ICA investigators—concerning the major problems in the Laos program, ICA took no significant remedial action.

11. Haynes Miller was "railroaded" out of Laos because he was on the verge of discovering the truth about the Universal Construction Company, its bribes, its virtual monopoly of U. S. aid construction projects in Laos, and its "woefully inadequate performance."

12. Through bribes to McNamara and the failure of other USOM/Laos officials to perform properly, Universal secured payments totaling over $1.6 million for "performance that was inadequate and did little to enhance the economy of Laos or the prestige of the United States."

13. USOM Director DePaul violated ICA contract regulations in several important respects, including one contract with a provision that the contractor (Universal) was not required to complete any work under the contract.

14. Laotian army pay raises in 1955 and 1958 added $3.8 million annually to the cost of the U. S. aid program in Laos. Justification for these raises is not clear. In both cases the State Department gave its approval after the fact—and then largely to avoid embarrassment because of unauthorized commitments made by USOM/Laos.

15. ICA officials sought to excuse deficiencies in the Laos aid program with the assertion that the program has saved Laos from going communist. "This assertion is purely speculative, and can be neither proved nor disproved. The subcommittee rejects the reasoning of ICA officials, and, on the evidence, believes that a lesser sum of money more efficiently administered would have been far more effective in achieving economic and political stability in Laos, and in increasing its capacity to reject Communist military aggression or political subversion."

In the remainder of its report, the committee discussed the above conclusions. The most significant aspects of the committee's findings are presented below.

1959 ARMY PAY RAISE

On August 31, 1958, Ambassador Horace Smith cabled the Department of State a request for financing a pay raise for the Laotian Army. The State Department denied the request. In another cable sent in December 1958, USOM/Laos recommended to CINCPAC (Commander in Chief, Pacific) that the pay raise be approved. On December 20, CINCPAC forwarded this recommendation to Washington with an affirmative endorsement. Before Washington replied to this cable, the Chief, Programs Evaluation Office, informed the Laotian Government that the pay raise would be acceptable. On January 5, 1959, the Laotian Government announced to the troops that the salary increase was forthcoming. Two days later, the Department of State gave a negative response to the request for the raise, but shortly thereafter it acquiesced on the basis of commitments already made. This pay raise cost the United States another $1 million a year.

NATURE OF THE AID PROGRAM

The level of United States aid to Laos was based primarily upon the cost of maintaining the Laotian military forces, for which the United States had assumed the full burden of support. To sustain the Laotian military, the United States injected approximately $40 million a year into the Laotian economy. According to two of ICA's own evaluation groups, this amount exceeded the absorptive powers of the Laotian economy; that is, it exceeded the total demand for goods and services. The Laotian accumulation of $40 million in dollar reserves supports this point. Speculative currency transactions, corruption, and capital flight took up the rest of the slack.

HIGHWAY PROGRAM

The highway program, the largest single project in the Laos aid program, afforded the United States an opportunity to present visible results of its aid to the average Laotian.

At the inception of the program, two contracts were signed. One provided for the procurement of $1.5 million worth of equipment; the other provided for the negotiation of a contract with an American engineering firm to give guidance to the Lao Ministry of Public Works, responsible for highway operation in Laos. ICA/Washington failed to coordinate the arrival of the equipment with the arrival of the contractor who was to use it, resulting in the presence in Laos of over $1 million worth of equipment with no one able to operate it. Cognizant of this situation, USOM/Laos Director dePaul asked for and received permission from Washington to negotiate a contract not to exceed $25,000 for the purpose of clearing a site for an equipment compound, conditioning the equipment for service, and performing emergency repair work on the Thadeua Road. This authorizing cable was the first step in Washington's loss of control of the highway program to the Mission. Pursuant to this authorization, the Mission signed a contract with the Universal Construction Company on October 4, 1956. Contrary to ICA regulations, this contract was let without bids. Subsequently, ICA auditors discovered that under the contract the contractor was not to be responsible for the completion of any work.

On October 10, 1956, the Mission, without fund authorization, signed

a second contract with Universal, this time for $15,950, to assist and expedite the reception, transportation, and off-loading of the highway equipment. Reversing ICA's contract procedure, the Mission negotiated this contract in the following steps:
1. Universal began performing the work in July, 1956.
2. The contract was signed October 10, 1956.
3. Invitations to bid were issued November 1, 1956.
4. Funds were authorized January 16, 1957.
Actually the Mission paid Universal $24,804.50 under this contract—$8,854.50 in excess of the contract limit. A U. S. Public Roads engineer, Robert S. Johnson, who reviewed Universal's operations, reported that Universal had not performed the work in a manner to insure proper receipt, disposition, maintenance and care of the roadbuilding equipment, and the facilities for the storage of the equipment had been neglected and were inadequate.

On January 26, 1957, the Laotian Government executed a contract directly with Universal to perform substantially the same services specified in a contract ICA/Washington was negotiating with an engineering firm named Vinnell, whose engineers were already arriving in Laos under a letter of agreement. The Mission turned over to the Laotian Government all the roadbuilding equipment procured with United States funds, the same equipment ICA/Washington had intended for Vinnell's use. The Laotian Government placed the equipment in Universal's custody. Since the work Vinnell was to do was actually being carried out by Universal under its contract with the Laotian Government, and since the Mission had relinquished control of the equipment, Vinnell was unable to do the work for which it had been hired. ICA/Washington did not learn of this contractual conflict until Vinnell complained about it in July 1957. USOM Director dePaul contended that the Mission merely acquiesced in the Laotian Government's contract with Universal. The Laotian Government stated that it had accepted Universal as reputable on the Mission's recommendation. The Laotian Government also claimed that the Mission had helped in negotiating the contract.

MCNAMARA'S ACCEPTANCE OF A GIFT FROM UNIVERSAL

From December 20, 1955, to November 3, 1957, Edward T. McNamara was public works and industry officer for USOM/Laos. He initiated and supervised numerous construction contracts, including those with Universal. He also influenced both the Mission and the Laotian Government to award contracts to Universal. He signed certificates of performance in connection with contracts between Universal and the Mission, although he inspected neither the work nor the equipment prior to signing the certificates. These certificates were necessary for Universal to receive payment. In return for these favors, Universal gave McNamara money, stocks, and airline tickets totaling at least $13,000.[26]

REMOVAL OF HAYNES MILLER FROM THE LAOS MISSION

Miller's investigations produced data that could have led ICA to McNamara's corruption and the deficiencies in the contracts and performance of Universal. ICA, however, reacted to Miller's reports by removing him from his position. "It is not apparent that ICA/Washington, any more than the USOM/Laos, made any use of the information obtained from Miller."[27] The following excerpt from a letter from Ambassador J. Graham Parsons to Kenneth T. Young, Office of Southeast Asian Affairs, Department of State, indicated that the American authorities ignored Miller's findings. The letter, dated April 24, 1957, refers to Universal's work on the road from Vientiane to Luang Prabang.

Apart from Souvanna and Petsarath, most of the Ministers and over half of the Chiefs of Mission accredited to Laos traveled either to or from Luang Prabang on the road. The trip dramatized American aid as nothing else has yet done in Laos. The contrast between unimproved stretches, stretches prepared for gravel surfacing and stretches where this work has already been completely provided, particularly with the rainstorms we encountered, a striking "before and after" demonstration. It was also an eye opener to encounter large roadmaking equipment working efficiently and around the clock up on the precipitous mountain slopes. The Okinawans are now famous in Laos and progress on the road is now a favorite topic of conversation.

From my own personal observation, I believe that the economic and social dividends from this operation will be considerable in this most important part of northern Laos. I also believe that it is by no means wildly optimistic to state as USOM people do that once the gravel surface is finished, it should be possible to keep the road open on a year-round basis with rather minimum maintenance crews and equipment spotted at a few points along the way. . . .

I repeat, for the first time American aid is producing something visible of major importance which has been brought to the inescapable attention of a large proportion of the key personalities in Laos. For the moment, our credit is high.[28]

Just over two years after the letter was written, the road had not yet been completed. The part that was finished was, as the committee stated, "most unsatisfactory."[29]

CIVIL POLICE PROJECT FOR LAOS

The United States undertook to enhance the capability of the Laotian police force to maintain internal security and simple law and order. The committee characterized this operation as "an example of one more ICA activity in Laos where accomplishments fell far short of expectations."[30]

OPERATION MEKONG

Establishment of adequate transportation and communication facilities, including facilities for ferrying commodities across the Mekong from Thailand, was of vital importance to Laos. As early as 1954, when the United States was aiding Laos through France, ICA issued a project agreement for $275,000 to cover the procurement of ferry craft. The procurement order contained inadequate specifications, however, and was allowed to expire on January 31, 1956.

Plans for the Mekong crossing were reactivated under the fiscal year 1956 aid program. ICA/Washington hired an American firm to prepare specifications for three pusher tugs and two barges. ICA instructed USOM Director dePaul that bidding invitations for contracts to build the craft must be sent to four American firms, among others. Stating that the project had an emergency status, dePaul asked ICA/Washington for a waiver of the necessity to extend bids to firms far from Laos. ICA denied the request. On August 3, 1956, the Mission issued an international call for bids with a submission deadline of September 1, 1956—a deadline that allowed American firms only fifteen days to prepare and submit bids in Laos. "By doing this, Director dePaul made it physically impossible for any American firm to submit a responsible bid, and accomplished his stated purpose of eliminating American competition."[31] DePaul's action violated ICA's regulations, which set a minimum of thirty days for the return of bids in such cases. When ICA/Washington requested the Mission to extend the deadline to October 1, 1956, dePaul replied that this was not feasible. Washington did not challenge this unsupported statement.

In early September the Mission selected the Hong Kong Transportation Company to build the ships. Despite the alleged emergency nature of the project, the contract was not signed until February 11, 1957. The subcommittee inquired why the Mission, which had precluded American firms from bidding on account of an emergency priority for the project, had then permitted initiation of the actual work to take so long. The subcommittee made the following findings. Two of the principals representing dePaul in the selection of the Hong Kong Transportation Company were

Edward T. McNamara, USOM Public Works Officer, and William E. Kirby, ICA Area Transportation Advisor. In July 1956, Kirby and McNamara went to Hong Kong to see what firms might be interested in submitting bids. Kirby, who had known officials of the Hong Kong Transportation Company prior to his employment with ICA, took an active role in promoting the company with the Mission. On the trip mentioned above, the men stayed in Hong Kong four days but visited no company except Hong Kong Transportation. On this trip, as well as on five or six others, McNamara's hotel expenses were assumed by a Hong Kong Transportation Company official. After McNamara's tour of duty in Laos, he was entertained in Hong Kong by the same official. The subcommittee also found that just before Kirby participated in the decision to award the contract to the Company, he had received $500 from it. Shortly after the contract was signed, Kirby left ICA to work for a subsidiary of the Hong Kong Transportation Company. Finally, the investigators discovered, dePaul lacked authority to approve a contract in the amount called for in the agreement with Hong Kong.

OPERATION BOOSTER SHOT

In an effort to rectify the aid program's neglect of the rural villagers, Ambassador Parsons in the fall of 1957 conceived Operation Booster Shot. This project, in essence a village aid program, was also motivated by an awareness that elections were coming in May 1958. Under Operation Booster Shot, ninety work projects were undertaken and 1,300 tons of food and medical and construction supplies were airdropped to Laotian villages. The operation cost approximately $3 million. Although Operation Booster Shot did not prevent a communist victory in the elections, it did, the committee said, "bring aid of a real and vital nature to some Lao citizens, other than the handful of officials and merchants who had previously been its primary beneficiaries. It also pointed the way to worthwhile modifications in the program, with more stress on economic and less on military matters. . . ."[32] In June 1958, Ambassador Smith wrote to the State Department about the results of Operation Booster Shot. He said it "has had a greater impact on Laos than any other aid program which the United States has undertaken in this area to date."[33] Concerning Operation Booster Shot and its discontinuance, the committee found:

> It apparently took an emergency situation [the 1958 elections] to evoke the only aid program that took account of the real needs of Laos. When the emergency was over, the program was abandoned. The lessons which should have been learned were promptly forgotten.[34]

SUMMARY OF FINDINGS

The Committee on Government Operations concluded its report with the following remarks:

In summary, the decision to support a 25,000-man army—motivated by a Department of State desire to *promote* political stability—seems to have been the foundation for a series of developments which *detract* from that stability.

Given that decision, the minimum size of the necessary aid program was inexorably established at a dollar value far beyond the estimated rate at which the Lao economy could absorb it. From this grew intensive speculation in commodities and foreign exchange, productive of inflation, congenial to an atmosphere of corruption, and destructive of *any* stability, political or economic.

With so much of the aid available for Laos earmarked for support of military forces, little attention was paid to programs which might reach the people of the villages. The aid program has not prevented the spread of communism in Laos. In fact, the Communist victory in last year's election, based on the slogans of "Government corruption" and "Government indifference" might lead one to conclude that the U. S. aid program has contributed to an atmosphere in which the ordinary people of Laos question the value of the friendship of the United States.

The army, which was too large for the economy to handle, was inadequate to perform its appointed mission. Against a much smaller force, it was unable to enforce Communist compliance with the Geneva agreements, which required evacuation of the two northern provinces and their return to the control of the central government. The presence of troops throughout the country may have assisted generally in the maintenance of order, but one may properly question, weighing all factors in the balance, if this was the most effective device.

The inability to remove the Communists from the northern provinces by diplomatic pressure or military force led to a compromise solution which admitted Communists to the Government and which established the Communist Party, Neo Lao Hak Xat, as a legal, above-ground political party.[35]

The committee did, however, detect some "hopeful" signs, such as the currency reform of October 1958, and the exclusion of communists from the Laotian cabinet in early 1959.

AIR AMERICA

One of the most controversial aspects of American aid has centered around an airline known as Air America, which has been flying missions in Laos for over a decade. The genesis of this company makes an interesting story in itself.[36]

Air America was the creation of General Claire Chennault. Chennault got his start in the airlines business in 1941. Before the United States entered World War II, President Roosevelt wanted to aid Chiang Kai-shek, then at war with Japan, and also give American flyers combat experience. The ideal arrangement would have been to lend the Generalissimo some American pilots. However, the Neutrality Act forbade American personnel from fighting for another government, so an alternative plan had to be devised.

This is where General Chennault came in.[37] Chennault went about recruiting American military pilots for a firm known as the Central Aircraft Manufacturing Company (CAMCO). The contracts said the pilots would help manufacture, operate, and repair airplanes. In private, Chennault explained to the men that they were going to fly combat missions in China.

CAMCO was actually owned by William Pawley, a former salesman for Curtiss-Wright, Inc., and then head of Pan American's subsidiary in China. In theory, the Chinese government was to pay for CAMCO's services; actually, the U.S. paid for the contract with lend-lease funds.

The CAMCO flyers later evolved into the famed "Flying Tigers," commanded by General Chennault, who compiled such an outstanding record in World War II.

After the War, Chennault saw financial opportunities in the formation of an airline to transport relief supplies into China's difficult-to-reach interior. Chennault went to Washington, where he obtained a partner and financial backing for an airline. Then he received a contract from the Chinese National Relief and Rehabilitation Authority, the Chinese government's agency in charge of distributing relief supplies. To help him get started, the United Nations Relief and Rehabilitation Authority (UNRRA) gave Chennault a $2 million credit. Using the airplanes and pilots from the "Flying Tigers," Chennault's airline began flying relief supplies into China in late January 1947. The new airline was known as Civil Air Transport (CAT).

From the very beginning, CAT became an instrument in the cold war; it first aided Chiang Kai-shek in his struggle with the Chinese communists and later flew missions in Korea and Indochina. This was as Chennault had intended, for his wife wrote,

I don't think either of us realized, as that first CAT plane became airborne, that the airline which had come into being would soon become the most powerful weapon in the Far East against another grim and determined enemy of China—an enemy more insidious and dangerous than the Japanese militarists: Communism. General Chennault, who had fought his way through two world wars, the Sino-Japanese War and World War II, was about to enter a third.[38]

The full exploits of CAT may never be known. What is known is that CAT pilots flew in supplies for United Nations forces in Korea and air-dropped medical supplies, food, and ammunition to French defenders at Dienbienphu. It is alleged that at Dienbienphu, CAT's airplanes and pilots were borrowed from the U. S. military. It is also alleged that, in a CIA operation in 1951, CAT ferried arms to the approximately 12,000 Chinese Nationalist Troops in northern Burma. The troops were supposed to use the arms to attack the Chinese communists. Instead, they went into the opium business and are now thriving, well protected by the arms they received.[39]

After Chennault died in 1958, CAT changed its name to Air America, Inc. However, the airline's cold war operations continued. At present the company operates in Vietnam, Thailand, Taiwan, and Laos.

In Laos, Air America has flown missions on behalf of the U.S. Government since 1960. Since the late 1960s Air America has become involved with the CIA-sponsored army of Meo tribesmen, commanded by General Vang Pao. Air America airlifts supplies to the Meos, transports them into battle, and according to some reports flies out the Meo opium crop to buyers in the cities.[40]

The exact relationship between Air America and the U. S. Government has remained a subject of lively controversy. Some say Air America is an arm of the CIA, since so many of Air America's operatives are (allegedly) former American military and intelligence personnel. Others insist Air America is a totally independent, private firm which happens to do some of its business with the U. S. Government, just as scores of other American corporations do. Whatever the exact relationship may be, one can be sure that the U. S. Government finds it very convenient to have Air America around. So long as the United States continues to have a role in the Laotian struggle, we can be sure that Air America, with its nearly 200 airplanes and over 10,000 employees, will have an active part to play.

EFFECTS OF AMERICAN AID

Before leaving the subject of American aid, it seems appropriate to consider the effects of such aid upon Laos.

Secretary of State Dean Rusk has testified as follows,

> Military aid, without real social, economic development is not likely to throw a shield around a society which is being subjected to subversion and penetration from outside; the real defense of the nation is the stake which its citizens feel and what they have in their own country; this has been one of the things that is missing in some stages of the Lao problem.[41]

American aid, according to the views of many, did not heighten the stake, to use Secretary Rusk's word, that Laotian citizens felt in their country. The reasons for this are discussed below.

American aid simply was not visible to many Laotians. Tan Chounlamountri, Secretary of State for the Ministry of Justice in 1959, said,

> The precious American aid is very much appreciated in Laos—only the way in which it is applied is often the cause of criticism. . . . The results are visible only to the government and the chiefs of the various national services. They are seen with difficulty by the mass of the people.[42]

American assistance flowed primarily to the military and the townspeople, although over 85 percent of Laos's population consists of peasants. "Aid activities having a direct impact on the rural villagers have been slight," a Congressional subcommittee concluded.[43] Benefits from commodity imports were limited to about 150,000 Laotians (out of a population of over two million). Only two projects that received significant amounts of money—police administration and road rehabilitation—were designed to produce basic improvements in Laos. The latter program was characterized by "corruption, maladministration, and poor performance."[44]

One prominent Laotian, Viceroy Tiao Phetsarath, commented on the concentration of aid in the following terms: "Our greatest danger of Communist subversion arises from the bad use of foreign aid we receive. . . . It enriches a minority outrageously while the mass of the population remains as poor as ever."[45]

Another reason for the failure of American aid to contribute more to the forging of closer links between the people and the government may be traced to corruption on the part of Laotian officials responsible for receiving the aid funds. As the House Committee on Government Operations concluded, "The aid program has not prevented the spread of communism in Laos. In fact, the Communist victory in last year's 1958 election, based on the slogans of 'Government corruption' and 'Government indifference' might lead one to conclude that the U. S. aid program has contributed to an atmosphere in which the ordinary people of Laos question the value of the friendship of the United States."[46] Champassak has said,

Black-market deals in American aid dollars reached such proportions that the Pathet Lao needed no propaganda to turn the rural population against the townspeople. The Chinese of Hong Kong and Bangkok and a few Lao officials profited from the American aid, while the poor Lao for whom it was intended stood by helplessly.[47]

A further reason why American aid failed to create closer ties between the government and the people was inflation caused by aid dollars. From 1953 to 1958 the cost of living doubled in Laos. In small market towns outside Vientiane, the price of 100 kilograms of polished rice rose from 450 kip in 1955 to 600 kip in 1956 to 950 kip in 1957. During the same time span, the price of a can of kerosene rose from 110 kip to 260 kip and the price of a chicken rose from 20 kip to 80 kip.[48]

Perhaps the most balanced assessment of the effects of American aid on Laos was offered by the International Cooperation Administration, which conducted its own study of American aid to Laos. The ICA report stated, "While serving the principal objective of preserving national independence of the State of Laos, the program was found less suited to promote other important U. S. objectives, such as to foster a stable and effective government with wide popular support and oriented toward democratic concepts, and to promote confidence in, and respect and friendship for, the United States."[49]

To be sure, contributing to the preservation of Laotian national independence represents an achievement that makes a certain number of deficiencies tolerable. However, the steps taken to keep Laos independent in the short run were to have unexpected effects on the long-run effort to contain communism in Laos. The United States kept pressure on the Pathet Lao by subsidizing the army, police, and civil administration. At the same time, however, the failure to forge strong links between the government and the population, as well as the alienation of many Laotians because of the way in which American aid was applied, created an internal situation that afforded the Pathet Lao unhoped-for opportunities. In other words, the United States, in devoting its attention to prosecuting the war against the communists, chose to ignore the very conditions that permitted a communist movement to exist and thrive. When these conditions reached a flash point, the explosion that ensued shook the international community with surprise and dismay. To these unexpected developments we now turn.

NOTES

1. This is not to say that the foreign aid program should be exempt from continued scrutiny and evaluation. Indeed, such close study is necessary in order to

render foreign aid as effective as it can be. The value of foreign aid to the donor country, even when such aid is administered without a flaw, is an entirely separate question which deserves greater attention than it has received.

2. As distinguished from military equipment.

3. This limit was observed in order to avoid inflation, which would have resulted had the United States merely poured money into the country. The cash grant program, to be discussed below, indeed brought about the feared inflation.

4. House Subcommittee on the Far East and the Pacific, *Mutual Security Program in Laos*, 1958, pp. 4 ff.

5. The discrepancy between the official exchange rate of 35 kip to the dollar and the black-market rate of 100 kip to the dollar led to the following dishonest practices. Under the cash grant system, an importer would exchange 35 kip for 1 dollar. Instead of using the dollar to import merchandise, the importer would take the dollar to a black marketeer and receive 100 kip for it. Thus he made 65 kip without even importing goods, the sale of which was supposed to limit inflation in Laos.

6. House Subcommittee on the Far East and the Pacific, *Mutual Security Program in Laos*, 1958, p. 6.

7. A subsequent GAO investigation showed that the U. S. Mission lacked knowledge of the number of Laotian troops receiving ration payments. Because the Lao Army would not let the Mission audit its financial records, the Mission could not verify that rations or financial support furnished to the Lao army actually reached the troops. Since the Mission did not know the number of soldiers in the Lao Army or the rate of consumption of supplies, programming over a period of time was difficult. "These deficiencies in data make it impossible to program prudently supplies and equipment for the Lao Army forces," the GAO report said.

Furthermore, GAO investigators found, military assistance material was being delivered in quantities that could not be utilized or properly stored by Lao forces. The Mission had no way to assure that such material was used and safeguarded after delivery. Depots in Laos lacked adequate storage space and provided only meager protection to equipment. Subcommittee on Foreign Operations and Monetary Affairs, *Hearings, United States Aid Operations in Laos*, 1959, pp. 239-47. The quotation appears on p. 244.

8. House Subcommittee on the Far East and the Pacific, *Mutual Security Program in Laos*, 1958, p. 31.

9. Parsons left this post February 8, 1958.

10. House Subcommittee on the Far East and the Pacific, *Mutual Security Program in Laos*, 1958, p. 34. Actually, the Pathet Lao and their political allies won 14 of the 21 seats up for election. Fighting resumed a year later, and the following year Laos established diplomatic relations with the Soviet Union, which provided economic and military aid.

11. In October 1958, the official rate was changed from 35 to 80 kip to the dollar.

12. DePaul was USOM/Laos Director from January 1, 1955, until July 1957.

13. House Subcommittee on the Far East and the Pacific, *Mutual Security Program in Laos*, 1958, p. 42.

14. *Ibid.*, p. 44.

15. *Ibid.*, p. 46.

16. *Ibid.*, p. 62.

17. Haynes Miller, "A Bulwark Built on Sand," *Reporter* 19 (November 13, 1958):11–16.

18. *Ibid.*, p. 14. Igor Oganesoff, correspondent for the *Wall Street Journal*, estimated that 50 percent of goods paid for never reached the Laotian market. See *Wall Street Journal*, April 9, 1958.

19. Miller, p. 15. When the Subcommittee on Foreign Operations and Monetary Affairs of the House Committee on Government Operations conducted hearings on American aid to Laos (see below), many of Miller's allegations were substantiated.

20. House Subcommittee on Foreign Operations and Monetary Affairs, *Hearings, United States Aid Operations in Laos*, 1959.

21. U. S., Congress, House, Committee on Government Operations, *United States Aid Operations in Laos: Seventh Report by the Committee*, 86th Cong., 1st Sess., 1959.

22. Another source states that, including illegal opium traffic of $3 million, Laotian exports in 1955 were approximately $5 million. (U. S., Congress, Senate, Special Committee to Study the Foreign Aid Program, *Foreign Aid Program*, "Southeast Asia," Clement Johnston, Survey No. 7, 1957, p. 1455.) With foreign aid approximating $40 million a year, Laotians were encouraged to import 8 times the value of the goods they could have imported with foreign exchange derived from exports.

23. Roger Hilsman has pointed out that the Laotian army would be unable to repel an open attack by either North Vietnam or Communist China. The Royal Army's most useful function would be to combat the anti-government guerrilla campaign being waged by the Pathet Lao. However, the United States did not equip and train an anti-guerrilla force, but instead formed the Laotian army into a conventional force designed to meet an armed attack from outside. The United States, for example, supplied the Laotian army with a complement of jeeps and trucks, even though most Laotian roads are impassable during the rainy season. A road-bound army could not, as Hilsman says, effectively suppress a guerrilla force that operated in the hinterland where roads did not penetrate. (Roger Hilsman, *To Move A Nation* [New York: Doubleday and Company, 1967], p. 113.)

24. In 1957 Laotian imports included dozens of cars, 4½ tons of feather dusters, 73 tons of sporting goods and $11,500 worth of musical instruments. (*The Wall Street Journal*, April 9, 1958, p. 1.) The Laotian government was supposed to approve import licenses only for goods that would raise living standards or stimulate economic development. A 1957 survey showed that only 2 percent of the Laotian people had heard of American aid. (Senate Special Committee to Study the Foreign Aid Program, *Foreign Aid Program*, 1957, p. 1439.)

25. On February 1, 1962, McNamara and two officials of the Universal Construction Company were indicted on charges of conspiring to defraud the Government on construction contracts in Laos. (*The New York Times*, February 2, 1962.)

26. GAO investigators failed to uncover McNamara's devious practices. Testifying in May 1958, a GAO official said, "We have no evidence at all that there was any fraud, malpractice, or wrongdoing on the part of the United States officials." (House Subcommittee on the Far East and the Pacific, *Mutual Security Program in Laos*, 1958, p. 10.)

27. House Committee on Government Operations, *United States Aid Operations in Laos: Seventh Report*, 1959, p. 28.

28. *Ibid.*, pp. 29–30.

29. Reporting in June 1957, on the status of the road, President Eisenhower, obviously misinformed, said, "Sufficient progress was made by June 1957 so that most of the road could be used the year round under all weather conditions." (U.S., President, *Report to Congress on the Mutual Security Program,* June 30, 1957, p. 15.)

30. House Committee on Government Operations, *United States Aid Operations in Laos: Seventh Report,* 1959, p. 33.

31. *Ibid.,* p. 43.

32. *Ibid.,* p. 46.

33. *Ibid.*

34. *Ibid.*

35. *Ibid.,* p. 50.

36. The best account of Air America may be found in a book by the wife of its founder. See Anna Chennault, *A Thousand Springs* (New York: Paul S. Eriksson, 1962). For a less sympathetic account, see Peter Dale Scott, "Air America: Flying the U.S. into Laos," *Ramparts,* 8 (February 1970):39–42.

37. This account follows Scott.

38. Chennault, p. 155.

39. Scott, pp. 39–42.

40. *Ibid.*

41. U.S., Congress, Senate, Committee on Foreign Relations, *Hearings, International Development and Security,* 87th Cong., 1st Sess., 1961, p. 86.

42. Joel M. Halpern, *Government, Politics and Social Structure in Laos* (Southeast Asia Studies, Monograph Series No. 4; New Haven: Yale University Press, 1964), pp. 136–7.

43. House Subcommittee on Foreign Operations and Monetary Affairs, *Hearings, U.S. Aid Operations in Laos,* 1959, p. 14. Dommen observes that of the $480.7 million obligated by the United States to Laos, only $1.9 million, or less than one percent, was spent on improving agriculture, the source of livelihood for over 96 percent of the Laotian people. (Arthur J. Dommen, *Conflict in Laos* (New York: Frederick A. Praeger, 1964), p. 107).

44. House Committee on Government Operations, *United States Aid Operations in Laos: Seventh Report,* 1959, p. 14.

45. Miller, *The Reporter,* 19:11.

46. House Committee on Government Operations, *United States Aid Operations in Laos: Seventh Report,* 1959, p. 50.

47. Sisouk Na Champassak, *Storm over Laos* (New York: Frederick A. Praeger, 1961), p. 64.

48. Dommen, p. 106.

49. House Subcommittee on Foreign Operations, *Hearings, U.S. Aid Operations in Laos,* 1959, p. 788.

11
KONG LE AND THE NEUTRALIST COUP

IN OCTOBER 1959, the Laotian monarch, King Sisavang Vong, died. The throne went to his son Savang Vatthana. Instead of being buried immediately, the old king's corpse was embalmed and placed on a bier for an indefinite period. Finally, in August 1960, nearly a year after King Sisavang Vong's death, the ranking members of the Royal Government[1] gathered in Luang Prabang to discuss his funeral arrangements. While the government was absent from Vientiane, elite paratroop Captain Kong Le and the 600 men of the Second Paratroop Battalion silently slipped into the capital in the pre-dawn hours of August 9. Seizing control of key installations, Kong Le announced to the world that he was now in control of the country. The *coup d'état* came as a surprise to everyone, except those who had come to expect the unexpected in Laos.

Five days after the coup, the National Assembly passed a no-confidence vote in the Tiao Somsanith regime. King Savang then requested Souvanna Phouma to form a new government. The National Assembly approved Souvanna's cabinet on August 17. The next day Kong Le turned over administrative powers in Laos to the new government headed by Souvanna, for it had been the Captain's wish that Souvanna become prime minister. The new cabinet, reflecting Souvanna's philosophy, was composed almost entirely of men opposed to the previous regime's pro-Western orientation and its militant anti-communism. Significantly Phoumi Nosavan, the strong man behind Tiao's government, was excluded from Souvanna's new regime.

204

KONG LE'S MOTIVES

Why did the 28-year-old captain engineer the *coup d'état*? Kong Le provided the first hints of his motives in a communique broadcast over Radio Vientiane on August 9, the day of the coup. The paratrooper said that the coup was "aimed at safeguarding and consolidating the Nation, the religion, the Throne, and the Constitution." He promised to "recognize all human rights," to "struggle against bribery," and to reorganize the parliamentary system and cleanse the administrative machinery. "The revolutionary group will oppose foreign intervention in the country's military affairs and will expel all foreign bases." Kong Le vowed to maintain a neutral foreign policy and to entertain "friendly relations with neighboring countries." He also promised to raise the people's living standards.[2]

The young Captain thought of himself as a Laotian nationalist who wanted to eliminate corruption, cast off foreign influence—which, at that time, was mainly American—and create a government dedicated to the establishment of better living conditions for all Laotians, regardless of political persuasion.

Speaking for neutrality, Kong Le declared,

> We want our government to be truly neutral. We will accept diplomatic relations with all countries.
> I hope the Government will lead our country to the path of neutrality. That means a government that will incline neither toward the free world nor the Communist world.[3]

One of Kong Le's principal targets was corruption. According to correspondent Keyes Beech, Kong Le said,

> Corruption must be stopped. . . . Leaders of government and the armed forces have more than once announced that those engaged in bribery, those living off the labor of others and those advancing their interests at the people's expense would be punished. But these evils continue to appear. I don't like these people.[4]

"I oppose corruption and persons who live on the sweat of others," he stated elsewhere.[5]

Kong Le bore a special grudge against the United States, whose aid he thought responsible for creating opportunities for Laotian officials to make illegal profits and for prolonging the Laotian civil war. This antipathy toward the United States was revealed in an interview with Wilfred Burchett, a journalist who generally sympathizes with communist positions. Burchett wrote that Kong Le said that "Laotian independence had always been a false independence. First we had the French on our backs, then the Americans." His Second Paratroop Battalion, he said, was created by Americans. "It was set up, financed, armed and trained by them. I knew the Americans wanted to influence me, to have me completely in their pocket. I let them think this was so, I had to hide my own feelings. But I didn't need their influence, I despised it."[6] The Americans, Burchett alleges Kong Le said, sent him to Thailand for military training.

> Later the Americans showered money on me. I took it and distributed it among the troops. They offered me a very nice civilian car. I said that as I was a military man my staff car was sufficient. By every possible means they try and butter up those they think will be faithful servants. In fact they despise our people and our army. The Americans have a "master race" complex and regard Laotians as inferior people.

Burchett said Kong Le told him that, after sounding the opinions of people in the areas where he was sent to fight, "I was soon convinced that over 90 percent of the people wanted one thing—peace and an end to foreign interference. They wanted a policy of neutrality. It was what I wanted too, and through contacts with the Pathet Lao I knew this was what they were fighting for. I determined to prepare a coup."[7]

Beech wrote that Kong Le had told him, "Lao must stop fighting Lao."[8] "I carried out the coup to end the war and end foreign interference in Laos," Kong Le told Burchett.[9]

Kong Le, then, wanted to place in power an honest government committed to ameliorating the lives of the Laotian people. He sought to bring an end to the civil conflict and to reduce foreign influence, especially American influence. He also believed that Laos should pursue a neutral foreign policy.

Kong Le and his followers were especially piqued at government corruption which, they said, would have been impossible without American aid. In other words, American aid was intimately related to the fact that leading government officials had displayed much zeal in squirreling away money for their own selfish purposes, to the neglect of the welfare of the people. This feeling in Laos puts into dramatic relief the statement by former ambassador Parsons to the effect that the United States should not be overly concerned with corruption induced by American aid, since the overall effect of that aid was to strengthen anticommunist forces in Laos. While the aid many have strengthened the army in the short run—and even this is debatable—American dollars also fostered conditions that alienated many Laotians from the Vientiane government, not to mention its sponsor in Washington. American aid thus had the unintended effect of driving many Laotians into the arms of the Pathet Lao.

The preponderance of military assistance over aid directed to the betterment of living conditions also antagonized a significant portion of the
Laotian population. Many Laotians believed that the conflict between the
Royal Government and the Pathet Lao would end if Washington would
stop financing and prodding the Royal Army to fight. If only the United
States would cease interfering in Laotian affairs, and instead confine itself
to bettering the lot of the people, peace would return to Laos—so argued
many of its people.

It seems, in sum, that Washington's perspective on aid to Laos was
decidedly shortsighted. Many Laotians, as Kong Le's popularity indicated,
disliked American aid because it fostered corruption and prolonged the civil
war. Parsons's justification of United States aid might have proved valid,
had the Royal Army been able to wipe out the Pathet Lao in a short period
of time. Over the longer haul, however, the aid gave rise to conditions
that only increased the Pathet Lao's appeal to the Laotian people. One
hopes that the foreign aid establishment has learned from the Laos experience that the manner in which assistance is distributed cannot be ignored
merely because the aid is going to groups "fighting communism."

KONG LE'S SUPPORTERS

Kong Le became the focus for liberal, noncommunist elements who
were disgusted by the corruption in Vientiane and who wanted an end to
the civil conflict. As a voice of protest, Kong Le attracted nationalists who
wished for a peaceful settlement and a regime that would govern in the
interest of the common man.

Another group that supported Kong Le was the Pathet Lao. It is not
clear whether they agreed with his policies or merely wished to promote
any movement against the succession of anti-communist, pro-Western regimes in Vientiane; the latter explanation seems the more convincing. At
any rate, the Central Committee of the NLHX declared their "full support" for Kong Le's coup. The NLHX offered to "help expand the coup
in various provinces" and proposed the establishment of a coalition government.[10]

PHOUMI TAKES HIS SUPPORTERS
TO SAVANNAKHET

When Phoumi Nosavan received news of the coup, he flew from Luang
Prabang to Bangkok to consult with his uncle, Thai Prime Minister Mar-

shal Sarit Thanarat, and from there to Savannakhet in southern Laos. There he was joined by twenty-one members of the National Assembly. These men formed a Counter Coup d'Etat Committee under the leadership of Phoumi, who had been promoted from colonel to general. On August 18 a transmitter in Savannakhet began broadcasting denunciations of Kong Le.

The political configuration in Laos was now drastically altered from what it had been before Kong Le's coup. Before Kong Le, Laotian politics could be depicted by a dumbbell, one of the globes representing the Pathet Lao and the other standing for the Royal Government. The government side was actually composed of many different particles—the liberals (Souvanna Phouma), the conservatives (Phoui Sananikone, Sisouk Na Champassak, Boun Oum and Phoumi Nosavan), and various others. Despite the conflicting pressures acting on the government side, the various factions had been able to hold together in the face of the severe political storms that had beset Laos.

Kong Le's coup was the hammer blow that shattered the Laotian government side of the fragile dumbbell. Souvanna Phouma, Kong Le, and the other moderates drew apart from Phoumi and the conservatives. The dumbbell image no longer applied. Instead, Laotian politics could now be represented by the design on the Laotian flag. The flag of Laos depicts three elephants standing under a white parasol. Each elephant, it could be said, stood for one of the political factions in Laos. On the left stood the Pathet Lao. Souvanna Phouma, backed by Kong Le and his followers, occupied the center position. To the right stood General Phoumi, who was only beginning to organize his supporters.

Souvanna Phouma wished to heal the breach between himself and General Phoumi. Accordingly, the new Prime Minister journeyed to Savannakhet for talks with the General. These conversations resulted in an agreement to form a new, expanded cabinet. On August 30 Souvanna broadened his government to include five members of the former Tiao Somsanith pro-Western regime. General Phoumi was appointed Deputy Prime Minister as well as Minister of Interior, Culture, and Social Welfare; Nhouy Abhay was named Minister of Education, Fine Arts, Sports, and Youth; and General Ouane Rathikone was designated Secretary of State for Defense.

On August 31 General Phoumi flew from Vientiane to Savannakhet, allegedly for the purpose of tending to personal affairs. For reasons that remain obscure, he did not return to participate in Souvanna's government but instead took up arms against it.

Upon Phoumi's return to Savannakhet, he helped organize a Revolutionary Committee to oppose the government in Vientiane. The Committee, whose nominal head was Boun Oum, half-brother to Souvanna, was in actuality a successor to the Counter Coup d'Etat Committee. Boun Oum declared the Souvanna Phouma government illegal and proclaimed himself head of the government. He charged that Souvanna had opened the country to communist aggression from North Vietnam.[11]

From this moment on, the three rival factions joined in the struggle for power in Laos. Each had its own army and its own political following. In the center stood Souvanna Phouma and his neutralist followers. The Pathet Lao remained on the left, willing to negotiate with Souvanna but opposed to dealing with Phoumi.[12] The rightists, under the political leadership of Boun Oum and military command of General Phoumi, refused to consider relations with either Vientiane or the Pathet Lao.

Fighting soon broke out. On September 19 Radio Pathet Lao announced that Souphanouvong's troops had been ordered not to fight troops loyal to Souvanna Phouma and suggested that the two factions join forces against Phoumi. Meanwhile, Kong Le's troops defeated 300 of Phoumi's troops at Paksane and pushed them down the Mekong Valley to the southern bank of the Ca Dinh river, where a front stabilized temporarily.

The political situation in Laos had thus become a three-sided struggle. Above the internal quarrels stood the international rivalries of the cold war. To these global complications we now shift our attention.

DISAGREEMENT IN WASHINGTON

SHOULD THE UNITED STATES SUPPORT
KONG LE OR GENERAL PHOUMI?

The new triangular Laotian conflict confronted Washington with the necessity to choose between lending support to the neutralists in Vientiane or General Phoumi in Savannakhet.

One could offer arguments for supporting either faction and, in fact, various agencies and departments in the foreign policy establishment held divergent opinions and even followed conflicting policies.[13]

Among the most ardent supporters of the neutralists was U. S. Ambassador Winthrop G. Brown, who had arrived at his new assignment in Laos one week before Kong Le's coup. Brown questioned the possibility of building a pro-Western bastion in Laos, as the directors of the containment strategy had planned. Instead, Brown leaned toward a scheme advanced by Souvanna for preserving Laotian independence. Souvanna, it will be recalled, had expanded his cabinet to include General Phoumi and four other members of the conservative Tiao Somsanith regime. Souvanna's strategy was to form a coalition between the center and the right, a coalition that could bargain advantageously with the Pathet Lao. Brown supported this plan although he knew it would probably result in a neutralist type of government for Laos. It might even lead to some measure of communist participation in the government, along the lines of the November 1957 agreements. The American Embassy in Vientiane stood behind the Ambassador in support of this plan.[14]

Brown's cables to Washington were not exactly calculated to please those officials who had worked so hard to defeat the settlement of November 1957. The opponents of neutralism were heavily concentrated in the Defense Department, the Pentagon, and the State Department, where former ambassador J. Graham Parsons headed the Bureau of Far Eastern Affairs. Leading officials in these three centers of power were anxious to back General Phoumi in his efforts to sweep Laos militarily.[15]

At least three fears troubled the opponents of Souvanna and neutralism. In the first place, it was felt that bringing even a few communists into a government, as Souvanna had done before and would no doubt do again, would lead to a communist takeover. Secondly, Souvanna was suspected of being either a communist sympathizer or a dupe of the Pathet Lao.[16] After all, what other reason could there be for trying so hard to include communists in the government? Actually, there were other reasons: the predominant one was that Souvanna could see no way of terminating the destructive civil conflict without allowing at least a few Pathet Lao to occupy government posts. For Souvanna, ending the civil war, even if it meant granting the Pathet Lao some of their demands appeared more urgent than containing communism. Furthermore, Souvanna considered the Pathet Lao to be more nationalist than communist. Souvanna was hopeful that, with help from the conservatives, he could limit communist influence and at the same time put an end to the fighting in Laos. In Washington, however, the preponderant view was that Souvanna was not to be trusted. The third difficulty that bothered American foes of Laotian neutralism was Kong Le, commander of Souvanna's military forces. Deemphasizing the paratrooper's nationalist feelings, these officials regarded him as a tool—whether willing or unwilling was not certain—of the communists. President Eisenhower wrote, "By October it appeared that Souvanna Phouma was either an accomplice or a captive of Captain Kong Le who, himself, was an accomplice of the Pathet Lao."[17] General Heintges, Chief of the PEO until January 1961, thought that Kong Le, rather than representing an independent force, was in league with the communists. The general referred to the August 9 coup as "the coup . . . where the Communists took over the government." Heintges went on to elaborate,

The Communists saw a golden opportunity to use Captain Kong Le's coup as a way of getting their foot in the door, . . .

And we knew Kong Le. I knew Kong Le personally, and I don't believe that he had the education or the intelligence to do some of the things that were done there. It was obviously a takeover by the Communists who built him up as a martyr, as a hero.[18]

In Washington the Defense Department, the Pentagon, and the State Department—especially the Bureau of Far Eastern Affairs—tended to support General Phoumi and his plan for military action.[19]

Despite the conflicting viewpoints taken by Ambassador Brown and the U. S. Embassy on one hand and leading officials at Defense, the Pentagon, and State on the other, the U. S. Government had to decide whether to support the neutralists or General Phoumi. As might be expected the disagreements over policy caused a temporary delay in the decision. On September 10, 1960, one month after Kong Le's coup, Washington issued its first public pronouncement on the unfolding Laotian situation. The United States said,

> The United States has in the past consistently supported duly constituted governments of Laos in their efforts to maintain the independence and integrity of Laos against Communist encroachment from without or within. It would regret a situation in which violence destroyed unity thereby increasing the danger of such encroachment. The United States has no desire to intervene in the internal affairs of Laos. . . . It would, however, be immediately concerned by the efforts of any other outside power, or the agents thereof, to take advantage of the disturbed conditions prevailing and to intervene directly or indirectly.[20]

The American statement did not indicate in which direction Washington intended to throw its support. It did, however, express regret that the noncommunists in Laos were exhausting their power against each other instead of combining against the Pathet Lao. The statement also warned against foreign intervention.

While Washington was trying to make up its official mind about what to do in Laos, Ambassador Brown and those working under him in Laos began to act. Their plan was to forge a coalition between Souvanna and Phoumi against the Pathet Lao.

Brown's first order of business was to prevent a split between Souvanna and Phoumi. On September 10, the day on which Phoumi announced the formation of the anti-Vientiane Revolutionary Committee, Brown sent a note to Savannakhet warning Phoumi that the United States would not support any revolutionary plans he might entertain.[21] At the same time, American agents tried to persuade Souvanna to abandon his efforts to form a government composed of representatives from all three factions and instead create a neutralist regime that leaned toward the West.[22] The Vientiane Embassy also dispatched two senior officials to Savannakhet, in an effort to persuade Phoumi to accept Souvanna's offer of the post of Deputy Prime Minister.[23] Souvanna said he would welcome a reconciliation with the General.[24]

While Ambassador Brown was pressuring Phoumi to join forces with the neutralists against the Pathet Lao, developments of another kind were transpiring at the General's headquarters in southern Laos. There is evidence that, at the same time Ambassador Brown was trying to deal firmly with General Phoumi and convince him to join with Souvanna, other Americans may have been encouraging the General to resist the Ambassador's pleas. Dommen, for example, avers that from mid-September unmarked C–46 and C–47 aircraft, manned by American crews, made several landings and takeoffs at Savannakhet airport. The planes, he said, belonged to Air America, Inc., "a civilian charter company with U. S. Air Force organizational support and under contract to the U. S. Government."[25] According to Dommen, the planes ferried military supplies from Bangkok to Savannakhet and from Savannakhet to Phoumi's outlying garrisons. Roger Hilsman supports Dommen's contention. He states that "aid transports of a civilian airline began a steady shuttle to Phoumi's base in Savannakhet."[26] Dommen also stated that 200 Laotian paratroopers trained in Thailand augmented Phoumi's troops. Despite Souvanna's request that these Royal Army soldiers be assigned to his forces, the American PEO routed them to Phoumi.[27]

Were Americans in Laos working at cross-purposes? While Ambassador Brown was trying to convince Phoumi to join Souvanna's coalition government, other American representatives were helping Phoumi maintain his own independent forces. In the end, Phoumi successfully resisted Brown's proddings. We may never discover why Phoumi was able to dodge the pressures exerted on him by Ambassador Brown, but we can at least suggest a reason. It would seem reasonable that Phoumi was emboldened to follow his own course by the assistance he was receiving through Air America and by such activities as the diversion of Royal Lao troops to his army. Certainly, these forms of assistance were not calculated to facilitate Ambassador Brown's task of forcing Phoumi to combine his resources with the neutralists. Arthur Schlesinger, Jr. seems to agree with this explanation, for he wrote that American "military support convinced Phoumi that, if he only held out, Washington would put him in power."[28] Schlesinger even goes so far as to say that Phoumi's original decision to take his followers to Savannakhet and denounce Souvanna may have stemmed from encouragement from Defense and CIA men in the field.

Judging from Phoumi's actions, contending pressures were being exerted upon him. It is known, for example, that Phoumi flew to Luang Prabang with the intention of joining Souvanna's government. However, a heavy bank of fog shrouding the airport, which lacked devices permitting an instrument landing, prevented Phoumi's plane from landing. Phoumi was thus compelled to fly back to Savannakhet, from where he resolved to oppose Souvanna instead of joining with him.

Can Phoumi's second thoughts about participating in Souvanna's government be attributed to persuasion by certain agencies of the U. S. Government? It is, of course, possible that Phoumi had intended to take up arms against Souvanna regardless of what Washington wanted him to do. However, Phoumi's debt to the United States, and more particularly his reliance upon American military support, render it unlikely that he would act in such a way as to endanger his lifeline to the United States.

UNITED STATES AIDS
RIVAL FACTIONS IN LAOS

As the fall of 1960 continued, the United States found itself in the unusual position of supplying aid to two factions in the same country, each of whom seemed intent on destroying the other. Before Kong Le's coup, Washington was giving financial aid to the Laotian government and training the Royal Army in the use and maintenance of American-supplied military equipment. After the coup, American policymakers decided to continue giving financial aid to the Laotian government, now under Souvanna Phouma, but to give military aid (equipment and training) to Phoumi's forces in the south.[29]

While Ambassador Brown went to work on General Phoumi to persuade him to join forces with Souvanna, Washington, or more particularly Assistant Secretary Parsons, decided to use American aid in an effort to force Souvanna Phouma to modify his policies. Such efforts at diplomatic blackmail are not new to diplomacy. In fact, one reason for giving aid is to place oneself in a position to use it for the sake of coercion should such use become desirable. This fact, it might be added, also explains why so many aid recipients view their benefactors with less than complete affection.

At any rate, on October 7, the State Department announced a suspension of aid to Laos, allegedly because it had suddenly become necessary to conduct a "review of the situation."[30] Funds for the payment of Souvanna's army were thus held up. Military equipment and training for Phoumi's troops, however, were not interrupted.

In reality, the halt in aid to Souvanna was meant to soften him up for a series of American demands that he was not likely to accept without some coercion. These demands were transmitted to Souvanna by none other than Parsons himself. On October 12, five days after the aid suspension, Parsons along with Assistant Secretary of Defense for International Security Affairs John N. Irwin II and Vice Admiral Herbert Riley, Chief of Staff at CINCPAC, went to Vientiane for the purpose of checking on alleged inconsistencies in policy towards Laos between different organs of the United States Government. While in Vientiane, Parsons talked with the Laotian Prime Minister. Sending Parsons to plead with Souvanna was a little like sending General Moshe Dayan to ask President Nasser to declare Yom Kippur a national holiday. Parsons was the individual who, as ambassador to Laos, had done his utmost to wreck the accords of November 1957, upon which Souvanna had placed his hopes for ending the conflict in his country. Souvanna, by all accounts, despised Parsons in return.

According to the man who was Souvanna's personal aide at the time, Parsons asked Souvanna to do three things:

1. Terminate talks with the Pathet Lao.[31]
2. Negotiate with General Phoumi with a view to bringing him and his followers into a pro-Western government.
3. Transfer the administrative capital to Luang Prabang.[32] (This shift was designed to place the formation of Laotian policy more under the influence of the conservative king.)

Souvanna rejected all three requests.[33] Later that month the leaders at State and Defense decided that Souvanna had to go.[34] The United States had finally made its commitment—to General Phoumi.

Meanwhile, Ambassador Brown, with Washington's approval, suggested to Souvanna that, in order to prevent the communists from capitalizing on the disunity among the noncommunist forces, he should acquiesce in deliveries of American military equipment to Phoumi in return for the resumption of cash-grant aid to the neutralists.[35] Souvanna assented on one condition, namely, that none of the military equipment delivered to Savannakhet would be used against the neutralists—it was to be used against the Pathet Lao only.[36] It was Souvanna's understanding that this condition was agreed upon, although how such a provision could be enforced once Phoumi possessed the equipment was not specified.[37] On October 17 the State Department announced that the United States was resuming financial aid to the Laotian government.

With the clairvoyant vision that hindsight provides, we can see that the fall of 1960, when Washington decided to back General Phoumi instead of Souvanna Phouma, was a time of opportunity missed for American policy. American champions of Phoumi assumed that the General, supported by American military aid and tactical assistance, was capable of overwhelming the remaining factions in Laos and turning that country into a bastion of the West. The events of 1961 and 1962 demonstrated, however, that Phoumi's proponents grievously miscalculated, for the General proved unable to defeat the neutralists and the Pathet Lao. In fact, as we shall see, American military advisors were to witness the total collapse of Phoumi's army under attack by the very forces over whom Phoumi was programmed to triumph. As a consequence, the pro-Western diplomats at the Geneva Conference in 1961–1962 were deprived of effective military force to support their diplomacy. Had the various organs of the U. S. Government united behind Ambassador Brown's efforts to persuade Phoumi to join Souvanna Phouma, instead of gambling on the General, there is a good chance that the Pathet Lao would not have acquired so powerful a voice in the Laotian government as it did in 1962.

VIENTIANE ESTABLISHES DIPLOMATIC RELATIONS WITH THE SOVIET UNION

American assistance to Phoumi's forces in Savannakhet did not pass unnoticed by other nations. On September 21 the Soviet Union issued a statement on what it called "the instances of flagrant intervention by the United States and its allies belonging to the aggressive S.E.A.T.O. bloc in the internal affairs of Laos."[38] The Soviet Union accused the United States of "egging on its placement to stage a rebellion" against the legal government of Souvanna Phouma. In support of this allegation, Moscow claimed that "the rebels are getting substantial supplies of American money, arms and ammunition, while American military advisers rule the roost among the rebel troops." Moscow also asserted that South Vietnam and Thailand were supporting Phoumi and stated, "The Soviet Government emphatically denounces the actions of the Government of the United States and its allies in the aggressive S.E.A.T.O. bloc in interfering in the internal affairs of Laos, and considers it necessary to warn them of the grave responsibility they are assuming by flagrantly violating the Geneva agreements of 1954."

In mid-September, Thailand placed an embargo on goods destined for Laos. This action seriously reduced Kong Le's capacity to prosecute the war against General Phoumi, because most of Laos's imports came across the Mekong River from the Nong Khai railhead in Thailand. Petroleum products became especially scarce after the imposition of the embargo. General Phoumi's forces were not affected because the United States supplied them directly with military equipment, whereas Washington was giving Vientiane funds with which the government had to purchase supplies from outside. Vientiane's logistics were also damaged by Washington's suspension of financial aid during October and November, on the ground that "procedural delays" were responsible.[39] Deprived of both American financial support and Thai shipping facilities, Vientiane was becoming desperate for supplies.

Souvanna Phouma informed the United States of his economic dilemma and asked for rice and oil; Washington refused.[40] Consequently Souvanna turned to the Soviet Union for help.

Moscow agreed to ease Laos's economic problems in return for the establishment of diplomatic relations. Souvanna assented. On October 13, 1960, Aleksandr N. Abromov became the first Soviet Ambassador to Laos.

The effect of Thailand's embargo[41] on shipments to Laos, combined with the suspension of American aid to Souvanna, was thus the establishment of diplomatic relations between Laos and the Soviet Union. An embargo on trade and aid can produce its intended results, but only when the country under pressure lacks alternative sources of supply. The actions taken by Washington and its SEATO ally in Bangkok remind one of the father who cut off his son's allowance, only to see a friendly aunt gain the boy's affections by slipping him an equivalent sum on the sly. In any event, the establishment of diplomatic relations between Moscow and Vientiane produced a glaring chink in Washington's shield of containment.

Soon after the Soviet Union and Laos exchanged diplomats, Souvanna concluded an agreement[42] with the Pathet Lao. The accord specified that "Laos must resolutely follow a line of peace and neutrality." The document said further that the Laotian Government should "request aid" from socialist countries and should establish diplomatic relations with Communist China and North Vietnam. The NLHX reiterated its support for Souvanna's government. "The armed forces of the former Pathet Lao fighting units will abide by the policies of the lawful government [that is, Souvanna's regime] in order to win victory in the struggle against the Phoumi–Boun Oum traitorous clique. . . ." The princes agreed on the necessity of forming a coalition government of all nationalities, patriotic parties, and groups, including the NLHX. "With the exception of Phoumi and Boun Oum, members of the so-called 'Revolutionary Committee' will be given suitable posts in the government. . . ." Souvanna sent a delegation to Savannakhet to win General Phoumi's assent to a tripartite government; the general refused.

The neutralist–Pathet Lao agreement once again modified the shape of the conflict in Laos. Before Kong Le's paratroopers seized Vientiane, the Laotian moderates, represented by Souvanna Phouma, had been inclined to join hands with the conservatives against the Pathet Lao. Now, however, Souvanna and the Pathet Lao were in league[43] against the conservatives. The cooperation between the neutralists and the Pathet Lao was embodied in the creation of a National Military Committee, formed for the purpose of directing joint military operations against Phoumi. Kong Le was named president of the Committee.

THE SOVIET UNION AIDS THE ANTI-PHOUMI ALLIANCE

Whereas the United States was giving supplies and training to General Phoumi's troops, the Soviet Union helped sustain the neutralist–Pathet Lao combined forces.

Soviet support for the neutralist–Pathet Lao coalition followed from Moscow's commitment to back wars of national liberation. Premier Khrushchev had announced this doctrine during his address to a meeting of Soviet Union Communist Party Organizations on January 6, 1961.[44] Distinguishing between wars fought among states and wars fought for the sake of national self-determination, Khrushchev said that "Communists support such just wars [that is, those fought for self-determination] fully and without reservations, and march in the vanguard of the peoples fighting for liberation." Moscow's support for the anti-Phoumi alliance was consistent with this policy.[45]

Another reason for Russian aid may have been to dilute Chinese accusations, leveled at the Moscow Conference of 81 communist parties in November 1960, that the Soviet Union was shirking its duties to promote global revolution.

According to the State Department, the Soviets flew at least 180 sorties to Laos during the period from December 15, 1960, to January 3, 1961; in addition, the Soviets made at least 34 flights to Vientiane between December 3 and December 14, 1960, the State Department said.[46]

GENERAL PHOUMI CAPTURES VIENTIANE

As 1960 drew to a close, the indecisive fighting between Phoumi and his opponents came to a climax. In early December, Phoumi's forces began to march from southern Laos through Thailand toward Vientiane. Meanwhile, 40 of the 59 deputies[47] in the National Assembly had elected to show their support for Phoumi by journeying to his headquarters. On the morning of December 11, as Phoumi's troops marched ever closer to Vientiane, Souvanna Phouma fled from the capital to Phnom Penh, after delegating his powers to others. Kong Le's troops remained in control of the capital city.

On December 12, the 40 deputies in Savannakhet called a special session of the National Assembly and passed a vote of censure against Souvanna Phouma's government. Then the King issued a royal proclamation entrusting the Revolutionary Committee—headed by Phoumi and Boun Oum —with the temporary conduct of the kingdom's affairs. Three days later the United States announced that it regarded the Revolutionary Committee as the legal government of Laos.

A new complication had thus been introduced into the already twisted Laotian conflict. Now there were two governments, Souvanna Phouma's and the Revolutionary Committee. Each claimed recognition as the Royal Government of Laos. Souvanna insisted that his censure at the hands of the deputies who met at Savannakhet was invalid because it had been passed at an extraordinary session held in neither the royal capital (Luang Prabang) nor the administrative capital (Vientiane). He dismissed the King's negotiations with the Revolutionary Committee as beyond royal authority. The Prince insisted that he was still Prime Minister. The Soviet Union said it would continue to recognize Souvanna Phouma as Prime Minister of the legal government of Laos.

Phoumi's troops, meanwhile, had reached the outskirts of the capital by December 13, where they set up their American-supplied artillery. Kong Le's forces, with their artillery (provided by the Soviet Union), were stationed near Vatthay airfield on the opposite edge of the city. An artillery duel began. By December 16 the city had been leveled by artillery fire from both sides. Over 500 civilian casualties were reported (more casualties than the fighting forces suffered) during the four-day battle. When the fighting ended, Phoumi's forces were in control of the city. Kong Le and his soldiers retreated to the north, but only after Kong Le had distributed 9,000 American-made rifles in royal arsenals to Pathet Lao irregulars.[48]

When the din of battle ceased, the diplomatic airwaves were filled with charges and counter-charges of American participation in Phoumi's attack. That the United States gave Phoumi some help in his campaign to take Vientiane seems certain. But the degree of support rendered by the United States remains a matter for speculation. Souvanna Phouma's personal aide told the author that in his opinion the United States gave Phoumi equipment, including helicopters, and even supervised the shelling of the capital. He also believed that the United States supplied vehicles for transporting Phoumi's troops to the assault on Vientiane.[49] Communist China estimated that American aid was instrumental in helping Phoumi win the battle for

Vientiane. The secret military journal, *Kung-tso T'ung-hsun,* published by the General Political Department of the Chinese People's Liberation Army, said that Washington supplied General Phoumi with 105mm. howitzers and M–24 tanks. The journal added that Phoumi was aided in the use of these weapons by technicians who secretly came from Thailand to instruct Phoumi's troops.[50]

The Soviet Union accused the United States of "providing broad military, material and technical, and financial assistance to the rebels of General Phoumi Nosavan. . . ."[51]

Souvanna Phouma, in an interview in January 1961, in Phnom Penh, said that the United States allowed General Phoumi to use American-supplied arms against him. He also complained that the United States plotted with the General to overthrow his government. "What I shall never forgive the United States for, however," the Prince said, "is the fact that it betrayed me, that it doublecrossed me and my Government."[52]

The evidence cited above is far from conclusive, inasmuch as the available sources remain biased against the United States. It does seem probable, though, that the United States provided some military assistance to General Phoumi. The exact amount of such aid remains in doubt and cannot be determined until more information becomes available. Of central importance, however, is the fact that *Souvanna* believed that the United States had given Phoumi military equipment that was used against the neutralist forces. It was on this belief that Souvanna based his future actions, whether or not his impression was correct. As far as Souvanna Phouma was concerned, the United States had "doublecrossed" him and was therefore to be regarded with suspicion in the future.

As we review the events discussed in this chapter, we find that during the fall and winter of 1960–1961 the United States made several important decisions that were to affect future American actions in Laos. Banking on Phoumi's ability—to be enhanced, of course, by American aid—to defeat the neutralists and the Pathet Lao militarily, the United States supported his policy of military confrontation. Washington's support of Phoumi, combined with Thailand's embargo on shipments to Laos, left Souvanna Phouma with no choice but to appeal to other sources for material aid and military assistance. When the Soviet Union offered to meet the needs of the neutralist forces, Souvanna accepted. The establishment of a Soviet embassy in Vientiane and the extension of Soviet aid to the neutralists soon followed. The Laotian civil conflict assumed the dimensions of a cold-war struggle between forces backed by the United States and the Soviet Union.

At first, these developments did not seem adverse to American interests, as Phoumi won the first major battle—the Battle of Vientiane—in the

Laotian civil war. The Soviet-supported group appeared to be on the decline, as Kong Le and his troops fled from the Laotian capital. Phoumi's army, however, was unable to inflict a final defeat upon the opposing forces, and a military stalemate took effect.

It is possible that, had Phoumi been able to drive the neutralist and Pathet Lao forces from the field once and for all, the United States would have engineered a stunning cold-war triumph. The installation of a pro-Western regime, resembling that of Phoui Sananikone, would probably have followed upon a final victory by Phoumi's forces. Lacking a military component, the Pathet Lao would have declined in political power to perhaps negligible proportions. In light of the magnitude of such a victory for Washington and the not improbable possibility of attaining it, the United States was taking what might be called a calculated risk. By no means could it be said that Washington was acting blindly or in complete foolishness. In selecting a foreign policy alternative, as in choosing a marriage partner, wisdom consists in acting on the basis of reasonable risk; in both cases, the desire for certainty would preclude any action whatever.

However, the fact remains that Phoumi was not able to deal a death blow to his opponents, and a military stalemate developed. As this stalemate persisted into the first quarter of 1961, the Soviet Union helped the neutralist–Pathet Lao coalition to consolidate their forces. Since he had failed to annihilate his opponents after the Battle of Vientiane, Phoumi was obliged to meet them at a later date, at a time when they had become strengthened by Soviet assistance. The United States, in the meantime, continued to give military and other assistance to Phoumi, to prepare him for a future showdown. On the outcome of this future battle, which would be fought in May 1962, the political complexion of Laos was to depend.

By most standards, the Laotian conflict seemed to be moving ever farther from a compromise settlement as the year 1961 progressed. Continuing and increasing external support for the Pathet Lao and General Phoumi reduced each side's incentive to conclude a compromise. Each side had reason to believe that it could use this external support for the purpose of bettering its own position, perhaps by a major military victory. So long as this hope remained, neither side was prepared to negotiate.

While the prospects for a compromise settlement appeared bleak, the very forces that created this impression were quietly giving birth to some of the foundations of the compromise that did in fact materialize in 1962. Most important was the emergence of a center group, headed by Souvanna Phouma, that stood between the Pathet Lao and Phoumi's pro-Western group.

The neutralists, led by Souvanna Phouma and Kong Le, were in a position to act as the keystone of a settlement that would embrace both the Pathet Lao and the pro-Western group. The policies espoused by the neutralists were ones to which the other two factions could accommodate themselves in case their maximum objective—exclusive control of the government—proved unattainable. Both extreme factions eventually reached this conclusion, and in June 1962 they tailored their political programs to those of the neutralists.

Another reason why the existence of the neutralists contributed to the 1962 settlement was that the neutralists were supported by a military force in being. The neutralist army offered hopes to extremists on each side that if they accepted a coalition government, the center had the power to prevent the usurpation of political power by the rival extreme element. Lacking military support, the neutralists could have served as a referee between the Pathet Lao and General Phoumi, but would have been powerless to protect one from the other. Such confidence was necessary in order for a coalition regime to come into being.

A third reason why the emergence of a middle faction proved conducive to a compromise settlement lay in the character of Souvanna Phouma. Souvanna had been prominent in Laotian politics since the birth of the nationalist movement following World War II. The Prince was a patriot whose methods were trusted even by those who disagreed with him on substantive grounds. His moderation was universally recognized. These attributes assume crucial importance for an individual who seeks to head a coalition embracing elements with fundamental differences.[53] In order for a coalition government to gain acceptance, the leader of the center must be trusted by both the right and the left. That the leaders of the Pathet Lao and the Phoumi–Boun Oum group had confidence in Souvanna Phouma was an important factor that led to the compromise settlement finalized in the summer of 1962.

NOTES

1. Tiao Somsanith became prime minister June 3, 1960, when Kou Abhay's caretaker regime stepped down after the elections in April 1960.

2. Communique No. 2 of the Second Paratroop Battalion, broadcast by Radio Vientiane on August 9, 1960, in Arthur J. Dommen, *Conflict in Laos* (New York: Frederick A. Praeger, 1964), p. 310.

3. *The New York Times,* August 13, 1960.

4. Keyes Beech, "How Uncle Sam Fumbled in Laos," *Saturday Evening Post* 234 (April 22, 1961) :89.

5. Joel M. Halpern, *Government, Politics and Social Structure in Laos* (New

Haven: Yale University, Southeast Asia Studies, Monograph Series No. 4, 1964),
p. 40.

6. Wilfred G. Burchett, *The Furtive War: The United States in Vietnam and Laos* (New York: International Publishers, 1963), p. 189.

7. *Ibid.*, p. 190.

8. Beech, *Saturday Evening Post*, 234:89.

9. Burchett, pp. 189-90.

10. Broadcast on August 12 over Radio Hanoi, reported in *The New York Times,* August 13, 1960.

11. *The New York Times,* September 12, 1960.

12. On September 5 Radio Pathet Lao announced five conditions for future negotiations with the Vientiane government:

1. Elimination of the Phoumists from the cabinet.

2. End of the fighting between the Pathet Lao and Vientiane.

3. Immediate freedom for all prisoners.

4. Royal Government acceptance of a policy of strict neutrality and agreement to have diplomatic relations with all countries regardless of their political systems.

5. Acceptance of all offers of aid if not accompanied by political conditions.

(*Le Monde,* September 6, 1960.)

13. "Each agency came to pursue its own programs and policies with less and less regard for the others, and with little relationship to an over-all American policy . . . neither the Lao nor our allies could tell who really spoke for the United States—whether it was the CIA, the military, the AID officials, or the Ambassador." (Roger Hilsman, *To Move A Nation* (New York: Doubleday and Company, Inc., 1967), p. 116.)

14. Arthur M. Schlesinger, Jr., *A Thousand Days* (Boston: Houghton Mifflin Company, 1965), pp. 326-37.

15. Schlesinger, p. 327; Dommen, pp. 157-58; Warren Unna in *The Washington Post,* December 15, 1960.

16. One wit referred to Souvanna as an oriental impotentate.

17. Dwight D. Eisenhower, *Waging Peace* (New York: Doubleday and Company, Inc., 1965), p. 608.

18. Senate Committee on Armed Services, *Military Cold War Education and Speech Review Policies,* Part V, 1962, p. 2049.

19. Schlesinger, p. 327; Dommen, pp. 157-58; Warren Unna in *The Washington Post,* December 15, 1960.

20. *Department of State Bulletin,* September 26, 1960, p. 499.

21. *The New York Times,* September 12, 1960.

22. Hilsman, p. 214.

23. *The New York Times,* September 24, 1960; *Le Monde,* September 25-26, 1960.

24. *Le Monde,* September 25-26, 1960.

25. Dommen, p. 154.

26. Hilsman, p. 124.

27. Dommen, pp. 154-55.

28. Schlesinger, p. 327.

29. *Ibid.*

30. *The New York Times,* October 8, 1960.

31. Eisenhower later wrote that the American mission made a "great effort" to persuade Souvanna not to bring the Pathet Lao into his government. (Eisenhower, *Waging Peace*, p. 608.)

32. Interview with Khamchan Pradith, Counsellor of Embassy, Permanent Mission of Laos to the United Nations, former personal assistant of Prince Souvanna Phouma, December 28, 1966.

33. *Ibid.*

34. Schlesinger, p. 328.

35. Dommen, p. 160.

36. Interview with Khamchan Pradith.

37. Later Souvanna alleged that Phoumi used the American-supplied equipment against the neutralist forces during the fighting leading up to Phoumi's capture of Vientiane in December, 1960.

38. Text of Soviet statement in *Documents on International Affairs*, 1960, pp. 516–17.

39. *The New York Times*, November 30, 1960.

40. Schlesinger, p. 328.

41. Thailand lifted the embargo at the end of October 1960.

42. Text in *Documents on International Affairs*, 1961, pp. 570–71, n. 3.

43. It should be pointed out that while the neutralists and the Pathet Lao agreed to combine forces, the two movements never merged under a single leader. In fact, the neutralists and the Pathet Lao came to blows after the 1962 Geneva agreements were signed.

44. Extracts from this speech may be found in *Documents on International Affairs*, 1961, pp. 259–72. President Kennedy regarded Khrushchev's speech as so significant that he circulated copies of it among the members of the Cabinet.

45. During this period the Soviet Union followed a militant policy on several fronts, including cancellation of the Geneva disarmament talks (after Russia shot down the American U-2 airplane), accusation of Western backing for Belgian intervention in the Congo, ICBM threats to the United States regarding Cuba, *de facto* recognition of the Algerian rebels, and shoe-banging at the United Nations.

46. *Department of State Bulletin*, January 23, 1961, pp. 114–15. Detailed descriptions of Soviet aid to Laos may be found in the following sources: *The New York Times*, December 5, 1960, and December 15, 1960; *Le Monde*, January 22–23, 1961; James Wilde, "The Russians in Laos," *Time* 77 (March 10, 1961) :26; Senate Committee on Armed Services, *Military Cold War Education and Speech Review Policies*, Part V, 1962, p. 2408 (testimony of General Heintges).

47. It should be recalled that these deputies were elected in April 1960, in elections supervised by Phoumi himself. We have already discussed seemingly indisputable allegations that these elections were rigged so as to yield a strongly conservative government. To the extent that the elections were dishonest, one could argue that these deputies, in coming to Savannakhet, did not in actuality represent the views of the people in their electoral districts.

48. Beech, *Saturday Evening Post*, 234:90.

49. Interview with Khamchan Pradith.

50. J. Chester Cheng (ed.), *The Politics of the Chinese Red Army* (Stanford: The Hoover Institute on War, Revolution, and Peace, 1966), p. 366. This collection, a translation of 29 issues of the journal issued between January 1, 1961 and

August 26, 1961, was distributed only to Communist Party cadres at the regimental level or above. The journal is not a propaganda medium and therefore the author includes it as evidence.

51. Soviet Note to the United Kingdom, December 22, 1960, in *Documents on International Affairs,* 1960, p. 528.

52. *The New York Times,* January 20, 1961. No doubt, Souvanna was referring to the arrangement, concluded in October 1960, that the United States would permit Phoumi to use American-supplied equipment only against the Pathet Lao, not against the neutralists.

53. The Secretary General of the United Nations, it seems, must also have a reputation for using fair methods and acting with moderation.

12
BACK TO GENEVA

THE MILITARY STALEMATE

GENERAL PHOUMI NOSAVAN'S capture of Vientiane was a source of great satisfaction to those American policymakers who had counseled against siding with Souvanna Phouma. Now the question in everyone's mind was whether Phoumi could sustain his momentum, destroy Kong Le's fleeing army, and deal the death blow to Pathet Lao soldiers quartered in northeastern Laos. If Phoumi could accomplish these tasks, then the American containment strategists would have cause to congratulate themselves on their achievements in Laos.

Phoumi's first objective was to decimate the forces commanded by Kong Le. The Battle of Vientiane, while delivering up the capital to Phoumi, was not so decisive an engagement as first had appeared. Kong Le had been able to evacuate his troops with few casualties and without impairing the effectiveness of his army. After the battle, Kong Le had led his troops to the Plain of Jars (a 500-square-mile grassy plain north of the capital, so named because large funeral urns were found there). The Plain occupies a strategic location because whoever controls it also controls land communications across Laos. Two vital roads intersect at Sala Phou Khoun on the Plain. A north–south road extends northward from Vientiane across the Plain, then to Luang Prabang, and on into North Viet Nam at Dien Bien Phu. The second road, Route Nationale 7, runs eastward across Laos from Sala Phou Khoun through Khang Khay and Nong Het and then into central North Vietnam. The Plain, which has one of the best airfields in Laos, can be easily supplied from North Vietnam by both Route Nationale 7 and air.

In early January, Phoumi attempted to capture the strategic Plain by a lightning paratroop drop. Kong Le's men, however, met Phoumi's paratroopers, took some of them prisoner, and sent the remainder fleeing back toward Vientiane. Kong Le had withstood Phoumi's offensive. In the next several weeks, Kong Le concentrated on enhancing the effectiveness of his fighting forces. The Pathet Lao army, meanwhile, had remained unscathed during the fighting of December and January. A military stalemate ensued, although at this point one could not be certain whether it would become a prolonged stalemate or only a brief prelude to a decisive victory by one of the parties.

While the pro- and anticommunists in Laos were wrangling on the battlefield, the United States and the Soviet Union, each joined by its respective allies, were exchanging diplomatic salvos. Just after the Battle of Vientiane, the United States sent a note[1] to the Soviet Union saying that it "condemns as a violation of every standard of legal conduct the recent Soviet action in airlifting weapons and ammunition in Soviet planes to rebel military forces fighting the loyal armed forces of the Royal Government in Vientiane" (that is, the government of Phoumi and Boun Oum). "It is communist and communist-fostered subversive activities, the guerrilla warfare of the Pathet Lao forces, and now the Soviet airlift of weapons which have led directly to the suffering and chaos which have befallen Laos," the note charged.

This communique was noteworthy not because of its standard denunciations of communist activity, but because it contained the first reference in the written diplomacy to the existence of two governments in Laos. The American note affirmed Washington's support of the Phoumi–Boun Oum regime, as opposed to Souvanna's group, as *the* government of Laos.

British Foreign Secretary Lord Home, a co-chairman of the Geneva Conference, announced his support for the American position on the government of Laos.[2] In the same speech, however, Lord Home enunciated a viewpoint that differed in an important respect from the American position. He said,

> It has been the policy of Her Majesty's Government ever since the rebellion of Captain Kong Le's troops in August of this year to try to encourage the Laotians to form a Government of national union. I think this is more desirable now than ever before. . . .[3]

A government of national union was precisely what the United States had been trying to prevent. Washington had been engaged in efforts to establish a strictly pro-Western regime that excluded Pathet Lao representation.

The Soviets and Chinese took a diametrically opposite position; they were attempting to bring about a leftist regime that did not include any pro-Western elements. Britain, it can be seen, stood in the middle. The position of Her Majesty's Government destined Britain to act as a linchpin in the 1962 settlement, which reflected the policy enunciated by Lord Home in December 1960.

In the heady days following their capture of Vientiane, the Laotian rightists, like their American well-wishers, were in no mood for compromise. Boun Oum, political leader of the military forces led by Phoumi, declared at a press conference that "neutrality is only a word." He said he did not envisage a coalition cabinet including the Pathet Lao because "the Pathet Lao are agents of communism." Souvanna Phouma, he stated, is "in same bag as Souphanouvong."[4]

On December 19 Peking joined the communist diplomatic offensive against alleged American actions in Laos. China attributed the outbreak of civil war in Laos to "the frenzied interference in the internal affairs of Laos by U. S. imperialism,"[5] a statement that could well have been stolen from Kong Le's lines. China echoed Russia's contention that Souvanna Phouma, not Boun Oum, was the head of the Royal Government of Laos, and added the usual allegations of American aid to Phoumi in the form of arms, ammunition, other military equipment, and military personnel.

The Soviet Union on December 22 issued another note, this time to Great Britain, urging her to join Russia in calling for a meeting of the countries that had attended the 1954 Geneva Conference; the Soviets also called for the reactivation of the ICC.[6] It said in addition that the cause of strife in Laos "is the crude interference in the internal affairs of Laos by the United States and some other members of the S.E.A.T.O. military bloc who, on the one hand, are rendering extensive military, material-technical and financial assistance to the rebels of General Phoumi Nosavan resisting the legitimate Laotian Government headed by Prime Minister Souvanna Phouma, and on the other hand have established a blockade of Laos."

The Soviet Union also explained why it regarded Souvanna Phouma as the head of the Laotian government. Moscow believed that "any decisions of a group of Deputies of the National Assembly or of the King, who are held captive by the rebels, have no legal force. Thus, the government of Prince Souvanna Phouma remains the legitimate national government of Laos. . . ." Since, the Soviets reasoned, Souvanna is the head of the Laotian government, and since according to international law only the government of a country is permitted to request external assistance, American aid to General Phoumi "is nothing but a flagrant violation of international law and the Geneva agreements on Laos. . . ." The note suggested that Britain and the Soviet Union, as the Co-Chairmen of the Geneva Conference, request the United States to withdraw its assistance to Phoumi. China supported the Soviet position.[7]

On the last day of 1960, the United States brought the mounting diplomatic chorus on Laos to a crescendo with two statements on the Laotian situation. The State Department warned that "the United States Government would take the most serious view of any intervention in Laos by the Chinese Communists or Viet Minh armed forces or others in support of the Communist Pathet Lao, who are in rebellion against the Royal Laotian Government."[8] President Eisenhower, about to vacate the Presidency, presented a more detailed picture of American policy. He said,

> For the moment here's what we must do: Induce Souvanna Phouma to resign as Prime Minister and if possible persuade him to leave Cambodia and depart for France. Get Boun Oum to allow the National Assembly to approve his government. . . . Alert the SEATO Council, but for the moment, do not request specific overt action by the alliance. Redeploy our own forces to bring them within striking range in the event they have to intervene against the North Vietnamese. We should then make a serious approach to the Russians, telling Ambassador Thompson to let Khrushchev know that we view these events with grave concern, that we are moving our forces to assure, if necessary, that the legitimate government of Laos will not be destroyed, and that if a major war comes, the United States will not be caught napping.
>
> We cannot let Laos fall to the Communists even if we have to fight, with our allies or without them.[9]

President Eisenhower, it must be understood, viewed the Laotian conflict in terms of an American–communist confrontation, not just as a localized civil war. The President's thinking on this issue is revealed in a letter he sent to French President Charles de Gaulle during the first week of January 1961. Eisenhower cited assistance to the Pathet Lao from both the Soviet Union and North Vietnam and said, "We take most seriously this evidence of an effort by the Soviet bloc to bring the Kingdom of Laos under its domination and control."[10] As the President saw it, North Vietnam and the Soviet Union were part of one overall "bloc," the former being subservient to the latter. These assumptions may prove to have been correct, but from today's perspective there is much room for doubt. Although Russia and North Vietnam cooperated in supplying the neutralist–Pathet Lao—Soviet planes flew from Hanoi to Laos—North Vietnam has exhibited a strong desire to maintain its freedom of action. This is best shown by Hanoi's refusal to take sides in the Sino-Soviet quarrel.

Eisenhower, in these closing days of his tenure in the White House, perhaps overestimated the determination of the Soviet Union to bring the Kingdom of Laos under its domination and control. To be sure, the Soviets opposed an American presence in Laos. However, Soviet calls for a reconvocation of the 1954 Geneva powers indicated that the Russians were willing to accept a compromise solution and had not ruled out a coalition government. Within a year both the United States and the Soviet Union were to subscribe to this arrangement.

Furthermore, it is doubtful that the Soviets exerted as much control in Laos as the United States presumed. Kong Le's rebellion did not start as a result of Soviet aid, which did not commence until over two months after Kong Le took control of Vientiane. Likewise, charges that communists dominated Kong Le and his followers seem misplaced. After gaining control of the capital, Kong Le did not offer political control to Souphanouvong but instead turned to Souvanna Phouma, rival of the Pathet Lao leader. Some Americans argued that Souvanna was a communist or that his policies so coincided with those of the Pathet Lao as to be nearly indistinguishable. However, the fact that the neutralists, led by Souvanna Phouma, have never merged with the Pathet Lao and have in fact been fighting them since 1962 unequivocally refutes the notion that Souvanna is a communist or is subservient to the communists. In fact, Souvanna and Kong Le represented an independent third force that the United States could have supported in an effort to reach a compromise settlement. But, as we have already seen, Washington preferred to gamble on Phoumi's ability to inflict military defeat upon the other two factions.

In the midst of all this diplomatic hassling, the Laotian National Assembly on January 4, 1961, passed a vote of confidence in the Boun Oum government. The King then completed the formal investiture proceedings. Boun Oum was named Prime Minister. Phoumi, the real strength behind the regime, became Deputy Prime Minister and Minister of Defense. Now, Boun Oum's backers said, the previous (Souvanna Phouma) government was ousted and the new (Boun Oum) government installed, all according to proper constitutional procedures. Souvanna Phouma, in voluntary exile in Phnom Penh, denied the legality of these proceedings. The Soviets backed Souvanna. For the time being, however, the question was important principally for propaganda purposes only. Although international law provides that only a legal government may request and accept outside aid, it is doubtful that the Soviet Union or the United States would have stopped assisting their Laotian protegés, even had either been convinced of the illegality of its actions. Both superpowers continued to act in accordance with their perceptions of their national interests, and international law be damned.

The dawning of 1961 brought forth a fresh round of American diplomatic statements concerning the Laotian conflict. On January 3 the State Department condemned "the extensive Soviet and North Vietnamese participation in the Communist military operations against the Royal Lao Government and the Lao people."[11] The statement accused the Soviets of conducting an "extensive airlift of war material" to communist forces. "Substantial numbers of north Vietnamese Communist personnel" were parachuted into Laos from Soviet and North Vietnamese aircraft, the State Department alleged. Washington said that Soviet and North Vietnamese aircraft had made 34 flights to supply the Souvanna Phouma regime between December 3 and 14, and at least 180 sorties since then in support of the Kong Le–Pathet Lao forces. During the period December 3–14, communist aircraft introduced into the battle for Vientiane "105-mm. howitzers, ammunition, gasoline, combat rations, and other war material. North Vietnamese military personnel were also landed or parachuted in to augment Kong Le's forces," the statement said.

On January 4 the SEATO Council met and "noted with concern the reports of increasing supply of war materials by Soviet aircraft from North Vietnam to Communist rebel elements engaged in operations against the Royal Laotian Army and the people of Laos."[12]

Three days later the Eisenhower administration published a lengthy valedictory statement on Laos.[13] Because this January 7 note so well summarized the American position, we are presenting a brief précis here.

By July 1959, in the face of increasing stability in Laos, the communists concluded that they had slight chances of "gaining control of Laos" through subversion, propaganda, and small-scale guerrilla activity, the American declaration said. Therefore, in mid-July they launched a military offensive, "made possible through external direction and assistance. Then, following a Lao appeal to the United Nations, this Communist military advance terminated almost simultaneously with the appearance on the scene of a subcommittee of the Security Council, and every attempt was made by the Communists to erase evidence of external support."[14]

After communist military efforts subsided, Laos returned to the path of increasing stability, until Kong Le's coup "plunged the country into chaos."

> Although originally there may have been some doubt concerning the inspiration for Captain Kong Le's action, his motivation and support, those doubts have been dispelled by the tragic events of the past few weeks. His initial collaboration with the Pathet Lao, including arming them from the Royal arsenals, his clandestine cooperation with foreign Communist governments, and the baneful effect on Laos are all now a matter of history.[15]

These events culminated in the flight of the Prime Minister and most of his cabinet between December 9 and December 15. "They thus abandoned any realistic pretense of fulfilling their responsibilities as a government."[16] Thirty-eight members of the National Assembly met in Savannakhet and voted no confidence in Souvanna's government.[17] The King dismissed that regime and appointed Boun Oum to form a provisional government, which was approved by the National Assembly on January 4, 1961.

During this period, the Soviets intervened by airlifting military supplies and personnel to Vientiane. After Kong Le's troops withdrew from Vientiane in December, the Soviets continued their airlift.

Laos cannot defend itself alone against the various kinds of overt and covert attacks which north Viet-Nam and the Communist Chinese with Soviet aid can mount against it. Under these circumstances, Laos can remain independent only if the non-Communist nations of the world render the assistance it has requested to maintain its independence.

American aid to Laos, unlike Soviet aid, has been legal because it was given to the allegedly legitimate government. American aid has been extended to further America's "basic objective of insuring the right of free nations to preserve their independence."

United States aid has been extended to Laos within the framework of existing international agreements and at the request of the Royal Lao Government. No United States aid has been given except pursuant to agreements with that Government, nor has any been given without its knowledge and approval.[18]

Soviet deliveries of munitions and military supplies to pro-Communist rebels is "illegal." "No government of Laos has ever asked for these deliveries which the Soviet Union is airlifting to Laos in growing quantities."

Communist policy in Laos has been motivated by "a determination to take over the country in line with the Communists' well-known and indeed oft-stated objective of ultimate global domination. If Laos should be seized by the Communists, the effects could be far-reaching and the implication for other small and vulnerable states all too evident."

The United States believes it can best contribute to a solution of the Laotian problem "by joining with other free nations to support and maintain the independence of Laos through whatever measures seem most promising."

In line with the January 7 statement, the United States began to render Phoumi more military assistance. In early January Washington supplied Phoumi with ten AT–6 observation aircraft, each armed with a pair of 30-caliber machine guns and two 2.36 rockets.[19] On January 30 the

United States announced that American military advisers would henceforth move with forward fighting units of Phoumi's army.[20] The United States, it seems, was becoming increasingly committed to a military victory by General Phoumi.

Despite these injections of American military aid, little action of significance was occurring on the ground in Laos. Outlying patrols from Phoumi's army skirmished halfheartedly with troops from Kong Le and the Pathet Lao during January. Such fighting as occurred brings to mind two youths who really don't wish to trade blows, but who want to maintain the spirit of bravado; each takes a belligerently defensive stand, hoping all the while that the other won't start punching. Accordingly, the military sparring produced no major engagements or critical victories. Meanwhile, however, new currents of diplomacy were beginning to break up the international logjam over Laos, produced by the confrontation between the United States and the communist powers.

MOVEMENT ON
THE DIPLOMATIC FRONT

On January 2, 1961, Cambodian Prince Sihanouk sent a proposal to the countries that had participated in the 1954 Geneva Conference. The Prince called for an international conference whose purpose would be "the determining of means by which the peace in Laos can be restored and an opportunity given to the Laotian people to make their choice freely and clearly of what path they intend to follow." Sihanouk suggested that the conference should be attended by the countries that had sent representatives to the 1954 Geneva Conference as well as the countries represented on the ICC and those nations that had a common border with Laos. The United States, he said, should also be represented.[21]

The Soviet Union endorsed Sihanouk's proposal, as did Communist China. Great Britain, on the other hand, demurred. The British felt that the situation in Laos was too urgent to allow for the slowness and cumbersomeness of an international conference. The first priority, Britain declared, was to end the fighting. In order to effect a cease-fire, Britain suggested, the ICC should be reactivated. "If at a later stage we feel that the time is ripe for a conference, I will certainly let you know."[22] France supported the Cambodian proposal.

While the diplomatic world was considering Prince Sihanouk's proposal to convene an international conference, the British and Soviets addressed their attention to a related matter, the ICC. On December 14, 1960, Indian Prime Minister Nehru had sent a message to both Co-Chairmen of the Geneva Conference, proposing that the ICC be reconvened. The possibility of revitalizing this body raised the question of which Laotian authority the ICC would be accredited to. The Soviets insisted that the ICC should be instructed to work with the Souvanna Phouma regime. The United States was just as adamant in demanding that the ICC should be told to work with Boun Oum. Britain adopted a position in between, suggesting to the Soviets that the Co-Chairmen send a message to Nehru asking him to appoint a representative to undertake an exploratory mission to the King of Laos—this would obviate the necessity of choosing between Souvanna Phouma and Boun Oum—proposing that the ICC be reconvened.[23]

On February 18 Moscow responded to the British suggestion. The Soviets said that the ICC could normalize the Laotian situation only in conjunction with an international conference, which would draft instructions to the ICC. Russia objected to the British plan, holding that the Laotian constitution gave the King no executive authority and that, anyway, he was "a prisoner of the rebels." Russia suggested that the ICC meet immediately in Delhi, and that the Co-Chairmen should supervise the work of the ICC.[24]

While the two principal diplomatic issues—convening the ICC and convocation of an international conference—were being debated in the capitals concerned, the feuding Laotian factions made a preliminary effort to sound each other's position. On March 9 and 10, General Phoumi went to Phnom Penh to confer with Souvanna Phouma. This meeting was the first official contact between the rival regimes since the battle of Vientiane in December 1960. On March 10 the two Laotians issued a joint communique, which said that the talks "took place in an atmosphere of good will and mutual understanding." The parties condemned foreign intervention and recognized that neutrality was the fundamental condition for peace and national accord. The meeting, however, did not bring them closer together on the basic issues that separated them.

A third feature of the developing Laotian situation—the other two being the Anglo-Soviet negotiations and the Souvanna-Phoumi meeting—was the military contest. By the end of February, the neutralist–Pathet Lao forces had consolidated their hold on the Plaine des Jarres. They also exercised military predominance in the provinces of Phong Saly, Sam Neua, and Xieng Khouang. In early March they seized the key road junction at Sala Phou Khoun, where the north–south road intersects the east–west road. Phoumi's troops were forced to flee, and the neutralists–Pathet Lao were in position to attack Luang Prabang and Vientiane.

In Washington, meanwhile, a new young President, John F. Kennedy, was busy organizing his administration to deal with the problems and opportunities of the 1960s. Phoumi's battlefield reversals confronted the Kennedy Administration with one of its earliest critical decisions—to intervene or not to intervene in Laos. In the words of the then Director of the State Department's Bureau of Intelligence and Research, "there were long and agonizing meetings in the Secretary of State's office and conference room. . . ."[25] Several proposals were made. Secretary of Defense McNamara suggested arming the AT–6 observation planes with hundred-pound bombs. Someone else suggested airlifting up to a division of U.S. Marines into the Plaine des Jarres. A third suggestion was to unearth a plan that had existed for some time: to use 60,000 Americans to seize the southern panhandle of Laos between the two large bends of the Mekong River.[26]

Roger Hilsman, who was a party to the debate, reveals that the discussion surrounding military intervention took place in a context that derived from the Korean War.[27] Many high-ranking military personnel considered the Korean War a humiliation. Restrictions placed on the use of force—especially limitations on bombing north of the Yalu River—prevented the military from winning an outright victory, or so many in the military believed. By 1961 the Joint Chiefs of Staff (hereafter: JCS) had come to feel that the United States should never fight a *limited* ground war in Asia. The majority sentiment within the JCS was that if the United States were to use force again in Asia, such force must be unlimited, including the use of nuclear weapons.

The debate on whether to use force in Laos was conceived within this frame of reasoning. If the communists gained control of Laos, it was thought, they would have access to the north–south route through Southeast Asia which lay along the Mekong lowlands, from which they could mount pressure on South Vietnam, Cambodia and Thailand. On the other hand, a limited commitment of American troops might result in another Korean type war, a lengthy and indecisive conflict. An unrestricted application of American force could escalate to World War III. None of these military alternatives looked especially inviting to the new President.

President Kennedy hoped to find a political solution instead of a military solution to the Laotian situation. In other words, he hoped that a negotiated compromise would obviate the need for military action. If a political solution proved unattainable, the United States still retained the option of a military response.

A political solution did not seem beyond reach. In Laos Souvanna Phouma, well known and commanding a considerable following, advocated a middle-of-the-road position upon which a political settlement could be based. The British and the Soviets were negotiating to find grounds for a compromise political settlement. The Co-Chairmen were considering, as preliminary steps, the convening of the ICC and the holding of an international conference. Active entertainment of these measures indicated that the Soviets[28] and the British, the latter speaking in part for the United States, were considering compromise instead of insisting on a settlement thoroughly unacceptable to the other side. Although Souvanna and Phoumi had been unable to reconcile their differences at Phnom Penh, the very fact of their meeting signified that they had not ruled out compromise.

The principal obstacles to a political solution seemed to be both General Phoumi's military weakness and the policies of Communist China and North Vietnam. Phoumi's inability to damage the neutralist–Pathet Lao fighting forces—in fact, the latter were hurting Phoumi—gave the neutralists–Pathet Lao little incentive to agree to a compromise. The same could be said for the Communist Chinese and the North Vietnamese, who were supporting their clients with military supplies and equipment. (Most Western experts believed, probably correctly, that North Vietnamese military personnel were actually fighting alongside neutralist–Pathet Lao soldiers.) A way had to be found to convince the neutralists–Pathet Lao, as well as Peking and Hanoi, to agree to a compromise settlement.

The answer seemed to lie in the threat of American intervention. In order to effect a political solution, as President Kennedy desired, the United States needed to persuade its adversaries in Laos that Washington would intervene, if necessary, to prevent the neutralists–Pathet Lao from gaining more ground.

But how was the United States to make a threat of intervention credible? Mere words would not do, for they might be interpreted as a bluff. The best way to make such a threat believable was to move American troops toward Laos. At the same time, the United States had to take care not to produce an overreaction by the neutralists–Pathet Lao. If the communists interpreted the threatened American intervention as motivated by a desire for outright victory instead of compromise, they would have no incentive to bargain.

After National Security Council meetings on March 20 and 21, Kennedy ordered the necessary steps preliminary to the movement of troops. A task force on Okinawa especially formed and trained to fight in Southeast Asia was placed on alert. A Marine force in Japan was readied. The Seventh Fleet steamed to the Gulf of Siam. At Udorn, the airfield in Thailand nearest Laos, a 500-man unit was sent to set up a helicopter base; a flight of helicopters arrived shortly thereafter. Stockpiles of equipment and supplies were sent to bases near the Laotian border.

These measures were designed to convince the neutralists–Pathet Lao that the United States would not permit them to overrun Laos. They also placed the world on notice that any compromise the United States made would not issue from a position of weakness or irresolution. Having thus demonstrated American determination to resist communist conquest of Laos, President Kennedy prepared to state terms that the United States would accept.

PRESIDENT KENNEDY ANNOUNCES NEW AMERICAN POLICY TOWARD LAOS

On March 23, President Kennedy held a news conference devoted to Laos. In a statement[29] which he read, the President accused the Laotian communists of disrupting Laos's progress toward unity and neutrality. In the last half of 1960, "the Communists and their supporters turned to a new and greatly intensified military effort to take over." In this effort, the President continued, the communists benefited from "increasing support and direction from outside."

> Soviet planes, I regret to say, have been conspicuous in a large-scale airlift into the battle area—over 1,000 sorties since December 13, 1960, and a whole supporting set of combat specialists, mainly from Communist north Viet-Nam—and heavier weapons have been provided from outside, all with the clear object of destroying by military action the agreed neutrality of Laos. It is this new dimension of externally supported warfare that creates the present grave problem.

After describing the existing situation in the terms above, President Kennedy redefined American policy.

> First: We strongly and unreservedly support the goal of a neutral and independent Laos, tied to no outside power or group of powers, threatening no one, and free from any domination. . . . If in the past there has been any possible ground for misunderstanding of our support for a truly neutral Laos, there should be none now.
>
> Secondly, if there is to be a peaceful solution, there must be a cessation of the present armed attacks by externally supported Communists. If these attacks do not stop, those who support a genuinely neutral Laos will have to consider their response.
>
> .   .   .   .
>
> Third, we are earnestly in favor of constructive negotiation—among the nations concerned and among the leaders of Laos—which can help Laos back to the pathway of independence and genuine neutrality. We strongly support the present British proposal of a prompt end of hostilities and prompt negotiation.[30]
>
> .   .   .   .
>
> I want to make it clear to the American people, and to all the world,

that all we want in Laos is peace, not war—a truly neutral government, not a cold-war pawn—a settlement concluded at the conference table, not on the battlefield.

President Kennedy thus modified American policy toward Laos in a major way. Under President Eisenhower, the United States had tried to create a pro-Western regime in Laos and had opposed the inclusion of communists in the government. In calling for "a neutral and independent Laos, tied to no outside power or group of powers," President Kennedy signified a willingness to accept a nonaligned Laos. In enunciating approval of the British proposal, the President hinted that the United States might be willing to consider a coalition government that included communists.

The British note, which, together with Kennedy's statement, should be considered as a single diplomatic package, also specified that "an *essential prerequisite* for the successful execution of the proposals which follow is that there should be an immediate cessation of all active military operations in Laos." (Italics mine.) Accordingly, the note said, the Co-Chairmen should issue an immediate request for a cease-fire. If this could be accomplished, the Co-Chairmen should ask the Indian Prime Minister to summon the ICC to meet in New Delhi as soon as possible. The ICC's task would be to verify the effectiveness of the cease-fire and report thereon to the Co-Chairmen. As soon as the ICC reported the existence of a cease-fire, the Co-Chairmen should call an international conference to consider a settlement of the Laotian problem.[31]

In addition to outlining the essentials of a Laotian settlement, President Kennedy at his news conference issued a warning to the communists. He said,

> My fellow Americans, Laos is far away from America, but the world is small. . . . The security of all of southeast Asia will be endangered if Laos loses its neutral independence. Its own safety runs with the safety of us all—in real neutrality observed by all. . . .
> Our response will be in close cooperation with our allies and the wishes of the Laotian Government. We will not be provoked, trapped, or drawn into this or any other situation. But I know that every American will want his country to honor its obligations to the point that freedom and security of the free world and ourselves may be achieved.

The military measures the United States took just prior to the President's news conference underlined Washington's determination to uphold this commitment.

The United States soon took further steps to signal its firmness. On March 24, SEATO's top military advisers, meeting in Bangkok, agreed that Laos must be defended at the Mekong basin, which includes Vientiane and Luang Prabang; all eight SEATO representatives later approved the principle. At the same time, the United States sent sixteen additional troop-carrying helicopters to Laos.

On March 26 President Kennedy and Prime Minister Macmillan, meeting in Key West, issued a communique which said in part,

> They agree that the situation in Laos cannot be allowed to deteriorate. They also agree that the recent British note to the Soviet Union contains proposals which, if implemented, would bring to an end the warfare in Laos and would pave the way for Laos to become the truly neutral country, which it is their joint wish to see.[32]

With reluctance, Macmillan gave Kennedy support for a limited intervention in Laos if it became necessary.[33]

On April 1 the Soviet Union replied to the British *aide-mémoire* of March 23. The Soviet note[34] approved the British suggestions for a cease-fire and the holding of an international conference. However, the Soviets differed with the British on the matter of whether verification of the cease-fire should precede the conference. The British note had emphatically insisted that no conference could be held until a cease-fire was reported. The Soviet reply stated, "Of course, a resumption of the Commission's work [the Commission was to report on a cease-fire] must in no way impede the convocation of the aforementioned international conference on Laos." The Soviets, in other words, were prepared to hold a conference whether or not a cease-fire existed. Moscow concurred in London's proposal that the ICC should meet in Delhi. The Co-Chairmen disagreed, however, on who was to represent Laos officially at the international conference. Moscow insisted that Souvanna Phouma was the Prime Minister of Laos, while Britain refused to recognize Souvanna's authority to represent his country. At the same time, the Soviets said that they "would favour negotiations among various political trends in Laos on measures to strengthen the country's national unity." If the Laotians did not form a unified government by the time the conference opened, Moscow said, the conference might assume as one of its tasks the rendering of assistance to the Laotians in reaching agreement.

President Kennedy called the Soviet note "a useful next step toward a peaceful settlement of a potentially dangerous situation." He said that "although the Soviet reply contains certain observations with which we cannot agree it offers hope that a way can be found to establish a neutral and independent Laos through negotiations." "The first need," the President said, "is to bring the present fighting in Laos to an end."[35]

During April the British and Soviets continued negotiations toward holding an international conference. Fighting in Laos continued, but neither side scored any strategic victories. The military stalemate persisted.

Souvanna Phouma, meanwhile, was circling the globe in an attempt to win support for a policy of neutrality for Laos. From April 16–22 he visited the Soviet Union, where he talked with Premier Khrushchev and other high Soviet officials. The joint communique issued at the conclusion of the visit stated that "both governments are of the opinion that real conditions exist for normalizing the situation in Laos. . . ." The parties agreed on convening an international conference, effecting a cease-fire, and reactivating the ICC. No mention was made, however, that these steps should occur in any particular sequence.

During the week of April 20, Washington's attention was diverted from Laos to the landing of anti-Castro fighters in Cuba. Kennedy had decided not to allow American troops to participate. Fearing that the communists in Asia might interpret this decision as irresolution, Kennedy decided upon a show of strength elsewhere. Accordingly, he instructed PEO personnel in Laos to doff their civilian clothes, put on uniforms and openly accompany Phoumi's battalions.[36] The PEO was converted into a Military Assistance Advisory Group.[37]

While Washington's eyes were turned toward the Carribean, Sir Frank Roberts, British Ambassador to Moscow, and Georgi M. Pushkin, Soviet Deputy Minister of Foreign Affairs, negotiated an agreement establishing procedures for settling the Laotian conflict. This agreement was issued in the form of three separate joint statements[38] from the Co-Chairmen of the 1954 Geneva Conference.

In one statement, addressed to the fighting forces in Laos, the Co-Chairmen stated that an international conference to settle the Laotian problem was to be called on May 12 and asked both parties "to cease fire before the convening of the international conference on Laos, and they call on appropriate representatives to enter into negotiations for concluding an agreement on questions connected with the cease-fire."[39]

The Co-Chairmen's second statement was addressed to the Government of India, asking it to convene the ICC in Delhi. "They [the Co-Chairmen] have in view that the commission will discuss the question of the tasks and functions which should be allotted to it after the cease-fire in Laos, and will present an appropriate report to the co-chairmen, who will consider the commission's report and give it directions on going to Laos to carry out the work of controlling the cease-fire."

The third statement consisted of an invitation to various countries to participate in an international conference on Laos to begin May 12 at Geneva. The invitations were sent to the following countries: Burma, Cambodia, Canada, the Chinese People's Republic, the Democratic Republic of Vietnam, France, India, Laos, the Polish People's Republic, the

Republic of Vietnam, Thailand, the Union of Soviet Socialist Republics, the United Kingdom, and the United States.

The State Department was quick to approve the British–Soviet agreements. However, continuing communist military attacks in Laos occasioned the following warning from the State Department:

> As the United States had made clear in the past, the first essential step is that a cease-fire be put into effect prior to the convening of the conference. The United States will, therefore, observe the situation on the ground in Laos very closely.

"Should a verified cease-fire be brought about," the statement continued, "the United States hopes to see emerge from the conference the peaceful, united, and unaligned Laos of which President Kennedy spoke on March 23."[40]

Thus, the United States endorsed the Anglo-Soviet agreements, but qualified its approval by reiterating its insistence that the cease-fire remained the first priority. The neutralist–Pathet Lao's continuing military aggressiveness made Washington fearful that the communist agreement to respect a cease-fire was either a trick to lure Phoumi's forces off guard for an all-out attack or that the neutralist–Pathet Lao forces were seeking to grab as much territory as possible before the cease-fire, in order to strengthen their bargaining position at Geneva.

Reports reaching Washington April 27 said the neutralists–Pathet Lao were attacking in force. The next day the National Security Council met to consider once again the possibility of sending American troops to Laos. The military, "chastened by the Bay of Pigs," to quote Schlesinger, left the impression that they did not want to deploy ground troops unless they could send 140,000 men armed with tactical nuclear weapons. Kennedy sent each of the Joint Chiefs home to prepare a written opinion on the deployment of American troops in Laos.

These written opinions were considered at a National Security Council meeting on May 1.[41] Although the opinions did not agree in all respects, the Chiefs favored a landing of American troops in Thailand, South Vietnam, and portions of the Laotian panhandle held by Phoumi's troops. If that action did not produce a cease-fire, the JCS said, the United States should undertake air attacks on neutralist–Pathet Lao positions and should employ tactical nuclear weapons on the ground. If North Vietnam or China intervened, the JCS recommended bombing their homelands. If Communist China mobilized troops, Washington should threaten nuclear bombing of China; if necessary, that threat would be executed. If the Soviets intervened, the Chiefs said, the United States should "be prepared to accept the possibility of general war." The Chiefs, however, assured the President that Russia "can hardly wish to see an uncontrollable situation develop." The opinions of the Chiefs reflected the military's objection to limited war in Asia.

During the May 1 meeting it was revealed that landlocked Laos had only two usable airstrips even in good weather. Neutralist–Pathet Lao control of the surrounding countryside would render troop landings hazardous, especially if hostile troops attacked before the entire American troop contingent could be placed on the ground.

As the talk continued, President Kennedy asked whether the United States would have to use nuclear weapons if China intervened in Laos. The Chiefs said yes. Kennedy then inquired whether the dispatch of American troops to Laos would weaken the Reserves for possible action in Berlin and elsewhere. Again the Chiefs answered in the affirmative.

Not yet having made up his mind on the wisdom of sending American troops to Laos, Kennedy sounded other opinions. General MacArthur as well as various congressional leaders were consulted and advised against a limited commitment of American troops.

After considering all the opinions he had requested, President Kennedy finally decided against sending American troops to Laos. In the view of Arthur Schlesinger, Jr., a close advisor to the President, Kennedy's decision was strongly influenced by the Bay of Pigs incident. Schlesinger wrote that before the Bay of Pigs, Kennedy was prepared to undertake limited intervention in Laos. But the failure in Cuba made Kennedy more cautious about a foreign policy adventure half-way around the globe. "If it hadn't been for Cuba," President Kennedy told Schlesinger on May 3, "we might be about to intervene in Laos."[42]

Although Kennedy decided against committing American troops to Laos, he felt it necessary to put his adversaries on notice that American will was not flagging. The President sent out another alert to American troops in Asia; the task force on Okinawa was alerted. The Russians were made well aware of these preparations, as was necessary in order to deter them from making the miscalculation that America was prepared to write off Laos.

Just after Kennedy had determined not to send American troops to Laos, representatives of the fighting factions there agreed to the cease-fire called for in the Co-Chairmen's message of April 24. On May 11 the ICC, having returned to Laos, said, "The Commission are satisfied that a general *de facto* cease-fire exists."[43]

As we look back on the first half of 1961, we notice the strengthening of various elements that would prove to be instrumental in making possible the compromise settlement of July 1962.

In the first place, the sporadic military skirmishing that lasted from December 1960, after the Battle of Vientiane, through May 1961 had produced no substantial military victories by either side. This is not to say, however, that the fighting was without consequence. As an experienced gambler can testify, the surest way of demonstrating that two boxers are equal is to let them fight. If a draw results, one has conclusive evidence that the fighters were equally matched. No amount of prefight analysis, from comparing weights to measuring punching power, can prove this fact so convincingly. In Laos, likewise, the prolonged draw showed that the fighting factions were approximately equal in military power. As the leaders of each side became convinced of the futility of battlefield victories, they became more prone to negotiate a compromise. Accordingly, Phoumi and the neutralist–Pathet Lao agreed to a cease-fire. The opening of the Geneva Conference followed soon after. This was one major result of the military stalemate.

These calculations grow more complicated when we introduce into the power equation a crucial quantity: foreign assistance. Both the neutralist–Pathet Lao and Phoumi were receiving foreign aid. This factor had two effects, which can best be explained by a return to the boxing analogy. Suppose that in the twelfth round of a championship fight, a fight which seems to be turning out a draw, one of the fighters is allowed to bring a friend into the ring to help him fight. In all likehood, the other boxer would withdraw—or suffer a bloody defeat. Returning to foreign aid, one of its effects may be to motivate the other side to give up.

Let us now make the situation more realistic by also allowing the second fighter to invite a friend into the ring. Either original fighter may well feel that his friend can punch better than the other fighter's friend. Thus outside help may lead each party to feel that it can eventually win if it holds out longer.

External assistance made both these effects felt in Laos in early 1961. On one hand, it led each side to fear that it would be defeated by its opponent. On the other hand, outside assistance encouraged each side to believe it might knock out the other party. Which of these contrary pressures would predominate in each camp could not yet be determined in 1961. More time was needed to assess the increment in fighting ability that each outside participant was providing. We can say this much, however: the mutual fear of being defeated by the other side, with the assistance of outside help, was strong enough to bring each party to the negotiating table for the start of talks. At the same time, each side's hope of eventual triumph acted as an impediment to compromise once the talks had begun. Only a stalemate lasting long enough to convince all parties that no significant change in military position was probable would induce the parties to compromise. That state of affairs had not yet arrived in Laos.

Another factor that made possible a compromise settlement deserves to be mentioned, namely, communication between the parties. The opposing factions had been out of direct contact between December 1960 and March 1961. On March 9 and 10, Phoumi met Souvanna at Phnom Penh, thereby reopening direct communications between the two sides. This step and the conversations that were to follow also promoted the chances for a compromise settlement.

A further reason why a start was made on a compromise settlement was the existence of a center group. We have compared the political lineup in Laos to the Laotian flag, with each of the flag's three elephants standing for one of the three political factions. By 1961, the center faction (Souvanna Phouma) had grown more friendly with the group on the left (Pathet Lao) than with that on the right (General Phoumi), but the three parties continued to retain separate identities. The existence of a center group enabled General Phoumi to discuss the ramifications of eventual negotiations with someone (Souvanna) who stood between him and his arch enemy, the Pathet Lao. It is doubtful that Phoumi would have journeyed to Pathet Lao headquarters for talks concerning a compromise settlement, for that would have led some to believe that Phoumi was ready to capitulate. Therefore the presence of someone standing between the Pathet Lao and Phoumi enabled the latter to communicate with the former without risking the embarrassment that might have ensued had Phoumi approached the Pathet Lao directly. Even though Souvanna Phouma and Phoumi were unable to reach any substantial agreements in the meeting of March 9 and 10, they did open a channel of communications. Without some form of contact among the opposing political factions, no compromise settlement in Laos would have been possible.

Souvanna, as the representative of a middle position, contributed to a compromise solution in another way. During his trip to various world capitals in April, he sought to generate support for a neutral Laos. It is not clear what importance the Prince's trip had in gaining adherents for such a solution to the Laotian problem. However, it seems doubtful that the leaders of either the Pathet Lao or the pro-Western group were in a position to champion such a cause in foreign chancelleries. The leaders of these two factions both hoped for exclusive political power, or at least for a preponderance of power over their extreme rival. Thus, they could not promote a solution giving equal power to all three factions without prejudicing their own cause. Souvanna, however, could do so without compromising the interests of the neutralists, who represented a position the

other groups could accept if their maximum objectives appeared unattainable.

It is worth noting, finally, that foreign powers played a decisive role
in arranging for a conference to settle the Laotian dispute. Great Britain
and the Soviet Union, Co-Chairmen of the 1954 Geneva Conference,
were most instrumental in this respect. The agreement of the United
States, as the backer of Phoumi's forces, was also required for the convening
of a conference. It is unlikely that, in the absence of these efforts by foreign
powers, a conference would have been scheduled. Neither the Pathet Lao
nor the pro-Western forces in Vientiane were as yet prepared to accept
the consequences of a compromise settlement, nor was Souvanna sufficiently
strong to compel them to attend a conference. The military stalemate had
not yet persisted for a sufficient period of time to convince them that
compromise was a more attractive alternative than continued fighting.

NOTES

1. Text in *Department of State Bulletin,* January 2, 1961, pp. 15-16.
2. Address to the House of Lords, December 19, 1960, in Great Britain, *Parliamentary Debates* (Lords) 227 (1960-1961) :692.
3. *Ibid.*
4. *Le Monde,* December 22, 1960.
5. *Documents on International Affairs,* 1960, pp. 525-26.
6. *Ibid.,* pp. 527-29.
7. Letter from Foreign Minister Chen Yi to the Co-Chairmen of the Geneva
Conference, December 28, 1960, in *Documents on International Affairs,* 1960,
pp. 530-31.
8. *Department of State Bulletin,* January 16, 1961, p. 76.
9. Dwight D. Eisenhower, *Waging Peace* (New York: Doubleday and Company,
Inc., 1965), p. 610.
10. *Ibid.,* p. 611.
11. Text of statement in *Department of State Bulletin,* January 23, 1961,
pp. 114-15.
12. *Ibid.,* p. 117.
13. Text in *Ibid.,* pp. 115-17.
14. In this manner the State Department sought to validate its claim that the
subcommittee's failure to conclude that North Vietnam had committed aggression
against Laos did not establish beyond doubt that such aggression had not been
committed.
15. The State Department, it should be noted, was arguing that Kong Le was
either a communist or was acting in complete accord with communists. In the
Department's view, Kong Le did not represent an independent force.
16. Washington seems to be saying that a regime cannot govern unless its

leaders remain in the capital, even under conditions of war. In addition, State Department officials chose to ignore the fact that Souvanna Phouma had delegated his governing powers to his subordinates, who remained in Vientiane until General Phoumi captured the city.

17. As pointed out previously, the April 1960 elections which returned these deputies were held under such suspicious circumstances that one could raise legitimate questions as to whether these deputies actually represented the wishes of the voters.

18. Since the identity of the legal government of Laos was in dispute, this claim remains open to interpretation. Furthermore, Souvanna Phouma later said that the United States "doublecrossed" him. By this he meant that Washington supplied aid to General Phoumi in the fall of 1960 and then, contrary to what Souvanna said was an understanding between himself and Washington, Phoumi used that aid against Souvanna in the campaign to take Vientiane. (*The New York Times*, January 20, 1961.)

19. *The New York Times,* January 11, 1961; January 13, 1961; January 21, 1961. A spokesman for the Boun Oum government claimed such aid was not illegal because the aircraft were not offensive weapons. (*Ibid.,* January 11, 1961.) Such "non-offensive" weapons, nevertheless, strafed and fired rockets at the neutralist–Pathet Lao forces. (*Ibid.,* January 13, 1961.)

20. *The Times* (London), January 30, 1961. As of January 24, the PEO had a staff of 125 Americans. Andrew Boyle, who until his arrival in Laos was a Brigadier General in the U. S. Army, succeeded General John A. Heintges as Chief of the PEO in January 1961. The military advisors were grouped into White Star teams. One team was assigned to each of Phoumi's battalions.

21. U. S. Department of State, *American Foreign Policy,* 1961, pp. 982–83. The list of countries invited to the 1961–62 Geneva conference conformed to Sihanouk's proposal.

22. Letter from British Prime Minister to Sihanouk, January 13, 1961, in Great Britain, Cmd. 2834, pp. 162–63. The British communication raised for the first time in diplomatic channels the issue of the relationship between the conference and a cease-fire. In May 1961, this matter assumed vital importance, inasmuch as the United States insisted that a cease-fire be verified before she would agree to attend a conference. The early British wish that a cease-fire precede a conference suggests that the United States and Britain were coordinating their efforts in the diplomatic exchanges leading up to the Geneva Conference. It should be noted that the British letter reverses previous British policy that the time was not opportune for the ICC to reconvene.

23. Great Britain, Cmd. 2834, p. 166.

24. *Ibid.,* pp. 166–68.

25. Roger Hilsman, *To Move A Nation* (New York: Doubleday and Company, Inc., 1967), p. 127.

26. *Ibid.,* p. 128.

27. See *Ibid.,* pp. 128–31.

28. On his first trip as Kennedy's roving ambassador, W. Averill Harriman reported from Moscow that Khrushchev had said he did not want a war over Laos. Two reasons accounted for Khrushchev's attitude. In the first place, he thought the communists would get Laos without war. "Why take risks over Laos?" he said to American Ambassador Llewellyn E. Thompson. "It will fall

into our laps like a ripe apple." The Soviet Premier also felt there were more important matters to be settled, such as Berlin. (Hilsman, pp. 130–31.)

29. Text of this important statement in U. S. Department of State, *Department of State Bulletin,* April 17, 1961, pp. 543–44.

30. British *aide-mémoire* to the Soviet Union, March 23, 1961, in *Documents on International Affairs,* 1961, pp. 564–65. The note called for a cease-fire and the formation of a "neutral Laotian Government of national unity," a reference to a broad-based regime with Pathet Lao participation. This note was drafted by the British in close consultation with the State Department. Secretary of State Dean Rusk and Britain's Foreign Secretary, the Earl of Home, agreed upon the final text in a telephone conversation on March 22.

31. Previously, the British had been reluctant to convene an international conference. The procedures outlined in the note were carried out during April and May.

32. *Department of State Bulletin,* April 17, 1961, p. 544.

33. Hilsman, p. 131.

34. Text in *Documents on International Affairs,* 1961, pp. 567–69.

35. *Department of State Bulletin,* April 17, 1961, p. 544.

36. Hilsman, p. 134. The PEO numbered between 250 and 300 men at the time.

37. According to *The Times* (London), April 20, 1961, the Boun Oum government on April 19 asked the United States to form a MAAG because of the "grave situation caused by rebel attacks on all fronts over the past 24 hours." The United States consented to the request. Commenting on the decision to establish a MAAG, Souvanna Phouma and Chou En-lai, in a joint statement issued during Souvanna's trip to China on April 25, 1961, said, "The two parties deemed it necessary to point out that the U. S. government while expressing itself in favor of settling the Laotian question peacefully, is still stepping up its military intervention in Laos. The recent decision of the U. S. government to establish a so-called 'military assistance advisory group' in Laos is a serious participation in the civil war in Laos. The two governments strongly protest against this step." (*Survey of the Chinese Mainland Press,* May 1, 1961, pp. 24–26.)

38. Texts in *Documents on International Affairs,* 1961, pp. 572–74.

39. Both Britain and the Soviet Union compromised on London's insistence that a cease-fire be verified before the conference could meet. Moscow agreed that a cease-fire should precede the conference, and Britain did not insist that a cease-fire be a precondition for the opening of the conference.

40. U. S. Department of State, *American Foreign Policy,* 1961, p. 1001.

41. This account of the May 1 meeting is adapted from Theodore C. Sorensen, *Kennedy* (New York: Harper and Row, 1965), pp. 644–46.

42. Arthur M. Schlesinger, Jr., *A Thousand Days* (Boston: Houghton Mifflin Co., 1965), p. 339.

43. Message to the Co-Chairmen from the ICC, May 11, 1961, in Great Britain, Cmd. 2834, p. 174.

13
THE GENEVA CONFERENCE

THE GENEVA CONFERENCE
CONVENES

ON MAY 12, 1961, representatives of the following countries gathered at Geneva for the opening of the international conference on Laos: Cambodia, Communist China, France, Laos, Soviet Union, United Kingdom, United States, South Vietnam, North Vietnam, India, Canada, Poland, Burma, and Thailand. (Only the first nine of these countries had attended the 1954 Geneva Conference.) The conference did not begin until May 16, however, because of disagreements over two crucial issues: Laotian representation and a cease-fire. Since these two matters were to provoke heated debate throughout the duration of the conference, it is most advisable to examine them first.

LAOTIAN REPRESENTATION

At the outset of the Geneva negotiations, a disagreement arose over which political faction in Laos was entitled to represent Laos. The United States contended that the Boun Oum government in Vientiane was the only authority to have the right to speak in the name of Laos.[1] The Soviet Union proposed that three delegations—the Pathet Lao, the neutralists, and the Boun Oum regime—represent Laos, with each faction having equal status.[2] Secretary Rusk, however, refused to permit the

247

Pathet Lao to enjoy equal status with the other two factions, on the ground that such an arrangement would be tantamount to recognizing the Pathet Lao as one component of the Laotian government that would emerge at the conclusion of the conference. Rusk did agree, however, to permit the Souvanna Phouma faction to sit as an equal with the Boun Oum group; the Pathet Lao, Rusk said, could sit as observers or as consultants to the neutralists.

The Co-Chairmen, the foreign ministers of Britain and the Soviet Union, succeeded in resolving this deadlock as follows. They decided that any Laotian political party could sit at the Conference, so long as that party was sponsored by a country (other than Laos) attending the Conference. According to this scheme, none of the Laotians so sponsored would sit as the representative of a government. Rather, the Laotians would join the Conference as representatives of political parties.

This device obviated the need to agree on which faction constituted the government of Laos. In accepting this compromise, the United States abandoned its attempt to prevent the seating of the Pathet Lao, which was sponsored by Communist China. The Soviets sponsored Souvanna; the United States, Boun Oum. All three Laotian factions were thus entitled to attend the Conference as equals. The Boun Oum–Phoumi group, then in control of Vientiane (although little else), reacted to this scheme by boycotting the Conference. When the negotiations began, therefore, the conservatives were not represented at Geneva.[3]

CEASE-FIRE

The United States, perhaps recalling that the Viet Minh had improved its bargaining position at Geneva in 1954 by defeating the French at Dienbienphu while the Conference was in session, demanded that a cease-fire be verified before the conference on Laos began. As we have seen, the ICC informed the Co-Chairmen on May 11 that the cease-fire had taken effect. After the Geneva Conference opened on May 16, the United States kept insisting that the Conference could continue only so long as the cease-fire existed. On May 17 Secretary Rusk, in his opening address at Geneva, said,

Information from Laos indicates that rebel forces continue to attack in a number of localities and that rebel troop movements are occurring which are prejudicial to an effective cease-fire. . . . An effective cease fire is a prerequisite to any constructive result from our proceedings; a failure of a cease-fire would result in a highly dangerous situation which it is the purpose of the conference to prevent.[4]

This statement, and others like it, was meant as a warning to the communists that the United States might take drastic action—perhaps in the form of American military intervention or withdrawal from the Geneva Conference—if the communists violated the cease-fire. The Americans realized that the neutralists–Pathet Lao were in a stronger military position than Phoumi's forces, and Washington wished to prevent Phoumi's adversaries from improving their position still further.

On May 27 the United States charged the Pathet Lao with over thirty violations of the cease-fire agreement and said,

> It is evident that the Pathet Lao are employing military pressure for political purposes at the very moment when this conference is endeavoring to secure the unity, independence and neutrality of Laos. At the same time, the Pathet Lao has obstructed I.C.C. efforts to investigate.[5]

Unable to bring about a genuine cease-fire by mere words, the United States sought an arrangement whereby the Co-Chairmen would give the ICC instructions enabling it to exert more control over the frayed cease-fire. Such instructions were designed to encourage the ICC to maintain a closer watch over the military forces of the feuding factions. The instructions would also call on the parties in Laos to cooperate with the ICC.[6] "In the view of my Government," Harriman said, "we cannot have an effective cease-fire agreement without the widespread investigation by the ICC and cooperation from the parties in Laos. . . ."[7] The Pathet Lao, however, refused to permit the ICC to inspect territory under its control and the Soviets would not, despite British urgings, agree to send instructions from the Co-Chairmen to the ICC as called for by the United States.

In early June, breaches of the cease-fire became still more flagrant. A Pathet Lao attack on Ban Padong, six miles south of the Plaine des Jarres, forced Meo tribesmen supporting Boun Oum to evacuate the area. The United States said Phoumi's forces had been under "almost continuous attack, consisting of heavy artillery fire combined with ground attacks," since April 22.[8]

The Ban Padong incident so incensed the Americans that they walked out of the Conference. This move was meant, no doubt, to signal the communists that the Conference would dissolve in failure if Pathet Lao attacks continued. One week later, a battlefield lull brought the American delegation back to the negotiating tables in Geneva.

KENNEDY MEETS KHRUSHCHEV IN VIENNA

On June 3 and 4 President Kennedy journeyed to Vienna for a summit conference with Premier Khrushchev of the Soviet Union. The two heads of state found little to agree upon except the desirability of a settlement for Laos, a subject that Kennedy introduced. Kennedy told the Premier that the United States wanted to reduce its commitment to Laos and that he hoped the Soviet Union wished to do likewise. Laos, the President said, was not important enough to warrant such heavy involvement by the United States and the Soviet Union. Khrushchev agreed. The President told Khrushchev that the United States sought a neutral and independent Laos; Khrushchev said that he would try to influence the Laotians to establish a truly neutral government. Kennedy then raised the issue of a cease-fire, and the Soviet Premier agreed to give it high priority. He promised to encourage both sides in Laos to stop fighting and resolve their differences. The two statesmen agreed, in short, that Laos should not become a major issue between them and that their common goal was a neutral and independent Laos.[9]

The joint statement issued at the end of the Vienna meeting reflected precisely the kind of settlement the United States hoped would emerge from the Geneva Conference. The statement said, "The President and the Chairman reaffirmed their support of a neutral and independent Laos under a government chosen by the Laotians themselves, and of international agreements for insuring that neutrality and independence, and in this connection they have recognized the importance of an effective cease-fire."[10]

Reporting to the American people on June 6 regarding his trip to Europe, the President said,

The one area which afforded some immediate prospect of accord was Laos. Both sides recognized the need to reduce the dangers in that situation. Both sides endorsed the concept of a neutral and independent Laos, much in the manner of Burma or Cambodia. Of critical importance to the current conference on Laos in Geneva, both sides recognized the importance of an effective cease-fire.[11]

Although we do not know what the Russians told their Pathet Lao allies after the Vienna meeting, it does seem likely that the summit conference had a mollifying effect on the course of events in Laos. As Roger Hilsman notes, "Not immediately but over time the Communist attacks lessened and the cease-fire became effective."[12]

RUSK'S STATEMENT AT GENEVA

During the first nine sessions of the Geneva Conference, the delegates heard policy speeches of the ministerial heads of delegations. Secretary Rusk, speaking for the United States, outlined a policy of neutrality for Laos.[13] After voicing his concern about breaches of the cease-fire and reiterating American support for the Boun Oum regime, Rusk presented a three-point plan designed to create a neutral Laos, having "the right to choose its own way of life in accordance with its own traditions, wishes, and aspirations for the future." The three points were as follows:

1. *A definition of neutrality for Laos.* Such a definition, Rusk said, must go beyond the classical definition of neutrality as nonalignment with contending parties. All foreign military personnel, except for those specified in the 1954 Geneva Accords, must be withdrawn from Laos. If international arrangements can be made regarding the withdrawal of foreign military forces and equipment, "there would be no problem on our side." Neutrality must be consistent with sovereignty and therefore must include safeguards against external subversion.

2. *Machinery for keeping the peace.* Those responsible for supervising the peacekeeping agreements must have full access to all parts of Laos without the need for the consent of any civil or military officials. They must have their own transportation and communication equipment. They must be able to act on any complaints from responsible sources, including members of the control body itself, officials in Laos, governments of neighboring countries and members of the Geneva Conference. The control body should act by majority rule. Effective methods must be found whereby the control body can inform interested governments in case the conditions of peace and neutrality are violated.

3. *Economic and technical development for Laos.* A better society and a better life for Laotians are necessary conditions for maintaining a neutral and independent Laos. The United States is willing to contribute economic assistance, which should be administered by an organization of neutral nations of the area.

Shortly after presenting his policy statement on May 17, Secretary Rusk departed from Geneva and left to W. Averill Harriman, as chief of the American delegation, the task of negotiating an acceptable settlement of the Laotian crisis.

For the next fourteen months, the diplomats at Geneva devoted their efforts to devising a solution that would satisfy, as much as was reasonably possible, all those concerned. By December 1961, the envoys had resolved most of their differences, so that they were able to approve texts of the

Declaration and Protocol in almost the exact form that these documents would take at the conclusion of the Conference in July 1962. The first phase of the Conference thus ended in December 1961. The final phase consisted of two meetings in January 1962 and five the following July.

There is no need to catalogue all the conflicts of interests, bargaining tactics, temporary delays, and final breakthroughs that marked the Conference. That task has already been ably performed.[14] We shall concentrate, instead, on the question of how the negotiations, as well as events in Laos, affected American efforts to realize their objectives in Laos.

EFFORTS TO FORM
A SINGLE LAOTIAN GOVERNMENT

Although the delegates had completed most of their work by December 1961, a settlement could not be effected until a universally recognized Laotian government had been formed and had signed the Geneva agreements. The issue of a new government became the most highly contested matter at the Geneva Conference. Each of the three factions involved was trying to gain control of Laos. In essence, this is what the fighting in Laos was all about.

Efforts to put together a new Laotian government were at first conducted by military representatives of the three factions, who met occasionally at the village of Ban Namone in Laos. Toward the end of June 1961, Souvanna Phouma, Boun Oum, and Souphanouvong gathered at Zurich to discuss the formation of a unified Laotian government. The three princes agreed in principle to form a provisional government of national union, which would then appoint a delegation to participate in the Geneva Conference. On the all-important matter of the composition of the government, however, the princes could agree to nothing more specific than that all three parties would be represented.

In October the three princes met again, this time at Ban Hin Heup in Laos. They decided to form a provisional government consisting of sixteen members and designated Souvanna Phouma as provisional prime minister. They could not agree, however, on the composition of the remainder of the cabinet.

During the next few months little progress was made in implementing the agreements made at Zurich and Ban Hin Heup. In the field, armed clashes were occurring. On December 2, the Co-Chairmen sent a message to the three princes, urging them to "do their utmost to implement promptly the agreements reached in Zurich and Ban Hin Heup to form a Government of National Unity, and to send a united Laotian delegation to the

International Conference at Geneva representing that Government." The Co-Chairmen also asked the rival factions to take appropriate measures to assure strict observance of the cease-fire. Two weeks later the Co-Chairmen sent an urgent appeal to the three princes, asking them to form a government of national unity as soon as possible so that the Geneva Conference— which had just finished drafting the documents to be signed by all parties, including Laos—could complete its work.

The principal issue dividing the princes was assignment of ministries in the coalition government. The two prized ministries were interior, which holds jurisdiction over the police and courts, and defense, which controls the army. The three princes scheduled a meeting in late December 1961 to continue their talks. However, just before these conversations were to begin, Boun Oum suddenly refused to participate, saying, "I have nothing more to say to Prince Souphanouvong and I see no more necessity for a princes' meeting. The Zurich agreement is finished." Souvanna, he said, had exhibited no proof of neutralism. The ministries of interior and defense would have to go to the conservative faction, Boun Oum insisted.[15]

The United States was not at all pleased with this breakdown of negotiations. A State Department spokesman said, "Really so much is at stake here—namely peace in Laos—the United States would view with deep regret the failure of the three princes to have a meaningful meeting."[16]

Differences were beginning to develop between the negotiating positions of the United States and its ally in Laos. Boun Oum, as we have seen, demanded that the conservatives retain possession of the ministries of interior and defense in a coalition government. Washington, however, was of the opinion that these two portfolios should go to the neutralists. In fact, on January 15 Harriman announced that he and Georgi M. Pushkin, head of the Soviet delegation at Geneva, had agreed that the neutralists should get the portfolios of interior and defense.[17]

Later that month, in response to a request from the Co-Chairmen, the three princes succeeded in arranging a meeting in Geneva. According to Souvanna Phouma's account of the meeting, Boun Oum showed signs of wavering. Boun Oum stipulated that if he could not have the ministries of defense and interior, he wanted to choose two portfolios from among foreign affairs, finance, and information.[18]

While these talks were proceeding, the cease-fire was becoming increasingly tenuous. At his news conference on February 14, 1962, President Kennedy voiced concern over this matter. "If the cease-fire should break down," he said, "we would have—be faced with the most serious decision."[19]

As the spring of 1962 advanced, the Boun Oum government returned to a more rigid stance, refusing to discuss the matter of a coalition government or allow the neutralists to occupy the ministries of defense and interior. In late March Sisouk Na Champassak, State Minister for Presidential Affairs in the Boun Oum government, reiterated his government's refusal to concede the two ministries to the neutralists.

The Boun Oum government's refusal to join a coalition government and yield on the question of the two ministries loomed as the principal obstacle to the final settlement of the Laotian problem at Geneva. The Conference had completed all its work and required only the presence of a unified Laotian delegation to sign the documents.

Boun Oum's policy created particular difficulties for the United States. Washington desired a compromise settlement of the Laotian problem and was willing to give the interior and defense ministries to the neutralists in a coalition government. Washington's Laotian ally, however, had assumed a more intransigent stance. Boun Oum now refused to join a coalition government and would not even consider giving up the two ministries. Washington was thus confronted with the problem of persuading Boun Oum to modify his position to conform with that of the United States. How could this be done? Mere words, in the form of diplomatic notes and official meetings, had failed. Probably the most reliable means would be to reduce American military and economic aid, upon which the conservatives depended for their very existence. But this alternative forced Washington to come to terms with an unpleasant reality. The more the United States undercut the conservatives' strength by reducing aid, the greater the likelihood that the Pathet Lao would be able to sweep Phoumi's military forces from the field. Furthermore, should a coalition government eventually materialize, the greatest limitation on Pathet Lao political power would be the strength of the conservatives. Curtailing American aid to Phoumi and Boun Oum would certainly weaken them, thereby undermining Washington's best hope of preventing a full-scale takeover by the Pathet Lao. In full realization of these eventualities, Phoumi and Boun Oum refused to compromise, hoping Washington's fear of communism would compel the United States to stand behind their intransigence. As one wag said, it was becoming increasingly difficult to distinguish the tail from the dog.

UNITED STATES HALTS AID
TO THE RIGHTISTS

In spite of the unpleasant eventualities described above, Washington decided that the risk of suspending aid was less than the risks involved in postponing, and perhaps even preventing, a settlement in Laos. Washington therefore suspended its aid to the conservatives on two occasions.

It will be recalled that in December 1961, Boun Oum surprised the diplomatic community by stating that he refused to hold further talks with the other two princes. On January 6, the Co-Chairmen addressed a message to the three princes, asking them to meet at Geneva and try to resolve their differences. Boun Oum, it seemed, needed some encouragement from the United States, for he would not enter into discussions as the Co-Chairmen had requested. On January 7 the State Department supplied the needed encouragement by announcing that it was holding back its monthly check of $4 million; non-cash aid, meaning military assistance, was continued, however.[20] Four days later, Boun Oum accepted the Co-Chairmen's proposal for talks. American financial aid was resumed within 48 hours.

Washington's second use of financial aid manipulation to influence the Boun Oum regime occurred the following month. Boun Oum had agreed to talk, but would not allow the neutralists to occupy the ministries of defense and interior. Therefore Averill Harriman recommended that Washington cease payments of money that Phoumi used each month to pay the salaries of his entire army; Kennedy agreed, and the funds were accordingly cut off.[21] However, the United States continued to give military equipment and training to Phoumi's forces during this interval.[22]

Despite the reduction in American aid, Phoumi and Boun Oum still refused to yield the interior and defense portfolios. This obstinance occasioned a visit to Laos by Harriman and his special assistant William Sullivan. Sullivan went to the Plain of Jars to see Souvanna Phouma and Souphanouvong. Harriman's assistant reported that both princes seemed willing to compromise. Harriman personally told Phoumi that he must accept a coalition government with Souvanna as prime minister.

One would think that, after suspending financial aid and sending a ranking official, the United States would be able to prevail upon the leaders of a relatively weak political faction in a mini-state to alter their policy. But as French Foreign Minister Maurice Couve de Murville once observed, "The weak who know how to play on their weakness are strong. This is the secret of women, and of the developing nations." It was also the secret of the right-wing faction in Laos. Boun Oum and Phoumi knew that the very weakness of their position vis-a-vis the neutralists–Pathet Lao compelled the United States to stand behind them. They fully realized that the United States could have halted military aid—ammunition, weapons, vehicles, fuel, training, and so on—in addition to financial aid. But they understood, as did Washington, that to cripple the rightists would only provide a clear field for a Pathet Lao takeover. Phoumi and Boun Oum, playing on their weakness, refused to join a coalition government or yield the ministries of interior and defense even after the United States suspended aid used to pay the soldiers in Phoumi's army. It took an event over which the United States had little control to convince Phoumi and Boun Oum to change their minds.

THE BATTLE OF NAM THA

Nam Tha was a Phoumi stronghold in northwestern Laos that had been under intermittent siege by the Pathet Lao since February 1962. For some time the United States had warned Phoumi not to concentrate additional troops at Nam Tha for fear of provoking a Pathet Lao attack on the town. Phoumi, however, ignored Washington's advice and proceeded to build up his forces at Nam Tha. In early May the Pathet Lao attacked the town, which by then held 5,000 of Phoumi's best troops. Two days later Nam Tha fell to the Pathet Lao while Phoumi's troops streamed in panic across the Mekong into Thailand.[23]

The Nam Tha incident raises the important question of why Phoumi ignored the advice of American military personnel, whom he presumably respected for their military judgment. Phoumi could have had no quarrel with the military advisers. They were not the ones who were asking him to make political concessions. Quite the contrary, the military advisers were doing all they could to strengthen Phoumi militarily.

It may have been the case that Phoumi simply had different ideas about the consequences of a buildup at Nam Tha. Such an explanation would be readily acceptable, were it not for reports that other factors influenced the General's thinking. Dispatches in both *The Times* (London) and *The New York Times* suggested that Phoumi agreed with the American opinion that a buildup at Nam Tha would invite a Pathet Lao attack. Nevertheless, the reports said, Phoumi concentrated his troops there in order to provoke an attack, which he hoped would compel the United States to intervene to save his army, the only remaining hurdle to a Pathet Lao takeover.[24] These newspaper reports gain added credibility from the fact that none other than President Kennedy accepted this interpretation.[25] To put the matter another way, Phoumi thought himself and his army to be so indispensable to the Americans that they would take unlimited risks to ensure the survival of his forces.

Other reports offered a variation on this theme. One account went so far as to say that CIA agents in Laos, opposed to Washington's official policy of establishing a coalition government, encouraged Phoumi to gather his troops at Nam Tha, hoping to force the United States to make a stronger commitment to the rightists. According to this version, the initiative for a troop buildup at Nam Tha issued from American officials, not from General Phoumi. The same report stated that Washington's suspension of financial aid to Phoumi did not have its desired effect because the CIA—without State's knowledge—gave Phoumi offsetting funds,[26] an accusation that the State Department denied.[27]

With the information presently available, we are unable to settle the issue of whether any American officials encouraged Phoumi to contravene American policy. Knowledgeable individuals, however, have hinted that such reports were truthful. In a personal letter to the author, Arthur M. Schlesinger, Jr. said, "My impression is that General Phoumi Nosavan was encouraged by Americans in the field to resist the formation of a coalition government, but I cannot say specifically whether these officials represented CIA or the Pentagon." Hilsman has written that Phoumi "set about to resist all pressures to participate in a coalition government. . . . And he undoubtedly also believed that this time, as in 1960, there would be a policy struggle in Washington in which he could count on the support of both the Pentagon and the CIA."[28]

These accounts by members of the Kennedy Administration, in addition to reports in the press, lead one to suspect strongly that there were American agents who prompted Phoumi to resist official policy. However, such a conclusion must remain tentative until the release of further information.

WASHINGTON RESPONDS TO THE PATHET LAO ATTACK

The Pathet Lao victory at Nam Tha caused considerable consternation in Washington. The battle destroyed whatever military balance of power had existed in Laos. The Pathet Lao attack sent Phoumi's best troops fleeing in disorganized fashion across the Mekong River, abandoning northwest Laos to the adversary. The Pathet Lao had unequivocally demonstrated its superiority over Phoumi's army. Another source of concern in Washington was uncertainty about communist objectives. Was the Pathet Lao assault the first stage of a general offensive to overrun all of Laos, or was it an isolated probe to demonstrate the Pathet Lao's military invincibility?[29] Before the battle at Nam Tha, Pathet Lao troops had captured the last airfield in northern Laos, at Muong Sing (May 3). On the following day they took an outpost a mile and a half east of Nam Tha. These incidents, combined with the Nam Tha victory, provided the basis for concern that the communists were planning to sweep across Laos as unopposed as a bolt of lightning slashing across the sky.

By May 11 the Pathet Lao had occupied all of northwest Laos, having taken Houai Sai without any resistance on the part of Phoumi's troops. Boun Oum's government remained in control of only these areas: a narrow strip of territory (including Vientiane) paralleling the Thai border along the Mekong River, Luang Prabang, and several pockets inside territory held by the neutralists–Pathet Lao.

The collapse of Phoumi's army and the new military situation confronted Washington with a dilemma of serious proportions. Unless something were done to halt the Pathet Lao's military advance, the communists would extend their hegemony over most of Laos. Pathet Lao military domination of Laos would dash American hopes of limiting Pathet Lao influence in a coalition government. Yet, given the demise of Phoumi's army, Washington lacked effective means of countering Pathet Lao advances short of direct military intervention.

An additional consideration pressed itself upon Washington. The Soviet Union was still committed to act in accordance with Premier Khrushchev's statement to Kennedy in Vienna in favor of a cease-fire and the formation of a coalition government. If the United States failed to convince the Soviets that the Pathet Lao breach of the cease-fire might have unpleasant consequences for the Soviet Union, then Russia would have little incentive to urge the Pathet Lao to respect the cease-fire and participate in a coalition government. Faced with these problems, the Kennedy Administration pondered its next move.

In preparing contingency plans for Laos, the State Department had produced a paper outlining possible pitfalls and various policies to avoid them.[30] The cardinal danger facing the United States in Laos, the paper said, was that the communists would underrate American determination to resist Pathet Lao conquest. If, after Phoumi's defeat at Nam Tha, the United States did not respond, the communists would continue their military advances. The paper went on to recommend a series of diplomatic moves designed to impress the communists with American determination to resist a Pathet Lao military takeover, to reestablish the cease-fire, and create a neutral Laos with a coalition government. Furthermore, the paper stated, any diplomatic efforts taken by Washington would prove ineffective unless backed by overt action to show that the United States meant what it said. The paper called for a package of moves intended to inform the communists that if they continued their military advance, the United States would occupy the Mekong lowlands and the territory held by Phoumi's troops at the time the cease-fire was agreed to. However, the moves should not be such as to convince the communists that America planned to occupy territory beyond the cease-fire line, for then the communists might be persuaded that the United States aimed to make Laos an American satellite. Such a perception on the part of the communists would not promote America's objective, a compromise settlement, but would only intensify the Pathet Lao's resolve to fight.

To realize this objective, the paper called for the following limited military moves: sending the Seventh Fleet to the Gulf of Siam, transferring a battle group of about 1,000 men immediately to Thailand, ostentatiously moving a battle group already in Thailand on SEATO military maneuvers up to the Lao border opposite Vientiane, and improving communications routes in northeast Thailand in case a partial occupation of Laos became necessary.

This strategy was predicated on the estimate that the communists, including the Chinese, would rather stop fighting and negotiate in pursuit of a neutral Laos under a coalition government than risk American military intervention. At the same time, the State Department figured that if the United States kept its moves limited, the communists would not fear that America intended to threaten their position in North Vietnam, China, or northern Laos; such an interpretation of American intentions would only provoke further escalation of the communist military effort, it was thought. The American military action had to show that Washington was determined to hold on to the territory already held by General Phoumi, but had no grander designs.

On May 10 the President met with the members of the National Security Council.[31] After the case for the policy paper described above was presented, the Pentagon countered with objections to using limited force in Asia. The Pentagon suggested a different plan. The United States, the Pentagon spokesman said, should move the Fleet—but not the troops—in combination with a series of diplomatic protests against communist breaches of the cease-fire. More basic to the Pentagon's thinking was its suggestion to reverse American policy toward General Phoumi. The Pentagon had never been enthusiastic about the idea of a coalition government for Laos. The military much preferred to see a decidedly pro-Western government in power. Realizing that this would have to be preceded by a rightist military victory, the Pentagon urged that the United States stop pressuring Phoumi to join a coalition government. Instead, Washington should embark on an all-out effort to revitalize Phoumi's army by providing it with more arms and equipment and a crash training program.

The Security Council remained deadlocked. Both the State Department and the Pentagon had recommended moving the Fleet to the Gulf of Siam, so the President ordered this action taken. Before proceeding further, Kennedy decided to await more NSC deliberation; he scheduled another NSC meeting for May 12. In the meanwhile, he sent CIA Director John McCone and Michael Forrestal, a Far Eastern specialist on McGeorge Bundy's staff, to see Eisenhower.

The former President said that he favored a show of strength, including, if necessary, the dispatch of American troops to Laos.[32] On May 12 the NSC met again, once in the morning and once in the afternoon. Secretary McNamara and General Lemnitzer (then Chairman of the Joint Chiefs of Staff), both just returned from Southeast Asia, supported the dispatch of a small number of American troops to Thailand and the improvement of communications and supply lines there. The President approved these actions.

Kennedy also ordered American naval, air and land forces, including a battle group of 1,800 marines, to move toward the Indochinese peninsula. At the same time the State Department announced that America's objective was limited to a restoration of the cease-fire and the formation of a coalition government.

Two days later a battle unit of 1,000 American soldiers, which had remained in Thailand since the close of earlier SEATO exercises, was moved to Udorn, thirty miles from the Laotian border, as a further signal to the communists that the United States meant business.

On May 15 President Kennedy, "barely going through the formality of asking the Thais to 'request' our help under the SEATO treaty,"[33] announced that he was sending 5,000 additional American troops to Thailand. The President couched this announcement in terms of the defense of Thailand against communist threats. The purpose of sending the American troops, Kennedy said, was "to help insure the territorial integrity of Thailand." At the end of his announcement, Kennedy reaffirmed that "there is no change in our policy toward Laos. . . ."[34]

On the same day the United States, attempting to demonstrate allied solidarity, asked Great Britain and other SEATO members to send token military forces to Thailand.[35]

During the next several weeks high officials in the Government debated what the United States should do in case the communists again violated the cease-fire. Although the communists never did so, Washington had to make contingency plans. Hilsman emphasizes the cleavage between the military approach—advocated by most Pentagon officials, in addition to Secretary McNamara and Presidential Assistant Walt W. Rostow—and the political approach, favored by the State Department. In time Secretary Rusk shifted toward the military position.

The military view opposed the limited use of force for political ends. Advocates of the military position felt that if it became necessary to use force, the United States should as a first step occupy the whole of the Laotian panhandle right up to the border of North Vietnam. Then, unless the communists surrendered immediately, the United States should attack North Vietnam itself. Although these planners did not specify an American reaction to Chinese intervention, they left the impression that they favored nuclear retaliation against the mainland.

Officials who supported the political approach believed that the United States should tailor its application of force to the limited goal of restoring the cease-fire and negotiating for a neutral Laos governed by a coalition cabinet. American military intervention should not concern itself with territory held by the communists. The cease-fire line divided Laos where the mountains descended to the Mekong lowlands. The communists held the mountains and Phoumi occupied the lowlands, which contained over half the Laotian population (including almost all those who were ethnically Laotian) as well as almost all the towns, commerce, and industrial production. Advocates of the political approach favored the occupation of the Mekong lowlands. This scheme suggested military advantages as well as political purposes. Occupation of the lowlands would prevent the communists from using the north–south road extending to Thailand and Cambodia. If hostilities should occur, Thailand could be more easily defended at the foot of the hills in Laos than from the Thai side of the Mekong River, which is fordable at many points for six months of the year. Denied use of the Mekong lowlands, the communists would be forced to move men and supplies through six or seven long, narrow defiles, which would present ideal bombing targets.

A further consideration bearing on the military–political dispute was an estimation of communist response. Intelligence specialists on Asian communism believed that if Washington introduced forces only into the Mekong lowlands, the communists would place additional forces—North Vietnamese and perhaps Chinese—in northern Laos but would not attempt to drive the Americans out. If, however, the United States tried to regain territory already held by the communists, then they would strenuously resist. If American troops attempted to take northern Laos or North Vietnam, the intelligence experts estimated that the Chinese would intervene.[36]

While leading officials in Washington were considering a further course of action, the United States was working through diplomatic channels to convince Moscow of the wisdom of persuading the Pathet Lao to accept a cease-fire. The United States explained to the Russians exactly why American troops were landed in Thailand—that the United States wanted a compromise settlement and would not accept outright defeat in Laos. On May 15 Soviet Ambassador Dobrynin conferred with Rusk and Harriman. The Soviets agreed on the need to maintain the cease-fire and to hold discussions among political leaders in Laos.[37] According to a later report, at the time of these conversations 5,000 additional American troops were sitting in transport ships at Okinawa, awaiting orders to sail for

Thailand. It was only because the Soviet Union had affirmed its peaceful intentions that these troops did not go.[38] On May 25 Premier Khrushchev announced that Moscow continued to support the establishment of a neutral Laos, thereby convincing the United States that Russia was doing what she could[39] to prevent the Pathet Lao from trying to seize all of Laos militarily.[40]

After dispatching 5,000 American troops to Thailand, the United States had just about run out of ways to convince the Pathet Lao to accept a cease-fire. The only alternative that remained was sending American troops to Laos to join combat with the Pathet Lao directly. This, of course, would mean the involvement of the United States in an open-ended land war in Asia, something that no President would wish to undertake except under the most compelling circumstances. Whether the United States would resort to this device depended on what the Pathet Lao would do next. Washington waited tensely.

Without issuing any major policy statements, the Pathet Lao gradually began to reduce the level of fighting. Then, on May 27, the Pathet Lao initiated a new series of attacks in northwest Laos (at Houai Sai) and in the south (at Saravane). Was a new general offensive about to begin? Would American troops have to go after all? Once again, without diplomatic fanfare, the communists broke off these attacks. From then on a tenuous cease-fire took effect.[41] Washington breathed a sigh of relief as piles of battle gear and procurement orders were set aside—for how long nobody knew.[42]

FORMATION OF
A COALITION GOVERNMENT

So long as Phoumi and Boun Oum possessed an army, they remained able to resist American pressures to join a coalition government. After the collapse of their army at Nam Tha, however, the rightists were faced with an entirely new situation. Now they were in the position of a tough gun-fighter who slaps leather, only to find his holster empty. The rightists were forced to go to the other side hat in hand, hoping to salvage as much as they could from their all-powerful opponent.

On May 14 the rightists sent a cablegram to Souvanna in Paris proposing the reopening of talks on the formation of a government of national union. These negotiations did not begin until June 7. In the interim Harriman made known to officials in Vientiane that the United States would prefer that Phoumi concentrate on improving the Laotian military forces and leave politics to others.[43] Harriman's remarks went unheeded in Vientiane, however.

On June 11 the three princes finally agreed on the composition of a coalition government. It was to include eleven neutralists, four rightists, and four members of the Pathet Lao. Of the eleven neutralists, seven leaned toward Souvanna's policies and four tended to support the positions taken by the Boun Oum government. The upper structure of the new coalition government resembled a pyramid. At the summit stood the ubiquitous Souvanna, who occupied the posts of Premier and Defense Minister. Two deputy-premiers formed the base of the pyramid. One of these deputy-premiers was General Phoumi, who also was Finance Minister. Souphanouvong was the other Deputy-Premier; he also held the post of Economics Minister. Quinim Pholsena, a leftist who had taken charge of the neutralist government in Vientiane just before Phoumi captured the city in December 1960, was named Minister of Foreign Affairs. A neutralist, Pheng Phong Savan, was given the position of Minister of Interior. The agreement also specified that the three heads of government—Souvanna, Phoumi, and Souphanouvong—must unanimously concur on every decision relating to activities of the ministries of defense, interior, and foreign affairs.[44]

On June 23 the new government assumed office and soon after sent a single Laotian delegation headed by Quinim Pholsena to Geneva, where the Conference resumed its meetings on July 2.[45]

THE GENEVA SETTLEMENT

On July 23, 1962, representatives of the fourteen states met at Geneva and initialed two documents, a Declaration on the Neutrality of Laos and a Protocol to the Declaration on the Neutrality of Laos.[46] These documents will be examined in turn.

The Declaration took note of a statement of neutrality issued by the new Laotian coalition government on July 9, 1962. In this statement the Government pledged:

1. To establish diplomatic relations with all countries, the neighboring ones first and foremost.

2. To refrain from entering into "any military alliance or into any agreement, whether military or otherwise, which is inconsistent with the neutrality of the Kingdom of Laos; it will not allow the establishment of any foreign military bases on Laotian territory, nor allow any country to use Laotian territory for military purposes or for the purposes

of interference in the internal affairs of other countries,[47] nor recognize the protection of any alliance or military coalition, including SEATO."[48]

3. To prohibit any foreign interference in Laos' internal affairs.

4. To require the withdrawal from Laos of all foreign military personnel and to prohibit the reentry of foreign military personnel into Laos, with the exception of French military instructors as designated in Article 5 of the Protocol.

5. To accept unconditional aid from all countries.

The remainder of the Declaration concerned the other countries represented at Geneva. They took note of the statement by the Laotian government and promised to:

1. Do nothing to impair the sovereignty, independence, neutrality, unity or territorial integrity of Laos.

2. Refrain from direct or indirect interference in Laotian internal affairs.

3. Refrain from bringing Laos into a military alliance or any other agreement inconsistent with Laotian neutrality.

4. Respect Laotian wishes not to recognize the protection of any military alliance, "including SEATO."

5. Refrain from introducing into Laos any military personnel.

6. Refrain from establishing in Laos any foreign military bases or strongpoints.

7. Refrain from using Laotian territory for interference in the internal affairs of other countries.[49]

The signatories also agreed to consult with the Laotian government and with themselves in order to consider measures that might become necessary to insure respect for the principles in the Declaration.

The Declaration was unsatisfactory to Washington in at least two respects. In the first place, the United States had wished to avoid specific mention of SEATO in the Declaration. More importantly, the Declaration disappointed Washington in that it failed to include a provision concerning the unification of the armies of the three Laotian factions. The United States had wanted the Declaration to describe in detail how the three armies were to be combined into a single national army. In the absence of such a specific plan, the United States feared, the communists might succeed in stalling off military integration indefinitely. So long as the communists fielded an independent armed force, they retained the capacity to upset the 1962 compromise. The communists, especially the Chinese and North Vietnamese, said the merger of the three armies was an internal matter for Laos and thus beyond the competence of the Conference.[50] The United States was eventually forced to accept the omission of any provision regarding unification of the three fighting forces. However,

Souvanna agreed to make a statement on this issue to the final plenary session of the Conference.[51]

The second document issued by the Geneva Conference was a Protocol to the Declaration on Neutrality. In the Protocol the signatories described in detail what courses of action they would follow so as to advance the principles set forth in the Declaration.

The first section of the Protocol concerned the presence of foreign forces in Laos. Foreign military personnel were to be withdrawn from Laos within seventy-five days (Article 2).[52] Reintroduction of any foreign military personnel into Laos was prohibited (Article 4).[53] The French were to transfer their military installations in Laos to the Laotian Government; if the Laotian Government considered it necessary, France was authorized to keep military instructors in Laos (Article 5). Introduction into Laos of war material, except conventional armaments the Laotian Government deemed necessary for defense, was prohibited (Article 6).

An innovation in the 1962 agreements was to formalize the role of the Co-Chairmen in exercising surveillance over the final settlement. Such supervision as had existed after 1954 was owing to ad hoc measures taken by the Co-Chairmen. It was decided to institutionalize the Co-Chairmen's functions. Article 8 of the Protocol listed the tasks of the Co-Chairmen. These tasks were:

1. To receive periodic reports from the ICC. The Co-Chairmen were also to receive special reports from the ICC concerning any violations or threats of violations of the Protocol, steps taken by the ICC in pursuance of the Protocol, and any important information the ICC could supply to assist the Co-Chairmen in carrying out their functions. The ICC could at any time seek help from the Co-Chairmen, and the Co-Chairmen could make recommendations to the ICC at any time.
2. To circulate to the members of the Conference any reports and other important information from the ICC.
3. To exercise supervision over the observance of the Protocol and the Declaration.
4. To keep the members of the conference informed and when appropriate consult with them.

A large portion (nine out of twenty articles) of the Protocol dealt with the powers and functions of the ICC. During the negotiations at Geneva the Western powers and the communist nations adopted different approaches to the ICC. The Western countries, lacking a military foothold in Laos, wished to provide the ICC with a broad grant of authority so that it could control anticipated communist attempts at subversion and infiltration. The communist nations wanted to minimize the ICC's prerogative.

The wording in the Protocol represented a compromise between these two positions.

The ICC was charged with supervising and controlling the cease-fire. Responsibility for execution of the cease-fire, however, remained with the three parties (Article 9).

The ICC was empowered to investigate, on its own initiative, all suspected cases of entry of foreign troops (Article 11).[54] In the case of suspected introduction of illegal war material into Laos, the ICC was authorized to conduct investigations only at the request of the Laotian government (Article 12).

On the crucial matter of ICC voting procedures, the communists managed to realize their objective, which was to make it as difficult as possible for the ICC to take action. This was done by requiring a unanimous vote in a wide range of cases. Article 14 stated that ICC decisions relating to violations of the following matters must be unanimous: withdrawal of foreign military personnel, introduction of foreign military personnel, introduction of war material, and the cease-fire. Conclusions on major questions sent to the Co-Chairmen, as well as all recommendations, were also to be unanimous. On other matters, including procedural questions and questions relating to the initiation and carrying out of investigations, ICC decisions were to be adopted by majority vote.[55] Article 15 described the procedure to be adopted regarding the conduct of ICC investigations. The ICC was empowered to carry out investigations when it deemed necessary in order to police the cease-fire and report on suspected entry of foreign military personnel and foreign military material, the latter task to be discharged only at Royal Government request.[56] When the ICC considered making an investigation on its own initiative, such a decision was to be adopted by majority vote,[57] a concession to Western demands. After the ICC conducted an investigation, it was to file agreed reports in which differences among ICC members could be expressed. Final conclusions and recommendations resulting from these investigations were to be adopted unanimously, however.

The ICC was provided with means of communications and transport, which were placed under its own administrative control (Article 17). This provision was included in order to allow the Commission to conduct investigations without having to await transport by an unwilling or paralyzed Laotian regime.

Within three years of July 1962, the Co-Chairmen were to present a report with appropriate recommendations regarding the termination of the ICC (Article 19).

THE UNITED STATES AND
THE GENEVA CONFERENCE

President Kennedy hailed the signing of the Geneva agreements, saying that they "can be a significant milestone in our efforts to maintain and further world peace. It is a heartening indication that difficult, and at times seemingly insoluble international problems can in fact be solved by patient diplomacy."[58]

Despite the President's sanguine tone, the Geneva Conference could not be considered a diplomatic triumph for the United States; nor, on the other hand, was it a total defeat. After the destruction of General Phoumi's army at Nam Tha in May 1962, the United States could restore a military balance only by sending American troops to Laos. President Kennedy, as we have seen, rejected this alternative, which the Joint Chiefs of Staff had recommended, and instead chose to seek a compromise settlement through negotiations. The American diplomats at Geneva were forced to negotiate from a position of weakness. Consequently, the United States was obliged to accept some demands put forth by the communists at Geneva, particularly that of a restricted role for the ICC. The United States did succeed, however, in gaining authorization for the ICC to undertake investigations by majority vote. Thus, the Polish veto could not totally immobilize the Commission.

Perhaps the most serious deficiency in the Geneva agreements, from Washington's point of view, was the absence of detailed procedures for the unification of the three Laotian armies. The workability of the Laotian settlement depended on cooperation among the three factions in the coalition government. So long as each faction retained a separate fighting force, it had the power to refuse to cooperate with the remaining factions. Such a situation could lead to a resumption of general hostilities.

UNITED STATES SUPPORTS THE
COALITION GOVERNMENT

The United States welcomed the Geneva settlement, despite its imperfections, and promised to support the new Laotian coalition government.

Laotian independence, President Kennedy said, will depend upon the efforts of Laotians themselves as well as "on the moral and material support it receives from the rest of the world. For its part, the United

States assures Laos of such support as that country enters this new phase in its history."[59]

The United States began to provide that support in mid-June 1962, when Washington made a payment of $3 million to the Boun Oum regime, which had just agreed to join the coalition government. This payment was America's first cash assistance to Laos since such aid was suspended in February 1962. In late August the United States made a $2 million contribution to the new coalition government. Harriman characterized this contribution as "an interim payment to help them with their grocery bills; we want to wait and see what other countries are prepared to do, and what the Lao financial program is, before we make any definite offer."[60] Harriman added that the United States was aiding refugees, of whom there were about 15,000, and giving assistance to the villages to help improve conditions there.

At the end of July 1962, Premier Souvanna Phouma paid an official visit to Washington. In a luncheon toast to the Laotian Prime Minister, President Kennedy said, "I can assure you, Mr. Prime Minister, that this country will do everything that is within its power to implement the commitment that it made in signing the Geneva accord."[61] On the last day of July, Souvanna and President Kennedy issued a joint communique which stated,

> Prime Minister Souvanna Phouma and the President welcomed the international accord which resulted in conclusion of the Geneva settlement and opened up a new era for Laos. They expressed the mutual determination of their two governments to meet the obligations imposed on them by the agreements and thereby to contribute to the maintenance of peace in Southeast Asia.
>
> . . . .
>
> The President confirmed the determination of the United States to work actively in supporting the independence and neutrality of Laos. He confirmed the willingness of the United States to offer in accordance with the spirit of the Declaration of Neutrality made by the Royal Government of Laos on July 9, 1962, its moral and material support to the Lao people toward achieving their aspirations with dignity and freedom through adherence to the stated course of strict neutrality.[62]

The United States, then, accepted the Geneva agreements as the most satisfactory settlement it could obtain short of American military intervention. Washington extended assistance to the new Laotian coalition government and expressed the hope that Laos would remain free to chart its own course.

NOTES

1. Note from Dean Rusk to Co-Chairmen of the Geneva Conference, Geneva, May 16, 1961, in *Le Monde,* May 17, 1961.

2. *The New York Times,* May 14, 1961.

3. Officially, the Boun Oum government never sent a representative to the Geneva Conference. However, after a meeting in Zurich in late June, 1961, among Souvanna Phouma, Souphanouvong, and Boun Oum, former prime minister Phoui Sananikone joined the conference as the representative of political parties in Vientiane (though not as the representative of the Boun Oum government). After the dissolution of the Boun Oum government in June 1962, and the subsequent formation of the government of national unity, Laos was represented at the conference by a single delegation.

4. *Department of State Bulletin,* June 5, 1961, p. 844.

5. *The New York Times,* May 28, 1961.

6. See W. Averill Harriman's statement at Geneva on May 31, in U. S. Department of State, *American Foreign Policy,* 1961, pp. 1012-14.

7. *Ibid.,* p. 1013.

8. *The Times* (London), June 8, 1961.

9. This account is based on Arthur M. Schlesinger, Jr., *A Thousand Days* (Boston: Houghton Mifflin Co., 1965), pp. 367-68; Theodore C. Sorensen, *Kennedy* (New York: Harper and Row, 1965), pp. 646-47; and Roger Hilsman, *To Move A Nation* (New York: Doubleday and Company, Inc., 1967), pp. 135-36.

10. U. S. President, *Public Papers of the Presidents,* 1961, p. 438.

11. *Department of State Bulletin,* June 26, 1961, p. 993.

12. Hilsman, p. 136.

13. Text in *Department of State Bulletin,* June 5, 1961, pp. 844-48.

14. The best comprehensive account of the Geneva Conference may be found in George Modelski, *International Conference on the Settlement of the Laotian Question 1961-1962* (Canberra: The Australian National University, 1962). Another valuable description, with emphasis on Chinese Communist negotiating behavior, is Arthur Lall, *How Communist China Negotiates* (New York: Columbia University Press, 1968).

15. *The New York Times,* December 28, 1961.

16. *Ibid.*

17. *Ibid.,* January 16, 1961.

18. *Ibid.,* January 20, 1962.

19. U. S. Department of State, *American Foreign Policy,* 1962, pp. 1068-69.

20. *The New York Times,* January 8, 1962.

21. The rightists did not receive this money during the months of February, March, April, and May. In explaining why these payments were suspended, Harriman said they were stopped "because we have felt that the Government was not negotiating in good faith for a coalition government." (U. S. Congress, Senate, Committee on Foreign Relations, Hearings, *Foreign Assistance Act of 1962,* 87th Cong., 2d Sess., 1962, p. 369.)

22. *Ibid.;* see also McNamara's testimony on p. 96 of the hearings; also *The New York Times,* February 17, 1962.

23. Souvanna Phouma, who was undergoing medical treatment in Paris, condemned the Pathet Lao attack as a violation of the cease-fire and told Souphanou-

vong to withdraw his troops from the town. (*The New York Times,* May 10, 1962.)

24. *The Times* (London), May 16, 1962; *The New York Times,* May 7, 1962.

25. *The Times* (London), May 16, 1962.

26. *The Times* (London), May 24, 1962.

27. *The Times* (London), May 25, 1962. Commenting on this denial, the *Times* correspondent—his name was not given—said, "Your correspondent is confident that the report was correct." (*Ibid.*)

28. Hilsman, p. 137. Hilsman added that after the Bay of Pigs incident, the CIA lost much of the President's confidence. The CIA, therefore, was not so powerful, vis-a-vis the rest of the Executive Branch, under Kennedy as under Eisenhower. As a result of Kennedy's determination to reduce CIA's influence, Hilsman says, the Pentagon was the stronger of Phoumi's two allies.

29. Harriman wrote that the communist motive "is not clear." If, he reasoned, it signaled an intention to abandon efforts to come to a peaceful solution of the Laotian problem and embark on a policy of military conquest, "the basis of our current policy will, of course, have to be re-examined." If, on the other hand, the attack on Nam Tha was just a single violent outbreak, the possibility of resuming negotiations remained. (W. Averill Harriman, "What Are We Doing in Southeast Asia?" *The New York Times Magazine,* May 27, 1962, p. 55.) President Kennedy said at his May 17 news conference, when talking about the attack on Nam Tha, "We did not know whether this was an indication of a general breach of the cease-fire which, of course, would immediately imperil Thailand." (U. S. President, *Public Papers of the Presidents,* 1962, p. 403.)

30. This paper is described in Hilsman, pp. 142–44.

31. This meeting is described in Hilsman, pp. 143–44.

32. *Ibid.,* p. 145.

33. Sorenson, p. 647. At his news conference on May 17, Kennedy said, "We are going into Thailand at the decision of the Thai Government." (*The New York Times,* May 18, 1962.) The Thai Foreign Ministry later said that Thailand had not formally asked the United States to send marines but had agreed when the United States suggested it. (*The Times* [London], May 19, 1962.) For text of the Thai announcement on the decision to receive American troops, see U. S. Department of State, *American Foreign Policy,* 1962, p. 1093.

34. U. S. Department of State, *American Foreign Policy,* 1962, p. 1094.

35. *The Times* (London), May 17, 1962. The British Foreign Office replied that Britain would consider such a request only if it came from Thailand. Thailand did make such a request, and Britain sent a squadron of Hunter jets to Thailand. New Zealand and Australia also sent forces.

36. Hilsman, pp. 146–49.

37. *The Times* (London), May 16, 1962.

38. *Ibid.,* December 6, 1962.

39. The United States "wondered if [the Russians] still controlled events on their side." (Sorenson, p. 647.)

40. Souvanna's personal aide at that time told the author that Peking and Hanoi had not planned a military takeover of Laos. They wanted the formation of a neutral government, which they believed the communists could then take over politically. (Interview with Khamchan Pradith.) Mr. Pradith did not identify the source for this information.

41. Precisely why the Pathet Lao finally agreed to a cease-fire remains a

matter of speculation. Was it because of Soviet pressure? Was it because the United States landed 5,000 troops in Thailand and was prepared to send additional forces? Did the Pathet Lao lack sufficient supplies, equipment, and manpower to seize and hold the entirety of Laos? Perhaps a combination of these factors induced Pathet Lao leaders to accept a cease-fire.

42. On July 1 the United States withdrew 1,000 marines sent to Thailand in May. Eighteen hundred more were ordered to leave on July 27, leaving a total American contingent of 2,200 army troops and 1,000 air force personnel. Owing to subsequent fighting in Vietnam, the American garrison swelled to over 40,000 military personnel by 1969.

43. *The Times* (London), May 25, 1962. Champassak, Foreign Minister in Boun Oum's government, said Harriman asked Prince Tiao Khampan, Laotian Ambassador to Washington, for the removal of Phoumi from Boun Oum's cabinet. American officials in Washington and Vientiane denied the report. (*The New York Times,* May 26, 1962.)

44. Not surprisingly, this arrangement did not work well once the new government was installed. Agreement proved the exception rather than the rule.

45. The formation of the coalition government occasioned an exchange of letters between Chairman Khrushchev and President Kennedy. Khrushchev's letter, dated June 12, said formation of the coalition government "may become the pivotal event . . . in the cause of strengthening peace in southeast Asia."

"The example of Laos indicates that, provided there is a desire to resolve difficult international problems on the basis of cooperation with mutual account of regard for the interests of all sides, such cooperation bears fruit. At the same time, the results achieved in the settlement of the Laotian problem strengthen the conviction that success in solving other international problems which now divide states and create tension in the world can be achieved on the same road as well."

President Kennedy replied, "I agree that continued progress in the settlement of the Laotian problem can be most helpful in leading toward the resolution of other international difficulties. If together we can help in the establishment of an independent and neutral Laos, securely sustained in this status through time, this accomplishment will surely have a significant and positive effect far beyond the borders of Laos. You can count on the continued and energetic efforts of the Government of the United States toward this end." (U. S. Department of State, *American Foreign Policy,* 1962, pp. 1072-73.) Neither statesman, it seemed, had any idea that the fighting in Vietnam would reach the enormous scale of the late 1960s.

46. Texts in Great Britain, Cmd. 2834, pp. 178-86.

47. This provision, inserted at American insistence, was not in Souvanna's original draft Declaration.

48. The United States wanted to avoid a specific reference to SEATO. The Americans proposed to omit the phrase "including SEATO" from the neutrality statement. In its place, the United States advocated an arrangement whereby SEATO itself would take note of Laos's neutral status. This action would invalidate the SEATO Protocol which extended SEATO protection to Laos. The United States was forced to yield on this point.

As Arthur Lall has pointed out, however, the phrase "including SEATO" lacked operational meaning. This was so because the SEATO Treaty and Protocol specified that the alliance did not have the right to intervene unless called upon by the country in question. The Laotian Government, in its statement of neutrality, pledged not to "recognize the protection of any alliance or military coalition." Just how this promise affects the traditional right of a country to request assistance from friendly governments remains to be seen. This right was recognized in Article 51 of the United Nations Charter. See Lall, p. 138.

49. "This article," said Harriman, "was designated specifically to prohibit Vietnamese infiltration through Laos into South Vietnam. . . ." (U.S. Congress, Senate, Committee on Appropriations, *Hearings, Foreign Assistance and Related Agencies Appropriations for 1963*, 87th Cong., 2d Sess., 1962, p. 711.)

50. *The New York Times*, July 5, 1962.

51. *Ibid.*, July 9, 1962. At the final plenary session on July 21, Souvanna listed the immediate tasks of his government as "the peaceful restoration of national unity and understanding by military as well as civil integration. . . ." (Modelski, p. 142.)

52. The ICC reported to the Co-Chairmen that 666 American military advisors had left Laos by the deadline, October 6. (*The Times* [London], November 12, 1962.) The United States said that by removing these 666 advisors, it had completed the withdrawal of its military advisors from Laos. "There remains considerable doubt whether all foreign Communist military personnel were withdrawn." (U.S. Department of State, *Laos Fact Sheet,* Publication No. 7484, 1963, p. 11.)

53. Foreshadowing future developments, General W. B. Palmer, Director of Military Assistance, International Security Administration, said, ". . . there is nothing in that treaty [the 1962 Geneva agreements] which prevents our giving military assistant [*sic*] to Laos at their request for the purpose of assisting in the formation of a sound regime in the country." (Senate Committee on Appropriations, Hearings, *Foreign Assistance and Related Agencies Appropriations for 1963*, 1962, p. 145.) If this interpretation is valid, then Articles 2 and 4 would seem to lack any meaning.

54. The Soviet draft (Article 7) envisaged such an investigation only on instructions from the Co-Chairmen, one of whom, of course, was the Soviet Foreign Minister.

55. The Soviets wanted unanimous decisions on all matters except procedural ones. (John J. Czyzak and Carl F. Salans, "The International Conference on the Settlement of the Laotian Question and the Geneva Agreements of 1962," *American Journal of International Law,* 57 [April 1963]: 314.)

56. Obviously, the ICC could not investigate reports of entry of foreign military material unless the Premier and two Deputy-Premiers in the Laotian government unanimously agreed to call for such inspection. One year later a U. S. Senate study concluded, "Because of internal factions within the Government, the International Control Commission . . . has found it impracticable to police the agreements." (U.S. Congress, Senate, Committee on Foreign Relations, Report, *Study Mission to Southeast Asia,* November–December 1962, 88th Cong., 1st Sess., 1963, p. 11.)

57. The Soviets had wanted such decisions to be unanimous.

58. U. S. President, *Public Papers of the Presidents,* 1962, p. 568.

59. *Ibid.*

60. Senate Committee on Appropriations, *Hearings, Foreign Assistance and Related Agencies Appropriations for 1963,* 1962, p. 714.

61. U. S. President, *Public Papers of the Presidents,* 1962, p. 582.

62. *Ibid.,* p. 587.

14
LOOKING BACKWARD

THE SIGNING OF THE 1962 agreements on Laos marked the close of a chapter in American policy toward that embattled land. American involvement began in 1954 with an effort to create a pro-Western Laos and ended with an agreement for establishing a neutral Laos, tied to no outside power.

Before passing on to events beyond 1962, which we shall examine in the next chapter, it would be well to pause and assess the pattern of events that unfolded between the Geneva conferences of 1954 and 1962. We shall consider the two aspects of the Laotian episode that have occupied us during the narrative thus far; namely, American policy and the prerequisites of compromise settlement.

EVALUATION OF AMERICAN POLICY

United States involvement in Laos commenced after the 1954 Geneva Conference and increased during the following eight years. The cardinal objective of American policy was to limit communist influence in Laos. Although the Eisenhower and Kennedy administrations interpreted this task differently—the former sought to eradicate communism in Laos while the latter accepted communism but tried to curb it—each President tried to reduce communist influence as much as he thought possible. In attempting to evaluate American policy, therefore, we shall use as the criterion of success or failure the amount of communist power in Laos.

273

The following indicators are proposed to measure the extent of communist power in Laos:

1. The Pathet Lao's numerical strength.
2. The degree of Pathet Lao participation in the Laotian government.
3. The amount of Laotian territory under Pathet Lao control.
4. The degree of international control over Laotian affairs.
5. Laotian relations with communist states.

Using these indicators, let us compare the Pathet Lao's power in 1954 and 1962.

PATHET LAO'S NUMERICAL STRENGTH

According to Souvanna Phouma, the Pathet Lao numbered 2,000–3,000 cadres after the 1954 Geneva Conference. By the time the 1962 agreements were signed, the Pathet Lao had grown to 15,000 members.[1] The Pathet Lao was much better organized as a fighting force in 1962 than in 1954. They also had a supply of Soviet weapons in 1962 which they did not have in 1954.

PATHET LAO PARTICIPATION IN THE LAOTIAN GOVERNMENT

In 1954 the Pathet Lao lacked representation in the Laotian government, although the government, in its Declaration on July 21, 1954, declared itself "resolved to take the necessary measures to integrate all citizens, without discrimination, into the national community. . . ."

In the coalition government formed in June 1962, the Pathet Lao occupied four cabinet positions, including one of the two posts of Deputy Premier.

TERRITORY UNDER PATHET LAO CONTROL

When the Vietminh withdrew from Laos, subsequent to the 1954 Geneva accords, the Pathet Lao did not have exclusive control over any territory in Laos. The 1954 Agreement on the Cessation of Hostilities in Laos designated the provinces of Sam Neua and Phong Saly as regroupment areas for the Pathet Lao. The language of Article 14 clearly indicated that the Pathet Lao were to occupy these provinces as a temporary measure; the Article states, "Pending a political settlement," the Pathet Lao will move into the two provinces. Thus, in 1954, the Pathet Lao did not exercise legal authority over any territory in Laos, but they did enjoy *de facto* control over the two provinces.

After the collapse of General Phoumi Nosavan's army at Nam Tha in May 1962, the Pathet Lao, allied with Kong Le's troops, enjoyed practically unchallenged military control of all of Laos except Luang Prabang and a strip along the Mekong River. Although in many parts of Laos no military forces from any faction actually maintained outposts or carried out regular patrolling, the forces arrayed against Phoumi had a secure grasp of the four-fifths of Laos in which they were dominant.

INTERNATIONAL CONTROL OVER LAOTIAN AFFAIRS

This indicator has been chosen on the supposition that the greater the degree of international supervision over Laos, the less chance one faction— whether pro-Western or pro-communist—would have of gaining power illegally. The principal agent of international control in Laos was the ICC. Hence, the extent of international control over Laos was primarily a matter of how much power the ICC wielded. The Co-Chairmen of the Geneva Conference also exerted some international control over Laos.

The 1954 Agreement instructed the ICC to establish a number of joint and mobile inspection teams. No specific arrangements were made to provide the ICC with means of transport and communication, although Article 26 said the ICC "shall have at their disposal such modern means of transport, observation, and communication as they may require." Recommendations of the ICC were to be made by majority vote, except for the following matters, on which recommendations were to be unanimous:

1. Amendments and additions to the Agreement on the Cessation of Hostilities.
2. Violations or threats of violation that might lead to a resumption of hostilities.
3. Refusal by foreign armed troops to effect the movements provided for in the withdrawal plan.
4. Violations or threats of violation by foreign armed forces of Laos's integrity.

The 1954 agreements gave the Co-Chairmen no formal role in the peacekeeping machinery of the Conference.

In the 1962 Protocol to the Declaration on the Neutrality of Laos, the Co-Chairmen were assigned specific functions: (a) to receive periodic and special reports from the ICC, (b) to give guidance to the ICC, (c) to circulate reports and other information provided by the ICC, (d) to exercise supervision over the observance of the Protocol and Declaration on Neutrality, and (e) to keep the members of the Geneva Conference "constantly informed" and, when appropriate, consult with them.

Unlike the 1954 accords, the 1962 documents institutionalized the role of the Co-Chairmen in the international supervision of the agreements. To this extent, international surveillance of Laos in 1962 was enhanced compared with the degree of such supervision provided eight years earlier.

The powers of the ICC, however, were reduced in 1962. The Commission was not instructed to set up fixed and mobile inspection teams; instead, the ICC was to dispatch inspectors when and where it judged necessary. Regarding alleged violations of the provision prohibiting the introduction of foreign military personnel into Laos, the ICC was empowered to undertake investigations upon its own initiative (by majority vote). The Commission was authorized to conduct investigations in the case of suspected violations of the provision disallowing the introduction of foreign military material only at the request of the Laotian government. Since the covert shipment of weapons and ammunition across borders is easier to effect than the dispatch of foreign troops, violations of the restriction on material may be expected to exceed violations of the restriction on military personnel. Yet, the ICC was not authorized to investigate alleged illegal shipments of material unless asked to do so by the Laotian government. Since such a decision on the part of the government would have to be unanimous, one faction could obstruct the inspection procedures with ease. Thus ICC power to conduct investigations of suspected entry of military material was tenuous at best.

In 1962 unanimous voting by the ICC was required for more categories of violations than in 1954. ICC decisions on the following matters were to be unanimous in 1962:

1. Failure to withdraw foreign military personnel by the deadline.
2. Deviation from specified withdrawal routes by foreign troops leaving Laos.
3. Introduction of foreign military personnel into Laos.
4. Introduction of war material into Laos.
5. Violations of the cease-fire.
6. Conclusions on major questions sent to the Co-Chairmen.
7. All recommendations adopted by the Commission.

Majority voting was provided for on other matters, including procedural questions and the initiation and execution of investigations of alleged illegal entry of foreign military personnel. However, conclusions and recommendations issuing from such investigations were to be adopted unanimously. As in 1954, majority and minority reports were to be filed when necessary. In 1962 means of transportation and communication were placed under the Commission's own administrative control.

In 1954 unanimous ICC voting was required essentially only on matters pertaining to illegal actions by foreign military personnel. In 1962, a unanimous vote was required on nearly all important issues. In short, the

ICC's authority was sharply curtailed in 1962. Since the ICC was the principal instrument of international control in Laos, the reduction in the ICC's authority meant that international control over Laos decreased in 1962 as compared with 1954. This decrease was only slightly offset by the increased supervisory powers accorded the Co-Chairmen of the Geneva Conference.

LAOTIAN RELATIONS WITH COMMUNIST STATES

In 1954 Laos did not have diplomatic relations with any communist state. The first communist state to establish diplomatic relations with Laos was the Soviet Union; the two countries exchanged diplomats in September 1960.

The 1962 Declaration on the Neutrality of Laos said Laos will "establish diplomatic relations with all countries, the neighboring countries first and foremost." By the end of 1962, the new Laotian regime had recognized Communist China, Poland, Czechoslovakia, North Vietnam and East Germany. The Vientiane government also agreed in principle to recognize North Korea, Outer Mongolia, Hungary, and Bulgaria. Laotian recognition of Peking caused Taiwan, which had opened diplomatic relations with Laos in June 1962, to sever these diplomatic ties. South Vietnam also broke its ties with Laos following the establishment of diplomatic relations between Laos and North Vietnam.

In 1954 Laos did not receive any aid from communist countries. Six years later the Soviet Union began to supply aid to the Souvanna Phouma regime. Soviet aid to Laos has continued after the signing of the 1962 agreements.

Between 1954 and 1962, as we have seen, Laotian relations with communist states increased markedly, including the establishment of diplomatic relations with six communist states—and the consequent severing of diplomatic relations with South Vietnam and Nationalist China.

Based on the extent of communist power in Laos as measured by the five indicators listed above, American policy in Laos between 1954 and 1962 was not a success. During the eight years between Geneva conferences, the Pathet Lao's numbers increased and the movement attained four posts in the government. The Pathet Lao wielded actual control over much of Laotian territory by 1962. The ICC, which by means of publicity might have been able to limit subversion and infiltration, enjoyed less latitude of action in 1962 than in 1954. Vientiane, which had diplomatic relations with no communist countries in 1954, had established relations with six such countries by 1962 and was receiving communist aid. If these indicators measure the extent of communist power in Laos, then we are forced to conclude that that power did increase in Laos during the period under consideration.

To a certain extent, the growth of communist influence in Laos was augured by the 1954 Geneva agreements. One of the declarations by the Laotian government issued at the end of the Conference stated that the government was "resolved to take the necessary measures to integrate all citizens, without discrimination, into the national community. . . ." Thus, the Pathet Lao was promised some leverage in Laos. However, the Pathet Lao did not have adequate military strength to demand a position in a coalition government until the communists overran Phoumi's army at Nam Tha in May 1962.[2] The increment in communist political power in 1962 as compared with 1954 was owing primarily to the growth in communist military capabilities.

The weakness of Phoumi's army rendered compromise with the communists inevitable unless the United States, SEATO, or some other outside agent sent troops to fight the Pathet Lao. Since no such external forces were forthcoming, there was no doubt that a compromise would be effected, in which the communists would realize at least some of their objectives. The only question was when the time would arrive for the noncommunists to negotiate the most favorable settlement with the Pathet Lao. Obviously, the worst time to arrange a deal would have been when the noncommunists were obliged to negotiate from a position of weakness. Yet, after the battle of Nam Tha, the pro-Western forces found themselves in exactly that position.

With the benefit of hindsight, one can suggest two occasions for concluding more favorable agreements with the Pathet Lao—more favorable, that is, from the standpoint of American interests. The first opportunity came in November 1957, when Souvanna Phouma and Souphanouvong reached an accord providing for the formation of a government of national unity. American concurrence in these arrangements would have signified American acquiescence in communist participation in the Laotian government. We have seen that, given the Eisenhower Administration's hostility to compromise with the communists, such American approval was unlikely. However, a compromise worked out in 1957 would in all likelihood have proven more compatible with American interests than the compromise of 1962, by which time the Pathet Lao had established itself as the foremost military power in the country. In 1957, when the communists were small in numbers and had not won one decisive military engagement, limiting communist influence in the government would have been easier.

In fairness to the decision makers in Washington in 1957, it should be admitted that it was then far from apparent that the Pathet Lao would overwhelm a Western-trained and Western-equipped army led by a general who had access to American military advice. In gambling that a buildup of indigenous anticommunist forces in Laos could deprive the Pathet Lao of political power, Washington was taking a not unreasonable risk.

Although the failure of such a strategy could not have been foreseen in 1957, when the effort was just beginning, three years later the United States should have realized how limited its influence was in Laotian affairs. The Phoui Sananikone regime, installed during the summer of 1958, adopted a staunch anticommunist policy. Encouraged by this course of events, as well as by the right-wing military coup executed by Phoumi in December 1959, the United States judged that its policy of sustaining anticommunist leaders in Laos was succeeding. However, Kong Le's coup in August 1960 upset the rightist ascendancy over the communists and brought about an entirely new situation. This coup proved that the United States exerted much less control over Laotian affairs than it had thought, and also that the policies pursued by Washington-backed political leaders had alienated a sizable proportion of the Laotian people. An accurate reading of the nature of Kong Le's coup, particularly its neutralist and nationalist content, might have given the United States a clue that the Laotian rightists and militarists, in power since the summer of 1958, had not won the support of significant segments of the Laotian population.

The United States must share the blame for alienating the neutralist nationalists. Of the $417 million in military and financial aid the United States gave Laos between fiscal 1954 and 1962, only $8 million, or 2 percent, was allocated to improving living conditions of the peasants, who constitute about 85 percent of the Laotian population. The remainder of American aid went to support the military effort against the Pathet Lao. The prime beneficiaries of American aid were the members of a few hundred families living in the major cities. Much of their wealth was gained through well-publicized corruption.

Many Laotians opposed American aid on the ground that it harmed more Laotians than it helped. Government corruption, made possible by American assistance, encouraged Laotian officials to neglect the interests of the people while filling their own pockets. Government dishonesty led, in turn, to increasing bitterness on the part of the rural population and consequently widened the seams of social division in a country already notable for its lack of social cohesion. Many Laotians, oversimplifying to be sure, viewed American aid as Washington's instrument for persuading Laotians to kill Laotians. Such slaughter, they thought, might have been in America's interest but was of questionable benefit to Laos.

Kong Le based his support on elements in Laos that were outraged by what American aid had brought in its wake. These individuals rallied to Kong Le because he seemed to be the only leader concerned with ameliorating the living conditions of the peasants and the impoverished city dwellers. Although Kong Le and the majority of his supporters were not communists, they allied themselves with the Pathet Lao in opposition to a common foe, the United States. Kong Le was bound to split with the Pathet Lao, as he did after 1962, because he and the Pathet Lao objected to Washington's policies on different grounds. For the period 1960–62, however, Kong Le and the Pathet Lao found it convenient to consolidate their forces to oust American influence. When this objective was largely achieved in July 1962, the Pathet Lao and the neutralists went their separate ways.[3]

In addition to a disaffected population, the United States had to contend with the Pathet Lao's growing army. Phoui Sananikone's inability to decisively repel the Pathet Lao's offensive in the summer of 1959 served notice that the Pathet Lao fielded a military force to be reckoned with. Furthermore, this strong separatist force was operating amidst a population disenchanted with the central government in Vientiane and therefore not unwilling to assist an anti-Vientiane movement.

One may question whether this combination of circumstances augured well for Washington's strategy of reliance upon right-wing military forces to defeat the Pathet Lao. Ambassador Brown perceived these difficulties in the fall of 1960 and accordingly recommended that the United States urge General Phoumi to join the coalition government proposed by Souvanna Phouma. Washington eventually overruled Brown and once again decided to rely on the ability of Phoumi—whose army had been unable to win any decisive victories against the Pathet Lao since the military coup of December 1959—to inflict military defeat upon the Pathet Lao. Policymakers in Washington continued to believe that if they only accelerated military aid to Phoumi, his army would rout the communists from the field. And so, in the fall of 1960, the United States rejected another chance to form a coalition government before the Pathet Lao had gained undisputed military superiority.

In this second instance of opportunity missed, the vigor of local nationalism to preserve Laotian freedom of action was more manifest than in 1957. Kong Le had galvanized the Laotian nationalists into a fighting force. Washington's key policymakers, operating under the philosophy of "if you're not with us you must be agin' us," erroneously concluded that Kong Le and his followers were merely an arm of the communists. Kong Le committed a costly error by his inflammatory denunciations of the United States. These statements, no doubt, were instrumental in persuading some influential American policymakers to oppose Kong Le instead of supporting him. The United States did not perceive that Kong

Le's objectives—national independence, honest government, and popular welfare—coincided with the long-run goals of America's Laotian policy.

In summary, the United States underestimated Pathet Lao strength, overestimated its own ability to control events in Laos, and refused to ally itself with the forces of local nationalism. The United States tried to contain communist influence in Laos by supporting right-wing anticommunists. However, in General Phoumi Washington backed a loser. This fact should have become apparent to the United States before March 1961, when President Kennedy realized it and consequently altered American policy. Unfortunately for Washington, the United States was obliged to compromise with the Pathet Lao from a position of weakness in 1962, whereas it would have been in a much stronger position in November 1957, or just after Kong Le's coup in August 1960.

In fairness to those officials who determined American policy toward Laos, it should be said that many of the developments that seem evident to the observer writing in the 1970s did not appear so clear to the men on the spot in 1954–62. It was impossible to know, for example, that Phoumi's army would be smashed by the numerically inferior forces of the Pathet Lao. Nor was it apparent that the Pathet Lao, ousted from the coalition government by Phoui Sananikone in January 1959, would amass sufficient power to gain an even more prominent position in a coalition government three years later. It can be argued that United States officials did not always make those choices that, from the standpoint of today, would appear the wisest. However, one cannot say that Americans responsible for Washington's Laotian policy did not earnestly attempt to accomplish what they deemed to be in the national interest. Foreign policy, like poker and marriage, is a matter of incomplete information, calculated risks, and unforeseen developments. One can only ask that the policymaker estimate carefully the likely outcomes of different courses of action, select the one that best suits his interests, and then choose the means most likely to bring this outcome about. Should that outcome fail to materialize, we may criticize the official for making a mistake, but we have no grounds for questioning his loyalty. With the exception of a very few dishonest officials, all Americans involved in Laos acted with the interests of the United States in mind. If we can fault them for anything, it may be that they acted not wisely but too well.

COMPROMISE SETTLEMENT

The 1954 Laotian settlement did not have the hoped-for effect of creating stability in Laos. After 1954, Laotian political leaders tended to drift toward the far left (Pathet Lao) or far right (pro-Western faction), with a few individuals, such as Souvanna Phouma, in the middle. Even Souvanna moved toward the left in late 1960. The Soviet Union and the United States gave their support to conflicting factions in Laos. The Soviets, along with the Chinese and North Vietnamese, backed the Pathet Lao; the Americans, the pro-Western faction. After Kong Le's coup of August 1960, the Soviet-American conflict intensified; each side sent arms and economic aid—as well as military advisers—to its adopted faction. Viewed from December 1960, when Phoumi's American-trained and equipped forces drove Soviet-equipped Pathet Lao and neutralist troops from Vientiane, the Laotian crisis seemed to be evolving toward a fight for total victory among irreconcilable parties.

As we know, however, the Laotian situation moved in the opposite direction—toward compromise.

WHAT FACTORS CONTRIBUTED TO A COMPROMISE SETTLEMENT OF THE LAOTIAN CRISIS?

In devoting attention to such a question, I find myself in the good company of other political scientists who have explored the phenomenon of compromise settlement.[4] One approach to this subject involves an attempt to discover preconditions that must be present in order for a compromise settlement to materialize. Once we have uncovered sufficient knowledge, it is hoped, we shall be able to advise policymakers what they must do in order to produce or prevent a compromise solution in any particular conflict. Perhaps political scientists flatter themselves in believing they can manipulate the stuff of politics with the deft precision of a skilled surgeon performing a difficult operation. It does not seem beyond the range of possibility, however, to hope that some day political scientists may be able to predict that if x is done, there is at least a high probability that y will result. In time we may even be able to attach a number to that probability, so that we could say if x is done, the chances are 8 in 10 that y will follow.

One method of accumulating the knowledge that might enable one to make such statements of probability is to examine various instances of compromise settlement and then extract those features present in all cases. We could then study these common characteristics in the hope of discovering which ones, if any, constitute the necessary and sufficient causes of compromise settlement. Perhaps such an effort will enable us to set forth a valid theory of compromise settlement of international conflicts. It is in this spirit that I have chosen to bring to light those factors which led to a compromise settlement of the Laotian conflict.

In conducting such an inquiry, it makes sense to build on and hopefully extend the findings of other investigators. Such a procedure will be followed here.

In a seminal essay on compromise settlement, George Modelski has suggested three "preliminary" and two "basic" conditions that must be present for a compromise settlement to materialize.[5] The three preliminary conditions concern the identity of the contestants, the duration of the conflict, and the degree of communication between the parties. Compromise settlement can occur, Modelski says, only if the identity of the disputing parties is well known, as is not always the case with the leadership and following of an insurgent movement. For example, the identity of the Burmese rebels, particularly the leaders, remains obscure. The same can be said for many Vietcong, who farm by day and fight by night. Turning to Modelski's second preliminary condition, a compromise is feasible only if the conflict has lasted a certain period of time. The conflict must persist long enough to allow each party to demonstrate its capacity to create difficulties for the other party for a long time to come. Usually, settlement follows upon an initial test of strength in which each party convinces the other that rapid victory is unlikely. A minimum duration is also necessary to permit third-party actors and conciliatory mechanisms to become involved. The third preliminary condition for compromise settlement is communication between the parties, for negotiations cannot be arranged unless both sides agree to hold them. Communication, of course, does not ensure that talks will be held, as the present impasse in the Middle East illustrates.

More important than the three preliminary conditions for settlement are Modelski's two basic conditions. The more crucial of these is stalemate, defined as "the state of affairs in which neither side, given its aims, has the resources to overwhelm the other (absolutely, or without incurring unacceptable losses)."[6] The second basic condition for compromise is a redistribution of aims. This means that each party must abandon some of its original objectives in favor of a position resting somewhere between them and the opening aims of the other side. The compromise finally accepted by both parties need not be exactly between the original demands of each side; it may well be more favorable to one party than the other. However, it must not satisfy all the original demands of either party, for then we would have total victory, not compromise. According to Modelski, the existence of stalemate facilitates the process of redistributing objectives. A third party—generally another state or an international organization— may play a catalytic role in bringing about a redistribution of aims.

Upon examining the situation in Laos that led to the 1962 settlement, one can detect the presence of Modelski's three preliminary conditions as well as his two basic conditions. The identity of the leadership and following of the contending factions was well known. The conflict had lasted eight years by 1962, a sufficiently lengthy period to persuade everyone concerned that a quick victory by any one party was not to be had. This eight-year span was adequate to permit third-party actors, such as the ICC and the Co-Chairmen of the Geneva Conference, to become involved. There was ample communication between the parties. During the crucial period while the Geneva Conference was in session, leaders of the three factions met at Zurich (June 1961), Ban Hin Heup (October 1961), and Geneva (January 1962). The three factions also maintained contacts on the military level at Ban Namone.

Modelski's two basic conditions for compromise—stalemate and a re-distribution of aims—accompanied the Laotian settlement. The precarious military stalemate that had persisted in Laos through 1962 was shattered in May of that year, when the Pathet Lao overran Phoumi's army at Nam Tha. After that battle, there was no Laotian force capable of pre-venting the Pathet Lao from gaining military control of the entire country. Stalemate had given way, so it seemed, to the likelihood of total victory. However, the stalemate was quickly restored, not by a recrudescence of Phoumi's army, but by the threat of American intervention. Washington put the communists on notice that American troops would intervene to prevent the Pathet Lao from taking over the entire country. The United States made its threat credible by sending troops to Thailand and taking other actions to indicate that it was serious about stopping the communists with force if necessary. Convinced that the United States was capable of inflicting unacceptable damage upon its forces, the Pathet Lao leadership called off its military campaign and agreed to negotiate.

The case of Laos thus lends support to the proposition that the existence of a military stalemate is an important contributing factor to the com-promise settlement of a dispute. The Laotian case shows that a foreign power can help to create a stalemate in an internal conflict.

Parenthetically, we might scrutinize the truism that one cannot win at the conference table what one has lost on the battlefield. A study of the Laotian conflict casts some doubt on this principle. In May 1962, the Pathet Lao defeated 5,000 of Phoumi's best troops at Nam Tha. Phoumi's army was broken, and his opponents were military masters in Laos. Yet one month later the three factions agreed to form a coalition government in which the losers at Nam Tha were accorded a position equal to that of their victorious adversary.

How did the rightists, militarily weaker than the Pathet Lao, emerge with equally strong positions in the coalition government? The answer lies in external support. We have seen that the United States restored the Laotian stalemate by threatening to intervene on behalf of General Phoumi.

We may conclude, then, that a party which suffers a decisive military defeat can still realize many of its objectives at the bargaining table if the defeated party has sufficient external support.

There are, of course, limits to what a defeated party can achieve during negotiations. The rightists, for example, had to agree to admit the Pathet Lao to the government and award them a position equal to their own.

Modelski's second basic condition for compromise, a redistribution of political aims, was also present in the Laotian settlement. The redistribution of political aims was greatly facilitated by the emergence of a strong center group, led by Souvanna Phouma and Kong Le, in August 1960. The neutralists provided a middle position, already in being, to which the Pathet Lao and the pro-Western group could adjust their objectives in case either party should decide against continuing to fight for its maximum demands. Because of the presence of a center faction, it was unnecessary for the yielding party or parties to place itself at the mercy of its direct opponents. This fact made concessions more palatable than they would have been if one party had been forced to appear on bended knee before another. The center group also facilitated agreement on the distribution of portfolios in the coalition government established in July 1962. The sharp dispute regarding control of key ministries, particularly interior and defense, was settled by awarding these portfolios to the neutralist faction. Thus neither right nor left "lost" this dispute. The formation of a coalition government was further facilitated by the availability of a neutralist, Souvanna, as Premier in the new regime.

It would seem, then, that one of the crucial factors making compromise settlement possible is the existence of a party representing a political position between those of the two extreme groups. Such a neutral party can serve as a locus about which a compromise settlement may develop as both of the conflicting groups soften their demands.

Another factor that contributed to a compromise settlement of the Laotian problem was the way in which the great powers, the United States and the Soviet Union, were involved in the dispute. It will be recalled that at Vienna Premier Khrushchev and President Kennedy agreed that Laos should not become the cause of a direct conflict between them. Each promised to urge its allied Laotian faction to conduct itself so as to promote a political settlement. This decision had considerable importance in bringing about the compromise embodied in the 1962 agreements.

By June 1961, when Kennedy and Khrushchev held their summit talks in Vienna, an international conflict had become grafted onto the Laotian civil war. There was a strong possibility that either the United States or Russia, or both, would encourage its faction in Laos to strive for a total military victory. Such a decision would no doubt have been accompanied

by massive increases in military aid, involving the likelihood that the other
cold war superpower would match the escalation. However, the two heads
of state agreed to turn the Laotian conflict in the other direction. This
decision, when communicated to the feuding parties in Laos, caused them
to realize that they could not expect the unlimited outside support each
needed to achieve total victory. Thus, the Kennedy-Khrushchev agreement
represented a significant contribution to the compromise that was con-
summated at Geneva.

Let us translate this finding into a generalized statement that can be
tested in other situations. We may phrase our hypothesis as follows: An
agreement, by major powers that sustain conflicting factions in an internal
war, to seek a compromise settlement contributes significantly to the likelihood of such a settlement.

One factor that inclined the Soviet Union and the United States to
reach the agreement made at Vienna lay in the manner in which each
superpower had managed the Laotian situation since 1954. Although both
Russia and the United States took specific and, at first, uncompromising
positions in the Laotian dispute, neither power had elevated the Laotian
matter to the rank of vital interest. By keeping the Laotian situation below
the level of vital interest and "sacred national honor," each superpower
could later afford to compromise without yielding what had been termed
unnegotiable. This analysis allows one to infer that if major powers
supporting conflicting factions in another country refrain from designating
their commitments as vital interests, a compromise settlement becomes
more likely to occur.

Thus far, we have confirmed or brought to light various conditions that
significantly contribute to compromise settlement. It would be advisable
to list these as follows:

1. Military stalemate.
2. Existence of a party representing a political position between those of
   the two contending sides.
3. An agreement to seek a compromise settlement by major external powers
   supporting the conflicting parties.

We have also noted the presence of Modelski's three preliminary conditions (knowledge of the identity of the parties, adequate duration of the
conflict so that rapid victory is ruled out and third parties may intervene,
and communication between the parties) and two basic conditions (stalemate and redistribution of aims) for compromise settlement.

A related matter calling for further investigation concerns the most
propitious time for consummating a compromise. Are people more inclined
to strike a bargain during a crisis period, when tensions run high, or are
people more likely to settle for a compromise during intervals of calm,

when reason has the opportunity to overcome the tuggings of emotion? Is compromise settlement more probable between parties of nearly equal military strength or between parties whose military might differs widely?

K. J. Holsti and Lloyd Jensen have addressed themselves to questions like the ones posed above. Two stages are involved in fashioning a compromise, Holsti says.[7] In the first place, both sides must agree that a partial withdrawal of demands is preferable to continued fighting. Then the parties can begin to discuss the terms of an agreement. These two types of accord are difficult to achieve in times of crisis, when each side tends to attach "symbolic value and importance" to the dispute, Holsti says. In such times, compromise is equated with the sacrifice of a great principle. Violence also impedes compromise by creating an atmosphere in which reconciliation becomes difficult. Holsti recognizes, however, that a military stalemate may induce one or both sides to reduce their demands rather than continue fighting. Whereas Modelski believes that stalemate is the most important prerequisite to a compromise, Holsti seems to feel that the fighting that could lead to a compromise might in itself create an ambiance impeding compromise.

The Laotian compromise casts doubt on Holsti's theorems. The 1962 Geneva agreements, particularly those regarding the composition of the coalition government, were effected in a time of crisis. Phoumi's army had just been defeated; American troops had landed in Thailand; a direct confrontation between the Americans and the communists was a not unlikely prospect. Yet, during those days of crisis and high tension, a compromise was worked out and put into effect. The Laotian situation calls for further study of the extent to which tension and violence block compromise settlement. Holsti's propositions, it appears, cannot be accepted at face value.

Lloyd Jensen has described what he considers to be the most propitious conditions under which negotiations may take place.[8] The optimum bargaining situation, according to Jensen, is one in which both sides have nearly equal strength (parity). Under such circumstances, each side will have little cause to hope for bettering its position. At the same time, inasmuch as neither side can remain fully confident of its security, both sides have an incentive for reducing their demands and agreeing to compromise. If, on the other hand, one party is demonstrably stronger than the other, negotiations leading to compromise are not likely to come about. The stronger party will feel no need to negotiate, since it may harbor realistic hopes of improving its position through the use of the superior military force at its command. The weaker side may also hesitate to negotiate for fear that its weakness would prevent it from being able to extract concessions from the stronger party. There is considerable evidence, Jensen says, to refute the theory that nations negotiate seriously from a position of strength. "One does not negotiate from strength; one may dictate from strength, but one does not negotiate."[9]

Jensen's propositions apply more closely than Holsti's to the Laotian case. After the battle of Nam Tha, the Pathet Lao forces were clearly far superior to the scattered remnants of Phoumi's army. As between these two parties, there was no parity. As has been seen, however, the United States threatened to intervene if the Pathet Lao did not stop their military actions and agree to negotiate. If one considers the balance of forces between the Pathet Lao on one hand and Phoumi, combined with the United States, on the other, then one perceives a situation of near parity. At the same time, neither side felt fully confident about its position. The pro-Western faction in particular had cause to worry, since its main force had been routed at Nam Tha. The Pathet Lao, although more secure than its adversary, could not discount the possibility of American intervention. It was exactly when these conditions took effect that serious bargaining leading to compromise occurred. Therefore, the Laotian case supports Jensen's contention that the optimum bargaining situation occurs when both side possess nearly equal strength and at the same time entertain doubts about their security.

Lewis Coser, a sociologist, offers another perspective on the relationship between conflict and negotiations.[10] Conflict, according to Coser, may actually promote the likelihood of settlement. In the course of violent conflict, the disputants make certain agreements; for example, regulations on the treatment of prisoners of war. Thus a pattern of cooperation is engendered. Violence may advance eventual accommodation in still another way. Coser accepts the postulate that a power equilibrium between two sides may advance the prospects for compromise. But how may both parties know with certainty that they possess approximately equal power? Power cannot be reliably measured, as spending power can be quantified in terms of dollars. How, for instance, can one determine that superior morale on one side will not offset greater firepower on the other? The only way to ascertain one's own strength, as well as that of one's opponent, is by mutual combat. Violent conflict between the two parties provides the most accurate measure of each side's relative power. If such fighting leads to stalemate, then the likelihood of a compromise solution is heightened, according to Coser. It is, moreover, nearly impossible to establish the fact of stalemate unless actual fighting takes place and results in a standoff. Such conflict may contain in itself the seeds of settlement.[11]

Confirmation of Coser's theorems can be found in the Laotian instance. However, his statements require further refinement in order to be of use to the managers of conflict. For example, it would be necessary to investigate other cases in order to determine if agreement on the treatment of prisoners and related matters has any actual bearing on whether negotiations on basic issues will occur and, if so, just how important such preliminary agreements are. Furthermore, may it not be said that Coser too readily makes the assumption that stalemate leads directly to a negotiated settlement? Additional work on the relationship between stalemate and compromise is called for. Indeed, one function of this volume is to break ground for further investigation in this area.

In this volume I have endeavored to extract from a study of the Laotian conflict those factors that contributed to a compromise settlement. Several generalizations, which students of conflict resolution may wish to test in other contexts, are presented below.

1. The existence of a party acceptable to conflicting groups and representing a position between those taken by the groups contributes to the settlement of a dispute.

2. A military stalemate between two opposing factions makes an important contribution to the conclusion of a compromise settlement between them.

3. Agreement to seek a compromise by major powers sustaining conflicting factions in another country contributes to a compromise settlement.

4. If major powers supporting conflicting factions in another country do not designate their commitments as vital interests, a compromise settlement is more likely than if the major powers had characterized their commitments as vital interests.

NOTES

1. *The Christian Science Monitor,* April 14, 1966.

2. The 1957 agreements, which provided for Pathet Lao participation in a coalition government, issued less from Pathet Lao strength than from Souvanna's desire to form a government of national unity.

3. According to Roger Hilsman, this fact largely vindicated American policy toward Laos under President Kennedy. Hilsman said that one of Harriman's aims was to create conditions whereby the neutralists would split with the communists and join the pro-Western forces. That is precisely what happened subsequent to the 1962 agreements. (Interview with Roger Hilsman, October 2, 1967.)

4. See, for example, Karl W. Deutsch *et al, Political Community in the North Atlantic Area* (Princeton: Princeton University Press, 1957) ; K. J. Holsti, "Resolving Inter-National Conflicts," *Journal of Conflict Resolution* 10 (September 1966) ; 272–91; H. L. Nieburg, "Uses of Violence," *Journal of Conflict Resolution* 7 (March 1963) ; 43–54; George Modelski, "International Settlement of Internal War," in James N. Rosenau (ed.), *International Aspects of Civil Strife* (Princeton: Princeton University Press, 1964) ; and Oran R. Young. *The Intermediaries:*

Third Parties in International Crises (Princeton: Princeton University Press, 1967).

5. George Modelski, "International Settlement of Internal War." Modelski reached his conclusion by comparing 100 internal wars fought between 1900 and 1962, including the one in Laos.

6. *Ibid.,* p. 143.

7. Holsti, *Journal of Conflict Resolution* 10:276.

8. Lloyd Jensen, "Military Capabilities and Bargaining Behavior," *The Journal of Conflict Resolution* 9 (June 1965): 155–63.

9. Kenneth Boulding, quoted by Jensen, p. 155.

10. Lewis A. Coser, *The Functions of Social Conflict* (Glencoe, New York: The Free Press, 1956).

11. *Ibid.,* pp. 133–37.

15
AFTER 1962

THE FRENCH ARE fond of a proverb which says, *"Plus ça change, plus c'est la même chose."* Roughly translated, this means the more something changes, the more it remains the same. This proverb applies with grim finality to Laos.

In the years after 1962, developments in Laos followed a course scarcely distinguishable from the chain of events we have found in the years preceding the new Geneva agreements. One new element—the intensified struggle in Vietnam—does enter the picture and modifies the Laotian situation somewhat. Yet the basic shape of the political confrontation in Laos has remained essentially unchanged since 1962.

We shall divide our examination of Laos after 1962 into five sections. First of all, we shall take account of the breakup of the coalition government. Then we shall look at America's involvement in Laos. Thirdly, we shall consider the one factor that was only barely present in the Laotian situation before 1962, namely, the symbiotic connection between Laos and the war in Vietnam. We shall conclude by examining the opium problem and the refugee situation in Laos.

THE COALITION GOVERNMENT
DISSOLVES

The regime established in 1962 depended for its success on cooperation among the Pathet Lao, the neutralists, and the conservatives. Indeed, the government could not act in the absence of unanimity among the neutralist

Premier, Souvanna Phouma, and the two Vice-Premiers, one from each of the other factions. Many people asserted that this arrangement was extremely fragile, given the depth of disagreement among the three factions in the years preceding 1962. These statements turned out to be only too accurate.

The coalition government foundered on the rocks of conflict between the Pathet Lao and the neutralists. This development surprised many, inasmuch as these two groups had cooperated and even joined arms against the right-wing faction before the signing of the Geneva agreements.

As was expected, the three parties in the coalition government began to vie for preponderant influence as soon as the fledgling government embarked on its first tentative flights into affairs of state. In the eyes of many, Souvanna and Kong Le held the key to dominant influence; that is, whichever faction could gain the support of the center could work its designs no matter what the third group did. This situation, to be sure, did not bode well for a government based on the unanimity principle. The veto privilege in the Laotian government set limitations on the leverage gained through preponderant influence. In like manner, the veto in the United Nations Security Council limits the payoff of influence politics. In both cases, one party can paralyze the body no matter how much pressure is brought to bear on the body.

Nonetheless, the three partners in the coalition government took their bows and began their minuet of power politics almost as soon as the new regime took over. The Pathet Lao immediately began to apply pressure upon the neutralists to solidify their previous *ad hoc* cooperation into a more regular pattern. The neutralists, anxious to live up to their nonaligned designation, resisted Pathet Lao advances. Tension between the two groups became manifest by late 1962.[1] The Pathet Lao began to share less and less of their rice, salt, and military equipment with Kong Le's troops. Finally, the Pathet Lao cut off all assistance to the neutralist army in late 1962.

The United States, meanwhile, had reentered the lists in Laos. Soon after the Geneva agreements were initialed, the Americans resumed sending aid to the country. The United States, like others in Laos, was operating on the assumption that the center faction was in a position to determine whether Laos would incline toward the objectives of the Pathet Lao or the conservatives. Accordingly, the Americans wished to exert influence upon the neutralists with their old standby, foreign aid. By late 1962, the neutralist troops had come to rely on American aid, since the Pathet Lao had terminated its assistance. In November, a plane flying American aid to the neutralists was shot down by a gunner who took his orders from none other than a neutralist colonel, Deuane Sipaseuth. How can this seemingly illogical incident be explained? It appears that the Pathet Lao's efforts to subvert the neutralists had paid off in part. Colonel Deuane, a high-ranking neutralist officer, had persuaded himself that the neutralists should detach themselves from Souvanna and join the Pathet Lao. Kong Le continued to support Souvanna as well as the principle of nonalignment. Colonel Deuane and Kong Le proved unable to reconcile their views, and a split developed within the ranks of the neutralist faction. Deuane finally broke with Kong Le and then took measures to overthrow him. This split within the neutralists explains why the plane carrying American aid to Kong Le was shot down by a neutralist (pro-Deuane) gunner. Shortly after the shooting incident, Colonel Deuane joined the Pathet Lao, taking about 500 neutralist followers with him. The rift between the neutralists and the Pathet Lao, a schism reflected in the affairs of the neutralist faction itself, was growing alarmingly wide.

In early 1963 relations between the neutralists and the Pathet Lao worsened. Military skirmishes between them occurred periodically. Then, in April, an incident took place that transformed the split into a gaping chasm that has not been bridged since. The Pathet Lao looked to one of its members, Quinim Pholsena, Foreign Minister in the coalition government, as a principal channel of influence over the affairs of the regime. On April 1, 1963, in retaliation for the murder of one of Kong Le's officers, a neutralist machinegunned Quinim to death in Vientiane. This episode spelled the end of the coalition government. The Pathet Lao withdrew its representatives from the government. Souphanouvong left Vientiane to join his Pathet Lao followers at their headquarters near the Plain of Jars. Souphanouvong, who has yet to return to participate in the coalition government, claimed that all government decisions made in his absence were illegal, since unanimity was lacking. Since Souphanouvong's withdrawal from the government, the Pathet Lao has denied permission for government officials to enter territory under communist control. The Pathet Lao regard their regions as autonomous from the administration of Vientiane and have succeeded in preventing the Royal Government from extending its control over communist territory. The coalition government, which was now defunct, had lasted less than a year.

Later in April 1963, new fighting erupted, as the Pathet Lao mounted an attack on Kong Le's troops, quartered near the eastern flank of the Plain of Jars. The fighting lasted over a year, and by the end of May 1964, the Pathet Lao was in full control of the strategic Plain.

The Pathet Lao, to sum up, made a bid to dominate the Royal Laotian Government by winning over the neutralist faction. The neutralists, however, with the exception of Colonel Deuane and his followers, took their neutralism seriously and successfully resisted Pathet Lao appeals. This power struggle resulted in a break between the Pathet Lao and the other two political factions. The Pathet Lao bolted the coalition government, which now existed in name only.

With the extreme left eliminated from the coalition regime—though not by any means from the politics of Laos—the conservatives moved to capture the government. In April 1964, two conservative generals, Siho Lamphouthacoul, 28-year old commander of the national security police, and Kouprasith Abhay, active in the Battle of Vientiane, staged a coup and declared the coalition regime suspended.[2] The two generals, acting on behalf of General Phoumi Nosavan,[3] wished to get rid of Souvanna, whom they regarded as weak and inept. Besides, General Phoumi had little love for his political rival who had triumphed to become Premier. The planners of the coup succeeded momentarily in capturing the government and then turned to Washington for support. The United States, however, had had enough of sustaining military governments in Laos. Washington, with support from Great Britain, Australia, and Laotian King Savang Vatthana, insisted that Souvanna be reinstated. The generals, who were on the verge of assassinating Souvanna, were compelled to step down, and Souvanna was placed in charge of the government once again. Souvanna did, however, agree to adopt a stiffer stance toward the Pathet Lao. The Vientiane regime, abandoned by the left and assaulted from the right, moved into the second year of its truncated existence.

It was widely known that General Phoumi had been the driving force behind the coup in April. After the coup, Phoumi was downgraded from Vice-Premier to Finance Minister. He was also stripped of his principal sources of income, his gambling casinos and monopolies in gold, perfumes, and liquor. In an effort to regain these privileges and boost his declining political fortunes, Phoumi mounted another coup in February, 1965. In this effort, Phoumi was assisted by General Siho, who was one of the principal figures involved in the 1964 coup. This time the coup failed from the start. Phoumi and Siho fled to Thailand, where the former has remained in exile ever since. Souvanna once again held onto his precarious position as chief of state. He has not been seriously challenged since the 1965 coup.

In July of that year elections for the General Assembly took place.[4] The Pathet Lao boycotted the elections and denounced them as invalid. After the elections, held on the basis of limited suffrage, Souvanna formed a new government. As required by the 1962 Geneva agreements, Souvanna offered the Pathet Lao one-sixth of the ministerial posts and one-quarter of the secretaryships of state. The Pathet Lao refused to occupy these positions.

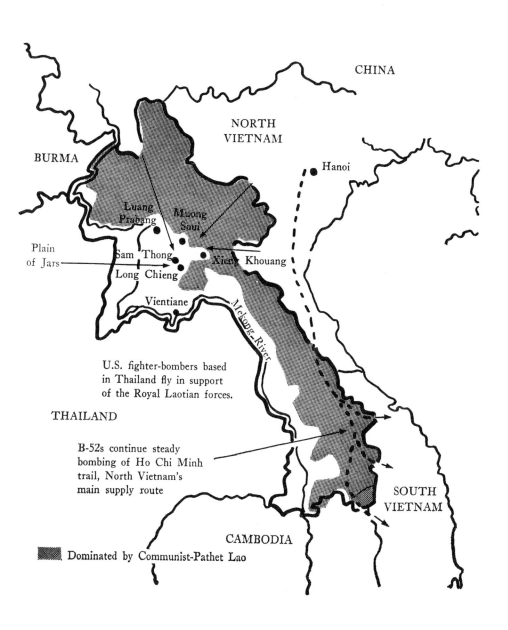

CHINA

NORTH
VIETNAM

BURMA

● Hanoi

Luang
Prabang   Muong
            Soui

Plain
of Jars

Sam Thong   Xieng Khouang
Long Chieng

Vientiane

Mekong River

U.S. fighter-bombers based
in Thailand fly in support
of the Royal Laotian forces.

THAILAND

B-52s continue steady
bombing of Ho Chi Minh
trail, North Vietnam's
main supply route

SOUTH
VIETNAM

CAMBODIA

Dominated by Communist-Pathet Lao

A final political settlement—to borrow a phrase from the 1954 Geneva agreements—has yet to occur in Laos. In all likelihood, no lasting solution will be found until the end of the war in Vietnam, if then. In the meanwhile, temporary political lines have been drawn and a quasi-partition of the country has taken place. There are, in actuality, two governments in Laos; each administers affairs in the territory under its control. The Pathet Lao, assisted by the North Vietnamese, remain in control of the northeast as well as a strip of territory which extends down the entire eastern boundary of Laos (see map, previous page). The neutralists and conservatives have merged into a single faction that stands somewhat to the right of center.[5] Souvanna continues to govern as head of this amalgam. He has not been troubled by serious attempts to topple his regime since the failure of General Phoumi's effort in February 1965. The Royal Government controls about two-fifths of the countryside, although a majority of the population live in government-controlled areas. Much of the territory in central Laos can best be classified as a no-man's land; control depends on the political and military tides of the moment. Fighting between the government and the Pathet Lao, often reinforced by the North Vietnamese, has been a recurrent motif in the orchestration of Laotian politics. Few battles of lasting significance are fought. Indeed, *plus ça change, plus c'est la même chose.*

Souvanna Phouma, as we have seen, has evidenced enormous staying power in the years before and after 1962. One is tempted to conclude that the urbane statesman is indispensable to government in Laos, regardless of what form that government takes. Kong Le has not proved so hardy; in November 1966, he resigned as commander of the neutralist forces and, disgusted by the continued killing of Lao by Lao, went to live in Indonesia and subsequently France. Phoumi resides in exile in Thailand. Boun Oum has remained in Laos and has held several appointive posts in the government. Phoui Sananikone, appointed by Souvanna as President of the National Assembly after the 1965 elections, continues to participate in the politics of Laos. Souphanouvong remains at the helm of the Pathet Lao. Of the principal figures in the pre-1962 political affairs of Laos, only Souvanna and Phoui, once formidable political rivals, still take an active part in government affairs. Souphanouvong, while he has refused to occupy the government post reserved for him, continues to represent an important quantity in the equation of Laotian politics.

It would seem in order to say a word or two about the ICC. At the 1961–1962 Geneva Conference, there was considerable wrangling over the authority and power to be accorded the ICC. In general, the ICC emerged from the conference with less authority than it possessed after the

1954 Geneva Conference. In retrospect, all the hassling and debate regarding the ICC seem rather pointless, inasmuch as events have rendered the ICC practically useless. The 1962 agreements were said to broaden the ICC's range of activities, in that investigations could be undertaken by majority vote. However, the decision to inspect was to be carried out only with the concurrence of the Laotian government. Since the Pathet Lao left the government in April 1963, the government has been unable to give unanimous approval to ICC inspections. Furthermore, the Pathet Lao has refused to permit the ICC to send officials into its territory, threatening to shoot "trespassers" should they enter Pathet Lao ground. In addition, the members of the ICC have found agreement nearly impossible to attain. According to the 1962 arrangements at Geneva, ICC conclusions and recommendations were to be unanimous. The Polish member, however, has rarely been in accord with his fellow-members from India and Canada. As a result, the ICC has agreed on almost nothing. The Soviet Union has published the Polish drafts, while Britain has published the drafts from the other members as well as Poland. The breakdown is complete. About the only undertaking carried out by the ICC recently has been the playing of badminton at its Vientiane headquarters.

AMERICAN INVOLVEMENT

The role of the United States, like the entire situation in Laos, remains consonant with the principle expressed in the proverb that begins this chapter. Looking at American policy today, one finds it scarcely different in objectives and means from the policy followed by President Kennedy. However, the extent of American involvement, particularly military assistance, has vastly increased.

To review briefly, from 1954 until President Kennedy assumed office in 1961, America sought to establish a pro-Western regime in Laos. In pursuit of this objective, the United States supported Phoui Sananikone and later General Phoumi Nosavan. President Kennedy modified American policy, opting for a neutral Laotian government even if it included some communists. The United States, in other words, was prepared to accept any solution in Laos short of a communist takeover. Presidents Johnson and Nixon have continued the Kennedy policy.[6] So long as communists do not control the government, the United States can be expected to support an independent Laos.

NONMILITARY AID

Washington's principal instrument of influence in Laos has been—both before and after 1962—military and economic aid. In this section we shall examine nonmilitary assistance. A summary of American military aid appears in the following section.

Tables 10 and 11 present a handy summary of American economic aid to Laos from 1962 through 1969.

Table 10 shows the amounts allocated to the support of specific projects, such as educational development and public health. In 1969, for instance, a total of $29,552,000 was spent by the United States on specific projects. Table 10 gives the full total of American economic assistance to Laos for each fiscal year. This figure is shown in the bottom line, labeled "Grand Total." The grand total for 1969 was $52,052,000. The difference between the figure for project assistance and the grand total represents aid designated nonproject assistance and may be found on the line labeled "Program SA" just above the grand total. In 1969 American nonproject assistance amounted to $22,500,000. This sum was spent in various ways to bring stability to the Laotian economy. The largest nonproject item ($18 million) was given in support of the multilateral Foreign Exchange Operations Fund (FEOF), sponsored by the International Monetary Fund. The remainder of the $22,500,000 was spent to support the foreign exchange budget of the Laotian government as well as miscellaneous other programs.

It should be noted that the above figures apply only to economic aid, dispensed by the Agency for International Development (AID). Additional funds were spent in support of military equipment, advisors, and operations; these sums will be discussed in the following section on military aid. As we have seen from earlier discussions of American aid, however, a large proportion of economic aid is designed to promote military objectives. For example, "economic" aid includes provisions for the army as well as a road-building program that enables the army to penetrate into Pathet Lao territory. In Fiscal Year (FY) 1968, for instance, the $62.9 million economic aid package breaks down as follows: $53.2 million for supporting assistance (that is, support for the military effort) and $9.7 for technological and economic development.

If one adds together American economic and military aid to Laos for a single year, the resulting figure is impressive indeed. In 1969, for example, American economic aid was $52 million and military aid was $90 million.[7] Additional American expenditures bring total American spending in Laos for FY 1969 to approximately $150 million. This figure matches one year's gross national product in Laos. On a per capita basis—using a figure

TABLE 10

AMERICAN AID: PROJECT ASSISTANCE, 1962–1969[a]
(IN THOUSANDS OF DOLLARS)

Project activities	Fiscal year—							
	1962	1963	1964	1965	1966	1967	1968	1969
Terminating activities[1]	673	654	262					
Education development	861	1,057	945	942	1,256	1,506	1,940	1,736
Public health development	200	500	1,785	2,839	2,790	1,698	2,665	2,454
Maternal child health—family planning								990
Development of rural economy	3,131	4,335	1,865	2,780	5,465	5,855	7,194	4,362
Refugee relief			2,277	4,550	4,112	4,554	3,565	2,117
Lao national roads	1,001	1,262	1,707	4,805	3,666	5,578	4,884	3,915
(BPR PASA-nonadd)		(318)	(485)	(576)	(850)	(925)	(1,159)	(900)
Civil police administration				900	557	654	445	466
Agriculture development			595	965	1,632	3,735	2,621	2,680
Public administration			136	93	142	254	202	275
Industry development						71	232	340
Military support			2,830	3,328	3,460	3,799	3,413	2,242
Air support			9,152	10,042	10,830	6,395	6,400	3,060
General technical support	1,952	10,763	2,999	4,282	5,746	5,160	5,281	4,915
Total	7,818	18,571	24,553	35,526	39,656	39,259	38,842	29,552

1. Project titles: Mining and Minerals, Vientiane Power Plant, RLG Air Services, Vientiane Airport, Telecommunications Construction, and Lao Photo Press. These were projects mainly involving construction and services which were initiated before the program was disrupted in 1962 by political events. The projects were completed between 1962 and 1964.

[a]*Laos Hearings,* 1969, p. 571.

TABLE 11

TOTAL AMERICAN AID, 1962–1969[a]

(IN THOUSANDS OF DOLLARS)

Program assistance	Fiscal year —							
	1962	1963	1964	1965	1966	1967	1968	1969
FEOF			4,000	4,000	10,000	13,800	18,600	18,000
USIP		14,500	10,700	7,400	5,000	1,900	4,500	3,700
POL		(3,000)	(2,700)	(2,500)	(2,800)	(1,300)	(3,500)	(3,100)
Commodities		(11,519)	(8,000)	(4,900)	(2,200)	(600)	(1,000)	(600)
Invisibles		2,000	1,800	3,700	2,500	1,500	1,000	800
Cash grants	21,100	2,000						
Program totals	21,100	18,500	16,500	15,100	17,500	17,200	24,100	22,500
SUMMARY								
Project:								
TA	1		8,429	11,825	11,135	10,400	9,742	9,400
SA	7,817	18,571	16,124	23,701	26,546	28,034	29,100	20,152
CF					1,975	825		
Program SA	21,100	18,500	16,500	15,100	17,500	17,200	24,100	22,500
Grand total	28,918	37,071	41,053	50,626	57,156	56,459	62,942	52,052

[a]*Laos Hearings*, 1969, p. 571.

of 2½ million for the Laotian population—American aid amounted to $60 per person in 1969. Laos was thus the largest recipient of American aid when measured on per capita standards. The average annual income of the Laotian is $70, only $10 more than American aid per person. Given the enormous American contribution to the Laotian economy, it is not difficult to understand why many Laotians—particularly those in position to make money from the American presence—wish the United States to remain in Laos indefinitely.

While tables 10 and 11 indicate the amounts of money spent on various aid projects, they do not supply a very complete picture of what happens to the funds once they reach Laos. In order to provide a clearer idea of what is done with this money, a brief description of some of the activities that fall under project assistance will be given. The reader is referred to Table 9 for the amounts allocated to each of the projects discussed below.

Education. This project is designed to strengthen the Laotian educational system, primarily through teacher training. As of the end of FY 1969, more than 3,000 Laotians had completed courses in AID-assisted schools. In-service training had been given to another 4,129 teachers. Furthermore, AID furnished hardware, tools, and tin-roofing material for hundreds of schools built by villagers throughout Laos. A basic text in Lao for each of the first six grades has been produced. At the secondary level, AID has helped the Ministry of Education establish "comprehensive" schools equivalent to American junior high schools. At the Laotian schools, students may take an academic track or study agriculture, mechanics, commercial skills, and the like.

Health. This project provides medical services through a country-wide system of AID-sponsored clinics and hospitals.

Rural economy. The objective of the rural economic development project is to strengthen rural support for the Laotian government in areas of political-strategic importance and economic potential. Emphasis is placed on self-help construction activities, well-drilling, irrigation, roads, and advisory services. It is hoped that through rural development the Laotian peasants will offer their loyalties to the Laotian government—which is trying to provide services desired by the farmers—rather than to the Pathet Lao.

Lao national roads. American personnel build and repair roads and train Laotians in these activities. Through a better system of national roads, the government hopes to ease the movement of government personnel into remote areas, link the people to each other and the central government, promote a market economy, and facilitate the movement of troops and military supplies. Obviously, this project serves both nation-building as well as military purposes.

Civil police. Under this project, the 5,000-man Laotian police force is trained to maintain order and provide internal security. A National Police Academy has been established.

Agricultural development. The aim of this project is to increase rice production through the distribution of improved seeds, fertilizer, and advice. The construction of irrigation systems and the expansion of credit and marketing systems have also occurred. Smaller programs relating to other crops and fish have been undertaken.

Public administration. Laotians are trained in such activities as budgeting, accounting, taxation, and modernized administrative procedures.

Military support. Food is provided to military forces that can be supplied by ground transportation.

Air support. Because of difficult terrain, risky security conditions, absence of railroads, and a road network largely impassable during the rainy season, much of Laos is inaccessible except by air. The air transport project pays for the air ferrying of personnel and commodities connected with the American aid program.

General technical support. This project supports all Mission programs that cannot be identified with any of the individual projects mentioned above. Housing, communications and so on fall under this category.

This extensive economic aid program is hardly a new phenomenon in American relations with Laos. Washington has been providing Laos with such assistance ever since the mid-1950s. One is inevitably led to inquire whether the aid program has paid off.

Such a question is more complex than it appears at first glance. We do not know what would have transpired in Laos in the absence of American aid, nor can we readily attribute specific events to American assistance. Another complicating factor involves the standard one should use in evaluating aid programs. Should economic growth be the proper measure? What of productivity or efficiency? Should the standard be the political objective supposedly served by economic aid? In the case of Laos, we can say that the prime purpose of American aid, since the Kennedy Administration, has been to help Laos exist as an independent state with a minimum of communist influence. More specifically, economic aid has been directed toward neutralizing communist power, fostering a spirit of nationhood where none existed, and permitting the economy to flourish with a minimum of dependence on outside support.

Have the fifteen years of American economic assistance forwarded these objectives? Information that would enable us to give a final evaluation of American aid is lacking. Utilizing the data at hand, however, one is left with the impression that, in the decade and a half during which the United States has contributed millions of dollars to Laos, little if any progress has been made. This position is supported by AID official Robert H. Nooter, Deputy Assistant Administrator of AID's Bureau for East Asia in 1969, who testified in the Senate hearings held in the fall of that year. According to Mr. Nooter, second in authority to the person in AID responsible for economic aid throughout East Asia, American economic aid efforts in Laos were being stymied by the following factors:

1. Widespread tax evasion.
2. Use of Laotian government positions—both civil and military—for personal gain.
3. Regional and family factionalism—a carryover from earlier days when Laos was organized along semi-feudal lines, with certain families ruling large areas—abetted by difficult transportation and communications problems, all of which keeps regions of the country isolated from one another and thereby frustrates efforts at nation-building.
4. Scarcity of trained capable officials. The French never took the trouble to prepare the Laotians for self-government.
5. A narrow tax base that provides insufficient funds for the Laotian government to pay adequate salaries, leading to the neglect of official duties owing to moonlighting and to the use of governmental positions for personal gain to supplement meager pay.
6. The deleterious effect of prolonged warfare.[8]

Mr. Nooter's overall assessment was as follows, "The Lao Government operates at relatively low effectiveness at both the national and local level."[9]

In view of President Nixon's Guam Doctrine, which presages an American disengagement from Asia, the situation in Laos looks grim indeed. The Laotian government is able to collect in taxes and other revenues only one-half of its expenditures. The deficit has been made up from contributions by other countries, 75 percent from the United States. It would seem that the United States has little choice in Laos other than a large-scale, open-ended economic commitment or a willingness to see Laos slip into economic chaos. In the event of the latter, there is strong likelihood that the communists will succeed in exploiting the situation so as to achieve what they have been unable to accomplish militarily. The mounting American disenchantment with foreign aid, coupled with the Guam Doctrine, renders the outlook for Laos anything but bright.

Perhaps one lesson that can be drawn from the American experience in Laos is that the United States should not undertake unilaterally to establish political and economic stability where none has existed previously. Restoring damaged stability—as the United States did in Western Europe and Japan after World War II—is quite a different undertaking from an attempt to create stability out of nothingness. Washington should perhaps pattern its behavior after the stockbroker who invests his money in a company that has shown some earnings, and who stays clear of a company that has just come into existence and can offer only promises.

American nonmilitary assistance has not been limited to economic aid. Another American effort has been to help the Laotian government in a propaganda campaign designed to create a popular feeling of national identity and to discredit the communists. The U.S. Information Agency is in charge of this program.[10]

The USIA works closely with the Lao National Radio. In 1968, for instance, the USIA prepared or assisted in preparing more than 800 hours of radio programming. These shows constituted one-third of total Laotian broadcasting time and nearly two-thirds of the nonmusical material on the airwaves. Most of the American-assisted programs contained nation-building material such as folksongs and folktales, which are designed to bind people together by making them aware of their common past.

The USIA also helps to produce a bimonthly magazine. This Lao-language publication, the most widely read periodical in Laos, has a circulation of 43,000. The circulation of the largest newspaper in Laos is 3,300. Other USIA activities in Laos include films, pamphlets, wall-posters, and leaflets which are air-dropped.

A disturbing feature of the USIA presence in Laos is that in most cases the material produced by the USIA or with its assistance contains no USIA attribution. In other words, a radio program carried over the Lao National Radio, and ostensibly produced by Laotians, may well have been conceived and recorded in a studio in downtown Washington. Similarly, there is no mention of the USIA in the bimonthly magazine referred to above. Such activities seem to be a distortion of the mission of the USIA, which is to create a favorable image of the United States in the minds of people over-seas. In the case of Laos, much of the work of the USIA has little or nothing to do with the image of the United States but rather with the image of the Laotian government among its own people. In other words, the USIA in Laos has been heavily involved in the propaganda effort of another government. All this would not be so unsettling if it were done openly. However, when the periodical with the largest circulation in Laos is produced with covert USIA assistance, and when a large percentage of the nonmusical shows on the Lao National Radio are created by the USIA without public attribution, one can only wonder how seriously Washington takes such principles as self-determination and government by the people. No amount of rhetoric or posturing can mask the fact that we do not always practice what we preach.

These considerations, however, must be weighed against the contribution the USIA broadcasts make to Laotian national unity. To the extent that a spirit of national purpose assists the RLG in preserving Laotian national integrity, thereby advancing American interests, can one condone the concealment of the origin of these broadcasts and publications? The RLG leaders knew who produced the material, and they could have stopped these activities had they so wished. This issue carries beyond Laos, for the USIA produces, without attribution, nation-building material in other countries as well.

MILITARY AID

In the years following the 1962 Geneva settlement, American military involvement in Laos has exceeded in effort and cost the nonmilitary assistance program described in the previous pages.

As mentioned earlier, the United States' military involvement in Laos reached a peak of $90 million in FY 1969. This sum represents the cost of supporting the military operations of the Laotian army. Additional money—the figure remains classified—was spent to finance American military operations in the country. Therefore, while the total cost of the American military effort in Laos is not publicly known, we can surmise it to be well above $100 million. The Laotian government, by contrast, spent approximately $17 million for defense in FY 1969.[11] Therefore, the United States spends at least six times as much money as the government of Laos on the security of the country. The evolution of America's military involvement in Laos since 1962 will be described in this section and the following one on Laos and Vietnam.

The ink had not long been dry on the Geneva agreements signed in July 1962 before the United States resumed military aid to Laos. In September of that year, Premier Souvanna Phouma asked the United States for supplies and spare parts to maintain American military equipment—vehicles, aircraft, weapons, and so forth—already in Laos. He also requested training ammunition and such supplies as oil, lumber, and clothing. In November, American Ambassador Leonard Unger informed Souvanna that the United States had agreed to his requests.[12] Such aid did not violate the Geneva agreements; Article 6 of the Protocol to the Declaration on the Neutrality of Laos authorized the introduction into Laos of "such quantities of conventional armaments as the Royal Government of Laos may consider necessary for the national defense of Laos." In order to operate the military aid program, a special section within the AID Mission was created with much secrecy. This new section, called the Requirements Office, was staffed mostly by retired military officers. Their duty was to work with Laotian officials to determine the kinds and amounts of materials needed. Souvanna had requested this assistance because, in the opinion of Assistant Secretary of State William Sullivan, he feared that the communists might try to topple the shaky coalition government.[13] According to Sullivan, who, before becoming Assistant Secretary had succeeded Leonard Unger as Ambassador to Laos, Souvanna was nervous because the North Vietnamese had not withdrawn from Laos pursuant to the Geneva agreements, and the communists had large stocks of Soviet equipment left over from previous fighting.

The presence in Laos of the Requirements Office, staffed by former military men, was a direct violation of Article 4 of the Protocol referred to in the paragraph above. Article 4 says, "The introduction of foreign regular and irregular troops, foreign para-military formations and foreign military personnel into Laos is prohibited." In order to avoid confusion regarding some of the terms in this statement, the Protocol in Article 1, section a, defines the term "foreign military personnel" as follows:

> The term "foreign military personnel" shall include members of foreign military missions, foreign military advisors, experts, instructors, consultants, technicians, observers and any other foreign military persons, including those serving in any armed forces in Laos, and foreign civilians connected with the supply, maintenance, storing and utilization of war materials.

The staff of the Requirements Office were clearly "foreign civilians [just barely] connected with the supply, maintenance, storing and utilization of war materials." The just-retired military personnel who staffed the Requirements Office also came under the description "foreign military advisors, experts, instructors, consultants. . . ." Instead of following the usual procedure of setting up a separate military assistance organization, the United States conceived the innocent-sounding title of Requirements Office and buried it within the AID Mission, because of the illegal activities it was performing.[14] To be sure, one should not hasten to condemn the United States for violating the Geneva agreements without mentioning that the North Vietnamese have also broken the accords by failing to withdraw from Laos within the agreed interval and by using Laotian soil for the purpose of interfering in the affairs of another country (South Vietnam). Indeed, the American violation of the Geneva agreements was a response to Hanoi's prior infringement.

As an additional subterfuge to conceal its illegal military aid activities, the United States established a headquarters in Thailand to serve as a liaison between the Requirements Office in Vientiane and higher echelons within the Defense Department.[15] This organization was called Deputy Chief, U.S. Military Advisory Group, Thailand. The Deputy Chief was a subordinate command of, and reported directly to, Commander-in-Chief,

Pacific (CINCPAC). In reality, the Deputy Chief and his staff were nonresident members of the American country team in Laos. In the fall of 1969, this office was composed of the Deputy Chief (a U.S. Army colonel), 38 other military officers, 78 enlisted men, 6 civilians, and a number of Thai employees. The Deputy Chief received all requests for supplies, services and training from the Requirements Office in Laos. He then arranged for the needs expressed in these requests. Presented graphically, the organization of American military assistance in Laos appeared as follows:

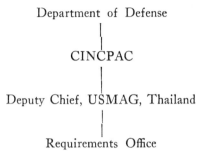

Department of Defense

|

CINCPAC

|

Deputy Chief, USMAG, Thailand

|

Requirements Office

A question is raised if one compares the number of people who worked in the Requirements Office with the number in the Deputy Chief's mission. One would think that the former would require a larger staff, since it held the responsibility for seeing that American military assistance is used properly throughout the territory of Laos. However, the Requirements Office had less than 30 ex-officers and noncoms, while the Deputy Chief's organization was composed of over 123 men, counting the Thais. One is led to wonder whether Laotians are brought to Thailand for training by members of the Deputy Chief's staff. It is known that in February 1964, Thailand permitted a United States Special Air Warfare unit to train Laotian pilots in Thailand for operations in Laos.[16] It would not be surprising if other kinds of training have taken place as well.

Thus far we have discussed the magnitude and organization of American military aid to Laos in the years after the 1962 Geneva agreements. We have yet to consider the specific programs carried out under the military aid arrangement. In order to make such a discussion more meaningful, however, it is necessary to consider the vital connection between the conflict in Laos and the war in neighboring Vietnam.

LAOS AND VIETNAM

At the beginning of this chapter, it was noted that the major factor that distinguished the pre-1962 situation in Laos from that of the years after 1962 was the war in Vietnam. As the 1960s waned, the struggle in Laos and the fighting in Vietnam blended into a single theater of operations. It is as impossible to understand the situation in Laos without reference to Vietnam as it would have been to comprehend the military situation in the Pacific in World War II without regard to the fighting in Europe. We therefore find it necessary to say a few words about events in Vietnam before returning to the situation in Laos and America's role there.

In late 1960, Hanoi formed the National Liberation Front and assigned to it the task of taking over direction of the already-existing insurgency in South Vietnam against the regime of Ngo Dinh Diem.[17] This step required that North Vietnam send its organizers south of the Seventeenth Parallel. Furthermore, ammunition, supplies, and equipment had to be transported to South Vietnam in order to sustain the mounting war effort there. The eastern flank of Laos, which rests alongside both Vietnams, was seen as a promising locale for developing a transportation corridor between North and South Vietnam. This the North Vietnamese hastened to do. The result was the famed Ho Chi Minh trail, perhaps the most well-known transportation system in our time. The Ho Chi Minh trail has become the principal route for the movement of men and supplies from North Vietnam to South Vietnam. The trail is in actuality a series of jungle footpaths and dirt roads that extend for about 250 miles. Largely concealed from the air, the trail passes from North Vietnam into Laos at the border near the strategic Mugia Pass north of Tchepone and thence into South Vietnam at various points. At the height of northern infiltration, about 17,000 men per month entered South Vietnam, most of them by way of the Ho Chi Minh trail. In the course of the fighting in Vietnam, approximately half a million men have tramped their way over the trail into South Vietnam.

In the course of time, the Ho Chi Minh trail assumed the function of an intravenous feeding tube, carrying essential sustenance from North Vietnam to its forces in the South. Thus the war in Vietnam spilled over into Laos. Control of eastern Laos, the region through which the trail passes, remains a prime North Vietnamese objective. One of Washington's cardinal aims in Laos has been to sever this lifeline. Much of the military action in eastern Laos, therefore, has been directly related to the war in Vietnam, rather than being a contest for control of Laos.[18]

In order to keep the Ho Chi Minh trail open, Hanoi has sent about 67,000 soldiers into Laos.[19] About one-third of these troops devote all their energies to keeping the trail free, engaging in such activities as road repair, bridge building, construction of storage depots for supplies and equipment, and the provision of medical care. The remainder harass the

Laotian army, particularly in northern Laos. In an effort to cleave the Ho Chi Minh trail, the United States has diverted to Laos B–52s and other aircraft that have also been used in North Vietnam. In addition, the CIA has trained Laotian trail-watchers to make traffic reports to relay stations in Thailand, which then call out the bombers to strike the trail. In February 1971, the United States helped sponsor an invasion of Laos by 20,000 South Vietnamese troops. The purpose of the South Vietnamese drive, which terminated in late March with a bloody rout of Saigon's troops, was to deny the North Vietnamese a sanctuary in Laos and to choke off the flow of men and supplies along the Ho Chi Minh trail. Widely hailed at the time by Saigon and Washington as a success, the short-lived invasion accomplished neither of its goals. Fighting in eastern Laos is likely to continue so long as the Vietnamese war goes on. Thus far, the North Vietnamese seem to be enjoying more success than the Americans regarding the trail. To be sure, American bombers are seriously complicating the task of moving men and supplies along the trail. Yet, the blow dealt by the Americans may more aptly be likened to a sprained ankle than a broken leg. Infiltration continues, although at a slower rate and under more difficult conditions than would obtain in the absence of bombing. In captured documents the North Vietnamese complain about the mental and physical strain imposed by the bombing of the trail. However, the flow of men and materials continues, highlighting more than ever the limitations of air power in jungle warfare.

One of the most dramatic cases of the intimate relationship between the fighting in Laos and Vietnam concerns a secret radar station in northeastern Laos at Phou Pha Thi. The events surrounding Phou Pha Thi sound as though they were taken from a James Bond thriller.

When the United States began to bomb North Vietnam after the Gulf of Tonkin incident in August 1964, it was determined that a radar installation would be needed to guide the bombers to their targets. The site selected was Phou Pha Thi, a mile-high mountain in Sam Neua province 190 miles northeast of Vientiane and about 160 miles west of Hanoi. This is one of the highest and most isolated mountains in the hilly northeast section of Laos. It is located 15 miles from the North Vietnamese border. The mountain faces a narrow valley where a 700-foot-long dirt landing strip was built. A cavern was dug inside the limestone summit to house electronic equipment and shelter the 20 or so Americans and their Laotian assistants who worked there.

Phou Pha Thi served several purposes. Its main function was to guide American bombers to their destinations in North Vietnam and electronically release their bomb loads when they flew over their targets. Pilots used the radar at Phou Pha Thi to determine the exact distance from their targets. This radar was especially useful at night and during bad weather. "Jolly Green Giant" rescue helicopters took off from the airstrip at Phou Pha Thi to rescue pilots and crewmen shot down over North Vietnam. The CIA used the base as a staging ground for American-led teams of Meo tribesmen who penetrated North Vietnam on special missions.

Phou Pha Thi was protected by CIA-directed Meo tribesmen who camped in the hills surrounding the secret installation. The communists made three unsuccessful attacks on the base, one in 1965, one in 1967, and one in January 1968. In the latter assault, four Soviet-made single engine biplanes (AN–2s) from the North Vietnamese Air Force tried to destroy the base. This was one of the few communist air attacks in the entire Laotian war. The attack failed, and the wreckage of one of the airplanes was displayed in front of the That Luang Monument, Vientiane's most important religious shrine, as evidence of North Vietnamese aggression.

The North Vietnamese finally succeeded in overrunning Phou Pha Thi in March 1968. The defenders fought in hand-to-hand combat to the last man inside the limestone cavern. The number of Americans killed in the struggle is uncertain. A Pathet Lao radio broadcast in March 1968 said 21 Americans were slain. Other sources give the figure of 19.[20]

Hanoi's ultimate objective with regard to Laos remains open to speculation. Is Hanoi's interest limited to maintaining the flow of men and supplies from the North through Laos to South Vietnam? Does Hanoi aspire to incorporate Laos into a greater Vietnam, perhaps to include South Vietnam as well? Does Hanoi merely use Laos to tie down forces that might otherwise be deployed in Vietnam, following General Giap's dispersal tactics that worked so well against the French? Or does Hanoi intend to assist the Pathet Lao in its drive to take over Laos, without bringing Laos into a political union with Vietnam? These questions are likely to remain unanswered until the Vietnamese war is settled. Ho Chi Minh's successors are unlikely to view control of Laos as sufficiently important to jeopardize their primary objective, which is to gain control of South Vietnam. Hence, the North Vietnamese are unlikely to step up their activity in Laos, unless they are convinced that the Americans will not meet such an escalation with an escalation of their own. So long as the war in Vietnam continues, Hanoi must refrain from taking the chance that an all-out drive in Laos would assist President Nixon in winning public support for an American build-up in Laos. The North Vietnamese would be much more clever to resist the temptation to mount a full-throated effort to take over Laos. Hanoi no doubt realizes that, once the Vietnamese war ends, the bird that will rule the roost in Washington will be neither the hawk nor the dove but the raven, which says, "Nevermore." Given a projected American post-Vietnam reluctance to become involved in another Asian land war, the North Vietnamese could then increase their efforts to grab Laos, if this is their final objective. The ultimate fate of Laos, insofar as North Vietnam is concerned, must await the end of the Vietnamese war.

In the meanwhile, however, North Vietnam has established an administrative apparatus by which they are able to wield considerable influence over the activities of the Pathet Lao.[21] This instrument, known as *Doan* 959 (Group 959), is located near Hanoi and receives its instructions from the Central Committee of the Lao Dong Party, the communist party of North Vietnam. *Doan* 959 then transmits these instructions to its forward command post, staffed by about 50 North Vietnamese, in Sam Neua Province, where the Pathet Lao have their central headquarters. Thus, *Doan* 959 guidance is carried down to province and district levels in Laos through the Pathet Lao organization. In addition, *Doan* 959 maintains a staff of North Vietnamese advisers attached to several Pathet Lao provincial headquarters. Further liaison between North Vietnam and the Pathet Lao is provided through periodic visits of Pathet Lao leaders to Hanoi. Using these various channels, the North Vietnamese provide military advice, military training, medical aid, agricultural assistance, logistic support and propaganda to the Pathet Lao.

The degree of North Vietnamese influence over the Pathet Lao defies quantification. Many facets of the Pathet Lao–North Vietnamese relationship remain obscure. For instance, Langer and Zasloff suggest that besides *Doan* 959 an important channel of North Vietnamese control over the Pathet Lao is the *Phak Pasason Lao* (PPL), the People's Party of Laos, which is said to be the communist party of Laos, clandestinely created in March, 1955.[22] The membership of the PPL, perhaps numbering in the hundreds, is largely unknown. At the top of the PPL stands a Central Committee, with about 20 members, headed by a Secretary, Kaysone Phomvihan. Another influential member of the Central Committee is said to be Nouhak Phomsavan. Prince Souphanouvong, perhaps a member of the Central Committee, possesses the family background and style to make him useful as a figurehead leader and international spokesman for the communists, but in reality his authority is shared with Kaysone, some allege. The PPL, in this view, directs the Pathet Lao and the Neo Lao Hak Xat, which is said to be a united front like the Viet Minh during Ho Chi Minh's early days of struggle against the French. Hanoi, it is further maintained, exerts much leverage over the PPL and through it the Pathet Lao and the Neo Lao Hak Xat. While Langer and Zasloff provide some evidence for this interpretation, final confirmation must await further investigation. Just how much influence is exerted through *Doan* 959 and the PPL remains a matter of conjecture. It does seem likely, however, that regardless of administrative structure, the superior knowhow and materiel of the North Vietnamese would confer upon them the role of tutor and guide for their less-well-endowed Laotian sympathizers.

As noted above, American activity in Laos has also been touched by the Vietnamese war, particularly as regards the Ho Chi Minh trail. Furthermore, Washington, like Hanoi, is thinking of the post-Vietnam situation in Laos, and seeks to take actions now that will promote the aims of its Laotian policy after the United States withdraws from South Vietnam. Let us, then, examine what the United States has been doing in terms of military operations in Laos.

AMERICAN MILITARY OPERATIONS

American objectives in Laos can be divided into two broad categories. Of more immediate importance, Washington wants to close the Ho Chi Minh trail to the infiltration of men and materiel from North Vietnam and deny the communists a sanctuary in Laos. In the longer run, Washington wants to lay the basis for a Laotian state capable of maintaining its independence and subduing the Pathet Lao, which will most probably continue to receive assistance from North Vietnam, China, and the Soviet Union. In pursuit of these objectives, the United States has provided Laos with considerable military (and nonmilitary) assistance.

American military aid to Laos has taken many forms: training the Royal Army, upgrading the Royal Laotian Air Force, and maintaining an army of Meo irregulars. Washington has also conducted operations of its own in Laos, with the involvement of American military personnel and equipment; most of these operations have involved the Air Force.

We have already referred to the Deputy Chief, U.S. Military Advisory Group, Thailand, and the 30 or so members of the Requirements Office in the AID Mission in Laos. Besides these Americans, there were about 218 U.S. military personnel in Laos in the fall of 1969. Of this total, 127 were military attachés working out of the American embassy. The remaining 91 were military personnel on temporary duty scattered throughout Laos.[23] (Figures for years following 1969 remain classified.) These men assisted the Royal Laotian Army in planning and logistics.[24] American majors and captains were stationed in the field with Royal Army units, where they devised battle plans, arranged for logistics and air support, and sometimes accompanied Royal Army units into battle. U.S. Air Force personnel would service, repair, and load bombs on the small T–28 bombers supplied by the United States and flown by Laotian pilots. The CIA had over 300 operatives stationed in Laos. Most of these men were former Special Forces soldiers with experience in Vietnam. They were assigned to train Laotian soldiers, command reconnaissance teams that would infiltrate enemy territory, and direct terrorist and psychological warfare operations.

In addition to providing assistance to the Royal Army, the United States has also called into being and sustained an army of irregulars which functions largely separate from the official army of Laos.[25] This special army, the brainchild of the CIA, is known as the *Armée Clandestine*. Commanded by Major General Vang Pao, a 40-year-old former sergeant in the French colonial army, it is made up mainly of Meo tribesmen from northern Laos. In 1969 there were about 40,000 soldiers in the *Armée Clandestine*. Of this number, 15,000 were full-time soldiers deployed throughout northern Laos, while the remainder stayed near their villages to fight when attacked. The *Armée Clandestine,* while organized and led by General Vang, is armed, equipped, fed, paid, guided strategically and tactically, and often transported into and out of battle by the CIA. Overall command control of Meo operations is exercised by the CIA chief in Vientiane, with advice from the head of the military mission in Laos.[26]

The CIA has attempted to insulate *Armée* affairs from the High Command of the Royal Laotian Army and from the Royal Government itself, owing to the CIA's doubts about the combat effectiveness of the Royal Army and about the incorruptibility and efficiency of the Royal Government (which would have to handle American funds and supplies). However, CIA does keep the High Command and the Royal Government informed of the *Armée*'s activities. AID cooperates with CIA by providing food and supplies to the Meo fighters, who usually travel with their families. Two allegedly private airlines, Air America and Continental Air Services, under contract to AID (and believed to be partly controlled by CIA)[27] transport the Meos from place to place and fly in supplies. Since much of Laos is impassable on foot, the prime means of transport for the *Armée Clandestine* is by airplane. Many pilots of the transport planes, small craft, and helicopters are American nationals. According to figures supplied by the American Embassy in Vientiane, Air America in Laos employs 207 Americans; Continental, 73. General Vang's operational base is at Long Chen, located about 80 miles north of Vientiane and just south of the Plain of Jars. The camp, surrounded by mountains, includes an airstrip suitable for the T–28s in the Laotian Air Force. Long Chen also serves as a communications center for CIA operations. In 1969, about 30,000 dependents of the Meo guerrilla fighters made their homes at Long Chen. A number of CIA officials are attached to the General's headquarters at Long Chen, while a few dozen others work in the field with his forces.

Laotian sources allege that Thais in the employ of the CIA give tactical guidance to the *Armée*'s forces. Filipinos help maintain equipment, and some of the radio men are South Vietnamese.

The *Armée Clandestine,* besides fighting the Pathet Lao, carries out reconnaissance on the activities of the North Vietnamese and Chinese, who are building roads from China into northern Laos. During the pre-November 1968 phase of American bombing of North Vietnam, the *Armée* manned observation posts on both sides of the Lao–North Vietnamese border, protected American installations such as Phou Pha Thi that guided attacking aircraft, and helped rescue American pilots.

In addition to the *Armée Clandestine,* the United States underwrites smaller irregular forces in southern Laos. Their principal mission is reconnaissance of the southern portions of the Ho Chi Minh trail. These trail-watchers radio information about convoys and coolie caravans to the CIA station at Udon, in northeast Thailand, which then activates planes at Ubon, Thailand, for air strikes against trail traffic.

Besides the operations already mentioned, the United States, particularly the CIA, has managed other paramilitary activities in Laos. A veterans' organization with branches throughout the country, capable of conducting propaganda, sabotage, and harassment operations, is subject to CIA direction. An intelligence team has been helping the Laotians to conduct psychological warfare and operate radio transmitters.[28]

Of all American military activities in Laos, the one whose presence has been most widely felt has been the air campaign over Laos. The origins of the American air war in Laos can be traced back to December 1963, when it was proposed that a special warfare unit be deployed in Thailand for the purpose of training Laotian pilots in counterinsurgency tactics.[29] The State and Defense Departments approved of this proposal. In March of the following year the Joint Chiefs of Staff directed that a U.S. Air Force air commando training advisory team be set up in Thailand to upgrade the capabilities of Laotian pilots. In May 1964, the first American air reconnaissance flights were flown over southern Laos, after consultation with Souvanna. These flights were extended May 21 to cover the Plain of Jars area in the north,[30] the scene of fighting between the Pathet Lao and forces loyal to Souvanna. Shortly after these reconnaissance flights were instituted, an unarmed reconnaissance aircraft was shot down in Laos by antiaircraft fire. On June 6, the date of the incident, President Johnson authorized the use of fighter bombers as escorts for the reconnaissance planes. Three days later the United States became involved in the shooting war in Laos, when these armed escorts fired on an enemy antiaircraft site in northern Laos.[31] Later that summer American ground controllers were introduced into Laos to support air operations.

The U.S. Air Force expanded its role in Laos in October 1964, when it began flying cover missions for Royal Lao Air Force planes striking targets in Laos along the Ho Chi Minh trail. On December 14, the United States flew its first strike mission in northern Laos other than the escort missions referred to above. This mission was flown in response to a request by Souvanna for more American pressure against the North Vietnamese operating in northern Laos.[32]

The year 1965 witnessed an enormous extension of American air activity in Laos, a development that reflected an alteration of American policy in both Laos and Vietnam. It will be remembered that the United States launched its first air strikes against North Vietnam in August 1964, in response to alleged attacks by North Vietnamese ships against American naval craft in the Gulf of Tonkin. In February 1965, Washington began to bomb North Vietnam systematically. The air campaign in Laos was intimately related to the air war in Vietnam. While American bombers pummelled North Vietnam and communist forces in the South, additional American aircraft bombed the Ho Chi Minh trail. The United States implemented this strategy in early 1965, after having received permission from Souvanna Phouma and King Savang to bomb the trail.[33] In northern Laos, American air strikes in 1965 increased a hundredfold over the handful of missions flown in 1964. In 1966 there were almost twice as many strikes in northern Laos as in 1965.[34] The extraordinary intensification of American direct military involvement in Laos starting in 1965 thus dovetails with the heightened American military involvement in Vietnam. This lends support to the contention that Laos and Vietnam are but two sectors of one overall military theater.

In order to provide proper control over American air operations in Laos, the United States introduced its own Forward Air Controllers into Laos in late 1966. This was a response to a Laotian request for increased American military aid.[35]

U.S. Air Force personnel in Laos—besides carrying out bombing, escort, and reconnaissance missions—have provided training and various other services for the Royal Lao Air Force. We have already referred to air training schools set up in Thailand to train Laotian pilots. In 1965 Americans began to train Laotians as forward air guides. United States personnel have also provided assistance to the Lao Air Force in maintenance, communications, medical aid, and command and control.

When the United States halted its systematic bombing of North Vietnam in November 1968, it vastly increased its bombing in Laos. According to one reliable report, the United States has flown as many as 500 sorties (a sortie is one flight by one airplane) of B–52s in Laos per day.[36] Thus, American bombing in Laos took up much of the slack left by the halt in the bombing of North Vietnam. Even after President Nixon resumed the bombing of North Vietnam in April 1972, aerial destruction in Laos has continued at a brisk pace. Souvanna Phouma's response to questions concerning American bombing reveals just how far he has moved away from his previous hostile attitude toward the United States. At a Paris news conference on July 15, 1969, Souvanna said that Laos had no agreement with the United States to conduct bombing missions in Laos. It sometimes happens, Souvanna continued, that American pilots have trouble locating the jungle frontier from the air; consequently, bombs occasionally fall on Laotian territory.[37] In taking this deceptive line, Souvanna was trying to head off charges that his government had illegally abandoned neutrality as stipulated in the 1962 Geneva agreements. The disingenuousness of the Prince's statement (there are no frontiers in northern Laos near American military targets, and there is no doubt that American pilots were instructed to bomb Laos in the east along the Ho Chi Minh trail) only serves to highlight his change of heart in favor of cooperation with the United States, at least for the time being. Souvanna also utilized the news conference to deny charges, levelled the previous day by Xuan Thuy, head of the North Vietnamese delegation at the Paris peace talks, that Laos had been invaded by 12,000 American troops, and that Thai troops were fighting on the side of the Laotian government. Subsequent news reports substantiated the accusations regarding the presence of Thai troops on the side of the Laotian government.[38]

On rare occasions the United States has flown defoliation missions in Laos. Four such missions were flown between June 1968 and September 1969.[39] Sometimes American planes have dropped napalm over areas in northern Laos. American aircraft are authorized to drop this horrendous substance on certain approved routes that the enemy is known to use on a regular basis. All other targets must be approved by the American Ambassador before napalm can be used.[40]

An outstanding example of American military assistance to Laos occurred in September 1969, when American-backed Laotian troops seized two strategic areas in Laos. One of the areas captured was the Plain of Jars, held by the Pathet Lao since the spring of 1964. The other key area lies on the rim of the Ho Chi Minh trail near Tchepone. The latter success, it was hoped, would enable the United States to increase its interdiction of traffic along the trail. These victories, it was reported, were the results of integrated American–Laotian planning as well as the most intense American bombing ever seen in Laos.[41] Some of the Lao units consisted of Thai soldiers wearing Laotian uniforms.[42] Aircraft from Air America, Continental Air Services, and the U.S. Air Force flew arms, supplies, and reinforcements to advanced combat areas. U.S. Army officers and CIA agents were busy advising local Lao commanders.[43]

It should not come as a surprise that the heavy American military involvement in Laos should have produced some American casualties. In disclosing these casualties, the Nixon Administration has been less than candid. In President Nixon's televised statement of March 6, 1970, on American involvement in Laos, the only reference to American losses was the following statement, "No American stationed in Laos has ever been killed in ground combat operations."[44] Subsequently, the White House acknowledged that an Army captain and 26 civilians had been killed or listed as missing in action as a result of enemy activity over the last six years. These figures clash markedly with statistics revealed in the 1969 Senate hearings on Laos. This document shows that between 1962–1969, somewhat fewer than 200 American military personnel were killed in Laos, while approximately 200 more were either missing in action or prisoners of war.[45] Of those killed in action, about one-fourth died as a result of operations in northern Laos, including the skirmish at Phou Pha Thi. During the years 1964–1969, American aircraft losses in northern Laos were slightly fewer than 80, while 300 American aircraft were lost in southern Laos, most of them in the region of the Ho Chi Minh trail.[46] The fate of the American crews of these airplanes was not given in the Senate hearings, but one can surmise that many of these individuals are among the 400 Americans listed as killed, missing in action, or prisoners of war as a result of combat in Laos.

The United States, to be sure, is not the only country to violate the 1962 Geneva agreements; neither is it necessarily the first. At least five other countries may be accused of disregarding the agreements. North Vietnam has failed to withdraw its troops from Laos and has sent additional troops to protect the Ho Chi Minh trail and to help the Pathet Lao fight the Royal Army. China and the Soviet Union supply these North Vietnamese troops with arms and other equipment.[47] South Vietnam provides bases for American air raids and ground actions along the Ho Chi Minh trail in Laos. In addition, South Vietnamese are reported to be working with the *Armée Clandestine*. Thailand has violated the Geneva agreements by allowing American planes to use Thai airfields for bombing, reconnaissance, and rescue missions in Laos. The Thais have also permitted the Americans to train Laotian pilots and ground troops on Thai soil. Finally, the Thais have agreed to accept up to $100 million a year from the United States to finance a 10,000-man fighting force in Laos.[48] The Thai Air Force, using equipment and ammunition supplied by the United States, has flown combat support missions in Laos. In order to conceal their Thai identity, these mercenaries assume Laotian names and don Laotian military uniforms upon entering Laos. The Thai government does not deny that Thai military personnel are fighting in Laos. However, Bangkok claims that these combatants consist of volunteers, ethnic Laotians residing in Thailand who wish to fight for Laos. A heavily censored Senate report by two staff members of the Senate Foreign Relations Committee, based on a study mission they made to Laos, Cambodia, and Thailand in January 1972, casts serious doubt on Bangkok's claim. The report indicates that these "volunteers" were recruited by the Thai Army from all over Thailand, and that no special efforts were made to select ethnic Laotians; that Thai officers went to Laos in separate Thai units, not as individuals; that both the CIA and the Thai Army maintain a headquarters at Udorn Air Force Base in Thailand which provides liaison with Thais fighting in Laos; that the "volunteers" were trained in Thailand by a 60-man detachment of U.S. Army Special Forces on temporary assignment from Okinawa; and that basic pay plus bonuses were made by the CIA to the Thai liaison unit at Udorn (suggesting a government-to-government, not a volunteer, relationship). Although the number of Thai mercenaries fighting in Laos is classified, Souvanna Phouma disclosed in a Voice of America interview in January 1972 that 15 or 16 battalions of Thais were already in Laos and that "in concurrence with the Americans we have planned for 25 to 26 battalions." There are about 370 men in a Thai battalion. The CIA has estimated that the annual cost of supporting a Thai battalion amounts to $4 million. Thus, when the full complement of 25 Thai battalions assembles in Laos, the annual cost of this operation to the United States will approximate $100 million.

The Chinese maintain a presence in Laos beyond that of providing supplies.[49] About 20,000 Chinese troops have been occupied in building roads in northern Laos. They have already completed a road running from where the Chinese border dips southwards into Laos to the market town of Muong Sai, 50 miles into Laos in an area controlled by the Pathet Lao. The Chinese are also working on two spurs from this north–south road. One spur runs east to link up with an existing road from China through Phong Saly province in Laos to Dienbienphu in North Vietnam. The other spur runs west along an old trail toward the border with Thailand. The Geneva agreements did not prohibit road-building as such. It is difficult to believe, however, that the Chinese are building these roads solely for the sake of Laotian economic development. No doubt the Chinese have learned from American road-building ventures how valuable access routes can be in moving men and supplies in Laos. Furthermore, as the communists lack air power equivalent to that of the Americans, roads are of even greater importance to the communist cause.

The Geneva agreements of 1962 are for all practical purposes as moribund as the spirit of compromise that gave birth to them. About the only purpose they serve is to act as a standard by which one country may accuse another of doing exactly what the first country has already done in violation of the accords. The fate of the Geneva agreements, like the destiny of the ICC, brings to mind Shakespeare's words about "a tale told by an idiot, full of sound and fury, signifying nothing."

As one looks back upon the history of Laos after 1962 and compares it with developments between 1954 and 1962, one has the feeling that he is watching an evening performance of the same drama he has seen enacted at that afternoon's matinee. Some of the leading roles have been changed, but not many. One or two alterations in the script have occurred, but the basic plot remains unchanged. The production is a bit more lavish and spirited, but the same fundamental story emerges. The confrontation between the Pathet Lao and the Royal Government goes on. Each side is supported by one of the superpowers, as well as several of its allies. The military struggle rocks back and forth, and neither side is able to win a decisive victory. Each element in the Laotian struggle pays lip service to the Geneva agreements, but dismisses them when planning actions of its own. The one new factor is the war in Vietnam, which has become enormously intensified in the years after 1962. This conflict has, however, not altered the fundamental shape of the struggle in Laos; it has only served to aggravate it.

Indeed, we are left with the conclusion, *"Plus ça change, plus c'est la même chose."*

OPIUM

It is one of the bitter ironies of American involvement in Indochina that America sent her boys abroad to plant the seeds of democracy and harvested instead a generation of drug addicts. To be sure, the war in Vietnam and the rebellious attitude that American youth developed toward it was not the only stimulus to the rising drug culture in the United States. But there can be no doubt that American military involvement in Indochina has been a major contributing factor to the greatly increased use of narcotics in the United States.

In the late 1960s, the pattern of drug use in America changed radically. No longer limited to the ghetto and bohemian society, drugs penetrated the middle class and even left their mark on high society.

The growth of a drug culture in America is intimately related to U. S. policy in Indochina, for that area—and Laos in particular—is one of the world's principal sources of heroin. Addiction to this substance has become a major problem in the United States, especially in large urban areas. At the beginning of the 1970s, the National Institute of Mental Health estimated that there were 250,000 heroin addicts in the United States, half of whom lived in New York City.[50] A survey taken in 1970 revealed that there were 10,400 heroin addicts in Washington, D. C.; by 1971, the number had risen 60 percent to 16,880. There were approximately 9,000 heroin addicts in Chicago in 1970. Military authorities estimated that in 1970 10 to 15 percent of American troops in South Vietnam were using heroin in one form or another; over 50,000 Vietnam veterans have returned home as heroin addicts. Besides its debilitating effects on the addict, heroin is the source of much crime. Based on a $30 daily habit, the quarter of a million American heroin addicts spend $7.5 million a day on the drug. In order to obtain this money, many of the addicts must resort to criminal activity.

Heroin is derived from opium, which in turn is extracted from the poppy. When the poppy blossom withers, a pod the size of an egg remains atop the stalk. To extract opium from the pod, the farmer makes an incision in the pod, using a three-bladed knife. The pod exudes a white substance resembling latex, which is allowed to thicken and dry on the pod for a day or two. Then it is scraped off. This is raw opium, which can then be boiled down and refined to yield heroin. Approximately ten pounds of opium are required to produce one pound of heroin. To satisfy the cravings of American addicts, between 40 and 50 tons of opium, yielding four to five tons of heroin, are required each year.

The total world production of opium amounts to about 3,000 tons annually.[51] Of this quantity, approximately 1,200 tons are used for pharmacological purposes, mostly in the form of heroin, morphine, and codeine. The remaining 1,800 tons are sold for illicit purposes.

The two main sources of heroin destined for the United States are the Middle East, particularly Turkey, and Southeast Asia. Mexico is another important source, accounting for about 15 percent of the heroin that reaches the United States.

In Southeast Asia the main poppy-growing areas are northern Laos, Burma, Thailand, and Yunnan Province in southern China. Most of the opium produced in this area is consumed locally, particularly by overseas Chinese, but considerable quantities are shipped to South Vietnam and the United States. A recent estimate stated that every year Burma produces 300–600 tons of opium; Laos, 80–150 tons; and Thailand, 200 tons.[52] These three countries comprise what is sometimes referred to as the Golden Triangle. The focal point of operations in the Golden Triangle is the area surrounding Ban Houei Sai in Laos, where the Laotian, Thai, and

Burmese borders join. At least 21 opium refineries exist there.[53] The most important ones are located near Tachilek in Burma, Ban Houei Sai and Nam Keum in Laos, and Mae Salong in Thailand. Much of the opium is brought to the refineries by mule pack trains, commanded by armed bandit gangs that buy opium from the hill tribesmen who produce it. At the refineries the raw opium is either refined into better-grade opium or processed into heroin. These products are then shipped to various outlets in Southeast Asia and Hong Kong.

Because of American pressure, officials in Turkey have been reducing the extent of areas where poppy growing is permitted. Although numerous violations of the Turkish restrictions undoubtedly occur, the result of this policy has been to accentuate Southeast Asia's importance as a source of heroin. This trend will assuredly continue as the 1970s progress.

Most of the heroin from Southeast Asia that reaches the United States travels by way of Hong Kong or Thailand. The heroin passes over numerous routes to reach these depots. Some of it is carried by mule train, aircraft, or other means from the Golden Triangle to Bangkok. Some heroin is airdropped into the sea, where Chinese boats carry it to Hong Kong. From Thailand and Hong Kong, the heroin is smuggled to the United States by couriers on commercial or U. S. military aircraft or through the G. I. mails. Recently, increasing numbers of American ex-military personnel have moved to Thailand to engage in the lucrative smuggling operations. A goodly proportion of heroin from the Golden Triangle is also smuggled into South Vietnam, where American G. I.'s find it readily available.

There are numerous reasons why the opium trade in Southeast Asia flourishes, including inadequate legislation and enforcement, high profits, and government corruption. We shall discuss these in turn, and we shall pay particular attention to Laos.

The principal international instrument for controlling opium production is the International Narcotics Control Board (INCB), which is charged with enforcing the provisions of the Single Convention of 1961. The Single Convention, which went into effect in 1964, is an international agreement calling for the signatories to control poppy cultivation by issuing licenses. The signers are also obligated to control trade in opium by granting export licenses only when the importer produces a permit signifying his government's approval to bring in opium. The Single Convention is not, however, a very effective restraint on illicit opium production, because the international agreement seeks to regulate only opium produced legally. Also, the Single Convention relies on voluntary restraints for the enforcement of its provisions. Laos, unfortunately, is not a member of the Single Convention.

If the illegal production and trading of opium is to be curtailed, national governments must do the job. On this level, legislation and enforcement are just as unsatisfactory as the practically nonexistent international controls. Opium production was declared illegal in Thailand in 1958, but there are no restrictions against it in Burma. In Laos, there was no law prohibiting the production of opium until August 1971, when the National Assembly passed legislation controlling the opium traffic. The new law, in large part the result of prodding by the American Embassy in Vientiane, calls for the phasing out of opium production in Laos over a five-year period. During these five years, ethnic minorities who dwell in the mountains and have traditionally consumed opium may grow opium for their own consumption; they may not sell it to others, however. Provincial governors are to issue licenses for this limited cultivation and consumption. Any consumption of opium by nongrowers is illegal, a measure that will theoretically close the over 100 opium dens that existed in Vientiane alone before the law was passed. The bill bans all sale and purchase of opium as well as the transshipment of opium and its derivatives in Laos. A schedule of fines is included to penalize violators of the new law.

It is unlikely that this new legislation will significantly reduce the amount of opium produced and traded in Laos. The law's greatest impact will no doubt be to drive up the price of opium and yield more payoffs for government officials charged with enforcing the law. There are several reasons why enforcement is likely to fail. First of all, the RLG exercises control over only about one-third of Laotian territory, so it cannot enforce the law in the remaining portion.[54] The RLG has practically no control over the thousands of miles of jungle border and over 600 miles of river frontier through which opium enters and leaves Laos. Another difficulty concerns the substitution of other crops for opium, a solution offered by some people for eliminating poppy growing. Tens of thousands of mountain tribesmen, particularly the Meos, depend for their livelihood on the opium trade. Once this traffic is halted, they must find other means of sustenance. However, what other crop produces so high a cash yield as opium? Even if the tribesmen agreed to switch to another crop, the lack of roads and markets in the mountain areas would severely limit the cash return the growers could expect. Perhaps the fear of antagonizing the tribesmen, who are constantly being courted by the Pathet Lao, is one reason why the Laotian government has assigned a low priority to control of the opium traffic.

There can be no doubt that, in Laos and elsewhere, the lure of huge profits and the prevalence of government complicity render any laws restricting the opium traffic nearly impossible to enforce. Obviously, the opportunity for enormous profit and the willingness of government officials to avert their eyes are related.

A kilo of opium can be purchased from a Southeast Asian poppy grower for $25–$75. On the streets of New York City, a kilo of heroin (which requires about ten kilos of opium to produce) sells for $220,000. This phenomenal markup allows plenty of margin for payoffs to law-enforcement officials.

Throughout Southeast Asia, high government officials and other respected citizens are directly engaged in the opium business. A singular case of international competition, involving ranking individuals in the opium business, occurred in Laos in 1968.[55] This incident, or "opium war," was the result of rivalry among three large opium syndicates in Southeast Asia. One syndicate, totalling between 4,000 and 6,000 heavily armed and equipped men, is led by two divisions of Chinese Nationalist (KMT) soldiers who left China in 1949. Many recruits from the local population have joined the KMT remnants to form a powerful opium syndicate. The KMT is said to control about 80 percent of the opium traffic in northern Burma. The KMT units, by the way, in the early 1950s received arms from the CIA, who hoped the soldiers would strike at the then still shaky Peking regime. Instead, they went into the opium business, well protected by the guns they received. The second syndicate is run by Chan Chi-foo, who is half Burmese and half Chinese. Fluent in several dialects spoken in opium-rich northwest Burma, Chan reportedly commands up to 2,000 heavily armed men who carry raw opium from northern Burma to refineries in the Golden Triangle. Chan's opium caravans sometimes extend for over a mile and include two hundred mules guarded by several hundred armed guards. Despite this armed might, Chan must pay thousands of dollars of protection to the KMT, so that they will let his caravans pass.

In 1968, it is reported, Chan refused to pay the KMT protection money. The KMT, in turn, ambushed one of Chan's caravans near Ban Houei Sai in Laos. While the fighting raged, yet a third opium kingpin entered the fray. This party was General Ouan Rathikoun, who at the time was Commander-in-Chief of the Royal Laotian Army, a post he vacated in July 1971. General Ouan, in addition to his military duties, is a major operator in the opium trade. In the midst of the battle between Chan's forces and the KMT, General Ouan diverted Laotian troops from their positions on the Plain of Jars, where their assignment was to engage the Pathet Lao, and sent them into combat against the KMT and Chan's men.

The participation in the opium traffic of such highly placed figures as General Ouan makes any attempt to restrict the trade practically hopeless. Unfortunately, official complicity is not limited to one or two individuals.

Although figures are unavailable, it is believed that many members of the Laotian and South Vietnamese armed forces, particularly the air force, are involved in illegal opium activities. As one recent U. S. report states, "In Laos, Government armed forces are major wholesalers of opium and heroin and have been directly involved in large-scale smuggling activities."[56] It is reported that planes and air crews from the Laotian and South Vietnamese air forces are heavily involved in the smuggling of heroin into South Vietnam for use by American servicemen. These airplanes, it is worth observing, have been supplied by the United States. Some heroin is smuggled into South Vietnam by Thai soldiers traveling on American and Thai military aircraft. Civilian officials are involved in the illicit opium traffic as well. U. S. Representative Seymour Halpern of New York, who visited Laos in April 1971 for the express purpose of investigating illegal narcotics activities, reported that the entire narcotics operation in Laos enjoys the protection of Prince Boun Oum, Inspector General of Laos. Mr. Halpern further reported that protection money is widely distributed to the Laotian police. Corruption, he said, is "endemic in every level of the Laotian hierarchy. As long as it continues, prospects for ending the narcotics traffic in Laos do not appear very bright."[57] It is difficult to dispute Mr. Halpern's conclusion, the new opium law in Laos notwithstanding.

American policy toward the drug traffic in Laos is at cross purposes with itself. On the face of it, the United States appears determined to do all it can to curb the flow of illegal drugs. To this end the U. S. Mission in Laos has established a top-level committee chaired by the Ambassador. This committee applied pressure on the Laotian government to pass the new drug law.

On the other hand, certain American activities in the field appear to be working in the other direction. This refers to the CIA and its sponsorship of the Meo army of irregulars in northern Laos. The Meo tribesmen have long depended on opium production for their chief source of revenue. In addition, the Meos smoke the substance themselves. The CIA, relying on Meo resistance fighters to stem communist advances in northern Laos, has not sought to eradicate Meo trafficking in opium. In fact, the question has been raised as to whether the CIA has not assisted the Meos in marketing their opium in exchange for military services. For instance, the headquarters of General Vang Pao's Meo army is Long Chieng, 30 miles south of the Plain of Jars. One correspondent has reported that at Long Chieng he saw "American crews loading T–28 bombers while armed CIA agents chatted with uniformed Thai soldiers and piles of raw opium stood for sale in the market."[58] According to seemingly reliable reports, U. S.

military aircraft and Air America planes pick up Meo opium couriers from outlying regions and fly them into Long Chieng. Some of the opium is purchased there by Meos living at the base, while the rest is flown to various outlets in Laos, Thailand, and South Vietnam. A congressional report states that heroin has been smuggled to South Vietnam aboard Air America aircraft, although the authors could find no evidence that any officials of the U. S. Government were involved.[59] One theory, which seems to have substance, suggests that opium is the adhesive that binds together the Meos, the CIA, and the RLG. The CIA does not interfere with, or perhaps facilitates, the Meos in their efforts to market opium. In return, the Meos, who also receive cash payments from the CIA, agree to fight the communists. Officials at every level of the RLG make such profit from the opium trade that they encourage the collaboration between the CIA and the Meos.[60]

At the very least, the CIA has averted its eyes in regard to the Meos' illicit opium operations. Judging from most reports, it would seem that the CIA goes farther, that it does assist the Meos in bringing opium to entrepôts such as Long Chieng and shipping it out to markets. In either case, the attitude of the CIA toward the opium traffic is clearly at odds with the stated position of the U. S. Embassy in Vientiane.

Can the U. S. Government do anything to curb illicit opium activity in Laos? The prospects for fruitful action are dim. So long as the CIA remains unopposed to the opium cultivation conducted by the Meos, few results can be expected. Even in the unlikely event that the CIA should reverse its attitude, corruption throughout the Laotian administration would in all likelihood neutralize enforcement efforts. It has been suggested that the U. S. threaten to cut off all aid to Laos unless the RLG curbs the drug traffic. This proposal is not likely to be accepted by the U. S. Mission, which regards the anticommunist struggle as too important to jeopardize by a halt in aid. Besides, it is improbable that Souvanna Phouma could overcome the corruption in RLG ranks to effectively curb illegal narcotics activities. One proposal that does merit consideration is that the United States or the International Narcotics Control Board purchase the entire Laotian opium output every year and encourage the tribesmen to shift to other crops. It is estimated that such a program would cost $10 million per year. While this tactic might curb the illicit sale of opium in Laos, it fails to recognize that the narcotics problem is one that must be attacked worldwide. To curtail the opium output only in Laos would merely drive up the price of opium and induce increased production elsewhere. Like the pollution of our planet, the pollution of our bodies by poisonous drugs must be attacked on a global basis or the campaign is destined to fail.

REFUGEES

One of the saddest episodes to emerge from the fighting in Laos concerns the sorrowful flow of refugees the war has produced. It is perhaps fitting to end this volume with a few words about these unfortunate individuals.

The plight of the refugees in Laos has been most systematically examined by Senator Edward M. Kennedy's Subcommittee to Investigate Problems Connected with Refugees and Escapees. We shall draw upon this and other sources in examining this matter.

The fighting that began shortly after the 1954 Geneva Conference led to the initial flow of refugees within Laos. Small groups of hill tribesmen began moving south out of Phong Saly and Houa Khong provinces. Most of these people were resettled in the provinces of Xieng Khouang and Luang Prabang.

The more intense fighting that began in mid-1959 generated a larger number of refugees, so that when the 1962 Geneva accords were signed, the Laotian government had about 125,000 refugees on its hands. After 1962, approximately 30,000–50,000 refugees were produced annually, until the widely expanded fighting of 1968. The United States, after halting for the first time the systematic bombing of North Vietnam in November 1968, greatly increased its bombing in Laos, sometimes flying up to 600 sorties in a day. On the ground, the North Vietnamese advanced as far as the Plain of Jars, farther than their ordinary dry-season probes. In the wet-season counteroffensive, General Vang Pao and his army of Meo tribesmen, aided by massive U. S. air support, pushed the communists back farther than usual. These two drives, combined with unprecedented use of American air power, generated a massive refugee crisis in Laos. People, particularly the tribal population in the north, fled from the military action that was destroying their homelands. As of July 1, 1970, AID reported there were 253,261 refugees in Laos.[61] Based on a total population of 2½ million, approximately 10 percent of the people of Laos were refugees at the time. This figure, of course, does not include the tens of thousands of Laotians who had been refugees at an earlier date and were now resettled, nor does it include refugees living in communist-controlled areas or civilian war dead. Senator Kennedy estimated, in April 1971, that 700,000 Laotians, or about one-fourth of the population, had become refugees in recent years.[62] By any standard, the war in Laos has dislocated a proportion of the civilian population rarely equalled in the history of human struggle.

The Laotian government has never been able to assemble enough resources to cope successfully with the refugees. Consequently, the United

States has gradually assumed the full task of caring for refugees in Laos.

Official American aid to Laotian refugees began in 1956 with a small resettlement program for Meo tribesmen in Xieng Khouang province. This project, located in Ban Khang Si, was actually conducted by an organization called International Voluntary Services (IVS), a private service organization similar to the Peace Corps. Under contract to AID, it performs development work in impoverished nations. Between 1956 and 1970, IVS placed approximately 300 dedicated young workers at dozens of locations in such fields as agricultural development, home economics, education, public health, and community development. In addition, no one has been able to calculate the amount of good will towards the United States that IVSers have generated.

The IVS pilot project in Ban Khang Si was expanded to neighboring areas in 1957–1959, as increased fighting produced larger numbers of refugees. In 1959, a refugee office was established in the AID mission to assist the Laotian government in caring for refugees. In October 1962, through an exchange of letters between U. S. Ambassador Leonard Unger and Prime Minister Souvanna Phouma, the United States assumed responsibility for refugee relief. As of 1970, AID managed virtually all facets of the refugee program, with the Laotian government providing labor and land for resettlement. According to Secretary of State William Rogers, the United States has provided $29.1 million for refugee relief through fiscal year 1970.[63] This figure does not include the cost of airdropping food and supplies to refugees. The full total, including indirect costs, is probably closer to twice the figure mentioned by Secretary Rogers.[64]

In addition to the U. S. Government, numerous private agencies operate refugee assistance programs in Laos. These organizations include the already mentioned IVS as well as Catholic Relief Services, CARE, Mennonite Central Committee, Thomas A. Dooley Foundation, Christian Medical Society, Meals for Millions, Asia Foundation, Boy Scouts, Damien-Dutton Society, Darien Book Aid, Volunteers of International Technical Assistance (VITA), and World Medical Relief.

In most countries, care for refugees is a strictly humanitarian, noncontroversial undertaking divorced from political considerations. In Laos, however, refugee relief has been tied to American military and political objectives from the beginning. This is not to say that no one has cared for the plight of refugees on purely humanitarian grounds. To the contrary, the provision of shelter, food, clothing, cooking utensils, seeds, tools, medical care, and other items of relief has all been directed toward the betterment of living conditions for the unfortunate souls uprooted by over ten years of war. Nevertheless, it is important to realize that the refugee program as administered by AID has had other, less altruistic objectives as well.

AID's refugee program has been closely tied to the CIA's efforts to support the Meo paramilitary force. The Meos have been very helpful to American military efforts; they act as trail-watchers and suppliers of intelligence on North Vietnamese and Pathet Lao activities; they help to defend such installations as the radar station at Phou Pha Thi; most important of all, they constitute the most effective fighting force against North Vietnamese and Pathet Lao penetrations in northern Laos. Small wonder, then, that a large proportion of refugee assistance has gone to the families of the Meo fighting men who, while soldiering, are unable to sustain their wives and children. In fact, much refugee relief has been distributed among the Meo fighters themselves, who often travel with their families close by. A report released by the General Accounting Office in April 1972, said that of 306,000 Laotians on refugee relief rolls, 20,000 were "paramilitary personnel" [meaning the Meos] and 105,000 were their dependents.[65] To a certain extent, therefore, the refugee relief program has acted as a cover to help the anti-communist guerrillas fighting under the banner of the CIA.[66] It is well known, moreover, that about 10 percent of the Americans listed as working for AID have actually been in the employ of CIA.

Furthermore, it appears that a certain proportion of the refugees have been deliberately removed from their homelands to areas where they would remain under tighter government surveillance and control. Some refugees were created by military decisions to deprive communist guerrillas of the population base they need to survive. Without it, the guerrillas find it difficult to obtain food, shelter, supplies, money, medical care, and other necessities that they generally extract from the local people. It is estimated that, as of 1970, approximately one-third of Laotian refugees were generated by Laotian government-sponsored village evacuations.[67] In theory, of course, when the Laotian Army prepares to move into a contested area, the population is given the choice of whether or not to be evacuated. In several cases, however, forced evacuations occur, in order to render the enemy more vulnerable.

On occasion, evacuations occur on a massive scale. Three such evacuations took place in early 1970, in connection with intensified military activity. In January 1970, 8,115 persons were flown out of the vicinity of Houei Tong Kho in southwestern Sam Neua Province. One month later, the Laotian government airlifted 13,840 persons from the Plain of Jars area. The largest evacuation occurred in March–April, 1970, when about 80,000 additional people were removed from the Plain of Jars. The Plain, it should be noted, has undergone a transition from a thriving (for Laos) area of 150,000 persons to a depopulated, crater-marked battleground where few people may be seen.

Another topic of controversy regarding the refugee issue is the reason why many refugees leave their villages and trek to government-held areas. Most observers agree that these population movements are related to the fighting. There, however, unanimity of opinion stops. Secretary of State Rogers voiced the viewpoint of many supporters of the RLG when he told Senator Kennedy's subcommittee in 1970 that villagers flock to RLG areas because they do not like life under Pathet Lao or North Vietnamese domination.[68] Very often, when the communists move into an area, they compel the villagers to contribute labor, food, money, and supplies. Sometimes the communists force peasants to carry heavy cases to the next village; they often conscript able-bodied men for fighting. The villagers know that the mere presence of communists places their village on the RLG target list, so they feel uncomfortable as long as the communists remain. All these factors would appear to support the conclusion that many peasants find it onerous to live in communist controlled areas. So, the argument goes, these people pack their belongings on their backs and walk to RLG territory. Once there, they are taken to a resettlement camp, where they receive the necessities of life and a feeling of security.

Quite another reason for the flow of refugees was enunciated by Senator Edward Kennedy in the course of his Senate committee investigations. The Democratic Senator from Massachusetts attributed the dislocations not to the peasants' preference for life under RLG authority; rather, the Senator cited American bombing and related military actions as the factors that give rise to refugees. In the Preface to his Senate subcommittee's 1970 report on refugees and civilian war casualties in Indochina, Senator Kennedy wrote,

> We are confronted today with a very serious regional crisis of people—millions of people—displaced within their country or fleeing across international boundaries. All are in urgent need of care and protection. And more than our government cares to admit, American military activities—especially the heavy bombing of many areas—is contributing much to this human toll of war.
>
> • • •
>
> The United States is great and powerful. . . . But the power to heal, to salvage and rehabilitate the hapless victims of conflict—and the responsibility to minimize our contribution to the inevitable human toll of war—has never been exercised in a measure commensurate with the other uses of our power in South Vietnam, Laos, or Cambodia.[69]

A sorrowful illustration of Senator Kennedy's statement concerns the former inhabitants of the town of Phong Savan on the Plain of Jars. When American planes began to bomb in the vicinity of Phong Savan in March 1969, the townspeople fled to the surrounding hills a mile or two away. There they dug caves and trenches, where they lived for six months. Most of the people lived in deep trenches shored up with planks and covered with corrugated iron roofing and dirt. The only time it was safe to come out was after dark, when the people would purchase rice and empty the buckets which served them as toilets. Even the farmers tilled their fields at night. Finally, in September 1969, these people were evacuated to Vientiane.[70]

While such harrowing tales are not common, the fact remains that thousands of Laotians have become refugees not because of the attraction of life in RLG territory, but simply because American bombing made life unbearable. To be sure, one cannot omit the fact that American bombers were called into action because of the presence of communists. But it is American bombing, not communist firepower, that drove these people from their homes. And the fact that so many villagers attempt to survive in caves and trenches near their homes only underscores their preference to remain there, despite the communist presence.

There can be no doubt that American military activity is to a large extent responsible for the refugee problem. This statement is confirmed by statistics on refugees supplied by AID. In August 1966, there were, according to AID, 147,500 refugees in Laos. This total shot up to 158,800 in August 1967 and then dropped to 128,200 in August 1968. But shortly thereafter, as intensified American bombing began to take its toll, the number of refugees rose steadily, except for a slight decrease in early 1970. Table 12 presents these figures in summary fashion.

Table 12 shows that the number of refugees parallels the intensity of American bombing in Laos. In light of America's heavy responsibility for the creation of these refugees, is the United States doing enough to care for the civilian victims of the war? The proposed U. S. budget request for fiscal year 1971 for refugee relief was $3.2 million.[71] This amount was less than three percent of the total aid—military and economic—proposed for Laos for that year. And, as the Kennedy subcommittee pointed out, the entire refugee relief budget for one year costs less than six days of bombing in Laos. (The average is 600 sorties a day.) It would seem that the United States could spare far more money to cope with a problem it has had such a large share in creating.

Of the many tragic episodes connected with the Laotian war, one of the saddest concerns the steady decimation of the Meo people and culture. In 1960 there were approximately 500,000 Meos in Laos. Ten years later, 40 to 50 percent of the men had been killed and 25 percent of the women and children had become war casualties.[72] With every Royal Army or communist offensive in northern Laos, the Meos are compelled to move. It is estimated that some families have relocated up to 18 times. According

TABLE 12

REFUGEES IN LAOS

Date	Total
1966	
August	147,500
1967	
August	158,800
1968	
August	128,200
1969	
February	157,000
April	187,000
June	206,000
August	232,000
October	250,000
December	235,000
1970	
February	204,000
April	246,000

Source: Senate Committee on the Judiciary, *Refugee and Civilian War Casualty Problems in Laos and Cambodia,* 1970, p. 63.

to AID information, during a long trek to a new home, one out of every five Meo families dies owing to malnutrition and the rugged terrain they must cross. Some people are hopeful that, upon the conclusion of the war, the surviving Meos will have the opportunity to return to their original villages in Laos. In all likelihood, however, the Meos will find their villages reduced to heaps of bombed-out rubble. Just where the Meos, as well as other refugees, will live when the war ends is anybody's guess. That is just one of the many problems that will confront the Laotians when peace returns to their land.

NOTES

1. See Eric Pace, "Laos: Continuing Crisis," *Foreign Affairs* 42 (October 1964): 64–74, and E. H. S. Simmonds, "Breakdown in Laos," *The World Today* 20 (July 1964): 285–92.

2. See Denis Warner, "Our Secret War in Laos," *The Reporter,* 32 (April 22, 1965): 23–26.

3. Bernard B. Fall, *Anatomy of a Crisis* (New York: Doubleday and Company, 1969), p. 234. The concluding section, from which this refercence was drawn, was written by Roger M. Smith. Professor Fall was unable to complete his book, because he was killed in Vietnam while covering the war.

4. See E. H. S. Simmonds, "Laos and the War in Vietnam," *The World Today,* 22 (May 1966): 202-03.

5. This is not to say that there are no political rivalries in the neutralist-conservative group. Such rivalry as exists, however, is closer to American intra-party disputes than gangland-style vendettas.

6. At a Senate hearing in October 1969, Deputy Assistant Secretary of State for East Asian and Pacific Affairs William H. Sullivan reiterated the American objective, saying, "Our policy is founded on the assumption that the interests of the United States are best served by an independent and neutral Laos. We do not seek to align the Royal Government with the United States." U.S. Congress, Senate, Committee on Foreign Relations, Subcommittee on United States Security Agreements and Commitments Abroad, *Hearings, United States Security Agreements and Commitments Abroad, Kingdom of Laos,* 91st Cong., 1st Sess., 1969, p. 376. (Hereafter referred to as *Laos Hearings,* 1969).

7. *Ibid.,* p. 526. Military aid is discussed in the next section.

8. *Ibid.,* pp. 569-70.

9. *Ibid.,* p. 569.

10. See *ibid.,* pp. 370, 586-87, from which the following account has been drawn.

11. *Ibid.,* p. 555.

12. See *ibid.,* pp. 441-42 for the exchange of correspondence.

13. See Sullivan's testimony in *ibid.,* p. 443.

14. Under questioning, Secretary Sullivan admitted that the United States violated the 1962 Geneva agreements on several counts, including the dispatch of military advisors, carrying out air strikes with American planes, and using the territory of Laos to intervene in the affairs of other countries. In regard to the last-mentioned activity, the Secretary was referring to American flights over Lao territory on bombing runs into Vietnam and the erection of navigational aids in Laos to assist these bombing missions. See *ibid.,* pp. 422-26.

15. Since 1968, American military aid to Laos has been taken out of AID and placed within the Department of Defense. This has led some to speculate that the reason for the shift was that congressional committees overseeing military aid are more willing to authorize such assistance than the committees that review the program carried out by AID.

16. *Laos Hearings,* 1969, p. 369.

17. For a valuable account of the organization and operation of the National Liberation Front, see Douglas Pike, *Vietcong* (Cambridge: The M.I.T. Press, 1966).

18. During the 1969 Senate hearings on Laos, Secretary Sullivan asserted that one reason for the American presence in Laos was to interfere with communist traffic along the Ho Chi Minh trail and to deny the communists a sanctuary in Laos. See *Laos Hearings,* 1969, p. 557.

19. The precise number of North Vietnamese troops in Laos remains in doubt. North Vietnam has never acknowledged the presence of any of its troops in Laos. At a news conference in Paris on July 15, 1969, Souvanna Phouma alleged that at least 60,000 North Vietnamese soldiers were operating in Laos. (*The New York Times,* July 26, 1969). President Nixon used the figure of 67,000 in his statement of March 6, 1970, on Laos. (*Ibid.,* March 7, 1970).

20. *The Washington Post,* March 16, 1970.

21. For the description of the following administrative structure I am indebted to Paul F. Langer and Joseph J. Zasloff, *North Vietnam and the Pathet Lao:*

Partners in the Struggle for Laos (Cambridge: Harvard University Press, 1970), pp. 106-23.

22. *Ibid.,* pp. 92-96.

23. *Laos Hearings,* 1969, p. 369.

24. *The New York Times,* September 28, 1969. The remainder of the information in this paragraph is drawn from the dispatch cited.

25. The following account is based on a dispatch filed in *The New York Times,* October 26, 1969, by Henry Kamm. It is interesting to note that the *Armée Clandestine* was scarcely mentioned in the released transcript of the Senate's 1969 hearings on Laos.

26. Memorandum from Brig. Gen. Edward G. Lansdale to Gen. Maxwell D. Taylor, in the *Pentagon Papers,* pp. 131-38. The memorandum is undated, but the author of the *Pentagon Papers* says it was probably written in July 1961.

27. For more details on Air America and Continental Air Transport, see pp. 196-98.

28. Memorandum from Lansdale to Taylor, in *Pentagon Papers,* pp. 131-38.

29. *Laos Hearings,* 1969, p. 457.

30. *Ibid.,* p. 370.

31. *Ibid.,* p. 476.

32. *Ibid.*

33. *Ibid.,* p. 370.

34. *Ibid.,* pp. 483-85. The number of strikes flown in each year remains classified. The strikes in northern Laos were in response to a request from Souvanna Phouma for additional American military assistance against communist logistics lines.

35. *Ibid.,* p. 439.

36. *The New York Times,* September 18, 1969.

37. *Ibid.,* July 26, 1969.

38. *Ibid.,* September 18, 1969.

39. *Laos Hearings,* 1969, p. 510.

40. *Ibid.*

41. Accounts of the two campaigns may be found in *The New York Times,* September 18, 1969.

42. A report in *The New York Times,* September 18, 1969, placed the number of Thai troops in Laos at 5,000.

43. In November, 1969, the Pathet Lao recaptured the Plain of Jars.

44. *The New York Times,* March 7, 1970.

45. *Laos Hearings,* 1969, p. 380.

46. *Ibid.,* p. 478.

47. A correspondent held captive for one month by the Pathet Lao in 1968 wrote, "During my long march I often met sizable detachments of North Vietnamese soldiers carrying Russian or Chinese arms. In all I may have seen 500 and generally it was the Vietnamese who directed operations." See Guy Hannoteaux, "The Savage Peace," *Far Eastern Economic Review,* 62 (November 21, 1968): 407.

48. The following information is based on a report in *The New York Times,* May 8, 1972.

49. See *Laos Hearings,* 1969, p. 372.

50. These figures and those that follow were reported in U. S. Congress,

House, Committee on Foreign Affairs, *The World Heroin Problem,* Report of Special Study Mission by Morgan F. Murphy and Robert H. Steele, 92d Cong., 1st Sess., 1971.

51. U. S. Congress, House, Committee on Foreign Affairs, *The International Narcotics Trade,* Report of Special Study Mission by Hon. Seymour Halpern, 92d Cong., 1st Sess., 1971, p. 23.

52. *Ibid.*

53. *Ibid.,* p. 26.

54. It is estimated that about 30 tons of opium are produced in RLG-controlled areas. Most Laotian opium is produced by Meos in areas controlled by the Pathet Lao.

55. The following incident is described in *Ibid.,* pp. 27–28. The author of the House report did not witness these events himself, but he cites accounts that he obviously feels are reliable.

56. House Committee on Foreign Affairs, *The World Heroin Problem,* p. 20.

57. House Committee on Foreign Affairs, *The International Narcotics Trade,* p. 46.

58. Carl Strock, "No News from Laos," *The Far Eastern Economic Review* 71 (January 30, 1971): 18.

59. House Committee on Foreign Affairs, *The World Heroin Problem,* p. 21.

60. See Frank Browning and Banning Garrett, "The New Opium War," *Ramparts,* 9 (May 1971): 32–39.

61. U. S. Congress, Senate, Committee on the Judiciary, *Refugee and Civilian War Casualty Problems in Indochina,* Report by Subcommittee to Investigate Problems Connected with Refugees and Escapees, 91st Cong., 2d Sess., 1970, p. 26.

62. U.S. Congress, Senate, Committee on the Judiciary, *War-Related Civilian Problems in Indochina,* Hearing before the Subcommittee to Investigate Problems Connected with Refugees and Escapees, Part I, 92d Cong., 1st Sess., 1971, p. 1.

63. Senate Judiciary Committee, *Refugee and Civilian War Casualty Problems in Indochina,* p. 75.

64. In testifying before Senator Kennedy's subcommittee, AID's Assistant Administrator for East Asia, Roderick L. O'Connor, cited the figure of $64 million total U. S. expenditures. U. S. Congress, Senate, Committee on the Judiciary, *Refugee and Civilian War Casualty Problems in Laos and Cambodia,* Hearings before Subcommittee to Investigate Problems Connected with Refugees and Escapees, 91st Cong., 2d Sess., 1970, p. 40.

65. *The New York Times,* April 23, 1972.

66. Senate Judiciary Committee, *Refugee and Civilian War Casualty Problems in Indochina,* pp. 22–24. In 1970 Secretary Rogers told Senator Kennedy's subcommittee that 40 percent of the refugees in Laos were Meos. *Ibid.,* p. 71.

67. *Ibid.,* p. 24.

68. *Ibid.,* p. 70.

69. *Ibid.,* pp. v, viii.

70. Dispatch by Henry Kamm in *The New York Times,* October 11, 1969.

71. Senate Judiciary Committee, *Refugee and Civilian War Casualty Problems in Indochina,* p. 76.

72. *Ibid.,* p. 27.

BIBLIOGRAPHY

BOOKS

Adams, Sherman. *Firsthand Report*. New York: Harper and Brothers, 1961.

Buttinger, Joseph. *Vietnam: A Political History*. New York: Frederick A. Praeger, 1968.

Burchett, Wilfred G. *The Furtive War: The United States in Vietnam and Laos*. New York: International Publishers, 1963.

Cameron, Allan W. (ed.). *Viet-Nam Crisis: A Documentary History*. 2 vols. Ithaca: Cornell University Press, 1971.

Champassak, Sisouk Na. *Storm over Laos*. New York: Frederick A. Praeger, 1961.

Cheng, J. Chester (ed.). *The Politics of the Chinese Red Army*. Stanford: The Hoover Institution on War, Revolution and Peace, 1966.

Chennault, Anna. *A Thousand Springs*. New York: Paul S. Eriksson, Inc., 1962.

Cole, Alan B. (ed.). *Conflict in Indo-China and Inter-National Repercussions, A Documentary History, 1945-1955*. Ithaca: Cornell University Press, 1956.

Collective Defense in South East Asia. London: Royal Institute of International Affairs, 1956.

Coser, Lewis A. *The Functions of Social Conflict*. Glencoe, New York: The Free Press, 1956.

De Gaulle, Charles. *The War Memoirs of Charles De Gaulle*. Translated by Richard Howard. 5 vols. New York: Simon and Schuster, 1960.

Deutsch, Karl W., *et al. Political Community in the North Atlantic Area*. Princeton: Princeton University Press, 1957.

335

Dommen, Arthur J. *Conflict in Laos*. New York: Frederick A. Praeger, 1964.

Drachman, Edward R. *United States Policy toward Vietnam, 1940–1945*. Rutherford, N. J.: Fairleigh Dickinson University Press, 1970.

Eden, Anthony. *Full Circle: The Memoirs of Anthony Eden*. Boston: Houghton Mifflin Co., 1960.

Eisenhower, Dwight D. *Mandate for Change*. New York: Doubleday and Co., 1963.

———. *Waging Peace*. New York: Doubleday and Co., 1965.

Fall, Bernard B. *Anatomy of a Crisis*. New York: Doubleday and Co., 1969.

———. *Street without Joy*. Harrisburg: The Stackpole Co., 1961.

———. *The Two Vietnams*. 2nd ed. New York: Frederick A. Praeger, 1963.

Farley, Miriam S. *United States Relations with Southeast Asia*. New York: American Institute of Pacific Relations, 1955.

Fifield, Russell H. *Southeast Asia in United States Policy*. New York: Frederick A. Praeger, 1963.

Finkelstein, Lawrence S. *American Policy in Southeast Asia*. New York: American Institute of Pacific Relations, 1951.

Giap, Vo Nguyen. *People's War, People's Army*. New York: Frederick A. Praeger, 1962.

Halpern, Joel M. *Government, Politics and Social Structure in Laos*. New Haven: Yale University, Southeast Asia Studies, Monograph Series No. 4, 1964.

Hilsman, Roger. *To Move a Nation*. New York: Doubleday and Co., 1967.

Hull, Cordell. *The Memoirs of Cordell Hull*. 2 vols. New York: The Macmillan Co., 1948.

Kahin, George M. *Governments and Politics of Southeast Asia*. 2nd ed. Ithaca: Cornell University Press, 1964.

———. *The Asian-African Conference*. Ithaca: Cornell University Press, 1956.

Lacouture, Jean, and Devillers, Philippe. *La Fin D'Une Guerre*. Paris: Editions du Seuil, 1960.

Lall, Arthur. *How Communist China Negotiates*. New York: Columbia University Press, 1968.

Lancaster, Donald. *The Emancipation of French Indochina*. London: Oxford University Press, 1961.

Langer, Paul F., and Zasloff, Joseph J. *North Vietnam and the Pathet Lao: Partners in the Struggle for Laos*. Cambridge: Harvard University Press, 1970.

Modelski, George. *International Conference on the Settlement of the Laotian Question 1961–1962*. Canberra: The Australian National University, 1962.

O'Ballance, Edgar. *The Indo-China War*. London: Faber and Faber, 1964.

Peace with Justice: Selected Addresses of Dwight D. Eisenhower. New York: Columbia University Press, 1961.

Pike, Douglas. *Vietcong.* Cambridge: The M.I.T. Press, 1966.

Roosevelt, Elliott. *As He Saw It.* New York: Duell, Sloan and Pearce, 1946.

Rosenau, James N. (ed.). *International Aspects of Civil Strife.* Princeton: Princeton University Press, 1964.

Sasorith, Katay D. *Le Laos.* Paris: Éditions Berger-Levrault, 1953.

Schlesinger, Arthur M., Jr. *A Thousand Days.* Boston: Houghton Mifflin Co., 1965.

Sorensen, Theodore C. *Kennedy.* New York: Harper and Row, 1965.

Young, Oran. *The Intermediaries: Third Parties in International Crises.* Princeton: Princeton University Press, 1967.

Zagoria, Donald S. *The Sino-Soviet Conflict.* Princeton: Princeton University Press, 1962.

ARTICLES AND PERIODICALS

Beech, Keyes. "How Uncle Sam Fumbled in Laos," *Saturday Evening Post* 234 (April 22, 1961) : 28ff.

Browning, Frank, and Garrett, Banning. "The New Opium War," *Ramparts* 9 (May 1971) : 32–39.

Czyzak, John J., and Salans, Carl F. "The International Conference on the Settlement of the Laotian Question and the Geneva Agreements of 1962," *American Journal of International Law* 57 (April 1963) : 300–317.

Dommen, Arthur J. "Laos: The Troubled Neutral," *Asian Survey* 7 (January 1967) : 74–80.

Dulles, John Foster. "Policy for Security and Peace," *Foreign Affairs* 32 (April 1954) : 353–64.

The Economist 202 (January 13, 1962) : 110.

Elegant, Robert S. "The Laos Blunder," *New Leader* 44 (June 5, 1961) : 5–6.

Fall, Bernard B. "The Laos Tangle," *International Journal* (Toronto) 16 (Spring 1961) : 138–57.

———. "Reappraisal in Laos," *Current History* 42 (January 1962) : 8–14.

Far Eastern Economic Review Yearbook, 1967.

Halpern, A. M., and Fredman, H. B. *Communist Strategy in Laos* (Santa Monica: The Rand Corp., RM-2561, 1960).

Hannoteaux, Guy. "The Savage Peace," *Far Eastern Economic Review* 62 (November 21, 1968) : 405–407.

Holsti, K. J., "Resolving International Conflicts," *Journal of Conflict Resolution* 10 (September 1966) : 272–91.

Jensen, Lloyd. "Military Capabilities and Bargaining Behavior," *Journal of Conflict Resolution* 9 (June 1965) : 155–63.

Lang, Nicholas. "The Chinese Communists in Laos," *Est et Ouest* 14 (June 1–15, 1962) : 16–18.

Le Monde, 1959–1962.

Miller, Haynes. "A Bulwark Built on Sand," *Reporter* 19 (November 13, 1958) : 11–16.

New China News Agency. August 25, 1956.

"New Government of Laos Expects U.S. Recognition," *Mundo* (World), No. 1158 (July 15, 1962), pp. 17–21.

The New York Times. 1954–1972.

Nieburg, H. L. "Uses of Violence," *Journal of Conflict Resolution* 7 (March 1963) : 43–54.

Pace, Eric. "Laos: Continuing Crisis," *Foreign Affairs* 43 (October, 1964) : 64–74.

Phouma, Souvanna. "Laos: le fond du problème," *France-Asie* 17 (March–April, 1961) : 1824–26.

Roberts, Chalmers M. "The Day We Didn't Go to War," *Reporter* 11 (September 14, 1954) : 31–35.

Scott, Peter Dale. "Air America: Flying the U. S. into Laos," *Ramparts* 8 (February 1970) : 39–42.

Shepley, James. "How Dulles Averted War," *Life* 40 (January 16, 1956) : 70–80.

Simmonds, E. H. S. "A Cycle of Political Events in Laos," *The World Today* 17 (February 1961) : 58–68.

———. "Breakdown in Laos," *The World Today* 20 (July 1964) : 285–292.

———. "Laos and the War in Vietnam," *The World Today* 22 (May 1966) : 199–206.

Strock, Carl. "No News from Laos," *The Far Eastern Economic Review* 71 (January 30, 1971) : 18.

Survey of the Chinese Mainland Press, April 28, 1961, and May 1, 1961.

The Times (London). 1954–1962.

Wall Street Journal. 1958–1962.

Warner, Denis. "Our Secret War in Laos," *The Reporter* 32 (April 22, 1965) : 23–26.

Wilde, James. "The Russians in Laos," *Time* 77 (March 10, 1961) : 26.

PUBLIC DOCUMENTS

GREAT BRITAIN

Parliamentary Debates (Hansard). Vol. CCXVII (1960–1961), pp. 692–95.

Parliamentary Papers. Vol. XXXI (Accounts and Papers, Vol. XII). Cmd. 9186. June, 1954. *Documents Relating to the Discussion of Korea and Indo-China at the Geneva Conference, April 27–June 15, 1954.*

————. Vol. XXXI (Accounts and Papers, Vol. XII). Cmd. 9239. August, 1954. *Further Documents Relating to the Discussion of Indo-China at the Geneva Conference, June 16–July 21, 1954.*

————. Vol. XIX (Accounts and Papers, Vol. XII). Cmd. 9445. May, 1955. *First Interim Report of the International Commission for Supervision and Control in Laos, August 11–December 31, 1954.*

————. Vol. XLIV (Accounts and Papers, Vol. XVI). Cmd. 9630. November, 1955. *Second Interim Report of the International Commission for Supervision and Control in Laos, January 1–June 30, 1955.*

————. Vol. XXX (Accounts and Papers, Vol. XII). Cmd. 314. December, 1957. *Third Interim Report of the International Commission for Supervision and Control in Laos, July 1, 1955–May 16, 1957.*

Parliamentary Papers. Vol. XXXIV (Accounts and Papers, Vol. XV). Cmd. 541. October, 1958. *Fourth Interim Report of the International Commission for Supervision and Control in Laos, May 17, 1957–May 31, 1958.*

————. (Accounts and Papers). Cmd. 2834. December, 1965. *Documents Relating to British Involvement in the Indo-China Conflict, 1945–1965.*

Documents on International Affairs, 1954–1961. London: Royal Institute of International Affairs.

PEOPLE'S REPUBLIC OF CHINA

Concerning the Situation in Laos. Peking: Foreign Languages Press, 1959.

REPUBLIC OF THE PHILIPPINES

The Signing of the Southeast Asia Collective Defense Treaty, the Protocol to the Southeast Asia Collective Defense Treaty, and the Pacific Charter. Manila: Manila Conference of 1954, Secretariat, Committee on Publicity, 1954.

UNITED NATIONS

Security Council. S/4236. *Report of the Security Council Sub-Committee under Resolution of September 7, 1959.* November 5, 1959.

Security Council. S/4216. *Resolution Adopted by the Security Council at Its 848th Meeting.* September 8, 1959.

UNITED STATES

Congress

House of Representatives, Committee on Appropriations. Hearings. *Operations Appropriations for 1962*. 87th Cong., 1st Sess., 1961.

House of Representatives, Committee on Foreign Affairs. Hearings. *Foreign Assistance Act of 1965*. 89th Cong., 1st Sess., 1965.

House of Representatives, Committee on Foreign Affairs. Hearings. *Foreign Assistance Act of 1967*. 90th Cong., 1st Sess., 1967.

House of Representatives, Committee on Foreign Affairs. Hearings. *Mutual Security Act of 1957*. 85th Cong., 1st Sess., 1957.

House of Representatives, Committee on Foreign Affairs. Hearings. *Mutual Security Act of 1958*. 85th Cong., 2d Sess., 1958.

House of Representatives, Committee on Foreign Affairs. Hearings. *Mutual Security Act of 1959*. 86th Cong., 1st Sess., 1959.

House of Representatives, Committee on Foreign Affairs. Hearings. *Mutual Security Act of 1961*. 87th Cong., 1st Sess., 1961.

House of Representatives, Committee on Foreign Affairs. *Mutual Security Program in Laos*. Hearings before the Subcommittee on The Far East and the Pacific. 85th Cong., 2nd Sess., 1958.

House of Representatives, Committee on Foreign Affairs. *The International Narcotics Trade*. Report of Special Study Mission by Hon. Seymour Halpern, October 24, 1971. 92d Cong., 1st Sess., 1971.

House of Representatives, Committee on Foreign Affairs. *The World Heroin Problem*. Report of Special Study Mission by Morgan F. Murphy and Robert H. Steele. 92d Cong., 1st Sess., 1971.

House of Representatives, Committee on Government Operations. *United States Aid Operations in Laos*. Hearings before the Subcommittee on Foreign Operations and Monetary Affairs. 86th Cong., 1st Sess., 1959.

House of Representatives, Committee on Government Operations. *U.S. Aid Operations in Laos*. Report by the Subcommittee on Foreign Operations and Monetary Affairs. 86th Cong., 1st Sess., 1959.

Senate, Committee on Appropriations. Hearings. *Foreign Assistance and Related Agencies Appropriations for 1962*. 87th Cong., 1st Sess., 1961.

Senate, Committee on Appropriations. Hearings. *Foreign Assistance and Related Agencies Appropriations for 1963*. 87th Cong., 2nd Sess., 1962.

Senate, Committee on Armed Services. *Military Cold War Education and Speech Review Policies*. Hearings before the Special Preparedness Subcommittee. 87th Cong., 2nd Sess., 1962.

Senate, Committee on Foreign Relations. Hearings. *Foreign Assistance Act of 1962*. 87th Cong., 2nd Sess., 1962.

Senate, Committee on Foreign Relations. Hearings. *International Development and Security*. 87th Cong., 1st Sess., 1961.

Senate, Committee on Foreign Relations. *Report of Senator Mike Mansfield on a Study Mission to the Associated States of Indochina, Vietnam, Cambodia, Laos.* 83rd Cong., 1st Sess., 1953.

Senate, Committee on Foreign Relations. Report. *Study Mission to Southeast Asia,* November–December, 1962. 88th Cong., 1st Sess., 1963.

Senate, Committee on Foreign Relations. Hearings. *United States Security Agreements and Commitments Abroad, Kingdom of Laos.* 91st Cong., 1st Sess., 1969.

Senate, Committee on Foreign Relations. Report. *Vietnam and Southeast Asia.* 88th Cong., 1st Sess., 1963.

Senate, Committee on the Judiciary. *Refugee and Civilian War Casualty Problems in Indochina.* Report by Subcommittee to Investigate Problems Connected with Refugees and Escapees. 91st Cong., 2d Sess., 1970.

Senate, Committee on the Judiciary. *Refugee and Civilian War Casualty Problems in Laos and Cambodia.* Hearings before Subcommittee to Investigate Problems Connected with Refugees and Escapees. 91st Cong., 2d Sess., 1970.

Senate, Committee on the Judiciary. *Refugee Problems in South Vietnam and Laos.* Hearings before Subcommittee to Investigate Problems Connected with Refugees and Escapees. 89th Cong., 1st Sess., 1965.

Senate, Committee on the Judiciary. *War-Related Civilian Problems in Indochina.* Hearing before the Subcommittee to Investigate Problems Connected with Refugees and Escapees. 92d Cong., 1st Sess., 1971.

Senate, Special Committee to Study the Foreign Aid Program. *Foreign Aid Program.* Clement Johnston, Survey No. 7, "Southeast Asia." 85th Cong., 1st Sess., 1957.

Other U. S. Sources

Agreement for Mutual Defense Assistance in Indochina between the United States of America and Cambodia, France, Laos and Vietnam. December 23, 1950.

Department of State. *American Foreign Policy: Current Documents.* 1956–1962.

Department of State. *The Bangkok Conference of the Manila Pact Powers.* 1955.

Department of State. *Department of State Bulletin.* 1954–1962.

Department of State. *Laos Fact Sheet.* U.S. Department of State Publication No. 7484. June, 1963.

Department of State. *The Situation in Laos.* 1959.

Department of State. *A Threat to the Peace: North Vietnam's Effort to Conquer South-Vietnam,* 87th Cong., 1st Sess., 1961.

Mutual Security Agreement with Laos. December 31, 1951.

Pentagon Papers, as published by *The New York Times.* New York: Bantam Books, 1971.

President. The Foreign Assistance Program: *Annual Report to the Congress, Fiscal Year 1968*. Washington, GPO, 1969.

President. *Public Papers of the Presidents of the United States*. 1954–1962.

OTHER SOURCES

Interview with Roger Hilsman, October 2, 1967.

Interview with J. Graham Parsons, September 16, 1969.

Interview with Khamchan Pradith, Counsellor of Embassy, Permanent Mission of Laos to the United Nations, December 28, 1966.

Interview with Charles Yost, August 28, 1969.

Letter from John F. Melby to the author, November 17, 1971.

Letter from Arthur Schlesinger, Jr. to the author, May 2, 1967.

INDEX